Praise for Ecclesiastes Through the (

"Christianson's study of Ecclesiastes's cultural impact is rich and rewarding. [He] beautifully exposits the material that he treats, and suggests by brief reference some other avenues of fruitful exploration. In these ways, Ecclesiastes Through the Centuries serves both as an excellent treatment of the title theme and a good model for other reception histories to follow. The book may be heartily recommended, without reservation."

Bible and Critical Theory

"Students of Ecclesiastes have been waiting a good many years for a book like Eric Christianson's study ... Not since the time of Christian David Ginsburg's magisterial commentary Coheleth (commonly called the Book of Ecclesiastes) in 1861 has there been such a thorough survey of the reception history of Ecclesiastes."

Lutheran Theological Journal

"With the text's many difficult and provocative passages, the reception history of Ecclesiastes is always going to be more interesting than that of many biblical books, and in this erudite but entertaining commentary, Christianson takes full advantage of the rich materials at his disposal ... The introduction and commentary proper cover many topics, from patristic and rabbinic exegesis through to modern science-fiction, with numerous stops on the way ... Christianson is a genial guide throughout, and his own enthusiasm is clear; the book is very well written and accessible, moreover, so that it should appeal to both specialists and a wider public ... Overall an excellent book."

Society for Old Testament Study Book List

"A fundamental resource on biblical interpretation, especially in the modern world, this book is a winner."

International Review of Biblical Studies

"The Bible's boldest dissonant voice, often muted in the interpretations of theologians, rings out clearly when amplified by the candid commentaries of such eclectic literary masters as Bunyan, Voltaire, Thackeray, and T.S. Eliot. Christianson's book draws the reader into the company of many distinguished earlier readers, admiring and critical alike. Those who, like me, appreciate the dissenting voice of Ecclesiastes will treasure this book as a new favourite about an old one."

Bernhard Lang, University of Paderborn

"Sophisticated and illuminating at every turn, this is an exemplary history of interpretation. A gem of a book."

Harold C. Washington, Saint Paul School of Theology

Blackwell Bible Commentaries

Series Editors: John Sawyer, Christopher Rowland, Judith Kovacs, David M. Gunn

John Through the Centuries
Mark Edwards

Revelation Through the Centuries
Judith Kovacs & Christopher Rowland

Judges Through the Centuries
David Gunn

Exodus Through the Centuries
Scott M. Langston

Ecclesiastes Through the Centuries
Eric S. Christianson

Esther Through the Centuries
Jo Carruthers

Psalms Through the Centuries: Volume I
Susan Gillingham

Galatians Through the Centuries
John Riches

Pastoral Epistles Through the Centuries
Jay Twomey

1 & 2 Thessalonians Through the Centuries
Anthony C. Thiselton

Six Minor Prophets Through the Centuries
By Richard Coggins and Jin H. Han

Forthcoming:

1 & 2 Samuel Through the Centuries
David M. Gunn

1 & 2 Kings Through the Centuries
Martin O'Kane

Psalms Through the Centuries: Volume II
Susan Gillingham

Song of Songs Through the Centuries
Fiona Black

Isaiah Through the Centuries
John F. A. Sawyer

Jeremiah Through the Centuries
Mary Chilton Callaway

Lamentations Through the Centuries
Paul M. Joyce and Diane Lipton

Ezekiel Through the Centuries
Andrew Mein

Jonah Through the Centuries
Yvonne Sherwood

Mark Through the Centuries
Christine Joynes

The Acts of the Apostles Through the Centuries
By Mikeal C. Parsons and Heidi J. Hornik

Romans Through the Centuries
Paul Fiddes

1 Corinthians Through the Centuries
Jorunn Okland

Hebrews Through the Centuries
John Lyons

James Through the Centuries
David Gowler

Genesis 1-21 Through the Centuries
Christopher Heard

Genesis 22-50 Through the Centuries
Christopher Heard

Deuteronomy Through the Centuries
Jonathan Campbell

Daniel Through the Centuries
Dennis Tucker

Ecclesiastes
Through the Centuries

Eric S. Christianson

WILEY-BLACKWELL

A John Wiley & Sons, Ltd., Publication

This paperback edition first published 2012
© 2012 Eric S. Christianson

Edition History: Blackwell Publishing Ltd (hardback, 2007)

Blackwell Publishing was acquired by John Wiley & Sons in February 2007. Blackwell's publishing program has been merged with Wiley's global Scientific, Technical, and Medical business to form Wiley-Blackwell.

Registered Office
John Wiley & Sons Ltd, The Atrium, Southern Gate, Chichester, West Sussex, PO19 8SQ, UK

Editorial Offices
350 Main Street, Malden, MA 02148-5020, USA
9600 Garsington Road, Oxford, OX4 2DQ, UK
The Atrium, Southern Gate, Chichester, West Sussex, PO19 8SQ, UK

For details of our global editorial offices, for customer services, and for information about how to apply for permission to reuse the copyright material in this book please see our website at www.wiley.com/wiley-blackwell.

The right of Eric S. Christianson to be identified as the author of this work has been asserted in accordance with the UK Copyright, Designs and Patents Act 1988.

Wiley also publishes its books in a variety of electronic formats. Some content that appears in print may not be available in electronic books.

Designations used by companies to distinguish their products are often claimed as trademarks. All brand names and product names used in this book are trade names, service marks, trademarks or registered trademarks of their respective owners. The publisher is not associated with any product or vendor mentioned in this book. This publication is designed to provide accurate and authoritative information in regard to the subject matter covered. It is sold on the understanding that the publisher is not engaged in rendering professional services. If professional advice or other expert assistance is required, the services of a competent professional should be sought.

Library of Congress Cataloging-in-Publication Data

Ecclesiastes through the centuries / Eric S. Christianson.
   p.   cm.—(Blackwell Bible commentaries)
Includes bibliographical references and indexes.
   ISBN: 978-0-631-22529-4 (hbk.)–ISBN: 978-0-470-67491-8 (pbk.)
   1. Bible. O.T. Ecclesiastes—
Commentaries.   I. Title.   II. Series.
   BS1475.53.C47 2007
   223′.807—dc22

                                        2006012585

A catalogue record for this book is available from the British Library.

Set in 10/12.5pt Minion by SPi Publisher Services, Pondicherry, India
Printed in Singapore by Ho Printing Singapore Pte Ltd

1   2012

For Juliana and Elliot

Contents

The Blackwell Bible Commentaries series, the first to be devoted primarily to the reception history of the Bible, is based on the premise that how people have interpreted, and been influenced by, a sacred text like the Bible is often as interesting and historically important as what it originally meant. The series emphasizes the influence of the Bible on literature, art, music, and film, its role in the evolution of religious beliefs and practices, and its impact on social and political developments. Drawing on work in a variety of disciplines, it is designed to provide a convenient and scholarly means of access to material until now hard to find, and a much-needed resource for all those interested in the influence of the Bible on Western culture.

Until quite recently this whole dimension was for the most part neglected by biblical scholars. The goal of a commentary was primarily if not exclusively to get behind the centuries of accumulated Christian and Jewish tradition to one single meaning, normally identified with the author's original intention. The most important and distinctive feature of the Blackwell Commentaries is that they will present readers with many different interpretations of each text, in such a way as to heighten their awareness of what a text, especially a sacred text, can mean and what it can do, what it has meant and what it has done, in the many contexts in which it operates.

The Blackwell Bible Commentaries will consider patristic, rabbinic (where relevant), and medieval exegesis as well as insights from various types of modern criticism, acquainting readers with a wide variety of interpretative techniques. As part of the history of interpretation, questions of source, date, authorship, and other historical-critical and archaeological issues will be discussed, but since these are covered extensively in existing commentaries, such references will be brief, serving to point readers in the direction of readily accessible literature where they can be followed up.

Original to this series is the consideration of the reception history of specific biblical books arranged in commentary format. The chapter-by-chapter arrangement ensures that the biblical text is always central to the discussion. Given the wide influence of the Bible and the richly varied appropriation of each biblical book, it is a difficult question which interpretations to include. While each volume will have its own distinctive point of view, the guiding principle for the series as a whole is that readers should be given a representative sampling of material from different ages, with emphasis on interpretations that have been especially influential or historically significant. Though commentators will have their preferences among the different interpretations, the material will be presented in such a way that readers can make up their own minds on the value, morality, and validity of particular interpretations.

The series encourages readers to consider how the biblical text has been interpreted down the ages and seeks to open their eyes to different uses of the Bible in contemporary culture. The aim is to write a series of scholarly commentaries that draw on all the insights of modern research to illustrate the rich interpretative potential of each biblical book.

John Sawyer
Christopher Rowland
Judith Kovacs
David M. Gunn

Preface

Qoheleth himself hints at the reality of the situation. The world may run its course with elegant regularity, but the stuff of interpretation – the articulation of words and the pursuit of understanding especially – is marred by fatigue, cognitive exasperation and endless publication. Rendering such boundless hermeneutical energy has required the use of fat paintbrushes, often resulting in far simpler lines than the subject would demand if examined more closely (though often that scrutiny has been more comprehensive than the lines suggest). In this respect I share wholeheartedly the views of James Barr in his preface to *The Bible in the Modern World*, that the phrases he found himself using (such as 'in the early church' or 'up to modern times') 'must be the abomination of the true historian' (1973: p. x).

It has of course not been possible to fully contextualize all of the examples of Ecclesiastes' reception presented here, but I hope that will not be conceived as a criticism. This commentary provides a portal of sorts to more in-depth investigation, and it is hoped that at least some of these examples will tempt readers to get out their spades and dig further. Indeed, this is precisely my own experience. In the course of research I was so enticed by the story of Voltaire's *Précis* of Ecclesiastes that I selected it as a case study for detailed scrutiny (the results of which are published in Christianson 2005). I have done my best, therefore, to point the way to studies that fill out the areas that this commentary has by necessity excluded. And with primary material I have spent many hours producing as full and as accurate references as I could manage.

As for selection, I do not pretend to have followed an objective set of criteria. I have, however, sought to indicate the ongoing relationship in Ecclesiastes' reading history between the well established and the subversive. While in many cases my own proclivities have biased me to showcase the latter, subversive readings nevertheless can say a great deal about what is conventional. Often the selection was driven by a moment of piqued curiosity or by the recognition of some strange and perceptive response to Qoheleth's words. In such a choice there is little in the way of science.

Readers would of course be right to recognize the inordinate swelling of the Introduction, an abscess that suggests some form of unchecked verbal abandon, but the growth comes from the inordinate attention given by readers to the person of Qoheleth and the tenor of the book. In the manner of Ray Bradbury's hero Guy Montag/Ecclesiastes in *Fahrenheit 451*, Ecclesiastes itself has become a byword for all sorts of critical ideas. The same can be said for the Testimonia chapter, which compiles citations on a range of subjects that authors have in some way related to 'Qoheleth' or the book as a whole. It is perhaps due to the manageable size of Ecclesiastes and its relatively easily grasped themes that writers have characterized its entirety with alarming frequency.

About seven years ago John Sawyer invited me to write this commentary. I immediately warmed to the spirit of the series but was wary of retreading material I had previously covered. Indeed, I set to work on a proposal for another book and surprised myself by coming to the conclusion that I did not want anyone else to write the Ecclesiastes volume! I am, then, immensely grateful to John for the invitation. The project has transformed my views on the nature of interpretation.

In charting this vast interpretive activity, I have been truly overwhelmed by the support of friends and colleagues who have been generous with their time, resources and skills. Among those who brought relevant material to my attention, I would like to thank George Aichele, Andy Benson, Jane Day, Paul Fiddes, Paul Joyce and Tina Nicolson. I would also like to thank those who have kindly made available to me their unpublished or soon-to-be published work (often in the form of old conference papers which their authors had presumed forgotten!): Rebecca Beal, Howard Clarke, Eric Eliason, Paul Flesher, Michael Fox, Larry Kreitzer, Scott Langston and Anthony Perry. I must offer particular thanks to Robin MacGregor Lane who allowed me to make use of his as yet unpublished translation of Jerome's commentary on Ecclesiastes. David Gunn, John Jarick, John Sawyer and Anthony Thiselton each gave of their valuable time reading portions of this book, and I am grateful for their many improvements (and I hereby exonerate them of any errors that follow). I am also grateful to those who kindly provided their translation skills: Andrew Dawson, Robert Evans, Terry McWilliams and Victor Morales (who also located some very useful material during a stint as research assistant). My own understanding of many of the odd occurrences of reception has benefited from conversations with friends and colleagues, for which I offer particular thanks to Trevor Dennis, John Jarick, Chris Partridge and Mike Williams. Mike's knowledge of classical music and perceptive listening skills was positively enlightening. Colleagues in the Department of Theology and Religious Studies at the University of Chester have supported this work in numerous ways, and I offer them my wholehearted thanks. And thanks as well to the editorial staff at Blackwell – in particular, Hannah Berry, Rebecca Harkin, Andrew Humphries, Karen Wilson, Jean van Altena and Cameron Laux – who have shown remarkable patience and support for this long-term project.

Of course a project like this requires exceptional resources, and many library staff have offered far more of their time and expertise than can reasonably be expected. They include: staff at St Deiniols library in Hawarden, North Wales (Peter Francis, Jenny Jones, Gregory Morris, Karen Parry, Nicola Pickett and Patsy Williams); staff in charge of rare collections at the Bodleian and University of Cambridge libraries; staff at the University of Chester library, in particular our indefatigable inter-library loan officer, Donna Crookall.

A special note of thanks must be offered to Catherine Milnes, who undertook a work placement as my research assistant in the early stages. It was not until I had reached the latter stages of writing that I came to realize the astonishing energy and detail of Catherine's work, particularly on the *vanitas* arts tradition. She was, it seems, as enamoured as I with this extraordinary interpretive history.

I would like to thank my parents, who continue to show their support across many miles of ocean. I also thank Bob and Carol Rowberry, my parents in-law. They will never know just how much their unstinting generosity has enriched my life in the UK. I can offer only the most inadequate thanks to my wife, Sonya, for once again enduring my obsession with Qoheleth, but also for showing me uncommon support (including late night coffee and toast!).

Finally, our children, Juliana and Elliot, have supported me no less with laughter and a steady stream of reality doses.

A Pragmatic Note

In the commentary proper each chapter begins with a brief *précis* of the passage and its literary context in Ecclesiastes. The remainder of each chapter charts its interpreters. These readings are arranged chronologically, but are not categorized under epochs or interpretive provenances (the only exceptions are the sections that deal with 1:1–2 and 12:1–7, which suited another scheme). Readers can, however, find extensive discussion of roughly conceived shifts of reading Ecclesiastes along such lines in the Introduction (e.g. Ecclesiastes in Renaissance readings, in modern literature etc.).

I have sought to preserve the variant spellings of early and pre-modern English, and I have not inserted '*sic*' where exclusive language occurs (I use it only sparingly to clarify sense). Such language is so frequent in the sources that it would have become tiresome to do so.

Eric S. Christianson
1 March 2006

It has been over five years since completing *Ecclesiastes Through the Centuries*. While I have been delighted by the volume's warm reception, it was inevitable that some shortcomings would become apparent to me almost immediately. Perhaps most importantly, I realized while looking at the Preface that I had introduced 'Qoheleth' in the first sentence without a word of explanation. As it is the hope of the writers and editors of this series that the commentaries will have an appeal beyond the guild of biblical studies, this was an embarrassing slip-up. So, for those outside of Hebrew Bible studies especially, 'Qoheleth' is a transliteration of the Hebrew term for the book's main character (alternatively transliterated as Qohelet, and more commonly in the past as Koheleth, Cohelet etc., and appearing at 1:1, 2, 12; 7:27; 12:8, 9, 10). A participle of the Hebrew verb *qahal* (to gather, assemble), most English translations of the Bible have alighted on a title such as 'the Preacher' or 'the Teacher' (and the 'titling' is supported by the prefixing of the definite article to *qoheleth* at 7:27 and 12:8). The majority of biblical scholarship, however, treats the word as a name, Qoheleth, and that is followed in this commentary.

Of course, some reviewers mentioned some of the gaps in the commentary's coverage (not so much as a criticism as a point towards even further directions for readers). In terms of the primary material, the most pertinent gap to me was that there was little coverage of discourse outside of the Western European and North American. This is fair, and something I tried hard to avoid. A couple of years into the research of the commentary I was blessed with a research assistant who had studied in South Africa, was originally from Mexico and had travelled extensively. We drafted a letter/email which was sent to as many of his contacts as possible and came up empty-handed. I also explored the routes of postcolonial Bible criticism, but again was disappointed. I am certainly not suggesting the discourse is not there, but its treatment will clearly have to wait for someone more resourceful!

In terms of the secondary literature, I was pretty satisfied by the coverage of the commentary. However, in the same *week* that this commentary was launched at the annual meeting of the Society of Biblical Literature 2006, I found a fascinating and relevant volume hidden in the depths of the massive bookstalls of the conference. This was Mark Swift's *Biblical Subtexts and Religious Themes in Works of Anton Chekhov* (Peter Lang, 2004). Remembering what I understood to be the fleeting presence of Ecclesiastes in the playwright's work, I had a leaf through, and Ecclesiastes' influence was plain to see. Swift argues that Qoheleth and Anton Chekhov shared 'an epistemological questioning about the limits of knowledge' and a form of 'scientific skepticism' accompanied by 'compassion, moral conviction and practicality' (178–79). Swift considers the thematic affinity of Ecclesiastes to selected stories ('The Steppe', 'Happiness', 'The Beauties' and 'Gusev') and finds that they all exhibit a search for meaning, the value of wisdom and learning, the method of epistemological observation, truth as a relative concept and the purposelessness of life, and these themes emerged from a direct relationship to the text of Ecclesiastes. Swift refers to Chekhov's attempt to dramatize Ecclesiastes in a notebook fragment entitled 'Solomon' (something that I *had* briefly covered in the commentary; see p. 68). Swift argues that the fragment is 'an adumbration of Chekhovian themes', such as the quest for meaning, the burden of wealth and fame and existential despair. In other words, these are the themes that occupied the playwright even at the height of his creative powers.

Two works that arrived too late for consideration are worth mentioning. James Limburg's *Encountering Ecclesiastes: A Book for Our Time* (Eerdmans, 2006) offers scores of mainly anecdotal, personal and compelling examples of readers engaging with Qoheleth, in times of grief (such as the carving of

Eccl. 7:2 on his grandfather's tombstone) and joy especially. Lastly, James T. Robinson has had a long-time interest in the Jewish medieval reception of Ecclesiastes and his work has come to a fruition of sorts in *Samuel Ibn Tibbon's Commentary on Ecclesiastes: The Book of the Soul of Man* (Mohr Siebeck, 2007). A key work in rabbinic exegesis that is touched on occasionally in this commentary (access to which was made possible through Robinson's earlier, less lengthy work on Tibbon), Robinson's translation will be of great interest to students of Ecclesiastes' reception history (and Robinson's Hebrew critical edition is apparently in the works).

I wish to thank Wiley-Blackwell for commissioning the paperback edition. Apart from some minor corrections and this second Preface, the text remains the same.

Eric Christianson
Chester, September 2011

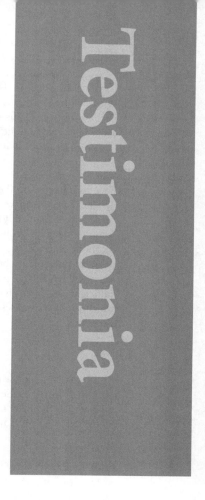

Testimonia

The Vagaries of Interpreting Ecclesiastes

For just as those who have trained in wrestling in the gymnasium strip for greater exertions and efforts in the athletic contests, so it seems to me that the teaching of Proverbs is an exercise, which trains our souls and makes them supple for the struggle with Ecclesiastes. . . . Indeed, one could think of every hyperbole and still not properly express in words what great struggles the contest with this scripture involves for the contestants, as they fight for a foothold for their thoughts, using their skill as athletes so that they may not find their argument overthrown, but in every intellectual encounter keep the mind on its feet to the end through the truth.

Gregory of Nyssa, *Homilies on Ecclesiastes*, c.380
(hom. 1, in Gregory of Nyssa 1993: 33)

[commenting on 1:9, 'There is nothing new under the sun':] A similar idea was suggested by the comic poet [Terence]: 'Nothing has been said which has not been said before.' Thus my teacher Donatus, when he would explain this verse, said, 'They can go to hell who have said my interpretations before me.'

Jerome, *Commentary on Ecclesiastes*, 388/9 (in Kraus 1999–2000: 183)

I, in my humility, have considered the writings and compositions of those who have commented on the book of Ecclesiastes, both the more ancient and those of later date, and have found that they divide themselves into several classes; some have explained it by strange and far-fetched primary interpretations; and some by deep and subtle scientific disquisitions; and some by the method of recondite interpretation have drawn from it just and right doctrines; but the phase of resemblance between them is, that they have all been forced to alter its sense with glossing expressions, and not one of them has given us reason by any sufficient causes which he alleges, to give it any higher praise than that of 'a rock which produces wholesome food'; or 'a strong lion from whence cometh forth sweetness'.

Isaac Aramah, *Commentary on Ecclesiastes*, 1492
(Preface, in Preston 1845: 14–15)

This book is . . . one which no one has ever completely mastered. Indeed, it has been so distorted by the miserable commentaries of many writers that it is almost a bigger job to purify and defend the author from the notions which they have smuggled into him than it is to show his real meaning.

Martin Luther, *Notes on Ecclesiastes*, 1532 (in Luther 1972: 7)

If we look upon this Sermon in the Text, or any of the rest in the whole Book, as the word of man, though as the wisest of men, for so was King *Solomon*, we shall finde work for our wits to censure it, if not for our wilfulness to contradict it; (for no one book in all the Bible hath been more upon the rack, more stretched upon the tenter-hooks, by all sorts of men, then [*sic*] this) . . .

Edward Hyde, *Allegiance and Conscience Not Fled out of England* . . . (1662: 18)

It was impossible to compare the interpreters together, without being struck at the wonderful diversity of their opinions, which the light Solomon's design and method appeared in to me gave me little room to expect . . . but the more I inquired into the grounds of every scheme that differed from mine, the more I found reason to conclude mine the most probable . . . For some find nothing in it but what appears to them perfectly agreable [*sic*] to the purest notions we can have of a revealed Doctrine; whereas others imagine they spy out Monsters, and discover many things which they can by no means reconcile with those notions, nor of consequence look upon as worthy of the holy Ghost.

A. V. Desvoeux, *A Philosophical and Critical Essay on Ecclesiastes*
(1760: pp. vii, 6)

For I have observed that nearly all the commentators who had preceded me have almost entirely failed in doing justice to their task of interpretation.

> Moses Mendelssohn, *Commentary on Ecclesiastes*, 1770
> (in Preston 1845: 73)

Every fresh commentator either actually or virtually regards all his predecessors as having misunderstood Coheleth.

> C. D. Ginsburg, *Coheleth* (1861: 73)

... the Book of Ecclesiastes [is] one of the wisest and one of the worst understood books in the Bible.

> Matthew Arnold, *A Speech at Eton*, 1879 (in Arnold 1973: 31)

Ecclesiastes passed formerly as the most obscure book of the Bible. This is only the opinion of theologians, and in reality is completely false. The book, as a whole, is very clear; only the theologians had a major interest to find it obscure.

> Ernest Renan, *L'Ecclésiaste* (1882: 15; my tr.)

... we have now reviewed the main lines of interpretation of this fascinating Book. I do not know how far any one of them has satisfied you, but none of them completely satisfies me.

> J. S. Wright, 'The Interpretation of Ecclesiastes' (1946: 21)

How many far-fetched theories have been hazarded by modern writers who are locked up in their own crippling presuppositions? Even the vagaries and extravagances of ancient exegesis can have a sobering effect on current scholarship.

> Roland E. Murphy, 'Qohelet Interpreted' (1982: 336)

It may be that in the last resort Qoheleth is a mirror which reflects the soul of the interpreter. If so, there is sufficient vanity in scholarship to appreciate reliable mirrors.

> James Crenshaw, 'Qoheleth in Current Research' (1983: 51)

Since one of Qohelet's themes is the inability of human enterprise to seize and hold, to take possession of a thing, it is perhaps no accident that the book eludes the attempts of interpretive activity to fix its meaning determinately ... It is always interesting to see where the 'interpretive sweat' breaks out in dealing with such an iconoclastic book.

> Carol A. Newsom, 'Job and Ecclesiastes' (1995: 190, 191)

Charting a Harsh Terrain

When . . . I had made myself, as I apprehended, a tolerable master of the subject [of interpreting Ecclesiastes], I set about the work, which, after all, proved a far more laborious task than I at first imagined, not only from the phraseology peculiar to this Book, which in many places, is dark enough in itself, and rendered still darker from the prodigious variety of arbitrary interpretations, but sometimes also from the difficulty of finding out the true connexion of the several parts, which, on a cursory view, seem to have no dependence on each other.

Anonymous, *Choheleth, or the Royal Preacher* (1765: p. vi)

It would be very difficult to distinguish the parts and arrangement of this produc-tion; the order of the subject and the connexion of the arguments are involved in so much obscurity, that scarcely any two commentators have agreed concerning the plan of the work. The style of this work is . . . singular; the language is gener-ally low, I might almost call it mean or vulgar; it is frequently loose, unconnected, approaching to the incorrectness of conversation; and possesses very little of the poetical character, even in the composition and structure of the periods.

Robert Lowth, *Lectures on the Sacred Poetry of the Hebrews*, 1787
(in Lowth 1995: 2.174–5)

[Ecclesiastes] reminds me of the remains of a daring explorer, who has met with some terrible accident, leaving his shattered form exposed to the encroachments of all sorts of foul vermin.

Paul Haupt, 'The Book of Ecclesiastes', 1894 (in G. A. Barton 1959: 28)

In the river of revelation these chapters of Ecclesiastes seem to lie in some quiet and shadowy backwater, far removed from the central stream.

Wilfrid Johnson Moulton, *c*.1925 (in Scott 1929: 74)

It is a sort of scrapbook collection of contradictory meditations on identical themes. Here the lore of the sages turns in upon itself, comments on and refutes itself . . . The effect of such a methodology is to open vacuous chasms in knowl-edge and experience. This is destructive criticism; even the alternative offered by Job is passed by . . .

Lawrence B. Porter, 'Bankruptcy: The Words of Qoheleth, Son of
David, King in Jerusalem' (1969: 3042)

. . . there is a tremendous interpretive pressure to raise the valleys and lower the hills, to make the way straight and level before the reader. But a reading faithful to this book, at least, should try to describe the territory with all its bumps and clefts, for they are not mere flaws, but the essence of the landscape.

Michael V. Fox, Qohelet and his Contradictions (1989: 28)

Inasmuch as it would be absurd to criticize a Rubik's Cube for the problems it presents to its user, so it is with the text of Ecclesiastes.

Gary Salyer, Vain Rhetoric (2001: 147)

Qoheleth the Philosopher

How then do I interpret the words, *Koheleth sought to find out words of delight?* Koheleth sought to pronounce verdicts from his own insight [lit. 'that are in the heart'], without witnesses and without warning . . .

Babylonian Talmud, c.450 (b. Rosh Hashanah 21b)

[Qoheleth] contemplates, teaches, mourns, comforts, imparts counsel, contradicts, and corrects himself . . . The author is no dogmatic and phlegmatic teacher, but a warm and animated examiner of truth. To a philosopher, it is essential to listen to the opposite opinions. He, without regarding his own system, listens to all objections which can be made, and does not fear the consequences of statements he admits . . . [He] candidly places before the eyes of the reader all the objections which he makes, and all that transpires in his inmost soul; *he is not afraid to think aloud.*

David Friedländer, Der Prediger, 1788 (in Ginsburg 1861: 79–80)

This book contains the investigations of several associations of literary men among the Israelites; it contains propositions which at that time formed the limits of philosophic speculation, and which seem to have been proposed intentionally, to agitate and to explain doubts, and thus to develop the intellectual faculties.

J. C. C. Nachtigal, Koheleth, 1798 (in Ginsburg 1861: 192)

It is an autobiography with a purpose. The book may seem unnatural, but it is because the life was a calculation . . . He seems to be a fool, but he is rather a wise man making experiments in folly – a philosopher blowing bubbles from which may come out the science of light.

James Bennet, The Wisdom of the King (1870: 5)

He was reverent, sincerely reverent . . . The joys of youth and friendship, of home and garden, are fleeting, but after all they are real, and in spite of all the sorrow in the world we need not hesitate to enjoy them while they last: they are God's gifts. Koheleth has not a satisfying philosophy of life. He has very little theology. He does have, however, something which in its intense earnestness and its steadfast allegiance to both reason and conscience, both mind and heart, well deserves to be called faith.

Millar Burrows, 'Kuhn and Koheleth' (1927: 97)

He stepped into the world of letters as a mature thinker. He had suffered much and seen much, and had formed the habit of looking at life analytically, searching always for an answer. He treated his own existence as an experiment to be lived out like a play. And he lived it alone.

Elizabeth Stone, 'Old Man Koheleth' (1942: 100)

Ecclesiastes . . . thinks it best to let sleeping dogmas lie . . . [He] is a free-lance humanist . . .

John Paterson, 'The Intimate Journal of an Old-Time Humanist' (1950: 245)

[Qoheleth] is 'disillusioned' only in the sense that he has realized that an illusion is a self-constructed prison. He is not a weary pessimist tired of life: he is a vigorous realist determined to smash his way through every locked door of repression in his mind.

Northrop Frye, *The Great Code* (1982: 123)

He is a man for the eighties, a private-sectorite. But being a personality who wears contradictions without discomfort, he has another side, one that suits another realm – the realm of the artist, where a restless spirit of inquiry soars beyond the walls of the *status quo*.

Daphne Merkin, 'Ecclesiastes: A Reading out-of-Season' (1987: 401–2)

Qoheleth is an 'intellectual' in a sense otherwise unknown to the Old Testament. In his remorseless determination to probe the nature of things he belongs to a new world of thought, though . . . his sense of God's transcendence ('God is in heaven, and you upon the earth', 5:2) is a Jewish inheritance which distinguishes him quite radically from the secular philosopher . . . To some extent . . . Ecclesiastes stands as a lonely beacon in a dark and largely uncharted literary ocean.

R. N. Whybray, *Ecclesiastes* (1989: 7, 8)

At most we could concede that the 'subjects treated' by Qohelet are also philosophers' favourite subjects – subjects that metaphysics has dealt with. But nothing more . . . Let us leave metaphysics to the metaphysicians, then, so that we can listen to Qohelet speak without metaphysicians' discourse interfering. This way we will see that he speaks differently from them.

Jacques Ellul, *Reason for Being: A Meditation on Ecclesiastes* (1990: 27)

Wrought by Melancholy

The Book of Ecclesiastes . . . is written as the solitary reflections of a worn-out debauchee, such as Solomon was, who looking back on scenes he can no longer enjoy, cries out *All is Vanity!* . . . From what is transmitted to us of the character of Solomon, he was witty, ostentatious, dissolute, and at last melancholy. He lived fast, and died, tired of the world, at the age of fifty-eight years . . . Seven hundred wives, and three hundred concubines would have stood in place of the whole book. It was needless after this to say that all was vanity and vexation of spirit; for it is impossible to derive happiness from the company of those whom we deprive of happiness.

Thomas Paine, *The Age of Reason*, II, 1794 (in Paine 1896: 4.127–8)

Ecclesiastes had diffused a seriousness and solemnity over the frame of his spirit [i.e. of Jesus Christ, who 'probably' studied this scripture], glowing with youthful hope, and made audible to his listening heart

> The still, sad music of humanity,
> Not harsh or grating, but of ample power
> To chasten and subdue.

Percy Shelley, 'Essay on Christianity', *c.*1820 (in Shelley 1880: 2.341; the lines Shelley cites are from William Wordsworth's 'Lines Written a Few Miles above Tintern Abbey' [1798], ll. 91–3)

The Book of Ecclesiastes has been called sceptical, epicurean; it is certainly without the glow and hope which animate the Bible in general.

Matthew Arnold, *Literature and Dogma*, 1873 (in Arnold 1968: 207)

He is an uncompromising pessimist, who sees the world as it is. Everything that seems pleasant or profitable is vanity and a grasping of wind; there is nothing positive but pain, nothing real but the eternal Will, which is certainly unknowable and probably unconscious. These truths . . . are the bitter fruits of that rare knowledge, increase of which is increase of sorrow.

E. J. Dillon, *The Sceptics of the Old Testament* (1895: 113)

The truth is, he was a disappointed man, and there are two sorts of disappointed men in life . . . The man who is disappointed because he has not got, may have still the fascination of his hopes before him. But the man who has got what he desires and is then disappointed, has pricked the bubble, and knows the meaning of emptiness and vexation of spirit.

E. E. Cleal, *Christian World Pulpit*, 1907 (in Nicoll and Stoddart 1910: 531)

A Chopin prelude always is saddening, and Milton's 'L'Allegro' never fails to liven up a leaden day. Koheleth, however, merely brings defeat and gladness into sharper outline in their relationship to each other, and does not deny or praise one or the other . . . His book is a record of profound personal disillusionment, which has ground him until he no longer feels it as anything but a faint taste of ashes in the mouth, and the red gone out of the sunset . . . Koheleth has not always been bored, and he participated passionately in the life around him, but in the end he set down his pen, and was only tired with life, and frustrated in his search to see something beyond it . . . Although the irony of his statements is apparent, I cannot think of them as being offered with a smile.

Elizabeth Stone, 'Old Man Koheleth' (1942: 99, 102)

There may have been many a melancholy streak in his nature that disposed him to look at the shadier sides of life. He is the original 'gloomy dean'. He had hung his harp on the weeping willows and it moaned in the breeze . . . Job is an eagle soaring in the face of the sun, but Ecclesiastes is a land-blown bird with bedraggled wings and no power of flight.

John Paterson, 'The Intimate Journal of an Old-Time Humanist' (1950: 251)

He is a pathological doubter of everything, stemming from a drastic emotional experience, a psychic disturbance. He is doubtful about himself as a person of worth and character. He has no self-esteem or value of himself. His doubt has destroyed all values. He is an inferior, of no account, and he demeans himself constantly. His doubts come from a parapathy, a disease of the mind which he shares with many neurotics.

Frank Zimmermann, *The Inner World of Qohelet* (1973: 8)

I cannot imagine what it is like to read Ecclesiastes on a sunny day under a clear sky. It is, however much the pious commentators bustle in with their ready assuagements, a depressive's lament – perfect reading for a gray day . . . Nothing suffices for this acquisition-happy malcontent, this Biblical character blessed with the dazzling 'life style' of a corporate raider but burdened with the wrong soul – the soul of a Flaubert. Like that other great connoisseur of *ennui*, Koheleth is acutely aware of the 'boredom and ignominies of existence', and would, I suspect, agree with the nineteenth-century writer's calibrated assessment: 'I admire tinsel as much as gold: indeed the poetry of tinsel is even greater, because it is sadder'.

Daphne Merkin, 'Ecclesiastes: A Reading out-of-Season' (1987: 393–5)

In Job, Job's friends and ultimately even God argue against Job, but in Qohelet, no such opposition – human or divine – ever appears to mitigate Qohelet's unrelenting pessimism.

Paul Flesher, 'The Wisdom of the Sages' (1990)

Preacher of Joy

. . . he quickly changes from an observing inquirer into an instructing and coun-seling senior friend, and to our great surprise advances the most beautiful maxims about caution and patience, fidelity and thoughtful industry . . . he at last concludes, from his observations, experiments, and researches, that there is no other lasting good for man than serene joy in God, comprising as it does everything else.

Georg H. A. Ewald, Sprüche Salomo's, Koheleth, 1837
(in Ginsburg 1861: 210)

We marvel at the prodigality of nature, but how marvellous, too, the economy! The old cycles are for ever renewed, and it is no paradox that he who would advance can never cling too close to the past. The thing that has been is the thing that will be again; if we realize that, we may avoid many of the disillusions, miseries, insanities that for ever accompany the throes of new birth. Set your shoulder joyously to the world's wheel: you may spare yourself some unhappiness if, beforehand, you slip the book of *Ecclesiastes* beneath your arm.

Havelock Ellis, The New Spirit, 1890 (in Ellis 1926: 33)

He looks at life in its vast sweep and, with a broad outlook on the world-order, sees not ground for despair, but order, reason, symmetry, and beauty – signs of an Infinite Wisdom and Goodness over all. He does not affirm that the world-order is meaningless, but, which is an altogether different thing, its meaning is beyond man's power utterly to fathom. This is not the impertinence of pessi-mism but the words of a real reverence, a mood of the spirit which we all do well to cultivate, in his opinion.

James A. Greissinger, 'The Worst-Understood Book' (1909: 740)

So much in the world seems but an endless and wearying and unrewarding cycle of no more substance than a breath of wind over the desert. But this is no sterile wind blowing over empty places. And Koheleth is not a creation of T. S. Eliot – he is no Gerontion, no 'old man in a dry month, being read to by a boy . . .' There is no sense of futility here. Puzzlement, perhaps, and a sense of the absurdity of the world. But no desire to reject the world because it contains so much ugliness and wrong. For the world of Koheleth contains beauty and joy as well.

> Joan Abramson, *The Faces of Israel* (in Abramson and
> Freulich 1972: 15)

In the popular mind a happy Koheleth is an oxymoron: how could the sage who was convinced that 'all is vanity' have been capable of enjoyment? It is true that an *ésprit de serieux* hovers over the intelligent thinkers, by and large, and Kohelet is no exception . . . The problem is that although thinkers such as Kohelet try to be holistic and integrative, most readers tend to think atomistically, in terms of either/or . . . [Kohelet's] is a religious vision embracing the insoluble tension between divine transcendence and human aspiration and responsibility . . . And when one reads Kohelet from the perspective of comedy, which is the upset and recovery of the protagonist's equilibrium, it becomes clear that his existential 'bottom line' is *not* 'vanity of vanities', but rather 'Sweet is the light, and it is good for the eyes to see the sun. And however many years a person may live, let him rejoice in them all . . .' [11:7–8]

> Étan Levine, 'The Humor in Qohelet' (1997: 82–3)

. . . Ecclesiastes advocates resignation without despair, that is, cultivating an inner attitude toward life that strives to transcend the tragic limitations and sorrows of existence through a frank and courageous acceptance that they cannot be transformed. Ecclesiastes thus promotes dedicating oneself to striving after joy in life, not so much for the reasons the idealistic pious believe, because it is a gift from God to be treasured, but because the search for joy is the only sensible goal considering the frustrating, tragic, and fundamentally futile nature of existence. Freud probably saw life in a similar way when he wrote that the purpose of psychoanalysis was to transform hysterical misery into common unhappiness.

> Paul Marcus, 'The Wisdom of Ecclesiastes and its Meaning for
> Psychoanalysis' (2000: 248)

True to Life

This book is like the basin which Moses made out of the mirrors of the women. For he taught not only to see men's faces in such mirrors, but to see their minds as well. Ecclesiastes also made this book out of the copper and the mirrors of women for the viewing of the minds of men . . . Therefore Ecclesiastes sees in this mirror whatever men do in the world.

> Rupert of Deutz, *Commentary on Ecclesiastes*, c.1110
> (in Eliason 1989: 74 n. 65)

This great Connoisseur of human nature would not have us to be always laughing, with *Democritus*, nor always weeping, with *Heraclitus*; but as, on some
occasions, to be very serious, so, on others, to indulge social Mirth with more
than ordinary freedom, provided we keep within the bounds of reason and
moderation.

> Anonymous, *Choheleth, or the Royal Preacher* (1765: p. xiii)

He speaks for humanity, and his words have always found an echo. His book is
a great monologue, which presents life to us in its energetic traits, and its laconic
style shews the profoundness of the thinker. It is scepticism softened by
maxims.

> S. Cahen, *La Bible*, 1848 (in Ginsburg 1861: 90)

This Preacher, I am willing to believe, had felt all that man's heart could feel; but
he had no suspicion of what man is allowed to know. The human mind in
his day overpowered science; in our day it is science that overpowers the
human mind.

> Ernest Renan, *c.*1870 (in Scott 1929: 78)

He has trodden the very paths we tread. He shares our craving and has pursued
our quest after 'that which is good'. He has been misled by the illusions by which
we are beguiled. And his aim is to save us from fruitless researches and defeated
hopes by placing his experience at our command.

> Samuel Cox, *The Book of Ecclesiastes* (1896: 209)

The Preacher belongs in the company of such spirits as Dante, Browning, Tennyson, Amiel, Paschal, and their like, who have through long years brooded on
the meaning of life. His dozen autobiographical pages, wrought with literary art,
replete with epigram, reveal a gentle, sensitive spirit, sincere, honest, reverent,
not without the saving grace of good humor, genial, urbane, cosmopolitan,
tolerant. The book is a wonderfully human document.

> James A. Greissinger, 'The Worst-Understood Book' (1909: 737)

Koheleth belongs to the small coterie of books that do not grow old . . . He is
almost brutally frank in holding the mirror up to life. For all that, he is neither
a scoffer nor a pessimist. He loves life and has intense sympathy with the struggles and sufferings of humanity, but he smiles at the attempts of zealous reformers to change human nature or to improve a state of things, which (as he believes)
follows logically from the conditions under which mankind carves out its career.
Koheleth is not a cold and severely logical philosopher, intent upon building up
a system of thought, but an easy-going dilettante who unfolds in a series of
charming, witty and loosely connected *causeries* his view of life, as gained by a
long and varied experience . . . Koheleth is serious in what he says, though he

always speaks with a slight ironical smile on his lips, but he does not want us to take him *too* seriously, just as he himself does not want to take life too seriously. The human interest of the book is all the more intense because of its main conclusion, that life itself is a paradox. Life is made to be enjoyed, and yet enjoyment is 'vanity'.

Morris Jastrow, *A Gentle Cynic* (1919: 8–9)

His words reveal a sensitive soul, sensitive alike to the joys of life and to its disheartening and inexplicable disappointments.

Millar Burrows, 'Kuhn and Koheleth' (1927: 95)

[Ecclesiastes] defeats all endeavors to force upon it interior self-consistency and harmony, and in its inclusion of many points of view, even though at odds with one another, it remains true to life.

Harry Emerson Fosdick, *A Guide to Understanding the Bible*, 1938
(in Fosdick 1965: 182)

Like a candleflame in mist, we cannot see him or touch him or name him, and yet he is there. And as surely as food gives a fragrance and drums resound, Koheleth gives us his own particular light, whether he is one or many men, whether the page has felt the point of one or many pens . . . Koheleth, illusive and fantastic and quixotic though he may be, has entrenched himself firmly in our life and background, and we may challenge his right to sit there, but he goes right on sitting. He, or it or they, belongs to us, and the warring philosophies tied into the few pages of the book of Ecclesiastes exist to contradict and augment each other and intrigue the critics and yet there is a completeness in the thing.

Elizabeth Stone, 'Old Man Koheleth' (1942: 98)

In the deepest sense, Koheleth is a religious book, because it seeks to grapple with reality . . . This cry of a sensitive spirit wounded by man's cruelty and ignorance, this distilled essence of an honest and courageous mind, striving to penetrate the secret of the universe, yet unwilling to soar on the wings of faith beyond the limits of the knowable, remains one of man's noblest offerings on the altar of truth.

Robert Gordis, *Koheleth – The Man and his World* (1955: 122)

Not to the nonsense-writers, the archaic conformists, the purblind antiquarians, for whom Koheles was and probably will ever be a nasty and a naughty word, shall we go for enlightenment . . . Koheles is a book of Jewish philosophy, Bible style . . . It is written as one speaks rather than as one thinks and, at a few points, the writer gets so emotionally involved that he becomes self-contradictory . . . [F]or those who want the story straight, who do not want to be flimflammed, bull-dozed or hypnotized by the so-called teachers of the many phony religious beliefs and practices that infest the earth, Koheles is one of the truly great (and there are not many of them) . . .

David Max Eichhorn, *Musings of the Old Professor* (1963: 2, 247, 254)

All he finds in [the world] is contradictions, which do not fit in with God. He cannot pile up enough contradictory concepts to describe the ambiguity of existence . . . All these contradictions he finds not following each other or accompanying each other, providing a meaningful solution to one or complementing each other, but confused and entangled with each other, entwined with each other in a meaningless way, cutting across and destroying each other in mutual hostility, apparently without end. The world he describes is enigmatic, discordant and contradictory – it is the world in which we live. But where is God in it?

Heinz Zahrnt, *What Kind of God?*, 1971 (in Short 1973: 76)

The man had so much insight into the absurdities of the world. His words strip away the rationalizations of life and yet leave us with all the more reason to live and to enjoy . . . He punctured the illusions of life – but always with a compassionate and never a barbed pen. Perhaps in so doing he could not allow himself even the shadow of an illusion so vain – he could not permit the thought that his own words might remain after him as his own immortality. It is possible. It is also possible that he is indulging his humor at our expense – that he is fishing; that he fully expects his reader to protest. I think he knew the value of his words.

Joan Abramson, *The Faces of Israel*
(in Abramson and Freulich 1972: 21)

Koheleth comes to us having faced down the existential void, the hollowness at the heart of the getting and spending that is the human enterprise . . . There is, to be sure, a bracing – even healing – aspect to the stark realism of the writer's vision, a way in which his resolute emphasis on the transience of all things human can be said to be a cloud-chaser. Still, the 'charm' of Ecclesiastes is a tonic charm, a somewhat bitter-tasting dose of our own dust-to-dustness . . . Koheleth cuts a less than imposing, recognizably human figure. Shamelessly inconsistent in his reasoning, though always a bottom-liner, with what relief we fall upon him!

Daphne Merkin, 'Ecclesiastes: A Reading out-of-Season' (1987: 396–8)

Ecclesiastes speaks to people in tough binds, people with vendettas, a bone to pick, no dog to kick, the sour-grapers, the hurt, those who've never shucked off

their adolescent angst. In general tones the preacher speaks to the bummed-out.
All is weariness, the soul cannot utter it.

Louise Erdrich, 'The Preacher' (1995: 235)

Qoheleth and Christianity

Everywhere Ecclesiastes, teaching us by dark sayings [*di 'ainigmatōn*], sends us
to the other life.

Olympiodorus, Commentary on Ecclesiastes, c.510
(on 3:21, in Hirshman 1958: 143 n. 16)

'It reminds me,' said Elder Staples, 'of the sad burden of Ecclesiastes, the mourn-
fulest book of Scripture; because, while the preacher dwells with earnestness
upon the vanity and uncertainty of the things of time and sense, he has no
apparent hope of immortality to relieve the dark picture. Like Horace, he sees
nothing better than to eat his bread with joy and drink his wine with a merry
heart. It seems to me the wise man might have gone farther in his enumeration
of the folly and emptiness of life, and pronounced his own prescription for
the evil vanity also. What is it but plucking flowers on the banks of the stream
which hurries us over the cataract, or feasting on the thin crust of a volcano
upon delicate meats prepared over the fires which are soon to ingulf us?
Oh, what a glorious contrast to this is the gospel of Him who brought to
light life and immortality! The transition from the Koheleth to the Epistles
of Paul is like passing from a cavern, where the artificial light falls indeed
upon gems and crystals, but is everywhere circumscribed and overshadowed
by unknown and unexplored darkness, into the warm light and free atmosphere
of day.'

John Greenleaf Whittier, My Summer with Dr Singletary, c.1866
(in Whittier 1889: 5. 229–30)

Ecclesiastes, like the first part of Goethe's *Faust*, may, with the fullest justice, be
called an apology for Christianity, not as containing anticipations of Christian
truth . . . but inasmuch as it shows that neither wisdom, nor any other human
good or human pleasure, brings permanent satisfaction to man's natural
longings.

T. K. Cheyne, Job and Solomon (1887: 249)

[Ecclesiastes] pushes the logic of a non-Christian position with tremendous
force, to all who feel keenly the misery of the world. More vividly than anything
else in the Old Testament, it shows us how imperious was the necessity for the
revelation of God in Christ.

A. S. Peake, The Problem of Suffering in the Old Testament (1904: 135)

Qoheleth and Justice

The author ... was a pious Israelite ... whose heart was greatly touched with the sufferings of his brethren, and who felt himself compelled to impart unto them his well-meant written counsel under these oppressions ... He was ... anxious, if not to remove, at least *to mitigate their misfortunes, by offering salutary precautions to his brethren for those fearful times.*

Georg H. A. Ewald, *Das Hohelied Salomo's überfeßt mit Einleitung,* 1826
(in Ginsburg 1861: 206)

... the book has been said, and with justice, to breathe *resignation at the grave of Israel.* Its author sees 'the tears of the oppressed, and they had no comforter, and on the side of their oppressors there was power; wherefore I praised the dead which are already dead more than the living which are yet alive.' [4:1–2] He sees 'all things come alike to all, there is one event to the righteous and to the wicked'. [9:2] Attempts at a philosophic indifference appear, at a sceptical suspension of judgment, at an easy *ne quid nimis*: 'Be not righteous overmuch, neither make thyself overwise! why shouldst thou destroy thyself?' [7:16] Vain attempts, even at a moment which favoured them! shows of scepticism, vanishing as soon as uttered before the intractable conscientiousness of Israel.

Matthew Arnold, *Literature and Dogma,* 1873 (in Arnold 1968: 207)

Qoheleth has his place in the long history of the battle of the Jewish conscience against injustice in the world. He represents a pause in the struggle.

Ernest Renan, *L'Ecclésiaste* (1882: 39–40; my tr.)

He has nothing of the flaming indignation of an Amos, nothing of the crusading spirit. He is not tough-minded. He cannot even blame corrupt officials: it is the system that is at fault, and the individual is helpless.

Millar Burrows, 'Kuhn and Koheleth' (1927: 96)

Here within the canon of Jewish Scripture ... popular fatalism and pessimism were given forceful and fearless utterance. Here the creed of those who cried, 'Where is the God of justice?' found an eloquent voice, and the spiritual insights by which the seers of Israel had tried to illumine the age-long problem of evil faced derisive denial.

Harry Emerson Fosdick, *A Guide to Understanding the Bible,* 1938
(in Fosdick 1965: 181)

Ecclesiastes was struck by the fact that time and again, according to his experience, it is as if man lives in an ethically indifferent universe. Ecclesiastes believed that there was a God who had creative and boundless power, but that He often did not wish to intervene in human history at the appropriate time, or if He did intervene, it was usually too little, too late. Ecclesiastes passionately protests against a world in which the powerful are evil and the weak vulnerable to victimization.

Paul Marcus, 'The Wisdom of Ecclesiastes and its Meaning for
Psychoanalysis' (2000: 236)

> So, naturalists observe, a flea
> Hath smaller fleas that on him prey;
> And these have smaller fleas to bite 'em,
> And so proceed *ad infinitum*.
> Thus every poet, in his kind,
> Is bit by him that comes behind.
> > Jonathan Swift, 'On Poetry'

There is something parasitic about the interpretive enterprise, be it either in what we call academic or cultural reception. Indeed, Qoheleth has been subject to all manner of 'biting', and it is a miracle that he has survived (his most influential interpreters have not escaped harm either, particularly Jerome).

But then it is entirely Qoheleth's fault. His story is simply too good for us fleas to pass up. Too inviting a feast lies before us. This is exemplified by the majority of instances that make up this commentary, in which readers from innumerable contexts have recognized Ecclesiastes as existentially valuable and simply charming. Above all, Ecclesiastes presents a profoundly ambiguous and yet oddly compelling argument, one that rests on Qoheleth's own self-portrait, and which demands decisions from readers. The dark terrain it surveys and demanding concepts it clarifies are rarely comfortable, which makes its magnetism all the more puzzling. As Carol Newsom observes, 'Ecclesiastes . . . makes people profoundly uncomfortable, a fact that renders its reception history particularly fascinating' (1995: 190).

Ecclesiastes' interpretive history discloses some salient features. First, readers have habitually engaged less with the complexities of Qoheleth's words and more with Qoheleth himself. This is partly due to what John Paterson diagnosed as Qoheleth's 'I trouble' (1950: 251), that overbearing sense of self that fills nearly every passage (see Christianson 1998a: 33–42 *et passim*). The portrait is a seductive one, drawn with great detail and conviction, and Qoheleth's path to wisdom has proved irresistible to his legion readers, on whose imaginations his persona has been indelibly inscribed. Second, Ecclesiastes exhibits both extremes and inescapably iterative themes, which is highlighted by O. Loretz's identification of 21.2 per cent of its verses as 'thematic' (1964: 179). Its very content has thus often effectively limited readers' responses to polarities: mostly, to be sure, of *hebel* (a word that appears some 38 times and that signifies, at the least, a deficit situation). Third, such responses have appeared with surprising regularity through the centuries. Indeed, most 'of the main ideas that modern interpretation ascribes to Qohelet', suggests Michael V. Fox, 'can be found, with differing emphases, in the interpretations of the earliest exegetes – a fact that seems to show that the essential themes of the book are clear' (1999: 349; cf. the similar views of Murphy [1982: 332] and J. R. Wright [2005: p. xxii]). Not only have the themes been relatively clear, but the hermeneutical issues that continue to vex Qoheleth (and generally biblical) studies surfaced surprisingly early on. So, for example, Gregory of Nyssa *c.*380 grapples with whether or not Qoheleth was a real or a fictive author (see p. 158); the Karaite commentator Yephet ben 'Ali *c.*990 observes that Qoheleth identifies himself as 'I' in 1:12 explicitly for the purpose of grounding his argument in experience (see pp. 31–32); A. V. Desvoeux anticipates a wealth of philological study in his richly detailed 234-page 'essay' on the subject (1760).

It is worth noting some territories that will not be explored in this commentary. Ecclesiastes' elusive structure is sparingly touched on in these pages, but it is fairly comprehensively covered in other literature (e.g. Fox 1999; Murphy 1992: pp. xxxv–xli; Salyer 2001: 143–64). Theories of direct influence (be it Hellenistic or Persian etc.), or of so-called Aramaisms in Qoheleth's Hebrew, have enjoyed a long academic life. Indeed, late nineteenth- and early twentieth-century studies were particularly enamoured with the idea of Qoheleth's Greek ideological (if not 'genetic') parentage, and those studies still raise stimulating questions (see the relatively lengthy and typical treatment by G. A. Barton, 1959: 32–43 [orig. 1908]; more recent surveys are, of course, readily available, e.g. Fox 1999; Newsom 1995; Murphy 1990, and subsequent editions in 1996 and 2001). This can be more loosely conceived, in that Qoheleth may have drawn on Egyptian, Greek or Babylonian sources to inform his thinking (it seems that he at least engaged in the same sort of questions with the same sort of language); but studies in this area continue to make themselves available (see e.g. Brown's recent discussion of parallels to the *Epic of Gilgamesh* [2000: 2–7] and Fischer's on the influence of Egyptian Harpers' songs [2002]). Whereas I am attempting to sketch Ecclesiastes' ongoing life as a fully formed book, this latter group of questions is really about the glint in the milkman's eye, and will therefore rarely surface here.

1   A History of Reception Histories

Interest in the reception history of Ecclesiastes has been, particularly since the late nineteenth century, vigorous, and shows no sign of abating. Indeed, it is unusual for commentaries not to have at least a brief overview. In order to clarify the focus of this commentary, it will prove useful to survey this rich vein of work.

From roughly the seventh century CE, catenas (commentary anthologies) were produced periodically. It seems that readers naturally come around to the desire to anthologize the interpretive enterprise, perhaps to better understand their own place in its 'scheme'. It will suffice here to highlight a few significant instances. One of the earliest to deal with Ecclesiastes is the work of Procopius of Gaza (*c.*650), which collected six early Christian commentaries on Ecclesiastes, and which shared some of the interpretive concerns of Jewish midrash (itself not unlike a catena; see Hirshman 1958). After Procopius's catena one might note the *Glossa ordinaria*, compiled by Anselm of Laon (*c.*1100), representing patristic and early medieval exegesis on the entire Vulgate Bible (and in the case of Ecclesiastes, heavily dependent on Jerome's commentary). Hugh of St Cher, *c.*1230–5, compiled a significantly broad range of views on Ecclesiastes from twelfth- and thirteenth-century commentators in order to supplement the *Glossa*. In the course of his own postil he let the cited views often take precedence over his own (see Smalley 1949: 345). The period of 1500–1700 sees a great deal of attention given to Ecclesiastes in moral, academic and poetic discourse (more on which below), but relatively little in the scrutiny of reception (Matthew Poole's *Synopsis Criticorum*, published 1669–76, is certainly an exception). It is worth noting, however, that several exhaustive commentaries appear, such as that of J. de Pineda (Seville, 1619), which offer an overview of patristic exposition of Ecclesiastes. (For surveys of commentaries of this period and earlier see, in particular, Geitmann 2004 and Philippe 1926.)

Several nineteenth-century studies show an acute interest in the contribution of pre- and early modern reading to concurrent interpretation. A good example is Theodore Preston's 1845 commentary that includes an English translation of Moses Mendelssohn's commentary (1770) and various other portions of rabbinic and Christian commentaries, such as Rabbi Isaac Aramah's preface to his 1492 commentary. James Darling's 1859 compendium *Cyclopaedia Bibliographica* is worth noting for its extensive list of commentaries and sermons ranging from the 1600s to the author's day (1859: 2. cols 555–76). In terms of its influence on subsequent reception scholarship, however, pride of place belongs to Christian D. Ginsburg's 1861 commentary (the product of 'seven years' labour', p. viii) with its sweeping 216-page overview of Christian and Jewish readings across the centuries. Its relevance is enhanced by the commentary proper's further engagement with those sources. Ginsburg's selections are nearly all translated into English, often with the original language provided and of a substantial length. At the least, Ginsburg provided tantalizing examples from readings as diverse as Gregory of Nyssa and the *Zohar*. While Ginsburg's work has undeniably proved its worth, it is not without its faults. As Sheldon Blank points out in his introduction to the 1970 reissue of Ginsburg, in 'reviewing the literature one meets with any number of works which he does not list' (1970: p. xi; note that Barton's 1908 commentary quite credibly brings Ginsburg up to date, for those 'who are interested in such curious details'; 1959: 18–31). No doubt readers will pass a similar judgment on this commentary, but I suspect that Ginsburg would agree that in neither case was some fantastic notion of totality either attainable or desired.

Just within the last 60 years or so there have appeared more than 60 studies that survey Jewish and Christian readings (see the Bibliography, pp. 275–80) and I will highlight a few of them here. Roland E. Murphy's long-time research and reflection on this area yielded invaluable results. He variously covered patristic commentary (1979, 1982), other traditional forms of exegesis (1982) and produced overall surveys (1992: pp. xlviii–lvi and 1993, both of which are summaries of earlier studies and more besides). Until his death in 2002, Murphy provided updates of academic approaches to Qoheleth in his introduction to wisdom literature, *The Tree of Life* (1990, and supplements in subsequent editions in 1996, 2001). Wide-ranging and well balanced, these remain perhaps the best surveys of recent Qoheleth scholarship.[1] Michael V. Fox (1999) has written a concise and detailed article in the *Dictionary of Biblical Interpretation*. There he outlines traditional Jewish and Christian approaches and modern critical studies. The brief treatments of Ben Sira's apparent knowledge of (and interaction with) Qoheleth and of the nature of the Septuagint translation are particularly useful (on which, see also Jarick in Gregory Thaumaturgos 1990: 5–6). For early Christian readings it is difficult to surpass the extensive treatment found in the recent Ancient Christian Commentary on Scripture volume on Proverbs, Ecclesiastes and the Song of Solomon (Wright 2005). As well as extensive bibliographical material for the patristic period, for Ecclesiastes there appears roughly 100 pages of selected translated passages ordered as commentary. The outstanding bibliographies that relate particularly to the history of reading are that of R. G. Lehmann in D. Michel's commentary (1989: 290–322), Marek Starowieyski's bibliographical list of 187 Christian (and some Jewish) works on Ecclesiastes up to the Middle Ages (1993: 424–40) and Thomas Krüger's 'Influence' section of his commentary bibliography (2004: 244–51).

Four works in particular make Jewish sources on Ecclesiastes more accessible. The first I have already discussed: Ginsburg's 1861 commentary, which has such useful items as a translation of the preface and first chapter of Ibn Ezra's commentary on Ecclesiastes (1861: 46–56). The second is Meir Zlotowitz's 1994 (orig. 1976) commentary in the Artscroll Tanach series. Writing from a strictly Orthodox perspective, Zlotowitz makes extensive reference to a large number of traditional Jewish exegetes – e.g. Rashi, Rashbam, Ibn Ezra, Saadia Gaon – and provides a helpful biographical supplement. The third is A. J. Rosenberg's Judaica Press edition of the Hagiographa (1992), which includes translation of all of Rashi's commentary as well as selections from Sforno, Rashbam, Ibn Ezra and various talmudic and midrashic sources. The fourth is Michael V. Fox's JPS commentary on Ecclesiastes (2004). The 'overview of interpretations' section of his introduction (pp. xxii–xxx) helpfully surveys the main rabbinic approaches and, as befits the remit of that series, informs the exegesis of the whole commentary.

As is the case with most biblical books, there has been little sustained attention given to the impact of Ecclesiastes *outside* Jewish and Christian traditions to include its frankly staggering impact on the arts (especially literature), and certainly nothing like an overview. Partial exceptions to this are volumes that survey *the Bible* in literature (e.g. Norton 1993 and Jeffrey 1992) and more

---

[1]   Murphy's 1993 survey of Qoheleth (and Proverbs) studies for *Currents in Research: Biblical Studies* is soon to be updated in that journal by Harold Washington.

than 30 specialist reception history studies (see Bibliography, pp. 281–3). Most of these are from literary or historical disciplines and have scrutinized Ecclesiastes in, for example, Chekhov, Donne, Eliot, Goethe, Melville, Thackeray, Wordsworth and Voltaire. Some of these studies have also sought a broader overview of a theme or body of work relating to Ecclesiastes in literature (e.g. Hattaway 1968, Matsuda 1989). During roughly the last 100 years, from that body has appeared a benign but aberrant growth: some now commonplace literary allusions to Qoheleth in articles and monographs. Chief among these are from Melville's *Moby Dick*, Shaw's *Man and Superman* and Thackeray's poem 'Vanitas Vanitatum'. In each case the primary authors engaged in a more careful and sustained reading of Qoheleth than the brief citations (always of the same proportion) suggest. These brief expressions of interest in Qoheleth's presence in the world of letters come only in passing and, much to my frustration, generally without bibliographic references. (A good example is the frequent, and it seems erroneous, reference to Tennyson's declaration that Ecclesiastes was 'the greatest poem of ancient or modern times'. In fact, the citation is even more frequently applied to Job, but no one, to my knowledge, has been able to locate it.) And so the distinct focus of this commentary, while a part of the rich tradition of reception history, is its attention to cultural impact, as broadly conceived as possible. And the comments of one scholar of medieval literature, at the conclusion of her study of the Solomonic corpus, its interpretive tradition and their collective impact on Dante and Chaucer, is particularly instructive here:

> while scholars have readily admitted the extensive influence of the Book of Scripture on the culture of the [medieval] period, the way in which that influence affected the literature of the period has yet to be clarified. If the tradition regarding the *libri Salomonis* is any guide, the Biblical books provided writers with paradigms for narrative structures, suggested means of obtaining thematic and aesthetic unity, and played a more crucial role than we have known in the referential context of the Middle Ages. (Beal 1982: 291–2)

If this commentary goes some way to 'clarifying' the cultural influence of the extraordinary little book of Ecclesiastes, it will have succeeded.

2   Reading Strategies and Lines of Influence

There are, to be sure, salient features of Ecclesiastes' reception in a given historical period, and these are, I hope, brought out clearly enough in this commentary. However, organizing the material along lines of historical

periodization alone has prove
employed a combination of
aware of the difficulties in a
larly that of historic 'perio
by the term 'Middle Ag℮
suggested should be r℮
survive quite well the
description, then, o'
cable here: 'the ol℮
ideas seemed ju℮
lenged. The c'
new science '
(2001: p. x℮
    I have

Pre-m
Early
Mo

conc℮.
the pre-m℮

℮e end, therefore, I have
℮ic organization. I am fully
℮tical categorization, particu-
℮cussion of the problems posed
℮–27), and the boundaries I have
℮eed, some interpretive paradigms
℮f subsequent shifts. Euan Cameron's
℮ of the European Renaissance is appli-
℮ot discarded overnight. Some of the new
℮cure as the medieval lore which they chal-
℮ quite elastic, and even exponents of the
℮hey clung to some of the earlier assumptions'

℮wing three periods:

℮00

℮w European shifts of thinking as construed in the broadly
℮ 'modernity' that continue to enjoy currency. As readings in
℮n period are defined almost entirely by Jewish and Christian
approaches, I have not sought to separate their treatment along these lines (this
more easily enables developmental comparisons). Jewish and Christian interpretive traditions exhibit, at least in part, patterns (due mainly to shared ideological commitments and the dominance of methods set out by influential
figures and schools – though even then, *pattern* is a strong word), but this is
far less the case in the multitude of other readings, especially those of poetry
and fiction. From almost precisely 1500, the relatively clear lines of Jewish and
Christian readings explode into more complex discourses, increasingly as art
for art's sake and increasingly political. For these reasons, in the other two
periods I have introduced thematic categories, such as, for example, Renaissance and Reform, Literature, Visual Art and so on.

Pre-Modern Reading: –1500

Two prominent features of Ecclesiastes interpretation in the pre-modern
period are worth noting here. The first is the working premise that Solomon
wrote the book. The second is the programmatic reading of Ecclesiastes as a
refutation of the vanity of the world. The latter of these is pretty well exclusively

Christian in provenance, while the former spans Jewish and Christian traditions. While there were exceptions, both features slowly faded from the interpretive horizon during the early modern period. At the same time as a host of changes were being rung in hermeneutics, pseudonymity of some sort gradually became an immovable fact of Ecclesiastes interpretation. And although the 'vanity of the world' reading proved more durable in the modern period, as a programmatic and exclusive reading, it too began to fade into obscurity during the early modern period. Since the 'raw materials' for both of these readings are found first in the book's opening verses, I deal with them as special sections of the first chapter of commentary.

Ecclesiastes, for whatever reason, did not engage the imaginations of the inhabitants of Qumran in the way that, say, the prophetic literature did (for what little is to be found in the Dead Sea Scrolls, see Martínez and Tigchelaar 1997: 289–90, and Christianson 1998a: 151 n. 77). After Qumran, the earliest interpretive traditions are likely preserved in the Mishnah, midrashim and even talmudim (more on talmudic readings in particular can be found throughout the commentary). Marc Hirshman (1958), in a study of remarkable insight, compares four early Christian commentaries to *Midrash Qoheleth* (itself a compilation of earlier sources, and which Hirshman dates *c.*600; 1958: 137), in the hopes of understanding the exegetical method and putative audiences of both traditions. Regarding the *Midrash*, Hirshman identifies 'five facets of its aggadic exegesis' (1958: 155–64): (1) Solomonic exegesis, which (creatively!) relates verses to the biographical material on Solomon in Kings and Chronicles; (2) identification, a close relative of allegory and typology, in which verses are related to 'a specific individual, event or object drawn either from the Bible or from the Midrash's contemporary surroundings' (p. 158); (3) anecdotes, usually revolving around rabbinic sages and illustrating 'moral or theological points' (p. 160); (4) *mashal*, 'generally translated "parable"', and defined by D. Stern as 'allusive narratives told for an ulterior purpose' (p. 161); (5) cataloguing, especially prevalent in *this* midrash, and concerned to 'collect and topically order diverse bits of information' in the form of lists and catalogues (p. 162).

Ecclesiastes only gradually took hold in the early Christian literature, and there is little sign of it, for example, in the 'Apostolic Fathers' writings of Ignatius, Polycarp et al. Perhaps it took time to relate Qoheleth to Christianity, but in the course of the third century the first substantial writing becomes available (see below; although J. R. Wright points to the work of Melito of Sardis in the late second century, 'of which little is known'; 2005: p. xxiv). When Christians broke ground on Ecclesiastes, the result calls to mind Ginsburg's caustic summary of this developing discourse as 'the monotony of patristic exposition'

(1861: 105; here said to highlight the 'relief' of the superior commentary of Olympiodorus, *c.*510). That assessment is fairly easily formed on the evidence of the relentless tendency to relegate Qoheleth's reflections to the perceived truths of Christian liturgy and doctrine. One of the earliest examples will become typical, from the *Commentary on the Beginning of Ecclesiastes* of Dionysius of Alexandria (*c.*200–*c.*265), a student of Origen. On Qoheleth's endorsement of eating and drinking in 2:24–5, he comments,

> And surely mere material meats and drinks are not the soul's good. For the flesh, when luxuriously nurtured, wars against the soul, and rises in revolt against the spirit. And how should not intemperate eatings and drinkings also be contrary to God? He speaks, therefore, of things mystical. For no one shall partake of the spiritual table, but one who is called by Him, and has listened to the wisdom which says, 'Take and eat.' (In Coxe 1978: 114; cf. the same reading in Augustine, *City of God* 17.20; the rabbis did not like the sentiment either and suggested that *all* 'the references to eating and drinking in this Book signify Torah and good deeds'; *Midrash Qoheleth* 2.24.1)

However, diversity is not too difficult to find, and Ginsburg's assessment does not do justice to some. In the third and fourth centuries we might begin to recognize in the work of Origen, Didymus the Blind, Gregory Thaumaturgos, Gregory of Nyssa, Theodore of Mopsuestia and Jerome the beginnings of more lengthy, influential and insightful readings. While Origen's commentary on Ecclesiastes is no longer extant, the other five of these offer the most substantial examples of early Christian interpretation of Ecclesiastes. Gregory Thaumaturgos's *Paraphrase* (*c.*245) is the 'earliest systematic Christian treatment of Ecclesiastes which has come down to us' (Jarick in Gregory Thaumaturgos 1990: 3). As a student of Origen, in whose footsteps Gregory Thaumaturgos envisioned his own work, his paraphrase offers some insight into Origen's lost commentary on Ecclesiastes. The paraphrase may have been borne of a need to address the perceived strangeness and inadequacy of the Septuagint, the only access to Ecclesiastes for Greek readers (Jarick in Gregory Thaumaturgos 1990: 5). As such, Gregory's *Paraphrase* is written for the benefit of the Church, with a vision of its 'unison with the general Christian tradition' (Gregory Thaumaturgos 1990: 315). Gregory refreshingly offers his own distinct interpretive voice, not always adapting, for example, the allegorical method that Origen's influence would imply. Didymus the Blind (*c.*313–98) is another interpreter on whom Origen exercised particular influence. Like that of Thaumaturgos, his commentary is complete (bar the last verses of ch. 12) and systematic, particularly regarding methodology (see Diego Sánchez 1990; note his seemingly prescient views on Ecclesiastes' authorship, below, p. 95).

Two other nuanced and perceptive patristic voices can be heard in this period. Gregory of Nyssa's eight homilies on Eccl. 1–3:13 (*c*.380) were also composed for the benefit of the church. Here Ecclesiastes looks 'exclusively to the conduct of the Church', for it 'gives instruction in those things by which one would achieve the life of virtue' (hom. 1, in Gregory of Nyssa 1993: 34). Consistently Gregory is at pains to relate the words of the Ecclesiast to a well ordered Christian life. Gregory sometimes uses the text of Ecclesiastes as a springboard for other subjects, notably in his extraordinary attack on slavery (the opening paragraphs of hom. 4; see below, pp. 158–9). Both Gregories pursue their task with originality and flair, and witness to the interpretive demands made by Ecclesiastes on the earliest readers (note Gregory of Nyssa's comment on the stamina required to wrestle with Qoheleth, in Testimonia, p. 1). Around the same time, we might note the unusually literal approach of Theodore of Mopsuestia (*c*.350–428), distinctly at odds with the already dominant allegorists. In his study of Theodore's Ecclesiastes commentary, John Jarick traces his condemnation by the Second Council of Constantinople in the sixth century (partly for denying the canonical status of some biblical books, including Ecclesiastes, an accusation Jarick argues was misguided) and the discovery of a Syriac version of his commentary in Damascus in the twentieth century (Jarick 1995: 306–7; Theodore's reading of 12:1–7 will be discussed below in the commentary section).

More influential than these commentators combined, however, is Jerome, whose commentary on Ecclesiastes (388/9) has received a good deal of critical attention (most recently and comprehensively in Hirshman 1996 and Kraus 1999–2000). It was designed, he tells us in his Preface, with a purpose:

> I remember just five years ago when I was still at Rome and studying virtuous Blesilla's book of Ecclesiastes that I taught her to think lightly of her generation and to esteem futile everything that she saw in the world. I remember too being asked by her to examine individually all the difficult passages in a short treatise so that she might be able to understand what she was reading without me always being present. Accordingly, since she was taken from us by her sudden death while I was still doing the preparation for my work . . . I then ceased from my work, silenced by the terrible grief of such a misfortune. Now though, situated in Bethlehem, clearly a more holy city, I can fulfil that promise to the memory of Blesilla and to you [i.e. his Roman disciples, a widow named Paula and her daughter Eustochium], and remind you briefly that I have used no authority in this work, but have rather translated directly from the Hebrew itself and have adapted it to the traditional language of the Septuagint in those passages which do not differ greatly from the Hebrew. Occasionally I have taken account of the Greek versions, those of Aquila, Symmachus, and Theodotion so that I do not deter the reader's enthusiasm with too much novelty. I have also not pursued

those streams of conjecture, which lack a factual basis, for I do not believe this to be sensible. (Jerome 2000: *ad loc.*[2])

Jerome describes here the thorough and unusually consultative approach that he employs throughout the commentary. J. N. D. Kelly admires Jerome's skill in edification and the brilliance of his style:

> On every page we come across . . . breath-taking transformations of the plain meaning of the Preacher's musings, all set out in colourful and rhythmic prose . . . For the modern student, intent on discovering what Ecclesiastes is really about, Jerome's brilliant exegetical essay is worse than useless. But judged by the standards of his age, when Christian men took it for granted that the true sense of the Old Testament was the spiritual one lurking beneath the surface which pointed forward to Christ and his Church, it was a *tour de force* of edification and illumination. (1975: 151–2; cf. 144–52 where other aspects of the commentary are discussed; cf. Ginsburg, who is even less charitable [1861: 101–3])

Kelly presumes a fairly limited horizon of expectation in his 'modern student' (can this really be 'worse' than 'useless'?). Jerome offers us in his comments, as Kelly admits, access to contemporary rabbinic exegesis. It is also fascinating to encounter Jerome's often detailed comments on the Hebrew and comparison to the Greek versions. Angelo Penna is impressed enough to call the commentary a 'milestone' for its use of Hebrew and rabbinic tradition, literal exegesis and sympathetic citation of classical authors such as Cicero, Horace and Virgil (1950: 41). Also noteworthy is Jerome's frequent procedure of dealing first with the literal interpretation of a verse and only then moving on to the spiritual. And in his thoroughness he is, by any contemporary standard, unusually respectful of the reader. So, for example, of the catalogue of times in ch. 3, Jerome comments, 'The Hebrews understand all that he has written about the contradiction of times . . . as concerning Israel. Because it is not necessary to go through each verse in turn here, commenting on how they are to be interpreted and what they mean, I will list them briefly, leaving a more detailed study to the reader's discretion' (2000: *ad loc.*).

There is no doubting the outstanding and lasting influence of Jerome's commentary, which is well captured by Murphy, who finds in it 'fairly liberal interpretation . . . erudite philology, command of the ancient Greek versions, lessons from his Jewish tutor, Bar Aqiba, etc.' (1992: p. li; Hirshman and Kraus share Murphy's enthusiasm). His translation of Ecclesiastes for the Vulgate (which reportedly, *along with* Proverbs and Song of Songs, took all of three

---

[2] *Ad loc.* is used throughout this commentary since the translation, by Robin MacGregor Lane (who has kindly permitted me to use it), is unpublished.

days to complete!) itself wielded its influence through, among other things, its reading of *hebel* as 'vanitas'. Indeed, Jerome's Preface (above), 'since it became one of the standard prefaces to the book in medieval Bibles, was probably the most widely read exegetical help on Ecclesiastes in the middle ages' (Eliason 1989: 41 n. 5). Examples from his commentary can be found extensively throughout this commentary, and Jerome's hugely influential monastic approach, to read Ecclesiastes as a refutation of the vanity of worldly things, will be taken up in detail in chapter 1 (see pp. 98–141).

A particularly influential mode of reading Ecclesiastes is first fully developed by Pope Gregory the Great in book 4 of his *Dialogues* (*c.*593). Here Gregory engages in a discussion with his deacon, Peter, on the question of the immortality of the soul. Gregory describes what is really behind the seeming contradictions of the book called Ecclesiastes:

> [W]hen there are many people holding opinions of various kinds, they are brought into harmony by the reasoning of the speaker. This book, then, is called 'the preacher' because in it Solomon makes the feelings of the disorganized people his own in order to search into and give expression to the thoughts that come to their untutored minds ... For the sentiments he expresses in his search are as varied as the individuals he impersonates ... Therefore we find that some statements of this book are introduced as inquiries, while others are meant to give satisfaction by their logic ... It is clear ... that one statement is introduced through his impersonation of the weak, while the other is added from the dictates of reason. (In Gregory the Great 1959: 193)

Such an approach allows Gregory to 'solve' troublesome passages. So, for example, Solomon 'writes, "Rejoice, O young man, while you are young." While a little later he adds, "The dawn of youth is fleeting" [11:9–10]. In criticizing what he has just recommended, he indicates clearly that the former pronouncement proceeded from carnal desires, while the latter was based on a true judgment' (1959: 194; cf. the 'ironizing' reading of this passage by Bonaventure, below, p. 221). Gregory works similar magic with other troublesome texts, such as 3:18–20 (the most developed example – see p. 178), 5:18[3] and 12:13.

Although this is not the first reading strategy to cope with Ecclesiastes' more unorthodox passages by proposing a fragmented discourse (Gregory Thaumaturgos anticipates it in his notion of the advice of the wicked being corrected by Solomon), it is one that influenced a host of commentators who followed. As Eliason comments,

---

[3]   All references to ch. 5 will follow the versification of English translations, which is one verse ahead of the MT (in which the English 5:1 is 4:17).

Gregory treats only a minuscule portion of the text of Ecclesiastes, but because he chooses a few of the most provocative cruces in the book and offers a powerful and attractive method for interpreting them, the influence of his work is out of proportion to its brevity. Alcuin [730–804] . . . , the *glossa ordinaria* [*c*.1100] (Eccl. 1.1), and Hugh of St. Cher [*c*.1230–5] . . . incorporate this section of Gregory's work into their commentaries in something close to its entirety. Throughout the Middle Ages, readers of Ecclesiastes label some opinions expressed there as deliberate falsehoods and choose to endorse the more orthodox opinions which follow such passages. (1989: 70)

The lasting influence of Gregory's reading can be discerned in much more recent work, notably by Anthony Perry (1993b). At the end of the exchange in the *Dialogues*, Peter humbly accepts Gregory's views, exposing a more subtle strategy: 'I am happy that I was ignorant on this point and proposed the question, for it provided an excellent opportunity for me to gain a thorough understanding. And now I beg you to bear patiently with me if I, too, like Ecclesiastes, impersonate the weak and continue the inquiry in their name in order to help them more directly' (1959: 196). In other words, here Gregory has used the dialogical approach to legitimate the same procedure in his *Dialogues*, in which others may represent 'the minds of the infirm' and Gregory the truly wise.

The Talmud's use of Ecclesiastes (like its use of the rest of the Hebrew Bible) usually focuses on practical application, often in support of the most banal observation. For example, of Eccl. 5:5, the Talmud at several points suggests that paying what one vows is to be preferred to vowing and not paying (and also to not vowing at all: *b. Nedarim* 9a; *b. Menahoth* 81a; *b. Chullin* 2a; cf. *b. Ketuboth* 72a; *b. Shabbath* 32b), which supports a pattern of authoritative praxis that tells us little about either the text or the community who read this way. Other readings are more informative in this regard. Qoheleth's activity as described in the epilogue is taken by the Talmud as both preservative and restrictive, and classical rabbinic commentary on the passage is rich and nuanced. Another area in which the Talmud does not disappoint is in its own personal interpretive voice, the imitable charm with which it woos its readers. Partly this is accomplished through its non-specificity, in that by not historicizing its illustrative exegesis it creates a space in which we can stand alongside the rabbis. Of course, the same qualities apply to the midrashim. For Qoheleth the patient of spirit are better than the proud in spirit (7:8b), which *Midrash Qoheleth* illustrates with a delightful story:

A Persian came to Rab and said to him, 'Teach me the Torah.' He [consented, and, pointing to the first letter of the alphabet] . . . , told him, 'Say aleph.' The man remarked, 'Who says that this is aleph? There may be others who say that it is not!' 'Say beth,' to which he remarked, 'Who says that this is beth?' Rab rebuked him and drove him out in anger. He went to Samuel and said to him, 'Teach me the Torah.' He told him, 'Say aleph.' The man remarked, 'Who says that this is aleph?' 'Say beth,' to which he remarked, 'Who said this is beth?' The teacher took hold of his ear and the man exclaimed, 'My ear! my ear!' Samuel asked him, 'Who said that this is your ear?' He answered, 'Everybody knows that this is my ear,' and the teacher retorted, 'In the same way everybody knows that this is aleph and that is beth.' Immediately the Persian was silenced and accepted the instruction. Hence . . . better is the forbearance which Samuel displayed with the Persian than the impatience which Rab showed towards him, for otherwise the Persian might have returned to his heathenism. (7.8.1)

The reading shows not just a response to Qoheleth's proverb, but an immersion in its language and logic, helping readers to internalize Qoheleth's words in their entirety.

As in various midrashism and talmudim, *Targum Qoheleth* (*c*.600) represents a relegation of Qoheleth's specific observations to tradition (namely, to the biographical life of Solomon) and to the study of Torah. As such, as Flesher argues (1990), this targum programmatically redefined wisdom (Qoheleth's, but also, in a representative sense, rabbinic wisdom). Indeed, the targumists were deeply uncomfortable with Qoheleth's many ambiguities:

> . . . the targum has transformed Qohelet's natural wisdom into learning based on torah . . . The document that should be the prime container of wisdom thought has been hollowed out and replaced by a post-talmudic rabbinism . . . The Qohelet Targum, which as a translation replaced the Hebrew Qohelet for the vast majority of Jews who did not know Hebrew, is no longer the cogent and relentless perpetuator of ideas dangerous to the rabbinic perspective, but the purveyor of a compelling statement of the rabbinic world view. (Flesher 1990)

While some examples of this mode are found in the commentary (particularly on chs 1 and 12), *Targum Qoheleth* represents one of the least adventurous readings of Ecclesiastes and, like so many pre-modern readings, a resistance to release the full force of his sceptical wisdom.

Jewish tradition has had a distinct way of articulating Ecclesiastes with Jewish life. The unusual grouping of Ecclesiastes with the other Megillot scrolls (Song of Songs, Ruth, Lamentations and Esther) has given it a long history of liturgical significance. Like the other scrolls, Ecclesiastes is read at a festival, in this case of Sukkot (Tabernacles). The practice seems to have been well in place by at least the eleventh century (Fox 2004: p. xv) and probably earlier. The Megillot grouping is unusual in that while the other books have a relatively clear relationship to the festival at which they are read (e.g. Ruth at *Shavuot*

[Harvest], Lamentations commemorating the destruction of the Temple on the ninth of Ab), the case of Ecclesiastes lacks such clarity. While the Talmud hints at some rationale for the choice (cf. e.g. *b. Chagigah* 17a, which relates Eccl. 3:1 to the appropriate keeping of the season, the eighth day of Tabernacles), the other four festivals had a logical textual partner, and Qoheleth was left, as it were, standing at the ball until Sukkot reluctantly agreed to dance (so Knobel, who does not quite put it in these terms; 1991: 4–5). It may well be that Ecclesiastes reflects the transient, fragile and joyful moods of Sukkot, which remembers the time in the wilderness of rootless wandering, unstable habitation (in 'booths', *sukkôt*; cf. Lev. 23:33–7) and the hope of a promised land (see the discussions in Fox 2004: p. xv, and Rosenberg 1992: pp. ix–xi; cf. Jarick [1997], who suggests a thematic correspondence of the liturgy with the season of autumn at which it is read).

Ginsburg surmises that 'numerous commentaries, which are now lost, have been written on this book in the tenth, eleventh and twelfth centuries' (1861: 56). A particularly intriguing extant example comes from the Karaite movement (for Hans Küng, a 'Jewish reformation'; 1992: 170–4): the commentary of Yephet ben 'Ali (written *c.*990). Yephet, the first Jew to write commentaries on the entire Bible, demonstrates a penchant for grammatical observations and an awareness of alternative interpretations (Frank 2000: 122). Richard Bland, in his translation and study of Yephet's commentary ('Ali 1969), argues that the key to understanding Yephet's approach to Ecclesiastes is his interpretation of 1:3, which is that only a person's 'performance of the precepts of God and his good works will benefit him in his hereafter. From this Yephet concludes that one should enjoy the blessings that God has bestowed upon him in this life' (1969: pp. v–vi). In this, suggests Bland, Yephet was 'in full accord with Saadia [Gaon, the leading opponent of the Karaites]' (p. vi). Bland continues in his assessment of the commentary proper:

> His commentary on Ecclesiastes . . . does leave much to be desired from the standpoint of modern critical methods, but as a popular commentary, one written to make the Book of Ecclesiastes an effective influence in the lives of his less literate co-religionists, it is outstanding. In this work which combines the best in the thinking of Yephet's predecessors with his own views, there is a unity and coherence which a mere eclectic could not hope to attain. ('Ali 1969: p. vii)

While very traditional in approach, the commentary is peppered with some remarkable and prescient insights. So, for example, on 1:12, Yephet observes that Qoheleth 'began with *I Qohelet* because he intends to relate from his own experience everything to which he refers in what follows . . . It was likely that it was he who first called himself *Qohelet*, the editor [*nwdm*, a term he uses several times] following his example' ('Ali 1969: 166–7; cf. Jerome, who comes close to this: 'here he returns to the subject of himself, and reveals who he was, and how he knew and experienced all things'; 2000: *ad loc.*). These are views that sit at ease among modern studies. It is worth noting, too, that Yephet's insight is made all the more remarkable by the fact that, according to Flesher (1990), classical rabbinic exegesis was ill at ease with Qoheleth's emphasis on experiential epistemology.

The main themes of Qoheleth interpretation, while modified, changed remarkably little throughout the Middle Ages. The book, however, seemed to hold a powerful sway over many. Eliason captures the appeal well:

> The modern reader is likely to be taken with the skeptical flavor of the book, and to feel a certain intellectual kinship with the un-biblical character of its thought. But the medieval reader could also feel an intellectual kinship with the book. No less than the modern reader he could find in the words of the Preacher a doctrine which fit his presuppositions, a project which was made easier by the fact that he read a text which had been translated by scholars who shared his neo-platonized understanding of the Old and New Testaments. (1989: 39)

Such appeal is evidenced by the immense popularity of Ecclesiastes among the Christian exegetes of the period, as has been so forcefully brought to light by the seminal work of Beryl Smalley. What Smalley finds to define thirteenth-century works on Ecclesiastes is that the 'ethical content, the observation on politics and on natural science to be found in the sapiential books do not stir the commentator's curiosity; he ignores the invitation to speculate' (1949: 323). At the same time, many writers were bringing the sapiential books to the fore in doctrinal dispute. 'In the twelfth century the Pauline Epistles had been the chief focus for doctrinal discussion. The sapiential books did not displace them; but they became second in the scale of importance, in so far as doctrine was attached to lectures on Scripture' (1949: 325; cf. her comments on William of Tournai and Bonaventure, 1950: 75).[4]

Among the key medieval commentators whom Smalley identifies, Hugh of St Victor, who was at the Abbey of St Victor in Paris c.1118 until his death in 1141, worked against the contemporary grain, privileging the literal sense of Scripture. His nineteen homilies on Eccl. 1:1–4:8 'originated in collations or conferences, preached to the brothers' (Smalley 1952: 98; cf. Holm-Nielsen 1976: 86–8). In the prologue to his homilies, Hugh makes his approach clear:

[4] More discussion of medieval approaches to Ecclesiastes is to be found in the *Vanitas Vanitatum* section of ch. 1 (pp. 102–106).

And so, in this work, I do not think that one should toil much after tropologies or mystical allegorical senses through the whole course of the argument, especially as the author himself aims less at improving, or at relating mysteries, than at moving the human heart to scorn worldly things by obviously true reasons and plain persuasion. I do not deny that many mysteries are included in the argument, especially in the latter part. As he proceeds, the author always, with increase of contemplation, rises above the visible ever more and more. But it is one thing to consider the writer's intention and his argument as a whole, another to think that certain of his *obiter dicta* [incidental speech], which have a mystical sense and must be understood spiritually, should not be passed over. (In Smalley 1952: 100)

A good example of his impressive attention to the style of Ecclesiastes is his explanation of the rhetorical change that occurs at the start of ch. 3, the catalogue of times: 'The words of a man are diverse, because the heart of a man is not one . . . Therefore Solomon, in disputing about vanity, changes the ideas in his speech frequently, so that he might show his attitude to be changed through love of vanity' (in Eliason 1989: 73 n. 64). According to Smalley, 'the *Homilies* became a classic. Teachers quoted and borrowed from them extensively' (1949: 320; cf. Lubac 1960: 434–5). Indeed, their impact was felt far and wide, beyond monastic settings, as is evident in their influence on the narrative poem of Guillame de Machaut, *Jugement dou roy de Navarre* (1349; see Ehrhart 1980).

Around the same time as Hugh, several key Jewish exegetes were flourishing in France and Spain. Perhaps most notable among these in the case of Qoheleth is the celebrated French exegete and Talmud scholar Rashbam (*c*.1080–*c*.1160), grandson of Rashi. Rashbam's commentary is a lucid and coherent treatment that is rightly credited for being the first to identify the presence of an edited frame in Ecclesiastes (see the discussion below, p. 249). Sara Japhet and Robert Salters draw attention to the commentary's 'well-structured, premeditated composition, the writing of which is guided by a literary insight into the book of Qoheleth' (in Rashbam 1985: 42). Like Hugh, Rashbam distinguished himself from the interpretive tradition to which he belonged. The principle applied with 'absolute consistency' throughout his commentary is to arrive at a literal meaning. 'A word, a phrase, a verse – when found in a given context – can have one and only one interpretation. Thus the practice which is so common in Jewish exegetical tradition, including medieval commentators, of suggesting several possibilities for interpreting a given text, is completely absent from Rashbam's works' (Japhet and Salters, in Rashbam 1985: 61–2).

Another outstanding Jewish work of this period was composed by Samuel ibn Tibbon, sometime between 1198/9 and 1221. James Robinson describes its scope and immense influence:

[The commentary] was one of the first major works of philosophical exegesis written in Hebrew and it exercised considerable influence in southern France, Italy, and Spain. It is a massive work [approx. 280 pp. 'in modern typeface'], comprehensive in scope, and shows why Samuel gained distinction not only as a translator but also as a philosopher and exegete. (2001: 83; cf. Kugel, who notes that it is Tibbon's commentary that contained 'one of the most influential' discussions of biblical poetry in the medieval period; 1979: 70)

The commentary begins with the ancient device of prooemium (prologue) in which Tibbon systematically explicates such questions as 'Solomon's' use of a pseudonym (further on Tibbon's view in this regard, see p. 96), the book's title, its rhetorical division and method of inquiry. The last item Tibbon takes to be a procedure of Qoheleth to relate 'one thing to another', which is embodied in the word *qhl*: '*Qohelet* signifies the bringing together of two premises in order to generate a conclusion, i.e. it is a word that means syllogism . . . [Tibbon] is clearly thinking of the Greek term for syllogism, which has the primary sense of bringing together' (Robinson 2001: 86, 87).

Like Tibbon, Italian theologian Bonaventure composed a commentary (1253–7) that resonated spectacularly well with its audience. Jeremy Holmes highlights the stimulating context in which Bonaventure found himself:

> The thirteenth century was an exciting time to be an exegete. Biblical studies were moving from the monasteries to the schools, the works of Aristotle were being introduced into Europe, and the new mendicant religious orders were leading the way in a gospel-driven intellectual revolution; these converging forces were accompanied by an explosion of theoretical and technical innovations . . . (2003)

Smalley suggests that Bonaventure's work 'illustrates how a single postill [commentary] could become a classic. I have seen a large number of postills on Ecclesiastes of the later thirteenth and early fourteenth centuries: all quote Bonaventure and all quote him anonymously' (1952: 274). For whatever reason, it seems that Bonaventure marked out Ecclesiastes for special attention (Holmes 2003). In perhaps the most developed mode of the reading, he follows the approach made so popular by Gregory the Great in his *Dialogues*, of postulating different voices in the book, such as the (repentant) fool, or that of an Epicurean. In Bonaventure's words,

> to understand what [Ecclesiastes] says, attention must be paid to two things, namely, *the reason* for speaking and *the style* of speaking. Further, he uses two styles of speaking, for he says some things *plainly*, others *ironically* . . . Ecclesiastes says some things *to approve them* . . . He says some things *to report* what *he*

has done ... Likewise, he says some things to report what *he has thought* ... He often uses this style in the book as if to report his temptations. Hence this book is a kind of meditation by Solomon. Just as a person moves from one meditation to another depending on diverse circumstances, as when someone thinks that this is good, and afterwards begins another line of thought. This is how Solomon speaks in this book. (Commenting on 5:17; 2005: 233–4)

The contribution of Bonaventure's literal approach was long-standing and far-reaching and managed to tackle the problems posed by Qoheleth in a more direct fashion than its predecessors (cf. Smalley 1952: 298). Indeed, Bonaventure's commentary 'was a brilliant summary of traditional teaching, yet also utilized the most recent developments in exegetical techniques' (Monti 1979: 84). Monti notes that some 'indication of its wide diffusion may be gathered from the forty-two extant manuscripts spread throughout Europe which contain this postill' (1979: 83). His commentary became the standard, displacing those of Jerome, Hugh of St Victor and Hugh of St Cher, and probably served as a significant aid to preachers and spiritual directors of the day (Karris and Murray in Bonaventure 2005: 7). Bonaventure's articulation of the *contemptus mundi* theme is discussed in chapter 1 (p. 103), and other examples can be found throughout this commentary.

The interest in Ecclesiastes of Bonaventure and many other medieval Christian writers was kindled in part by surrounding philosophical inquiries, as Karlfried Froehlich explains:

A real shift in the exegetical treatment of the 'Books of Solomon' ... occurred with the reception of the *libri naturales* into the arts curriculum in the first decades of the thirteenth century which stirred theologians and exegetes to a new interest in the scientific aspects of biblical teaching. The interpretation of Ecclesiastes, which was concerned with the 'nature of the things of this world', was bound to reflect this trend ... The new interest in the sapiential literature was easy to understand. Its content was closer than that of other biblical books to the secular sciences being explored at that time. The questions which the literal sense of the Solomonic books raised often paralleled the philosophical material taught in the arts faculties ... Thus, the thirteenth century interpretation of Ecclesiastes did not discard the older exegetical tradition. It enriched it by making room for the discussion of a wider range of issues. (2000: 530–1; cf. the example of the interpretation of 1:4–7 below, pp. 145–6)

Intriguingly, this rich articulation between Ecclesiastes and concurrent questions of science and philosophy (i.e. the pursuit of knowledge broadly conceived) would recur with particular urgency and scope in the Renaissance period, constituting one of the most momentous themes of Qoheleth's reception history.

There are, however, other kinds of readings in this period to consider, readings not limited to strictly religious contexts. From as early as the Old English poem *The Wanderer* (from the 'Exeter Book', c.975), Ecclesiastes appears to have influenced literary works in terms of theme and structure. Paul de Lacy suggests that the difficult structure and thematic disparity of *The Wanderer* is best accounted for by Ecclesiastes being a 'primary influence' on the poet (1998: 125), and hence it shares some of its key features. So, for example, *The Wanderer*, too, reflects on the transitory nature of existence, the futility of human endeavour and expresses 'a strong declaration of the hopelessness engendered by mutability' (1998: 131). Indeed, the mournful reflections on wisdom recall Qoheleth's concerns:

> And so to grow wise
> one must spend
> a few winters in this world . . . The sage gets
> how ghastly it will be
> when all the world's estate
> is standing in ruin
>   (In Romano 1998)

And towards its end appear bleak reflections on destiny that also mirror Qoheleth's thought:

> All is suffering
> in this earthly realm.
> Things wend to the worse
> in this world under the heavens.
> Here fortune is not given.
> Here friend is not given.
> Here man is not given.
> Here maid is not given.
> All this earthly abode
> ends in emptiness
>   (In Romano 1998)

The similarities lead Lacy to conclude that the poet 'knew about' aspects of the philosophy, imagery and structure of Hebrew wisdom, especially Ecclesiastes.

Qoheleth-like reflections on human transience and death are also reflected in a poem by Bishop Patrick, 'To a Friend on the Frailty of Life' (*ad amicum de caduca vita*, c.1079), which begins,

The painter, alas!, shall die sooner than the painted page,
   Unless fire devour it or heavy water drown it:
And this skin which I have scored with my own hand for a short while,
   Ah me!, shall outlast my brief life.

He goes on to suggest themes more directly from Ecclesiastes:

As one man dies another, doomed to death, is born:
   So are man's birth and end ever with us.
. . .

The present wipes out the past, and the future the present:
   Who once was mighty, lo! that he lived is unknown.
. . .

Now in time of weeping he laughs: in time of laughter
   Soon he may weep and grieve that he has not grieved before.
We all know these truths, but few of us dread them in our hearts,
   For the heart of man is harder than rock.
(ll. 1–4, 19–20, 29–30, 41–44, in
Patrick 1955: 79, 81; translated
anonymously in 1585)

Such themes on the brevity of life and its fickle workings, which resonate so naturally with Ecclesiastes, are picked up again in the Vernon manuscript, a collection of anonymous Middle English 'mortality lyrics' of the fourteenth century (*c*.1325–50). These, too, provide a counterpoint to the more controlled readings of the abbeys. In contrast to the more orthodox theological exegesis of the twelfth and thirteenth centuries, the mortality lyrics interpret Ecclesiastes with little concern for theological palatability. As Matsuda puts it, the 'poems on death and transience not only borrow directly from Ecclesiastes but depend on it to provide them with the dignified and personalized generalizations on death and transience, expressed with the lyrical grandeur and the simplicity of images characteristic of the Sapiential Books' (1989: 193).

Two poems in particular, 'For Each Man Ought Himself to Know' and 'And Some Time Think on Easter Day', engage with Ecclesiastesan themes and ideas, while 'This World Fares as a Fantasy' (lit. 'This World Passes like a Dream') draws its language more directly from Qoheleth:

> The passage of the sun, we may well know
> > Arises in the East and goes down West;
> the rivers run into the sea,
> > and [the sea] is never increased;
> winds rush here and there
>
> . . .
>
> This world passes like a dream.
> > > (ll. 13–17, 24, in
> > > Brown and Smithers
> > > 1952: 160–1; my tr.)

One of its dominant themes is the illusory nature of the world. 'This world is false, fickle and frail', laments the poet (l. 83, 1952: 162; further, see the commentary below on 8:17). Sitwell traces the lyrics' concerns to mid-fourteenth-century conflict about the question of God's foreknowledge (1950: 290). Matsuda discusses the particularly distinct interpretive approach to Ecclesiastes found in the lyrics:

> Ecclesiastes . . . proved challenging to medieval commentators for the somewhat unorthodox eschatological assumptions it maintained, especially because it appeared to lack the perspective which extends beyond death and remains sometimes ostensibly indifferent to the fate of the afterlife. Unlike late medieval commentaries on Ecclesiastes, the Vernon series makes little attempt to alter such problematic points, but rather adopts, whether consciously or not, similar indifference towards the afterlife. One may say that the Vernon series owes its non-homiletic quality basically to the fact that it regards, like Ecclesiastes, death and salvation primarily as problems of this world. (Matsuda 1989: 193–4; cf. the similar assessment in Sitwell 1950: 288)

Not only did Ecclesiastes provide these poets with a framework for reflecting on the darker themes of human existence, but they even anticipate modern approaches in their recognition and emphasis on the 'self-examining' aspects of Ecclesiastes (Matsuda 1989: 199; cf. Brown 1996 and Christianson 1998a: 173–215).

Other discourses of the period distinguish themselves from the more common examination of Ecclesiastes' relevance to points of doctrine, even by adopting and transforming the approach typified by the abbeys. The tripartite programme of reading the books of Solomon (Proverbs, Ecclesiastes, Song of Songs) originated with Origen and was developed by various medieval exegetes. In such schemes Ecclesiastes inhabited a middle, transitional stage of moral or spiritual development. As Eliason puts it,

> In Origen's view of the process of education, Ecclesiastes holds a mediating position between the most basic religious instruction – good conduct – and the most

sublime religious achievements – the mystical contemplation of divine things. Or, in other words, Ecclesiastes pertains to those whose religious instruction is already significantly under way, but who have yet to attain the highest goals of that instruction. It is the next to last stop in the project of learning to love. Jerome, faithful to Origen, expands these ideas in his commentary . . . and from this source they pass into the works of Alcuin . . . , *glossa ordinaria* (Eccl. 1.1), Hugh of St. Victor . . . and Honorius of Autun. (1989: 49)

It is such a structure that, according to Rebecca Beal, exercised a substantial influence on Dante in his composition of *La commedia* (composed between 1308 and 1321) as well as Chaucer's *Troilus and Criseyde* (*c*.1385). So with *La commedia*, the

> formal organization of the [medieval Solomonic corpus] into three books arranged in a 'necessary' order and identified as 'three songs' corresponds exactly to Dante's organization of the *Commedia* into the three *cantiche* of *Inferno*, *Purgatorio*, and *Paradiso*. Solomon's composition reflects the *triplex status hominis* [developed in Hugh of St Cher's Ecclesiastes commentary] (man at the three levels of his spiritual ascent) . . . Against the background of the three states Dante sets his pilgrimage, an allegorical presentation of the soul's progress to perfect wisdom. (1982: 107)

In the application of such an approach Dante may have been directly influenced by the popular postils of Hugh of St Victor (between 1118 and 1141) and Bonaventure (1253–7) in particular. But for Beal, 'correspondences between the *libri Salomonis* and the *Commedia* go beyond the external or even formal parallels. The Biblical tradition provides a literary vehicle which Dante appropriates and adapts to his own similar subject, the journey of the soul to God' (1982: 108; Beal goes on to develop in detail the ways in which Dante's 'allegory and narrative progression' mirrors the medieval approach to the Solomonic corpus). Beal detects a more direct and complex engagement with Eccl. 12 in Chaucer's *Troilus and Criseyde* (on which, see below, pp. 233–4).

It is perhaps sadly fitting to close this section on pre-modern readings with an example wracked with pre-modern superstition. Qoheleth's words made a very brief appearance in one of the most malignant and destructive texts of Western culture (and one which exercised enormous influence). The *Malleus Maleficarum* (*Hammer of Witches*), published by two Dominicans (Jakob Sprenger and Heinrich Institoris) with the blessing of Pope Innocent VIII in successive editions between 1430 and 1505, became 'an immediate best-seller . . . second only to the Bible [and] . . . remained "the" text which any detractor of the witchcraze must confute' (Fontaine 1998: 161–2; cf. the comments of Peter Paolucci in McNeil 1999). Under the heading *Concerning*

Witches who copulate with Devils, and addressing the question, *Why it is that Women are chiefly addicted to Evil Superstitions*, the *Malleus* suggests that

> It is this which is lamented in Ecclesiastes vii, and which the Church even now laments on account of the great multitude of witches. And I have found a woman ... [the whole of 7:26 is cited] More bitter than death, that is, than the devil ... More bitter than death, again, because that is natural and destroys only the body; but the sin which arose from woman destroys the soul ... [and again, because] bodily death is an open and terrible enemy, but woman is a wheedling and secret enemy. (In Sprenger and Institoris 1928: 47)

The *Malleus* goes on to develop the idea of the female anatomy as 'snares and nets', referring to the actual practice of 'binding' men through witchcraft (an oddly similar though inverted idea in relation to this text is found in the *Zohar*, *c.*1290: 'From women come all kinds of divination and sorcery ... And were it not for the fact that their "hands are bound" [7:26], in that they are prevented by heaven, women would be continually murdering and killing the world's inhabitants'; in Lachower and Tishby 1989: 3. 1358). Qoheleth's primary metaphors, then, offer a way of 'expositing' the dangers of witches. It is certainly the case that, as Brian Noonan (1998) has shown, Qoheleth's words are not a favourite source for the *Malleus* (this is his only appearance), and indeed Proverbs and Job appear far more frequently, but this particular use of the text is highly developed and sustained (more so, for example, than other biblical texts in this section). While such a use of the text is hardly evidence in itself of any inherent misogyny, it does lay bare the power of Qoheleth's emotive language, which seemingly lies in wait to be 'exploited' for suppression.[5]

Early Modern Reading: 1500–1800

A.   Renaissance and Reform
... we sometimes feel that there is something ominous in the changes rung on Ecclesiastes during the sixteenth century.

Michael Hattaway (1968: 512)

---

[5] Ecclesiastes has, thankfully, not proved a useful source for religious propoganda. There is a subtle instance, however, in a provocative and latently anti-Semitic statement from French philosopher and historian Ernest Renan, which is oft cited in late nineteenth- and early twentieth-century commentaries, usually without accompanying comment: Ecclesiastes is a 'charming book, the only likeable book [*le seul livre aimable*] ever written by a Jew' (Renan 1873: 101; my tr.). Renan went on to produce a translation and study of the 'age and character' of Ecclesiastes (1882).

The impact of Ecclesiastes, particularly from the early modern period (1500–1800) onwards, has restricted itself mainly to Western discourse, particularly in works of Renaissance and reform. Qoheleth's themes, as we shall see, suited thinkers in this period tremendously well. Indeed, Renaissance thinking (particularly scepticism) and the book of Ecclesiastes enjoyed (if that is the right word) a terribly complex relationship. In unpacking that relationship, I have been helped by the exhaustive work of Michael Hattaway (1968) and Robert Rosin (1997b). As a rough overview, Hattaway's comments on the significance and appeal of Ecclesiastes (and other 'books of Solomon') to Renaissance learning provide a useful starting point:

> Humanist writers did not go to Ecclesiastes merely because the doctrine it contained was particularly suited to their theological quarrels with the schoolmen. At a time when the reading of the Bible was by no means unrestricted, the books of Solomon were, it was felt, texts that could safely be put into the hands of a young man to teach him moral philosophy and eloquence . . . Sir Thomas Elyot [who moved in the circles of Sir Thomas More and Henry VIII in the 1520s to 1530s] prescribed them along with the *Ethics* of Aristotle and the works of Cicero and Plato, they were studied and annotated by Henry VIII, recommended by his Tutors to Edward VI, and by James I to his son Henry. William Lily in his Grammar cited them as suitable texts to turn into Latin, and generations of schoolboys must have absorbed Solomon's proverbial learning in class. (Hattaway 1968: 510)

As well as for these reasons, Ecclesiastes, with its empirical form of scepticism, seemed to fit the cautious yet energetic approach to the new sciences embodied in humanist and reform thinking. Indeed, the long-acknowledged personal approach to knowledge exemplified in its pages would resonate with a new critical change, 'when the evidence of observation came to be accepted as more compelling and credible than inherited wisdom and authority: when natural philosophers quite literally insisted on believing the evidence with their own eyes' (Cameron 2001: pp. xxiii–xxiv; cf. Luther's comments, below). This appeal to Ecclesiastes is bound up with the quest to legitimize the pursuit of the new human sciences (see commentary below on chs 1, 3 and 8 especially).

Rosin's in-depth survey of Renaissance scepticism in relation to the Ecclesiastes commentaries of Luther, Brenz and Melanchthon notes the energetic bundle of attitudes towards scepticism dominant at the start of the Renaissance revival (1997b: 3):

> Skepticism . . . was nothing extraordinary. As the reformers viewed skepticism, it grew from a common human problem . . . Viewed thus, classical skepticism

did not differ from more spontaneous radical doubt in the 16th century. Natural, garden variety doubt could multiply, questioning order and direction in the world and eventually challenging divine purpose and providence in life. Interest in skepticism emerged with the burgeoning Renaissance, resurrecting from classical antiquity a philosophical approach not simply to epistemology but to life. In general, the 16th-century understanding of 'skepticism' echoed the original precept: philosophical non-dogmatism refused to make assertions and shied away from definition, disputing the ability to attain certain knowledge and allowing only a suspension of judgment ... Broad tributaries contributed to a skeptical revival ... – philosophers with their striving for lofty anthropological heights, some common, popular attitudes, plus thinkers with their misgivings on the darker side of man's nature – fostered a natural interest in skepticism. (1997b: 6–7, 76)

Ultimately it was to the implications of this epistemological relativism that Luther, Brenz and Melanchthon felt compelled to respond. But it was not only the reformers who would engage with Qoheleth. A broad range of humanist thinkers would recognize the same dangers but would also see in Qoheleth a safe bridge from the sacral world of Scripture to the intoxicating danger of the new sciences. The luminous figure of Solomon, one who had experienced the heights of learning and of royal authority, would of course enliven this capacity of the book to connect, making his judgment regarding the great sorrow brought on by the increase of knowledge (1:18) simultaneously a humanist battle-cry and lament.

Luther's *Notes on Ecclesiastes* were delivered as a series of lectures in 1526, and he had hoped to publish them himself later (see Luther 1972: pp. ix–x). Although Luther is the progenitor of the attack on the (exaggerated perception of the) monastic approach to Ecclesiastes, in a period of increasing intellectual freedom, Luther also uses Ecclesiastes to cast a generally positive light on the new sciences:

> ... we should not follow the imaginations of the interpreters who suppose that the knowledge of nature, the study of astronomy or of all of philosophy, is being condemned [in Ecclesiastes] and who teach that such things are to be despised as vain and useless speculations. For the benefit of these arts are many and great, as is plain to see every day. In addition, there is not only utility, but also great pleasure in investigating the nature of things. (1972: 9)

Luther further sees Ecclesiastes as a book against free will and therefore in support of his dispute with Erasmus. This is evident in his oft-repeated notion that God frustrates the vain plans of humans, exemplified by Solomon's failures. Commenting on 2:4–11, Luther demands that 'everyone freely enjoy the things that are present, as God has given them. Let him permit them to be granted or withdrawn, to come or go, according to the Lord's will' (1972: 38; cf. his comments on ch. 3 below, pp. 165–6). A few years earlier, Luther commented in his *Fourteen Comforts* (1520) that Ecclesiastes describes a 'whole tragedy' when declaring 'All is vanity and vexation of spirit': 'How many of our plans miscarry? How many of our desires mock us!' (in Luther 1956: 23). Rosin summarizes Luther's approach in relation to Ecclesiastes' anthropology (even if in the process he summarizes Qoheleth's words rather too simply):

> If the text is taken apart from the faith perspective suggested by the book's closing verses and solomonic authorship, then it is an expression of abysmal despair and abject skepticism. Luther is intent on guarding against such a plunge. On the other hand, when Ecclesiastes is read as the wise reflection of a believer, trusting in God's larger, constant control, then the text becomes a humbling lesson in man's limitations while directing attention instead to the proper relationship between God and man. Such an outlook preserves against skepticism and is just what Luther wants to underscore. (1997b: 124; cf. Murphy 1992: pp. lii–liii)

The consistency with which Luther conceived of Qoheleth's fatalism finds echoes in modern scholarship (see especially Rudman 2001; cf. William of Auvergne [*c.*1220] and his arguments on Ecclesiastes *not* teaching determinism, in Smalley 1949: 334–5). In fact, Rosin sees in Luther's *Notes* full correspondence with his earlier writing on human will, and especially with his debates with Erasmus (1997b: 106–8, *passim*). And Ecclesiastes was even more than these things to Luther. In places he uses the text to address those in authority, 'counselling them to fear God and endure bravely amid the trials of their position; it is a sort of *liber politicus*' (Kraeling 1955: 19). (Luther's approach relating to the *contemptus mundi* reading is discussed below, pp. 106–7.)

Johannes Brenz's commentary (written in 1526, published in 1528) addresses some of the same questions as Luther's, but from a distinct angle, and one that is more deeply informed by the classics and classical scepticism (Rosin 1997b: 185–93). Brenz also seeks to apply Ecclesiastes directly to his own political situation in a manner distinct from Luther (see the example below, p. 203). Of the three reformers, however, it seems that it is Philip Melanchthon who takes the threat of scepticism to task most earnestly in his treatment of Ecclesiastes (1550):

> A vigorous critic of skepticism as it touched the *studia humanitatis*, Melanchthon was also a staunch opponent of skepticism as it threatened theology . . . The truths revealed [in Scripture] are beyond human ability to prove or understand without faith. The specific message of Ecclesiastes concerning divine control and purpose is a case in point. Attempts by man to establish his own criterion for understanding and controlling the odd workings of the world are doomed

to fail . . . Only through the theology of life as presented in his exposition of Ecclesiastes can a person hope to cope with life's problems and combat doubt . . . Skepticism looms when man's desire to understand or to control life completely clashes with his inability to do just that. (Rosin 1997b: 266, 284)

Years before Luther turned his attention to Ecclesiastes, Erasmus found his own use for Qoheleth's unique take on wisdom. Writing in what had become an established genre (fool's literature, in which a jester represents the weaknesses and vices of society), Erasmus offered his *Moriae Encomium* (*The Praise of Folly*) in 1509, which was to be reprinted fifteen times before 1517 (Brigden 2000: 92). The fool of *Folly* is deluded by a sense of his own wisdom and knowledge. A lengthy example here is instructive in understanding just how well suited was Ecclesiastes to Erasmus's subtle task of satirizing misguided perceptions of wisdom and folly:

> When he cries, 'Vanity of vanities, all is vanity', what do you suppose he meant, if not, as I was saying before, that human life is a puppet show containing *nothing* but folly? Thus he confirms that celebrated vote cast by Cicero in my [i.e. the fool's] favor . . . to the effect that 'The world is full of fools' . . . 'The heart of the wise is in the house of mourning, but the heart of the fool is in the house of mirth' [7:4]. That makes it clear that he thought mere knowledge of wisdom insufficient without knowledge of me [Folly] as well. And if you don't believe me, here are his very words . . . : 'I gave my mind to know wisdom and to madness and folly' [1:17]. In this passage you must particularly note that folly is given the highest praise because she is placed last in the sentence. Ecclesiastes wrote it, and you know that the ecclesiastical ordering always places the person of highest dignity in last place . . . Now consider this: the scriptures attribute to the foolish a candid and generous mind, while the wise man thinks himself superior to everyone else. That at least is the way I interpret what Ecclesiastes wrote in his tenth chapter: 'When he that is a fool walketh by the way, his wisdom faileth him, and he saith to everyone that he is a fool' [10:3]. Now don't you think that a mark of exceptional candor, to think everyone your equal, and instead of puffing yourself up, to share your merits with everybody else? (In Erasmus 1989: 75–7)

A more significant and sustained engagement with Qoheleth comes from another towering figure of Renaissance learning, Michel de Montaigne, who has frequently been compared to Qoheleth (e.g. Perry 1993a, 1993b; Fisch 1988; Mills 2003). The themes of the limits of human knowledge, of vanity, of the role of wisdom in the formation of the self – all appear throughout his *Essays*, composed between 1580 and 1592, and often keenly resonate with Qoheleth (e.g. essays 1.2, 20, 36, 39; 2.12, 28; 3.9). Just as quotes from Ecclesiastes adorned his personal library (e.g. a loose paraphrase of 9:2, 'Of everything which is under the sun, fortune and law are equal, Eccl. ix'; in Montaigne 1991: 252 n. 1), so they are peppered throughout the *Essays*, sometimes elusively (e.g. in 1.36, 39; 2.12; 3.9). In the course of his most lengthy and carefully argued essay, 'An Apology for Raymond Seybond' (2.12), he writes, 'A line of ancient Greek poetry says "There is great convenience in not being too wise" [Sophocles, *Ajax*, 554] . . . So does Ecclesiastes: "In much wisdom there is much sadness, and he that acquireth knowledge acquireth worry and travail"' (1991: 552). A few pages later comes the familiar Renaissance lament that so echoes Qoheleth: 'It is so far beyond our power to comprehend the majesty of God that the very works of our Creator which best carry his mark are the ones we least understand' (1991: 555–6). At least part of his solution comes when he summarizes Qoheleth's thought while giving the impression of citing it: 'Ecclesiastes says: "Accept all things in good part, just as they seem, just as they taste, day by day. The rest is beyond thy knowledge"' (1991: 565).

At a deeper level, Montaigne's contradictory and querulous approach as articulated in his *Essays* mirrors Qoheleth's own style, a feature that Fisch recognized when he suggested that Qoheleth could say with Montaigne, 'It is my portrait I draw . . . I am myself the subject of my book' (1988: 158). Perry goes as far as to suggest the fundamental influence of Ecclesiastes' rhetorical form on the genre for which Montaigne is famous, the essay: 'This was perhaps the only new literary genre that the modern age had ever produced, alongside the novel' (Perry 1993a: 265; tr. V. Morales). Perry goes on to argue that Montaigne mines Ecclesiastes to forge his distinctive style of writing, which would produce the modern essay. 'When . . . the author writes, "I, Kohelet . . .", he gives to the literary world the first instance of the genre that Montaigne was about to discover' (ibid., tr. V. Morales). Montaigne gives notice to his self-aware approach throughout the *Essays*, and one can recognize the imprint that Perry has argued for. So, for example, in 'On repenting', Montaigne anticipates Emerson's famous dictum that 'foolish consistency is the hobgoblin of little minds' (in his own *Essays*!):

> Constancy itself is nothing but a more languid rocking to and fro. I am unable to stabilize my subject: it staggers confusedly along with a natural drunkenness. I grasp it as it is now, at this moment when I am lingering over it . . . I must adapt this account of myself to the passing hour . . . This is a register of varied and changing occurrences, of ideas which are unresolved and, when needs be, contradictory, either because I myself have become different or because I grasp hold of different attributes or aspects of my subjects. So I happen to contradict myself, but . . . I never contradict truth. (3.2, 1991: 907–8)

If Perry is right, Montaigne anticipates far more than Emerson's insight, but more significantly (if indirectly) that growing pool of scholars who have recognized that what holds together Qoheleth's disparate sayings is nothing less than the thread of his consciousness. And even though, as for Montaigne, Qoheleth's consciousness is cohesive, it may also be seen to stagger along 'with a natural drunkenness' (on Montaigne and the *vanitas* theme, see pp. 107–8).

More evidence of Ecclesiastes' appeal in the European Renaissance comes from Portugal. In 1538, Damião de Góis published his translation and commentary, *Ecclesiastes de Salamam*. For five months in 1534, Góis, one of the most prominent Portuguese scholars of the period, was a guest of Erasmus, whose intellectual influence is evident in *Ecclesiastes* (Earle 2001: 42–4). As Earle suggests, it may even be that Erasmus suggested the choice of text for translation (p. 45). It seems clear that Góis, like Erasmus, recognized the rhetorical brilliance of Ecclesiastes and its subsequent suitability to the intellectual climate, evidenced partly by the fact that *Ecclesiastes* is published with his translation of Cicero's *De Senectute*. The significance of the pairing would not have been lost on readers. As Earle comments,

> There is plenty of evidence that Góis's translations, particularly of Ecclesiastes, were intended to be read especially, if not exclusively by those who could understand their hidden significance. They at least would have the wit to appreciate for themselves the community of spirit which links Ecclesiastes and Cicero, and makes of the two translations a satisfying literary whole. (2001: 47)

Góis, like his European counterparts, saw in Ecclesiastes a validation of the pursuit of humanist sciences, and the translation itself may even suggest that 'the religious tradition of Portugal is not as Orthodox as is sometimes supposed' (p. 44). Commenting on 1:8, Góis offers what Earle suggests is 'something of a watershed in Portuguese intellectual and religious history' (p. 48): 'Some ignorant people interpret this passage as Solomon wishing to denigrate the studies of the philosopher, through which we can reach and understand the secrets and courses of nature; but the sentence is this: to be so much vanity and human inquietude that no meaning can be comprehended or expressed' (in Earle 2001: 48; tr. A. Dawson). Like Luther, Góis also uses Ecclesiastes to combat what he regards to be the corrupt teaching of the Church, in this case that Ecclesiastes teaches contempt of the world.

The appeal of Ecclesiastes to Renaissance thinkers relates in part to a social malaise. Rosin traces the Renaissance obsession with misery, death and contempt of the world, as well as the mass experiences of war, famine and pestilence (1997b: 28–33). We might further note the contribution of Pope Innocent III's *De Contemptu Mundi sive de Miseria Condicionis Humane*, published nearly 400 years previously (1195; it was adapted and translated in the

Renaissance by George Gascoigne as the first section of *The Droomme of Doomes Day* in 1576). As Robert Lewis has shown, the extensive influence of *De Contemptu* is difficult to understate. It is quoted, referred to, translated and adapted in hundreds of works throughout the Middle Ages (Innocent III 1978: 2–5). To this we can add works that propound the general theme of the 'vanity' of the world, suspicion of material wealth and wisdom, such as the numerous 'vanity poems' in one of the most popular collections of verse in the sixteenth century, *The Paradise of Dainty Devices*, which went through ten editions between 1576 and 1606 (see Rollins 1927). Further, Hattaway surveys a range of Renaissance humanist scholars and poets who saw in their own work some affinity with Qoheleth. For example, around the time of Thomas Elyot, Cornelius Agrippa von Nettesheim published his influential *Of the Vanitie and Uncertaintie of Artes and Sciences* (*De vanitate et incertitudine scientiarum et artium*, 1530), a work that explored the limits and perceived superstitions of occultism and other sciences (i.e. common and concurrent means of accounting for human experience). The book further served the Renaissance revival of scepticism, and because it was reprinted in his day, scepticism's champion, Montaigne, drew heavily on it (Screech, in Montaigne 1991: p. xxxiii). On its title page, *Vanitie* bore the words of Eccl. 1:1: 'All is but most vaine Vanitie: and all is most vaine, and but plaine vanitie.' As Hattaway comments,

> Their discontent with contemporary ways of recording experience had provoked the desire of the earlier humanists to explore the learning of the ancient world, which had in turn given rise to the flowering of arts and sciences we associate with the Renaissance. But as the skepticism of Solomon had been applied to the wisdom of the schools, now it was applied to the wisdom of the humanists themselves. (1968: 511)

(For Agrippa's most sustained encounter with Qoheleth, see below, p. 204.)

A particularly poignant reading of this period shows the theme of the limits of knowledge in amended, personalized and political form. In the spring of 1546, Henry Howard, Earl of Surrey, cousin of the by then executed (in 1541) Queen Katherine Howard, came under suspicion of Catholic allegiance at a time when Henry VIII's death was imminent and evangelicals, among whom he was counted a friend, were jostling for power. Surrey hatched a scheme that his sister should become the king's mistress. His sister, taken aback, reported it to Howard's friends, who further distanced themselves from him (Brigden 2004). Howard could see the wheels of conspiracy moving against him, for charges regarding Howard's misrepresentation of heraldry were soon to be trumped up against him with the help of those closest to him. But just before that, Howard composed his remarkable *A Paraphrase of Part of the Book of*

Ecclesiastes (i.e. chs 1–5), a book he found well suited to reflect on the misery engendered by the pursuit of knowledge, which included his bewilderment at the betrayal of friends and loved ones.

> I, that in David's seat sit crowned and rejoice;
> That with my sceptre rule the Jews, and teach them with my voice,
>   Have searched long to know all things under the sun;
> To see how in this mortal life, a surety might be won.
>   This kindled will to know; strange things for to desire.
> . . .
> Defaults of nature's work no man's hand may restore,
> Which be in number like the sands upon the salt floods shore.
>   Then vaunting in my wit, I gan call to my mind
> What rules of wisdom I had taught, that elders could not find.
> . . .
> Thereby with more delight to knowledge for to climb:
> But this I found an endless work of pain, and loss of time.
>   For he to wisdom's school that doth apply his mind,
> The further that he wades therein, the greater doubts shall find.
>   (Ch. 1, in Howard 1815: 1.67)

Editor G. F. Nott suggests that throughout the poem the 'subjects of his complaint are principally the insincerity of friends, the malice of enemies, and the instability of worldly greatness. The whole bears evident marks of haste' (in Howard 1815: 1.377). James Simpson finds in the paraphrase an attempt by Howard to express his sense of frustration and powerlessness in the face of his impending demise:

> . . . these royal monologues [are] . . . a fascinating attempt to appropriate the king's voice and to imagine the position from which that royal voice expresses nothing but its own grief and the near-despair of power . . . Surrey forces . . . a royal self-recognition here, which clearly perceives the futility and injustice of its own exercise of power. He speaks with the voice of an aged king in order to rebuke 'aged kyngs wedded to will, that worke with out aduice' (Ecclesiastes 4; 51.36) . . . Surrey's Ecclesiastes paraphrases, then, would seem here to have been welcomed in an evangelical environment. They did so presumably because they offered a space for attacking the king even from within a discursive space that ostensibly belongs to the king himself. The king's voice attacks the king. (Simpson 2004)

Simpson's theory finds support from Brigden's comment that 'Surrey inhabited a range of voices in his poetry . . . and the predicaments of his speakers often seemed to be his own' (2004). Howard himself was well schooled in the humanities and would no doubt have been familiar with the themes of social malaise and frustrated endeavour that had come to be so intrinsically linked to Ecclesiastes. Howard did not achieve recognition in his lifetime as a poet (although his Ecclesiastes paraphrase is widely believed to have influenced the ballad of the Protestant martyr Anne Askew, 'I Am a Woman, Poor and Blind', in the summer of 1546), and his poems were not published until 1557. It is at least clear that Howard, who developed the sonnet form to be used by Shakespeare, had produced one of the finest paraphrases of Ecclesiastes of his age (further examples are found throughout this commentary).

Other figures of the period would use Ecclesiastes to critique the endeavour of human learning especially. In this regard we might note Antonio de Corro, a Spanish-born Reader in Divinity at Oxford, who in 1578 published *Solomons sermon of mans chief felicitie* (so the English title, published 1586), a commentary on Ecclesiastes (which would become very popular) in which he 'denied that human knowledge could bring truth or felicity':

> Either for that [man] cannot attain to the ful & absolute knowledge of things, because they are lapped & inwrapped in so manifold knots & marveilous difficulties, & beside the things themselves be so infinite in number: or for that there happen so many perverse, crooked, and overthwart chances in the life & doings of men, which by no reason can be ordered or amended. (In Hattaway 1968: 521)

A similar spirit of intellectual critique can be noted in the 'Treatie of Humane Learning' by Fulke Greville (1554–1628; the 'Treatie' was published posthumously in 1633 and 'written in his Youth'), a philosophical poet and courtier. While the vanity of knowledge-oriented endeavours is a key theme of the poem, he makes no *direct* reference to Ecclesiastes (though see below). However, as an expression of the age it helps us further to understand the broad appeal of Qoheleth's themes. Here epistemological scepticism is given pretty full expression in the opening stanzas (behind which echo the themes of Eccl. 3, 7 and 8 in particular):

> The Mind of Man is this worlds true dimension
> And *Knowledge* is the measure of the minde:
> And as the minde, in her vaste comprehension
> Contains more worlds than all the world can finde:
>   So Knowledge doth it selfe farre more extend,
>   Than all the minds of Men can comprehend.
>
> A climing Height it is without a head,
> Depth without bottome, Way without an ende,
> A circle with no line inuironed,

> Not comprehended all it comprehends;
> Worth infinite, yet satisfies no minde,
> Till it that infinite of the God-head finde.
> (Greville 1633: 23)

One verse in particular suggests Ecclesiastes as its subtext:

> *Salamon* knew nature both in herbes, plants, beasts; . . .
> Let his example, and his booke maintaine:
> *Kings, who have travail'd, through the Vanity,*
> *Can best describe vs what her visions be.*
> (Greville 1633: 48)

It is Francis Bacon, however, who sheds perhaps the brightest light on Ecclesiastes' significance to Renaissance thinkers and their concerns in his monumental and unprecedented (in English) *Of the Proficience and Advancement of Learning, Divine and Human* (1605). His overarching treatise on the sciences of knowledge begins with extensive reflection on Qoheleth's themes. After a lengthy dedication to the king, Bacon sets out to correct the manner in which the 'dignity of learning' has been woefully mishandled by divines, politicians and 'sometimes in the errors and imperfections of learned men themselves' (in Bacon 1730: 2. 415). He takes issue with those who say that 'knowledge hath in it somewhat of the serpent', and who would cite Solomon as giving 'a censure, *That there is no end of making books, and that much reading is weariness of the flesh* [12:12]: And again in another place, *That in spacious knowledge there is much contristation, and that he that increaseth knowledge, increaseth anxiety* [1:18]' (ibid.). He then sets out to 'discover . . . the ignorance and error of this opinion' and makes immediate recourse to Ecclesiastes, but this time in support of his view, that

> *Solomon* speaking of the two principal senses of inquisition, the eye and the ear, affirmeth that the eye is never satisfied with seeing, nor the ear with hearing [1:8] . . . so of knowledge it self, and the mind of man, whereto the senses are but reporters, he defineth likewise in these words, placed after that kalendar or *ephemerides*, which he maketh of the diversities of times and seasons for all actions and purposes; and concludeth thus: *God hath made all things beautiful or decent in the true return of their seasons: Also he hath placed the world in man's heart, yet cannot man find out the work which God worketh from the beginning to the end* [3:11]: declaring not obscurely, that God hath framed the mind of man as a mirrour of glass, capable of the image of the universal world, and joyful to receive the impression thereof, as the eye joyeth to receive light . . . If then such be the capacity and receipt of the mind of man, it is manifest, that there is no

danger at all in the proportion or quantity of knowledge, how large soever . . . but it is merely the quality of knowledge . . . And as for that censure of *Solomon*, concerning the excess of writing and reading books, and the anxiety of spirit which redoundeth from knowledge . . . let those places be rightly understood, and they do indeed excellently set the true bounds and limitations, whereby human knowledge is confined and circumscribed. (In Bacon 1730: 2.415–16)

What is so crucial and telling here is that Bacon uses Ecclesiastes exclusively (though he somewhat superficially cites as well Paul's warnings that '*we be not seduced by vain philosophy*' and that '*knowledge bloweth up*') to defend his approach to knowledge, knowing that it is in the framework of Ecclesiastes that many of his readers, divines and learned men, have formulated their 'erroneous' epistemology. Ecclesiastes, then, set the terms for what many regard as the first significant work of philosophy in English (further on the theme of knowledge in Renaissance readings, see the commentary on 1:17–18 and 8:16–17 in particular).

English statesman William Temple echoes these themes as well in his essay 'Upon the Gardens of Epicurus, or of Gardening in the Year 1685', in which he suggests that Solomon's 'natural philosophy' has not been improved upon:

How ancient this Natural Philosophy has been in the World, is hard to know . . . The first who found out the Vanity of it, seems to have been *Solomon*, of which Discovery he has left such admirable strains in *Ecclesiastes*. The next was *Socrates*, who made it the business of His Life, to explode it, and introduce that which we call Moral in its place, to busie Human Minds to better purpose. And indeed, whoever reads with Thought what these two . . . have said, upon the Vanity of all that mortal Man can ever attain to know of Nature, in its Originals or Operations, may save Himself a great deal of Pains, and justly conclude, That the Knowledg of such things is not our Game; and (like the pursuit of a Stag by a little Spaniel) may serve to amuse and to weary us, but will never be hunted down. (1690: 83–4)

By this time the Solomon of Ecclesiastes can with ease be spoken of in the same breath as 'Socrates', and together they are seen to stand as a stalwart warning not to exasperate oneself in the fruitless pursuit of 'Knowledge'. Indeed, one might as well chase after wind.

B.   Sixteenth- and Seventeenth-Century Verse
Poets of the sixteenth and seventeenth centuries had a particular fondness for Ecclesiastes. Among the poems I will touch on here are those by Henry Lok (1597), John Donne (1610s and 1620s), George Sandys (1632), Francis Quarles

(*c*.1644) and Alexander Brome (*c*.1648). (There are of course more poets in this period who engaged with the Preacher, and some are found elsewhere in this commentary – e.g. Edmund Spenser, Fulke Greville, Henry Howard, Anne Bradstreet and An Collins.)

In 1597 Henry Lok, a poet and 'intelligencer' (Doelman 1993: 1), published his *Ecclesiastes*, a long paraphrase in sonnet form. At the end of this work appear sixty 'dedicatory' sonnets to 'all the members of the Privy Council and various influential courtiers and ladies of the court' (Doelman 1993: 1). Within the paraphrase itself, Lok is careful not to be offensive to any of his audience, and on the whole the text follows no adventurous lines. But through this work Lok sought specifically to advance himself in the Queen's illustrious courts, for 'it seems that Lok's primary concern in 1596–1597 was to attain a position both dignified and sufficient to relieve his financial needs [which were severe]. It is in this context that *Ecclesiastes*, along with its dedicatory sonnets, was published' (Doelman 1993: 7). Lok takes frequent opportunity to use Ecclesiastes' fairly conservative – at least on the surface – notions of monarchy (the power with which Qoheleth invests the monarch may be deeply ironic) implicitly to give praise to Elizabeth herself. So, for example, on 8:1 ('Who is like the wise . . . ?') he comments,

> It [wisdom] teacheth man his dutie vnto God,
> And how with ciuill men he should conuerse,
> With neighbours how to haue a kind abode,
> Or with a people that are most peruerse:
>   To know what doth beseeme in euery case,
>   And how to walke, to win our soueraignes grace.
>
> It will aduise thee (as I also do)
> To be attentiue to thy Prince behest,
> To be obsequious also there unto,
> So farre as may accord with all the rest,
>   Of lawes of God, of nature, and of state,
>   And to attend his pleasure rare and late.
>   (Lok 1597: 74; ch. 8, ll. 15–26)

To 'win our soueraignes grace' it seems was the thrust of the whole work. Ultimately Lok failed (quite spectacularly, according to Doelman) to gain the favour he sought. (Lok's instance makes for a curious footnote to Bishop John White's sermon on Eccl. 9 at Queen Mary's funeral some 40 years previous [see pp. 208–10] – it was not the first time that Qoheleth had made political manoeuvres in Elizabeth's courts!)

So enamoured was John Donne with Ecclesiastes that, as Robert Bozanich suggests, 'Donne not only saw his problems in terms of Solomon's but . . . he used the very language of Ecclesiastes to describe his own predicament . . . [T]he

Book of Ecclesiastes exerted a profound and lifelong influence on Donne himself' (1975: 274–75). Furthermore, an

> awareness of his vanity overwhelmed Donne during the years of aimlessness that followed his marriage and the utter ruin of his hopes for courtly preferment. Conscious of his abilities but unable to find a direction in which to put them to use, Donne came to think of himself as a mere nothing, as vanity itself; the terms are synonymous and recur obsessively in the letters of this period. (Bozanich 1975: 271)

Bozanich recognizes this appropriation by Donne in several passages of the sermons, his poetry (the *Anniversaries* series – 1611–12 – is 'heavily indebted' to Ecclesiastes; 1975: 273) and in letters, such as the following to Sir Henry Goodyer in 1608: 'I begun early, when I understood [undertook?] the study of our laws; but was diverted by the worst voluptuousness . . . an hydroptic, immoderate desire of human learning and languages' (in Bozanich 1975: 271). Bozanich goes on to show (p. 274) that this language was also influenced by one of the more influential commentaries on Ecclesiastes of Donne's day, that of Johannes Lorinus (in several editions from 1606 to *c*.1642), itself steeped in the tradition of *contemptus mundi*. Donne's readings of Ecclesiastes throughout his work constitute a sparkling example of early modern reading that engages with the text as a literary and thematic whole, recognizing the impact of Qoheleth's autobiographical strategy (another good example of this is Donne's handling of the *vanitas* theme; see below, p. 122). Bozanich highlights evidence of this quality in a passage from *Of the Progresse of the Soule: The Second Anniversary* (*c*.1611–12), Donne's first published work:

> Thirst for that time, O my insatiate soule,
> And serue thy thirst, with Gods safe-sealing Bowle.
> Bee thirsty still, and drinke still till thou goe;
> 'Tis th'onely Health, to be Hydropique so.
> Forget this rotten world; And vnto thee,
> Let thine owne times as an old story be,
> Be not concern'd: study not why, nor whan;
> Do not so much, as not beleeue a man.
> For though to erre, be worst, to try truths forth,
> Is far more busines, then this world is worth.
> (ll. 45–54, in Bozanich 1975: 273)

Clearly Donne had a subtle grasp and appreciation of Qoheleth, but this did not stop the Archbishop of Canterbury (1633–45) William Laud judging, somewhat ironically, Donne himself to be of an inferior quality to Ecclesiastes. In a letter to Thomas Wentworth, who was a collaborator with Laud in imposing the official religion of Charles I, Laud comforted him in his discouragement over lack of success in implementing Charles's policies:

> But once for all, if you will but read over the short book of Ecclesiastes, while these thoughts are in you, you will see a better disposition of these things, and the vanity of all their shadows, than is to be found in any anagrams of Dr. Donne's, or any designs of Vandyke [Dutch artist Van Dyck, who was living in England since 1632 and painted a portrait of Charles I in 1638]; so to the lines there drawn I leave you. (Letter 153, Lambeth, 14 May 1638, in Laud 1857: 6. 523–4)

Many of the paraphrases of this period exhibit little in the way of imagination, seeking a plainly conservative line of thought, taking the edges off Qoheleth's unorthodoxy. Others, however, in their rhetorical brilliance and willingness to read Qoheleth's hard words at something like face value, stand out. George Sandys's brief paraphrase, published in 1638 (composed in 1632), is a sterling example. Here Sandys renders 7:13–14 in tightly constructed turns of phrase:

> Gods works consider: who can rectifie,
> Or make that streight which he hath made awry?
> In thy prosperitie let joy abound;
> Nor let adversitie thy patience wound:
> For these by him so intermixed are,
> That no man should presume, nor yet despaire.
> (1638: 9)

From this one can read with recognition the *Account of the English Dramatick Poets*, in which Gerard Langbaine says of Sandys's scriptural paraphrases that 'I have heard them much admired by Devout and Ingenious Persons, and I believe very deservingly' (1691: 438). Qoheleth's text in the last verse (14b) goes, 'God has made the one [a day of joy] as well as the other [a day of adversity], so that mortals may not find out anything that will come after them' (NRSV). Sandys's paraphrase subtly pushes Qoheleth's logic further: in bringing adversity and joy together in such close proximity, God has in fact 'so intermixed' the two as to confound humanity.

Unlike Donne and Quarles, Brome was not a religious poet, but was known rather for his drinking songs and political poetry, for which he was highly regarded in his day (Anselment 1984: 39). His early poetry was witty and lighthearted, and it was the English Civil War that brought out a more serious response to the world around him. In Anselment's terms, 'the poems written near 1648 and after abandon their light-heartedness and develop increasingly the skeptical, questioning manner of Ecclesiastes' (1984: 46). Brome wrote an extensive paraphrase of the first chapter of Ecclesiastes (*c*.1648). A brief example, of 1:9–11 will suffice here:

> And ther's no new thing underneath the Sun;
> There's no new Invention; that which we stile wit,
> Is but remembrance; and the fruits of it,
> Are but old things reviv'd. In this round World,
> All things are by a revolution hurl'd.
> And though to us they variously appear,
> There are no things but what already were,
> What thing is there within this world that we
> Can justly say is new, and cry Come see?
> (ll. 48–56; Brome 1982: 1. 336)

Brome recognized the balance of Qoheleth's themes (as, according to Anselment, he did throughout all of his work): 'taken as a whole, the political poems reveal a deeper understanding of this biblical wisdom. Sceptical and realistic, light-hearted and facile' (1984: 49). One might also discern, as in so many of the works I have here reviewed, a reflection of Brome's culture of the mid-seventeenth century, a time when so much had been lost and destroyed, and one was always being reminded of the 'vanity of ambition and of the hopeless struggle against time' (Parry 1989: 174).

In comparing Brome's work to the paraphrases of Sandys and Quarles, Dubinski comments that like 'Brome's, these two paraphrases are in decasyllabic couplets' (in Brome 1982: 2. 120). To give some indication of the differences in the interpretive style of the four (Lok, Sandys, Quarles, Brome), it will be instructive here to offer the others' renderings of the same verses, 1:9–11.

Henry Lok's paraphrase (1597) differs from the others in that the verses are followed by stanzas of commentary:

> *9. What euer hath bene, shall be done: for there is nothing new:*
> *10. What may we say is now, the which was not before thinke you?*
>
> For proofe, let me demaund but this of you,
> Who most haue searched natures secret powre?
> And you who are conuerst in stories true,
> And you obseruers of ech day and howre,
> Haue ye not found, that time doth all deuour?
>   And that new times the like things doth produce,
>   As any former ages had in vse.

We dreame of secrets daily, newly found,
And of inuentions passing former wits,
We thinke our world with wisedome doth abound,
And fame (for knowledge) vs much rather fits,
But ouer-weening thoughts this toy begits:
   Their longer liues more temperately led
   In holy studie, sure more knowledge bred.
[two more expository stanzas follow] . . .

11. Things past forgotten are we see, and future so shalbee.
. . .

But they forgotten are, as ours once shall,
Mans few and euill dayes with cares of mind,
Make many worthy things to dust to fall,
And vs to predecessors grow vnkind,
Whose fames with theirs shall vanish with the wind,
   And as our stealing wits would clips their fame,
   Deuouring time, shall desolate our name.

For what more equall recompence is due,
To such as others merits doe depraue,
Then that like base contempt, do them insue,
And of successors they like guerdon haue,
And so we see fame leaues vs at the graue:
   Build then his happinesse on earth who will,
   He but himselfe with care and scorne shall fill.
(ll. 121–66; Lok 1597: 5–6)

George Sandys (1632):

What is, hath beene; what hath beene shall ensue:
And nothing underneath the Sun is new.
Of what can it be truely said, Behold
This never was? The same hath beene of old.
For former Ages we remember not:
And what is now, will be in time forgot.
(In Sandys 1638: 1)

Francis Quarles (*c.*1644):

The Thing that heretofore hath been, we see
Is but the same that is, and is to be:
And what is done, is what is to be done;
There's nothing that is new beneath the Sun.

> What Novelty can Earth proclaim, and say,
> It had no Precedent before this Day?
> No, no, there's nothing modern Times can own,
> The which precedent Ages have not known:
> The Deeds of former Days expire their Date
> In our collapsed Memories, and what
> Times early Sun-shine hath not ripened yet,
> Succeeding Generations shall forget.
>
> (ll. 27–38, in Quarles 1739: 4)

For the most part Quarles's extensive paraphrase is unimaginative, and the several examples of Ecclesiastes in verse from his earlier, and hugely popular, *Emblemes* (1635) and *Hieroglyphikes* (1638) are at least somewhat unconventional (for examples, see below, pp. 113–14, 222–3).

These creative treatments of Ecclesiastes in verse can still function as useful reflective prompts for interpreters. They seek not so much to translate Ecclesiastes as to capture its tenor and spirit, and as such they are works of exegesis that often provide remarkable insight. To view Qoheleth's words 'There is nothing new . . . it has already been', through the lens of Brome ('There's no new Invention . . . All things are by a revolution hurl'd') is to re-encounter Qoheleth's world with a fresh and urgent new language.

Because of the prominence of Ecclesiastes in the early and middle discourse of this period, a list of key works follows overleaf for convenience of reference.

C.   On the Way to Modernity

In the eighteenth century those who debated the value of the humanist sciences continued to make recourse to Ecclesiastes, particularly now in relation to rationalism, deism and theism. Henry Bettenson describes the following as 'typical' (1963: 439) of the kind of arguments used by eighteenth-century rationalists (from Matthew Tindal's *Christianity as Old as the Creation, or the Gospel, a Republication of the Religion of Nature*, 1730):

> And if the *Holy Ghost*, as Bishop Taylor says, *works by heightening, and improving our natural Faculties*; it can only be by using such Means as will improve them, in proposing Reasons and Arguments to convince our Understanding; which can only be improv'd, by studying the Nature and Reason of Things: *I apply'd my Heart* (says the wisest of Men) *to know, and to search, and to seek out Wisdom, and the Reason of Things* [Eccl. 7:25]. (In Bettenson 1963: 440)

An anonymous author in 1765 produced an intriguing and lengthy rendering of Ecclesiastes in verse. It is variously ascribed in commentaries to Walter

Ecclesiastes in Renaissance and Reform Works: Key Examples

Predecessors
Jerome (*c*.347–419/20), *Commentary on Ecclesiastes* (388/9)
Bernard of Cluny (?), *De Contemptu Mundi* (*c*.1140)
Pope Innocent III (1160/1–1216), *De Contemptu Mundi* (1195)
Anonymous religious lyrics from the Vernon MS (*c*.1325–50)
Thomas à Kempis (1379/80–1471), *Imitation of Christ* (*c*.1440)
Giannozzo Manetti (1393–1459), *De dignitate et excellentia hominis* (1452)

Academic and moral discourse
Desiderius Erasmus (1469–1536), *In Praise of Folly* (1509)
Martin Luther (1483–1546), *Notes on Ecclesiastes* (1526/32)
Agrippa von Nettesheim (1486–1535), *On the Vanitie and Uncertaintie of Artes and Sciences* (1530)
Johannes Brenz (1499–1570), *Commentary on Ecclesiastes* (1538)
Damião de Góis (1502–74), *Ecclesiastes de Salamam* (1538)
Philip Melanchthon (1497–1560), *Commentary on Ecclesiastes* (1550)
George Gascoigne (1525–77), *The Droomme of Doomes Day* (1576; adapted tr. of Innocent III's *De Contemptu Mundi*)
Antonio de Corro (1527–91), *Solomons Sermon of Mans Chief Felicitie* (1578)
Michel de Montaigne (1533–92), 'Of Vanity' and other essays (*c*.1580–92)
Theodore Beza (1519–1605), *Ecclesiastes* (1588)
Henry Smith (*c*.1560–1591), 'The Triall of Vanitie' (*c*.1590)
Pierre Charron (1541–1603), *Of Wisdome Three Bookes* (1601)
Francis Bacon (1561–1626), *Of the Proficience and Advancement of Learning* (1605); 'Of Vicissitude of Things', *The Essayes . . . Civill and Morall* (1625)
Pierre du Moulin (1568–1658), *Heraclitus, or, Mans Looking-Glass and Survey of Life* (*c*.1605)

Poetry
William Dunbar (*c*.1460–*c*.1530), 'Of the World's Vanitie' (*c*.1500)
Henry Howard (1517–47), *A Paraphrase of Part of the Book of Ecclesiastes* (1546)
Fulke Greville (1554–1628), 'Treatie of Humane Learning' (pub. 1633, 'written in his Youth')

Henry Lok (*c*.1553–1608), *Ecclesiastes, Otherwise Called the Preacher* (1597)
John Donne (1572–1631), 'Anniversaries' (1611–12) and other works
George Sandys (1578–1664), *A Paraphrase upon the Divine Poems* (pub. 1638, orig. 1632)
George Herbert (1593–1633), 'Vanity (I)' (1633)
Francis Quarles (1592–1644), *Emblemes* and *Hieroglyphikes* (1635, 1638), *Solomon's Recantation* (*c*.1644)
Alexander Brome (1620–66), 'Ecclesiastes 1' (*c*.1648)
Anne Bradstreet (*c*.1612–72), 'The Vanity of All Worldly Things' (1650)

Fine arts
Vanitas still life painting tradition, fl. *c*.1530–1650
Vanitas choral music, fl. *c*.1600–50

Bradick (or Brodick) or Dennis Furley. The *Oxford Dictionary of National Biography* in its entry for Walter Bradick sheds some fascinating light on the mystery of its authorship:

> An obituary in the *Gentleman's Magazine* claims that Bradick was the author of *Choheleth, or, The Royal Preacher* (1765), an anonymous paraphrase of Ecclesiastes in Miltonic blank verse, dedicated to George III. However, according to a manuscript note by the Methodist preacher Joseph Sutcliffe in a copy of the 1824 reprint of *Choheleth*, the poem was written by Dennis Furley, said to be the merchant whose miraculous escape from death in the Lisbon earthquake is recounted in John Wesley's Journals (8 February 1768). His son was John Wesley's disciple and correspondent, the Revd Samuel Furley (1732?–1795). Peter Hall (1803–1849) suggested that the Hebrew scholar Robert Lowth (1710–1787) wrote *Choheleth* . . . [!] (Sambrook 2004)

If Peter Hall was right, then Lowth's assessment of Ecclesiastes 22 years later, that its 'language is generally low . . . mean or vulgar . . . [possessing] very little of the poetical character' (see Testimonia, p. 4, for the full citation), represents either a whole change of heart, a catastrophic lacuna of memory or a bit of ironic play. Whoever wrote the 1765 volume exhibited a profound appreciation of Qoheleth as a whole (cf. especially the comments on ch. 9, p. 211 below). The perceptive quality of the volume itself is striking, and I am not alone in my assessment, as John Wesley's journal entry shows:

> Monday, Feb. 8, 1768. I met with a surprising poem, intituled *Choheleth, or the Preacher*: it is a paraphrase in tolerable verse on the Book of Ecclesiastes. I really

think the author of it (a Turkey merchant) understands both the difficult expressions and the connection of the whole, better than any other, either ancient or modern, writer whom I have seen. (In Spurgeon 2004)

The anonymous author's work was inspired by the 'accidental' discovery of another anonymous poem of Ecclesiastes, published in 1691. The 1765 author was moved to do justice to Ecclesiastes in the light of what he regarded to be a 'specimen . . . very indifferent, that, were it our design to make the Reader smile, we might quote a great number of passages . . . indeed . . . that Poetry, which has nothing else to recommend it, but a mere jingle of words, and this, for the most part, extremely harsh and dissonant, is but a dull entertainment' (Anonymous 1765: pp. i–ii). The 1765 work is remarkable for, among other things, a unique feature: a critique of a basically non-religious attempt to render Ecclesiastes in verse, namely of Prior's 'Solomon':

> I perused the whole piece, in hopes at least of finding some new lights struck out from such copious matter, by one of his fertile genius; but must confess, that the beauty of his Poetry made me no amends for the disappointment. He has not only passed over the most striking passages, which would have greatly embellished his Poem . . . but given to others a sense so low and grovelling, and so widely different from that of the sublime original, as would scarce be pardoned in the most ordinary Writer. (Anonymous 1765: pp. iii–iv)

After providing an example from chapter 12, our author goes on to make an intriguing point:

> We do not intend what we have here said, as a reflection on that justly admired Writer's poetical talents, but . . . had he taken but half as much pains in studying and copying the beauties of this sacred Book, as he had done with those of the Classics, particularly his favourite Horace, we should probably have had a much finer Poem, beyond all comparison, than we have at present . . . [W]ithout depreciating [the poem's] merit . . . we see too much of *Prior* in it, and too little of *Solomon*. (1765: pp. iv–v)

Further examples from this sparkling volume appear in the Testimonia section and chapter 9 of this commentary.

Two representative writers of the eighteenth century in particular engaged with Ecclesiastes at the edges of received readings: Jonathan Swift (1667–1745) and Samuel Johnson (1709–84). Whereas in Swift one finds very little direct engagement with Ecclesiastes, critics of Swift have noted the way in which his work can be seen to, in Brian McCrea's terms, redact Ecclesiastes. So in *Gulliver's Travels* (1726), the 'various "situations"' in which Gulliver finds himself redact that of the Preacher in Ecclesiastes: "And I gaue my heart to seeke and search out by wisdome, concerning all things that are done vnder heaven . . ." [1:13]' (2000: 477; cf. Campbell 1975). In his sermon, 'On the Poor Man's Contentment', Swift generalizes in a manner that seems to have Qoheleth clearly in mind:

> The holy Scripture is full of Expressions to set forth the miserable Condition of Man during the whole Progress of his Life; his Weakness, Pride, and Vanity; his unmeasurable Desires, and perpetual Disappointments . . . the Corruptions of his Reason; his deluding Hopes, and his real, as well as imaginary Fears . . . the Shortness of his Life . . . and the wise Men of all Ages have made the same reflection. (In Campbell 1975: 60–1)

James Campbell sees a progression from Swift to Johnson, in which one might discern 'increasing sympathy with and closeness to Koheleth's melancholic reflections about man's condition, his ability or inability to know God and God's will, and his chance of finding satisfaction, happiness and meaning in his life' (1975: 32). Indeed, Johnson's engagement with Qoheleth is far more direct and wide ranging.

The Vanity of Human Wishes (1749) is widely regarded to be Johnson's finest work, and it is discussed in chapter 1 (see pp. 123–4). As in that poem, in *Rasselas* (1759) Johnson systematically exposes the pursuit of meaning and lasting hope, articulated in its opening sentence: 'Ye who listen with credulity to the whispers of fancy, and pursue with eagerness the phantoms of hope; who expect that age will perform the promises of youth, and that the deficiencies of the present day will be supplied by the morrow; attend to the history of Rasselas prince of Abissinia' (in Johnson 1823: 3. 299). Campbell traces not only the influence of Ecclesiastes in *Rasselas*, but also striking parallels in theme and structure between it and *The Vanity of Human Wishes* (1975: 100). One remnant work that sheds incomparable light on both, however, and perhaps the most light of all on Johnson's engagement with Ecclesiastes, is his sermon on Eccl. 1:14 (regarded as 'undateable'). The editorial note makes the connections clear: 'This, a quintessentially Johnsonian sermon – a prose *Vanity of Human Wishes*, a *Rasselas* without narrative – exposes, as does no other work of SJ, the orthodox Christian foundation that underlies his philosophy of human life and effort and that supports the entire structure of his morality' (in Johnson 1978: 127 n. 1). Like so many others, Johnson sees human frustration writ large in Qoheleth's words: 'That all human actions terminate in vanity, and all human hopes will end in vexation, is a position, from which nature with-holds our credulity, and which our fondness for the present life, and worldly enjoyments, disposes us to doubt; however forcibly it may be urged upon us, by reason or experience' (in Johnson 1978: 127). Johnson goes on to develop the idea that humanity continually deludes itself into 'holding out' for happiness, despite the overwhelming evidence of our failure to acquire it. This frustration of desire is founded on a certainty, that human 'wisdom has . . . exhausted its power, in giving rules for the conduct of life; but those rules are themselves but vanities' (p. 131). Johnson's ultimate aim is to demonstrate the vanity of 'all human purposes', for to 'live in a world where all is vanity, has been decreed by our Creatour to be the lot of man, a lot which we cannot alter by murmuring, but may soften by submission' (p. 134). The sermon concludes with a fairly orthodox citation of Eccl. 12:13, but the sense of failed quest is its permeable theme.

Oliver Goldsmith's poem *The Deserted Village* (1770) offers parallels to Johnson's famous poem, and perhaps to Ecclesiastes as well. Behind its concern for the oppressed within the decaying village of the poem, its concern for companionship, its symbolic imagery of light and dark, Jack Wills (1973) sees the source of Ecclesiastes.

> Vain transitory splendours! could not all
> Reprieve the tottering mansion from its fall?
> Obscure it sinks, nor shall it more impart
> An hour's importance to the poor man's heart.
> Thither no more the peasant shall repair
> To sweet oblivion of his daily care;
> No more the farmer's news, the barber's tale,
> No more the woodman's ballad shall prevail;
> No more the smith his dusky brow shall clear,
> Relax his pond'rous strength, and lean to hear;
>   (ll. 237–46, in Goldsmith 2003)

While the detail of the parallels is not entirely convincing, in these lines that observe the decay of village life the restless spirit of Qoheleth does seem to be present (cf. Eccl. 12:2–5).

The case of Voltaire's *Précis* of Ecclesiastes (1759) makes for a fine conclusion to readings of this period. I have published a full study and translation of the *Précis*,[6] and so will only outline my findings here. In 1756 Voltaire was invited to write a paraphrase of the Psalms for the recent Christian convert and influential mistress of Louis XV, Madame de Pompadour. With the sub-

---

[6]   See Christianson 2005, in which I provide a fulsome account of the context for the composition of the *Précis*, making use of the *Précis* itself and undertaking some exposition of the *Zeitgeist* of Voltaire's era. Also included is a full translation of the *Précis* by Terry McWilliams, with critical notes.

tlest touch of satire, Voltaire reportedly replied that he was 'not the right man for the Psalms'. The idea seems to have taken root in some form, since in 1759, in what appears to be an unsolicited act, he wrote two striking *précis* of biblical texts that perhaps suited his temperament more clearly: Ecclesiastes and Song of Songs. In his Ecclesiastes text Voltaire translated portions from the Hebrew and arranged them by theme, with opposing stanzas of reflective verse. Voltaire's reading is remarkably free from the polemical and satirical approach he takes in almost all of his other published work on the Bible. It is also unorthodox in its empathetic and inventive approach to Qoheleth's themes. Indeed, from his opening summary and throughout the *Précis*, Voltaire shows himself a careful exegete of the nuances of Qoheleth's experience:

> In my burning youth
> I searched for pleasure,
> I savoured its intoxication.
> Sickened by my happiness,
> in its enchanting cup
> I found vanity.
> (In Christianson 2005: 476)

Voltaire proceeds subtly to align his own disillusionment (with the confidence of science and the doctrine of Optimism) with that of Qoheleth:

> I wanted to penetrate
> the obscurity of science . . .
> O nature, immense abyss,
> you leave me without clarity.
> I resort to ignorance;
> knowledge is vanity.
> (Based on 1:17;
> in Christianson 2005: 476)

One of the more intriguing features of this episode is the suggestion of some critics that Ecclesiastes was a 'favourite text' of Frederick the Great, king of Prussia 1740–86. So, for example, E. H. Plumptre: 'Voltaire dedicated his paraphrase of [Ecclesiastes] . . . to Frederick II, as that of a book which was the king's favourite study' (1881: 9); Paul Haupt: 'It was a favourite book of Frederick the Great, who referred to it as a Mirror of Princes' (1905: 1); J. S. Wright: 'to Frederick the Great [Ecclesiastes] was the most precious book of the Bible' (1946: 253). The 'Épitre dédicatoire' to Frederick, which now prefaces the *Précis*, was not original to it. It first appeared in a 1775 edition (Voltaire 1877: 9.482) and has been attached to the work ever since. The person to whom Voltaire 'presents' the *Précis* in the original foreword (the 'esteemed personage') is Madame de Pompadour. The exceptionally flowery 1775 dedication likens Frederick to Solomon:

> We attribute to the third king of Judah the little book of Ecclesiastes. I dedicate the *Précis* of this work to the third king of Prussia, who thinks as Solomon seems to think, and who frequently expresses the same thoughts with more method and more energy . . . [Y]ou reconcile all that is, as we say, the best that is on earth . . . [Your majesty] has the advantage over Solomon of being able to write in verse, and of not being tempted by 700 wives, apparently legitimate, and by 300 scamps, apparently concubines . . . which is not the most appropriate thing for a sage. (Voltaire 1877: 9.483; my tr.)

The intent of this dedication is difficult to discern. As David Fraser comments, neither Voltaire 'nor Frederick would have been deceived by gracefulness of compliment – this was a game which it was well-mannered to play' (2000: 255). Furthermore, Frederick and Voltaire's relationship was a volatile one. After a long correspondence, with tutelage from Voltaire and expressions of mutual admiration (again, not always easily interpreted), in 1750 Voltaire was 'installed' as intellectual and poet in Frederick's court. In 1753, under a cloud of controversy, Voltaire left (or perhaps was pushed), and relations vacillated between the two until Voltaire's death in 1778. Around the time of the *Précis*, early in 1759, the two enjoyed a brief restoration of friendship at the death of Frederick's sister, Wilhelmina, for which Voltaire offered sincere and well-received sympathy. The restoration was short-lived, however, when around June of 1759 the two began 'to quarrel again, for no adequate reason' (Besterman 1970: 394; cf. Fraser 2000: 406). Their relationship from this period until Voltaire's death is brilliantly described by Gustave Lanson: Voltaire 'made up with the king of Prussia while still keeping one fang bared for him' (in Voltaire 1991: 91). In any case, the academic lore of Frederick's affection for Ecclesiastes must be considered suspect.

To summarize, sometime between 1756 and 1759, a period of momentous change for Voltaire, Ecclesiastes somehow insinuated itself into his way of thinking, of corresponding and relating to the world. His engagement with it may even have significantly informed the resolution of Candide's dilemma (see Christianson 2005: 470–2). In any case, it is evident that from this period onwards he was habitually engaged with Ecclesiastesan themes, which was made possible in part by the rhetorically open structure of Qoheleth's reflections. As so many other readers have done, Voltaire placed himself in the position of Qoheleth's implied reader, who has no name and who will empathize with Qoheleth's disillusionment with the quest for real wisdom. Ecclesiastes as scripture offered Voltaire the peculiar luxury of sacred scepticism, free from the destructive presence of barbed satire (further, see below, pp. 124–5). As such, Voltaire might be recognized as the emblematic reader of Ecclesiastes who anticipates modernity while relating Qoheleth to the vital intellectual disputes of the day.

Modern Reading: 1800–

A. LITERATURE

Ecclesiastes seems to have influenced 'English literature' in two senses. First, it has through various modes of quotation and theme made its way into many of the 'canonical' works of poetry and prose. The second sense is of osmosis. This is still discernible in the daily discourse of Western culture, in which 'there is nothing new under the sun', or 'il n'y a rien de nouveau sous le soleil' or 'geschieht nichts Neues unter der Sonne' have somehow entered the vocabulary as descriptors of a broad range of experiences (see the examples compiled in the Appendix, 'The Quotable Qoheleth'). Of course this is partly due to the fact that, as Walter Brueggemann puts it, 'the dominant images and metaphors still governing public life are largely and powerfully shaped by the Bible' (2005: 13). At this 'dawn of modernity' of the nineteenth century, references to biblical texts were often part of a complex intellectual game of sorts. What Rosemarie Morgan says of Thomas Hardy's allusions to classical and biblical literature applies to many works of the period:

> Invariably thought-provoking, frequently ironized and often delightfully picturesque, it was not necessarily the aptness of the allusion or the brilliance of the literary analogue so much as its familiarity as part of a shared cultural heritage which excited the interest and pleasure of Victorian readers. The more esoteric the allusion, the more intense the reader's bright moment of recognition; the more ironic the implications, the greater the reader's satisfaction and pleasure – even the unschooled were familiar with Bible stories and classical mythology. (In Hardy 2000: pp. xxii–xxiii)

This provided a (now largely absent) rich context in which novelists and poets could use biblical texts to make social comment (particularly in Hardy's case) and otherwise reflect on human experience.

Nonetheless, Ecclesiastes in particular provided a specific language, a way of thinking and of scrutinizing the stuff of literature.[7] Michael Edwards (1990a)

---

[7] While this survey is broad ranging, a good deal of modern literature, particularly poetry, is also discussed in relation to the *vanitas* theme in chapter 1, pp. 125–38 and throughout the commentary.

offers an insightful description of this phenomenon in modern literature, as well as its appeal:

> Ecclesiastes, with its insistent refrain: 'vanity of vanities; all is vanity', and its string of quotable, unflattering remarks on the human condition, has always proved attractive. It has entered English literature through a number of titles, some of them recent (*Many Inventions, The Golden Bowl, The Sun Also Rises*), and, more importantly, it has provided an atmosphere, a vocabulary, for works as disparate as Johnson's 'The Vanity of Human Wishes' and, I suppose, the whole *oeuvre* of Beckett. (*Murphy*, for example, opens with a Beckettian recasting of one of the famous phrases: 'The sun shone, having no alternative, on the nothing new'.) (1990a: 79)

Edwards captures the pervasive sense in which Ecclesiastes has slipped into the language of literature, not only in vocabulary but in tenor and style. Indeed, because it captures so brilliantly the reality of disillusionment and the frustration of expectations on a scale that is both personal and universal, Ecclesiastes has been a natural choice of literary sparring partner for legion men and women of letters (cf. the discussion of the psychological appeal of Qoheleth in the Hermeneutical Postscript).

In the spirit of Renaissance interpreters, the nineteenth century sees Ecclesiastes and/or the Preacher himself coming gradually to signify a general spirit of inquiry that is as intoxicating as it is dangerous or frustrating. This is evident in the way in which writers such as Percy Shelley found kinship in Qoheleth's observations, seeing increasingly that the world is a 'spectacle of emptiness' (Quinney 1990: 177). This was sometimes coupled with a profoundly frustrating sense of futility, such as in Shelley's 'Sonnet' (1818):

> Lift not the painted veil which those who live
> Call Life: though unreal shapes be pictured there,
> . . .
> I knew one who had lifted it – he sought,
> For his lost heart was tender, things to love,
> But found them not, alas! nor was there aught
> The world contains, the which he could approve.
> Through the unheeding many he did move,
> A splendour among shadows, a bright blot
> Upon this gloomy scene, a Spirit that strove
> For truth, and like the Preacher found it not.
>
> (In Shelley 1887: 3. 413)

In describing the one who 'lifted the veil' (the figurative 'seeker'), who 'strove for truth', Shelley has recourse to Qoheleth, whom he might also have seen as 'a splendour among shadows'.

William Makepeace Thackeray (1811–63) engaged frequently with the idea of vanity (on which, see below, pp. 125–8), and also with Ecclesiastes' larger program of sceptically examining the world. One of the lesser-known examples appears in Thackeray's novel *The Newcomes* (1853–5). R. D. McMaster sees 'hovering' over the work 'the tone and perspective of Ecclesiastes with its themes of recurrence and frustration' (1987: 22). The opening of the novel, an 'overture' before the appearance of 'a drinking chorus', has the narrator, partly in the 'voice' of Solomon ('"Then in what a contemptuous way", may Solomon go on to remark, "does this author speak of human nature!"'; Thackeray 1962: 1. 4), reflecting on the repetition of things:

> What stories are new? All types of characters march through all fables . . . So, the tales were told ages before Aesop; and asses under lions' manes roared in Hebrew . . . The sun shines today as he did when he first began shining . . . There may be nothing new under and including the sun; but it looks fresh every morning, and we rise with it to toil, hope, scheme, laugh, struggle, love, suffer, until the night comes and quiet. And then will wake Morrow and the eyes that look on it; and so *da capo*. (1962: 1. 4–5)

It is worth noting that the list of morning intentions ('toil, hope' etc.) recalls Qoheleth's key vocabulary. McMaster highlights other points at which the Preacher seems to loom, and given Thackeray's affection for the book elsewhere that presence makes sense.

From writers like Thackeray it seems clear that reference to Qoheleth's words assumed reader familiarity and required no contextualization. Thomas Hardy's *Far from the Madding Crowd* (1874: ch. 4) is a particularly good example from the period. Farmer Oak, an upstanding Wessex Christian gentleman, finds that local comely lass Bathsheba Everdene 'soon made appreciable inroads upon [his] emotional constitution' (Hardy 2000: 21–2). Unfortunately, Oak, because he 'had one-and-a-half Christian characteristics too many to succeed with Bathsheba' (p. 29), makes his feelings known too quickly and naïvely. Upon hearing her devastating rejection of his declaration of love ('"I don't love you – so t'would be ridiculous!" she said, with a laugh'), Hardy's narrator describes his subsequent 'bearing': 'No man likes to see his emotions the sport of a merry-go-round of skittishness. "Very well," said Oak, firmly, with the bearing of one who was going to give his days and nights to Ecclesiastes for ever. "Then I'll ask you no more"' (p. 29). This light comment has a serious undertone as well. It is a small part of the tapestry of divine determinacy that Hardy weaves throughout the novel. As Morgan comments, 'local superstitions, traditional omens and ancient portents intersect with Ecclesiastes and Job, providing a delightfully incongruous series of signs pointing the way, quite arbitrarily, towards Destiny' (in Hardy 2000: p. xxix). (On Hardy's engagement with the vanity theme in *Tess of the d'Urbervilles*, see below, p. 130.)

As the Bibliography shows, numerous, highly specialist literary reception studies of Ecclesiastes have been published, and some have unearthed spectacular artefacts. One of the most notable is Peter Rossbacher's study of a 'fragment' in Anton Chekhov's notebook, *c.*1892. The fragment outlines the idea for a play about Solomon. As Rossbacher argues, the notes seem to have found their genesis in Ecclesiastes. I have indicated in brackets points at which the fragment resonates with Qoheleth:

> Solomon (alone) 'Oh, how dark life is. No night during the days of my childhood has ever terrified me so much with its darkness, as has my incomprehensible existence. My God, you gave my father David only the gift to combine words and sounds, to sing and to praise you on a harp, to weep sweetly, to make others weep and to enjoy beauty, but why have you given me also a pining spirit and hungry thoughts which cannot sleep [5:12; 8:16]. Like an insect, born from dust [3:20–1; 12:7], I hide in darkness, in despair, trembling all over and growing cold with terror [12:3, 5]. I see an incomprehensible mystery in everything [3:10–11, *passim*]. Why does this morning exist? Why does the sun rise from behind the temple and gild the palm? Why are my wives so beautiful? [cf. 2:8, 11] Where does this bird hurry, what is the purpose of its flight, if it itself, its nestlings, and that place where it is hurrying must turn into dust, as I must? Oh, better not to have been born or to be a stone, to which God gave neither eyes nor thoughts [6:3–5; cf. 4:2–3]. To exhaust my body for the night, I spent all day yesterday like a simple worker, carrying marble to the temple, but now night has come and I cannot sleep [5:12; 8:16] . . . I will lie down once more. Forzes told me that if you imagine a running flock of sheep and think of it incessantly, your mind will get confused and fall asleep. I will do this . . .' (He goes away.) (X, 534–535.) (In Rossbacher 1968: 27)

One can only wonder with regret both at what this may have become and at what other lost attempts to dramatize Qoheleth existed. As far as I know, this is as far as anyone has got, and the fact that it went no further from a playwright so attuned to Qoheleth's themes, and who approached the idea at a time of great personal literary creativity (Hingley 2004), indicates the enormity of the task. (Note that Salyer and I have separately published the notion that Ecclesiastes can helpfully be imagined as a one-man play: Salyer 2001: 186–7; Christianson 1998a: 257–8.)

Like that of Donne and Thackeray before him, T. S. Eliot's work, as Michael Edwards argues, seems to breathe the world-weariness of Qoheleth:

The work held Eliot's imagination before he was converted, to the extent that the statement: 'he that increaseth knowledge increaseth sorrow' (1:18) might stand as an epigraph to his early poems; and to the extent that a Dantean reference to '*nostra vanitate*' does stand in the epigraph to his first book. It continued to speak to him, after his conversion, of a reality not to be ignored. Is it an exaggeration to think that the first of his *Collected Poems* was actually written under the sign of Ecclesiastes? (1990a: 79; cf. T. Wright 2005)

The most prominent influence Edwards recognizes is in Eliot's *Four Quartets* (1943) and (less so) *The Wasteland* (1922), both widely regarded as his most influential works (1990a: 80–1; examples can be found in this commentary on chapters 1, 3 and 12).

Other modern writers have found in Ecclesiastes a fruitful, creative resource. Ernest Hemingway's novel of 'Lost Generation' expatriates in Spain, *The Sun Also Rises* (1926), opens in its title-pages first with a citation from Gertrude Stein ('You are all a lost generation') and then with Eccl. 1:4–7 (and of course the title takes its cue from 1:5). More significantly, several critics have recognized other influences of Ecclesiastes on the novel. So, for example, it may be that Hemingway rendered the main character Robert Cohn as an embodiment of the fool of Ecclesiastes – that is, as one who lacks moderation, who is dead to life's possibilities, and whose lack of wisdom causes him to 'walk in darkness' (so Cowan 1983; cf. also Cochran 1968 and Ross 1972–3). When adapting Hemingway's novel for the screen, the potential of the connection to Ecclesiastes was not lost on the film's producers:

'Twentieth Century-Fox suggested to theater managers that they ask local clergymen to preach sermons on the famous Ecclesiastes text from which Hemingway took his title.' It is doubtful that if the film had followed the language of the novel, the clergy would have approved of Brett's dialogue and would not have been interested in promoting the film, but probably would have condemned it. (Ferrell 2000: 177; citing Frank Lawrence)

Hemingway also considered Ecclesiastes-inspired titles for 'A Farewell to Arms' (1929), namely: 'Thing that Has Been' [1:9]; 'Knowledge Increaseth Sorrow' [1:18]; 'The Peculiar Treasure' [2:8]; 'One Event Happeneth to them All' [2:14]; 'One Thing for them All' [3:19]; 'Nothing Better for a Man' [2:24]; 'A Time of War' [3:8]; 'One Thing is Certain' [2:14]; 'The Long Home' [12:5] (Smith 1982: 75). Other titles appear in his list of possibilities, but Ecclesiastes seems to occupy a special place. As Paul Smith comments, 'One might argue that Hemingway first returned to his source for The Sun Also Rises, picked up the Preacher's stoic sayings in the following verse, and started listing phrases that seemed to capture some of his sense of the narrative's burden' (1982: 76).

American poet Louis Untermeyer takes on Qoheleth's voice in intimate style in his 1928 poem 'Koheleth':

> I waited and worked
> To win myself leisure,
> Till loneliness irked
> And I turned to raw pleasure.
>
> I drank and gamed,
> I feasted and wasted,
> Till, sick and ashamed,
> The food stood untasted.
>
> I searched in the Book
> For rooted convictions
> Till the badgered brain shook
> With its own contradictions.
>   (Untermeyer 1928: 242;
>   cf. the remaining lines,
>   cited in the commentary
>   on ch. 9, p. 210)

Untermeyer is typical of readers who narrate Qoheleth's words as though they were their own, who wish to suggest a seamless symmetry between Qoheleth's experience and their own. Intriguingly, as in so much of the *vanitas* poetry (e.g. of Anne Bradstreet, Christina Rossetti and Lord Byron), this takes place with the darker themes of Qoheleth and rarely if at all with Qoheleth's exposition of joy. In these readings the 'I' of the poet manages to commandeer Qoheleth's voice while expanding his or her own autobiographical voice.

Thomas Wolfe also finds some kindred spirit in Qoheleth in the penultimate chapter of his (posthumous) novel *You Can't Go Home Again* (1940), and he proves to be a careful reader of Qoheleth's themes. Wolfe's protagonist, novelist George Webber, writes to his friend Fox as he reflects on how his own experiences have shaped and changed his philosophy:

> [O]f all that I have ever seen or learned, that book [of Ecclesiastes] seems to me the noblest, the wisest, and the most powerful expression of man's life upon this earth – and also earth's highest flower of poetry, eloquence, and truth. I am not given to dogmatic judgments in the matter of literary creation, but if I had to make one I could only say that Ecclesiastes is the greatest single piece of writing I have ever known, and the wisdom expressed in it the most lasting and profound. (In Wolfe 1968: 732–3)

This at first appears to be like a poor undergraduate essay, as Wolfe's character does not state *why* Ecclesiastes rings with such poetic wisdom. But he goes on to build his case, appealing to Fox's inclination to 'agree with' a 'few precepts' (which he draws from 1:1, 8–9, 17; 3:1; 7:1; 9:10). In his friend Fox he has seen 'every syllable of it . . . a thousand times' (p. 733). And, what is more, Ecclesiastes is his epitaph and his portrait. He finds in both his friend and in Qoheleth a 'philosophy of *hopeful* fatalism. Both of you are in the essence pessimists, but both of you are also pessimists with hope . . . I learned from both of you the stern lesson of acceptance . . . but, having accepted [my lot], to try to do what was before me, what I could do, with all my might' (p. 734). And so gradually the passage becomes something of a compelling exegesis of chapter 9 especially, but George wants to suggest that change is possible as well, and he criticizes Fox's tendency to accept 'the order of things as they are' (and George is right in lumping Fox and Qoheleth together in this view):

> In everlasting terms – those of eternity – you and the Preacher may be right: for there is no greater wisdom than the wisdom of Ecclesiastes, no acceptance finally so true as the stern fatalism of the rock. Man was born to live, to suffer, and to die, and what befalls him is a tragic lot. There is no denying this in the final end. *But we must, dear Fox, deny it all along the way.* (Wolfe 1968: 737)

In his 'Koheleth' (*c.*1944), Canadian poet A. M. Klein, part of the 'Montreal group' of poets in the 1920s and 1930s, also recognizes little beyond Qoheleth's most gloomy themes:

> Koheleth, on his damasked throne, lets weary exhalation follow
> The weary inhalation. He finds breath a toil of no reward.
> As hollow as the rotted gourd is the heart of the monarch hollow . . .
> His weakened voice drops weariness, that slowly falls, word after word:
>
> 'Take your black quill, O Scribe, and write in wormwood and with gall –
> That I am but erected dust that flutters to a roofless tomb;
> That even on the loveliest the unparticular worm will crawl;
> And that this sun, this splendid sun, is nothing more than whitened gloom.'
>
> . . .
>
> 'Speak of the pleasures of the wise, verily I have known these once;
> The glories of the goblet, yea, these, too, have been a part of me,
> The ecstasies of damosels, these also have been Solomon's,
> Who waking and with sleeping cries: These things are wind and vanity.
>
> . . .

Death is a tall, a stripped and oil-anointed Negro chamberlain
Standing behind the throne; he makes grimaces underneath his palm;
Behind the royal back he scoffs; his gestures they are more than plain . . .
Koheleth turns his head, and lo, Death stands most dignified and calm.

(Selected verses; complete text in Klein 1974: 20–1)

Few writers have imputed such bitterness to Qoheleth as Klein. Gone here is
a larger redemptive strategy, or joy or repentance (indeed, the monarch's heart
is hollow) that might drive us beyond the hateful conclusion of chapter 2 (cf.
2:17–18). Qoheleth here only meets death, and we can easily envisage Qoheleth's defeat, and can no longer apply Frank Crüsemann's perfect summary of
the death theme, that in Ecclesiastes it makes life shine more brightly (1979:
67). Klein is also unique among modern literary interpreters in recognizing
Solomon as a rhetorical device, subtly combining that voice with Qoheleth's
(see the discussion below, p. 98).

A new kind of short-hand use of Qoheleth arrives in several works from the
post-war boom in science fiction. Easily the most accomplished among these
is Ray Bradbury's *Fahrenheit 451* (1953). Bradbury imagines a future culture
in which information feeds the masses in digestible thought-free morsels, in
which its inhabitants are all levelled by the fact that they desire nothing to
engage their minds. In this world Guy Montag is a fireman whose job is to
burn books and the buildings that house them. All books are banned, and their
readers are to be imprisoned, or more likely, burned 'accidentally' with their
books. Montag's 'bright and clear' fire is there to cleanse the masses from the
pollution of knowledge. As Montag's Captain lectures him, 'Cram them [the
masses] full of non-combustible data, chock them so dammed full of facts they
feel stuffed, but absolutely "brilliant" with information . . . Don't give them
any slippery stuff like philosophy or sociology to tie things up with. That way
lies melancholy' (1993: 68). And so for everyone in this book, and in every
sense, even for Montag who is reborn by and suffers from thinking for himself,
the thesis is borne out: 'in much wisdom is much grief: and the one that
increases knowledge increases sorrow' (1:18). Ecclesiastes' haunting spirit over
the first half of the novel gradually becomes embodied. Montag steals books
from the hoards that he burns, and among these is a Bible, perhaps the
last Bible. Montag consumes of the Bible what he can, in order to memorize
and therefore be rid of the hard evidence. In the closing scenes, after Montag
has done what is 'right' in killing his captain and fleeing the city, he comes
across other fugitives, the bums of the outland whose leader's name is
'Granger', and discovers their subversive strategy to revive their culture: they
each have memorized a book. When asked what Montag has to offer them, he
replies,

'Nothing. I thought I had part of the Book of Ecclesiastes and maybe a little of Revelation, but I haven't even that now.'

'The book of Ecclesiastes would be fine.' . . . Granger turned to the Reverend. 'Do we have a Book of Ecclesiastes?'

'One. A man named Harris of Youngstown.'

'Montag.' Granger took Montag's shoulder firmly. 'Walk carefully. Guard your health. If anything should happen to Harris, *you* are the Book of Ecclesiastes. See how important you've become in the last minute!' (Bradbury 1993: 158)

While all of Montag's drama is played out, a war is also being undertaken. Not long after the above scene, the final bombs are struck, and these are witnessed by the band of fugitives. Knocked to the ground, Montag's memory slowly returns:

Yes, yes, part of the Ecclesiastes and Revelation. Part of that book, part of it, quick now, quick, before it gets away . . . Book of Ecclesiastes. Here. He said it over to himself silently, lying flat to the trembling earth, he said the words of it many times and they were perfect without trying . . . it was just the Preacher by himself, standing there in his mind, looking at him . . . (1993: 168)

The fugitives march on in silence, because

there was everything to think about and much to remember . . . Montag felt the slow stir of words, the slow simmer. And when it came to his turn, what could he say, what could he offer on a day like this to make the trip a little easier? To everything there is a season. Yes. A time to break down and a time to build up. Yes. A time to keep silence and a time to speak. Yes, all that. But what else. What else? Something, something . . . [he cites Rev. 22:2] (1993: 172)

With that final scene Montag, with his recurring 'yes', has become Ecclesiastes and now embodies its active call to think, to spurn a tacit engagement with the world. Bradbury first published *Fahrenheit* in shorter form as *The Fireman* in 1951, in which Montag was not Ecclesiastes, but Job (Baker 2005: 498). Ecclesiastes, then, represents a very deliberate and deeply embedded idea in the final work. Bradbury returned cryptically to Ecclesiastes in a brief poem entitled 'Long after Ecclesiastes', which opens

> Long after Ecclesiastes:
> The First Book of Dichotomy,
> The Second Book of Symbiosis
> What do they say?
> Work away.
> Make do.
> Believe . . .
>
> (Bradbury 1984: 249)

Philip K. Dick's *The Man in the High Castle* (1962) is set at the time of the novel's composition in the USA and explores the 'what-if' scenario in which the Allies lost the Second World War. In this world, Hawthorne Abendsen writes his own 'what-if' novel which imagines the Allies' victory: *The Grasshopper Lies Heavy* (from Eccl. 12:5). The novel is banned by the Nazi and Japanese authorities in the USA, but is available in some states. One of the main protagonists, Juliana Frink, becomes obsessed with the world this book describes (a world which in its detail is actually different from what readers would expect, i.e. it is not the 'real world', but one in which, for example, Hitler is tried in Munich after the war). In the end Juliana discovers that Abendsen's novel was in fact written by an oracle, the *I-Ching* (which, like *The Grasshopper*, features throughout the book), with Abendsen acting as a sort of nominal cypher. In the end, it is the oracle that informs her and Abendsen that the *Grasshopper* world is in fact 'true'. Readers are left uncertain as to what world is the 'real world' (and to whom), and this may be the significance of the oblique reference to Ecclesiastes (which is acknowledged in the novel only by the line from one of its minor characters, 'That's a quote from the Bible' [Dick 2001: 69]). In other words, its appropriateness may lie once again in Qoheleth's crushing theme of the inaccessibility and unreliability of knowledge about the world (further, see DiTommaso 1999 – there is an element of serendipity to John Jarick's study [2000] in which he notes a number of intriguing similarities between Ecclesiastes and the *I Ching*).

A less oblique (though even more odd) engagement with Ecclesiastes came a year later in the science-fiction 'novelet' 'A Rose for Ecclesiastes' by Roger Zelazny (1963). The story is told by its protagonist, Gallinger, an arrogant poet and linguist who is sent to Mars in order to catalogue and notate its language and culture. In the process he is given access to its 'Temple' and is asked to offer some of his own poetry (from Earth) in Martian 'High Tongue'. On reading some of their sacred texts, he is struck by a likeness: 'They wrote about concrete things: rocks, sand, water, winds; and the tenor couched within these elemental symbols was fiercely pessimistic. It reminded me of some Buddhist texts, but even more so, I realized from my recent *recherches*, it was like parts of the Old Testament. Specifically it reminded me of the Book of Ecclesiastes' (1963: 12). Like some Elizabethan paraphrast, he decides that a rendering of Ecclesiastes into verse would be a suitable poetic offering for the Martian 'royalty'. When some verses are ready, Gallinger reads them to Braxa, a Martian female with whom he has formed a relationship, and receives an unexpected reaction: '"These are the first three chapters of the Book of Ecclesiastes", I explained. "It is very similar to your own sacred books." I started reading. I got through eleven verses before she cried out, "Please don't read that! . . . He is so sad . . . like all the others"' (1963: 22–3). In the course of his 'research',

Gallinger discovers that the Martian race is on its way to extinction and that they have decided as a people to accept their fate. He decides that he might change their minds by exposing them to a pessimism to match their 'sacred texts of Locar': a full reading of Ecclesiastes in the Temple. But before this he argues that Earth has overcome its pessimism through survival, that all was, indeed, not vanity after all. After reading Ecclesiastes, he is told that he has fulfilled a prophecy, 'The Promise of Locar'. When he asks how, he is told, 'You read us his words, as great as Locar's. You read to us how there is "nothing new under the sun". And you mocked his words as you read them – showing us a new thing . . . You are the [prophesied] Sacred Scoffer' (1963: 34). And so Ecclesiastes saves a whole planet because it has, as the earth-bound rabbis had recognized so long ago, the power to defile!

Writers understandably engage less and less with Qoheleth, probably because they engage less with the Bible, though it is worth noting that its influence is still found in titles of books that themselves do not engage directly with Ecclesiastes, such as Mark Jarman's collection of poetry *Questions for Ecclesiastes* (1997), Judson Mitcham's collection of poems, *Somewhere in Ecclesiastes* (1991), or Elie Wiesel's memoirs, *All Rivers Run to the Sea* (1996), *And the Sea is Never Full* (2000).

B.   Visual Art, Music and Film

Ecclesiastes has been given relatively little attention in the arts. This is partly due to its lack of narrative action and its focus on character. Without exception, then, visual artists have rendered it either in abstract terms or in terms of its protagonist alone.

The most sustained and voluminous artistic engagement with Ecclesiastes is found in the (mainly Dutch) *vanitas* painting tradition (see below, pp. 119–22). Apart from that tradition, there are very few significant visual renderings of Ecclesiastes. What can be found, however, is a slight if rich vein of illustrations that focus on Qoheleth the man. First I would note the beautifully illustrated Solomon preaching *vanitas* in a thirteenth-century glossed Latin Bible (plate 7, p. 102). Of other examples I would highlight the following.

The illustrative sketch as frontispiece to Thackeray's 1855 poem *Vanitas Vanitatum* (plate 9, p. 127), shows a scythe-wielding skeletal Qoheleth, crowned and sitting on a coffin, clearly comfortable with the iconography of death. He is positioned 'under the sun' and, in a sense, 'over' death. A 1965 wood engraving by Stefan Martin, based on a drawing by Ben Shahn (plate 1), relates a proclamatory, royal Qoheleth, connected inexorably to Solomon and holding forth the Hebrew of his opening words in 1:1–2a.

Plate 1 Ben Shahn's 'Koheleth', 1965. © Estate of Ben Shahn/DACS, London/VAGA, New York 2006

As one might expect, in his illuminated Bible (1964–7) Salvador Dali offers the most fantastic rendering, a kind of cosmic Qoheleth (plate 2), royal, all-encompassing and universal. Renowned illustrator Barry Moser rendered a particularly appealing sceptical and direct Qoheleth (plate 3) for the Viking Studio edition of the Pennyroyal Caxton Bible (1999).

Taken together, these pieces can be seen to comment on modern takes of Qoheleth the man, as king (Shahn), as representing a universal wisdom (Dali) and (my personal favourite) an uncluttered and direct confrontation with a face that sparkles with sharp intelligence (Moser). (I would also note here a brief but insightful graphic treatment of Ecclesiastes in the Great Bible Discovery Series [adapted from the *Découvrir la bible* series, 1983], vol. 17. It is probably the only visualized reading that makes a meaningful distinction between Qoheleth and Solomon, and exploits it to significant rhetorical effect.)

In 1984, artist Philip Ratner founded the Israel Bible Museum, in Safad. Included in its permanent collection are a series of paintings representing the time poem of chapter 3 (plate 11, p. 171), and the rather hopeful rendering of Qoheleth, simply entitled *Ecclesiastes* (plate 4).

Two photographic essays on Ecclesiastes (Abramson and Freulich 1972 and Short 1973) have creatively juxtaposed photographs with the text in the form of commentary. Both works take seriously the manner in which Qoheleth 'speaks' to modernity as an existential protagonist. Short, in recognizing the epistemological significance of the extensive use of *r'h*, 'to see/observe', in Ecclesiastes, likens Qoheleth to a photographer. Indeed, for Short, 'Ecclesiastes was the Henri Cartier-Bresson of the Old Testament' (1973: 4). While the photos have an understandably dated look, on most pages Short has created a thoughtful juxtaposition between text and image. Here the images relate to 9:3b–7 (plate 5).

Music is another area in which Qoheleth has received little attention. As discussed below (pp. 120–1), Ecclesiastes' *vanitas* theme became a reflective interest to choral and string music of the first half of the seventeenth century. But other examples are worth noting here. In May 1897, less than a year before his death, Johannes Brahms (1833–97) composed what R. Wehner calls one of his 'most compelling and mature compositions' (in the sleeve notes to Brahms 1992), *Vier ernste Gesänge*. The first two of these 'Four Serious Songs' are based on Eccl. 3:19–22 and 4:1–3 respectively. The next two move to the like-minded Sir. 41:1–2, and then the more uplifting 1 Cor. 13:1–3, 12–13. The songs are, as Wehner puts it, 'as far removed as possible from the nineteenth-century art song'. Musically sparse, with a solitary baritone and piano, they present a graphic reflection on the eventuality (and levelling power) of death and its subsequent conquering by love.

PLATE 2   Salvador Dali's 1964–7 illuminated Bible. © Salvador Dali, Gala-Salvador
Dali Foundation, DACS, London 2006

PLATE 3   Barry Moser's 'The Preacher', 1999. © Barry Moser

PLATE 4   Philip Ratner's 'Ecclesiastes'. © Philip Ratner, reprinted with permission

Other classical composers have been attracted to Qoheleth. British composer Granville Bantock, in his a cappella choral work *Vanity of Vanities* (1913), rendered selections from the whole book in seven movements. A peer of Elgar, Bantock was best known for his full treatment of the poetry of Omar

...madness fills
their hearts
while they live...

...and then they go
down to the dead.

4 But only the living have any hope; and therefore a living
dog is better than a dead lion.

5 At least the living know that they will die, but the dead
know nothing at all. Nor does anything good come to the
dead. They are utterly gone *and* forgotten.

6 Their loves, their hates, their jealousies, are all stopped
short; nor will they ever again take part in anything done
under the sun.

7 Go to it then, eat your food with enjoyment, and drink your
wine with a merry heart; for it is God's good pleasure that
you find enjoyment while you live.

PLATE 5   From Robert Short's photographic essay, 1973

Khayyam, a work frequently compared to Ecclesiastes. The piece is noted for its ambition. Diana McVeagh describes the scope of the intended performance: 'Choirs then were usually very large: for one Bantock performance there were 400 singers. In *The Vanity of Vanities* Bantock asks for a 12-part choir . . . When he brings the whole chorus to a climax, in a sequence of crushing chords spread over the choir's full compass, the grand sweep is overwhelming' (sleeve notes to Bantock 1996). Like Joio later, Bantock seeks to match the tenor of the music to its text, though unusually finishes on the note of vanity instead of on the orthodoxy of the epilogue. As McVeagh notes, 'Elgar, fondly, called him "the arch-heretic" . . . There is no redemption here, no resurrection. Such a setting might lead to despair, but the tone, though pessimistic, is astringent, grave and stoical' (ibid.).

In 1916, Jewish composer Ernest Bloch composed '*Schelomo*: Hebraic Rhapsody for Cello and Orchestra'. Abraham Karp fleshes out the context:

> Bloch was thirty-six years old when he completed his masterpiece in his native city. Later his work took him to the United States, to France, and back to America.
>   Bloch recalled how he turned sketches which lay dormant into the *Schelomo*: One day I met the cellist Alexander Barjansky and his wife . . . I played my manuscript scores for them, *Hebrew Poems, Israel* and the Psalms, all of them unpublished and about which nobody cared. The Barjanskys were profoundly moved . . . The Ecclesiastes was completed in a few weeks, and since legends attribute this book to King Solomon, I named it *Schelomo*. (Karp 1991)

Finally, American composer Norman Dello Joio won the 1957 Pulitzer Prize for Music with his 1956 composition *Meditations on Ecclesiastes* ('for string orchestra'). Based on Eccl. 3:1–8, it is discussed in the commentary below (along with other music based on ch. 3, such as The Byrds's rendition of Pete Seeger's *Turn! Turn! Turn!*).

Apart from *Turn! Turn! Turn!*, Ecclesiastes seems to have made little impact on popular music. One notable exception, however, *may* be the case of U2. Lead singer Bono comments that 'I always felt like "The Fly" [from the 1991 album, *Achtung Baby*] was this phone call from hell. It took U2 fifteen years to get from Psalms to Ecclesiastes, and it's only one book!' (this is possibly anecdotal and is cited on numerous websites, such as Bono 2004). Bono also explains that the lyrical idea behind 'Miss Sarajevo' (for the soundtrack to the 1995 documentary film of the same name) 'invokes – and maybe undoes – the spirit of the book of Ecclesiastes, a "time for everything under heaven"' (*Three Sunrises* 2004, which further references 'All Passengers Present and Correct', *Propaganda*, 23 August 1995). The song employs the refrain 'is there a time for . . .', couched in the form of a question. Finally, Bono is reported to have likened the track 'The Wanderer' (with Johnny Cash, on the 2002 album *The Essential Johnny Cash*) to 'The Preacher' (so Waters 1994).

It is mostly understandable (though to a cinema enthusiast like myself, bitterly disappointing) that Qoheleth has never been 'filmed' as such. His direct 'filmability' is an intriguing potential to reflect on (I see Ed Harris in the role, personally), but there are other senses in which he has been rendered in celluloid.

A recent conference demonstrated interest in Ecclesiastes' relationship to film. *Reel Spirituality: Cinematic Wisdom and the Book of Ecclesiastes* was held in September 2000 by the Theology through the Arts group at the University of Cambridge. Speakers were not suggesting that Ecclesiastes had directly influenced filmmakers (it has, though only rarely and in small doses), but rather films such as *American Beauty*, Ken Loach's *Ladybird, Ladybird* and *My Name is Joe*, *Shirley Valentine* and *Pleasantville* were all identified as films that manage, after the manner of Qoheleth, to hold together the themes of joy and despair. (The most intriguing aspect of the conference was to hear Ecclesiastes 'performed', when portions were read out to a hugely receptive audience of about 350. Laughter occurred where I did not expect it, such as at 1:18 – this was probably the nervous laughter of recognition – and it was clear that the text was winning over an audience that, on the whole, had probably never closely read it.)

Christopher Deacy's book *Screen Christologies* (2001) starts by recognizing film as both a bearer and a locus of religious meaning and reflection. Deacy develops the idea of *film noir* being particularly concerned with the *activity* of redemption. Films provide viewers the opportunity to examine the human condition as 'privileged witnesses' (2001: 18, with reference to Paul Gallagher; cf. pp. 13–15, 21–3). Early in his study Deacy develops a comparison of *noir* to Ecclesiastes, suggesting that for Qoheleth, as in *noir*, there is little hope under the sun except for finding a way out through a transformation of everyday existence (pp. 59–64). In some sense this comparative approach can be seen to continue in Robert Johnston's *Useless Beauty: Ecclesiastes through the Lens of Contemporary Film* (2004). Johnston (who was the organizer of the film conference discussed above) offers not so much a sustained dialogue as a sampling of themes that spark off one another, particularly in relation to the companionship sayings of Eccl. 4:9–11.

Ecclesiastes has been a relatively fruitful location for filmmakers seeking titles: *A Fly in the Ointment* (1924 [Fr.], 1933 [Fr.], 1943, 1955 [Fr.], 2003 [Swed.]); *Rejoice in Thy Youth* (1939, Swed.); *A Time to Kill* (1954, 1996); *The Sun Also Rises* (1957); *A Time to Love and a Time to Die* (1958); *A Time to Live and a Time to Die* (1963, Fr.); *Pick up on 101* (aka *A Time to Every Purpose* [1972]); *A Time to Die* (1982, 1985 [Ital.], 1986); *A Time to Remember* (1987);

Under the Sun (1992); *A Time to Love* (1999, Ital.). Also, novels with Ecclesiastes connections have made their way to the screen: *Vanity Fair* (1915, 1922, 1923, 2004; see pp. 125–6); *A Farewell to Arms* (1932, 1957; see p. 69); *The Sun Also Rises* (1957; see p. 69); *Tess* (1979; see p. 130). Ecclesiastes as part of the dialogue has made its way into a few films. So, for example, in the silent film *Intolerance* (1916), during which portions of chapter 3 appear as graphics. Too innumerable to mention are occurrences of the phrase (usually in a funeral context), 'Ashes to ashes, dust to dust', which is an amalgamation of the imagery in Gen. 3:19 and Eccl. 3:20 and 12:7. More significant examples of dialogue are discussed in the commentary: *Babette's Feast* (1987, Dan.), *Darrow* (1991) and *Rembrandt* (1936) on chapter 1 (pp. 138–41); *Gattaca* (1997) on chapter 7 (p. 192); *Final Destination* (2000) on chapter 9 (p. 215); and *Platoon* (1986) on chapter 11 (p. 224).

C.   COMPARATIVE STUDIES

Since the nineteenth century a whole range of comparative interpretive exercises have been undertaken (see Bibliography, pp. 283–5). Although it is outside the remit of this commentary to undertake such interpretation, examples of others doing so are clearly part of the book's reception history. Indeed, they can produce impressive results, since they are 'not just curios, but serious functional analogies, such as evolutionary biologists use' (Michael Fox in Carasik 2004). Such studies include comparisons (sometimes in detail) to Beckett, Camus, various Egyptian Instructions, the *Epic of Gilgamesh*, Flaubert, Goethe, Hemingway, the *I Ching* (ancient Chinese *Book of Changes*), Omar Khayyam, Montaigne, Nabokov, Pascal, Shakespeare, *Uncle Tom's Cabin*, Yeats (two comparative studies on Ecclesiastes and film, discussed above, show that such study is not limited to literature: Deacy 2001 and Johnston 2004). A few examples will suffice to highlight this popular critical strategy.

E. H. Plumptre (1881) finds parallels to Qoheleth's thought and style in a range of world literatures and highlights these in three appendices (pp. 231–64) on Shakespeare, Tennyson and the twelfth-century Persian poet Omar Khayyam (a figure who features prominently as a comparative counterpoint, even extending to rendering Qoheleth in Khayyam's metre [e.g. Buchanan 1904 and Moore 1924]). Plumptre delineates in detail what he finds to be echoes of Qoheleth's mood and tenor and melancholic type of meditation. F. W. Nichols (1984) compares Ecclesiastes to Beckett's work, particularly *Waiting for Godot*. Dickens's *A Tale of Two Cities* is thought to share some of Qoheleth's concerns as well as narrative procedure (so Friedman 1988: 149–50). Larry Kreitzer (1994) develops a comparison of the themes of birth/death and life/loss to Hemingway's *A Farewell to Arms*. Comparisons in terms of Ecclesiastes' genre include that to Pascal's *Pensées* (Murphy 1955) and Marcus Aurelius's *Meditations* (J. S. Wright 1946: 249; Christianson 1998a: 141–2).

In a lengthy and stimulating article, Arthur Kirsch (1988) identifies some intriguing affinities between Shakespeare's *King Lear* and Ecclesiastes. Although *Lear* is frequently compared to the book of Job, Kirsch finds Ecclesiastes a more useful point of comparison. In particular he picks up on themes of death and the extremities of experience (expressed as thematic polarities in both works). Kirsch offers a careful reading of Ecclesiastes' themes, highlighting Qoheleth's frequent reference to the 'landscape' of the heart (citing from the 1560 edition of the Geneva Bible, which was probably the Bible that Shakespeare read). Kirsch sees in both texts 'the pain of protest as well as of resignation . . . And perhaps most important, if most obvious, *vanitas*, the theme that echoes endlessly in Ecclesiastes, and that *King Lear* catches up in its preoccupation with the word "nothing"' (1988: 158). Kirsch grasps the significance of Qoheleth's extremes: 'For like Ecclesiastes, *King Lear* is composed of oppositions, oppositions between weeping and laughing, seeking and losing, being silent and speaking, loving and hating. The characters embody such contrasts: Cordelia is schematically opposed to Goneril and Regan, Edgar to Edmund, Kent to Oswald, Albany to Cornwall' (1988: 159).

Deborah Pierce, in a literature PhD thesis, offers a particularly illuminating comparison of Ecclesiastes with Gustave Flaubert's 1881 novel *Bouvard et Pécuchet* (Pierce 1992: ch. 3). '[U]pon examining the two works it can be concluded that the import of *Bouvard et Pécuchet* is comprehended in a verse from *Ecclesiastes* which Flaubert might well have used as an epigraph: "And I applied my mind to seek and to search out by wisdom all that is done under the heavens; it is an unhappy business that God has given to the sons of men to be busy with" [1:13]' (1992: 77). Flaubert's novel depicts the experiences of two copyists living in Paris who become inseparable friends, one of whom inherits a substantial fortune. In love with the idea of an idyllic country life, they set out to live 'off the land' on a farm in the town of Chavignolles, Normandy, in 1841. The novel follows their attempts at learning to achieve wealth and success through the aid of knowledge, particularly, if not solely, from books. When they cannot understand the way the world is working, they turn to books of every kind under the sun. Such was the story's encyclopedic range that Flaubert is said to have consulted more than 1,500 volumes in its writing, taking 'assiduous' notes on each, even causing his eyesight to go bad (Pierce 1992: 101, 104; Krailsheimer in Flaubert 1976: 9). Flaubert spent 16–18 years writing the novel in the late 1860s and 1870s up until his death in 1880, but never completed it, leaving us instead with an enticing plan, written in point form, of the final, incomplete tenth chapter. While it is unlikely that Flaubert drew directly from Ecclesiastes for his inspiration, he was aware of the book, stating in the novel that 'our two worthy men, after all their disappointments, felt the need to be simple, to love something, to find peace of mind. They tried Ecclesiastes, Isaiah, Jeremiah. But the Bible frightened them with its prophets roaring like lions, the thunder crashing in the clouds, all the weeping in Gehenna, and its God scattering empires as the wind scatters clouds' (Flaubert 1976: 223). (Further on the Flaubert comparison, see Christianson 1998a: 235–42.)

Finally, mention should be made of the fact that not a little attention has been given to the idea that Qoheleth is a precursor of sorts to existentialism. This notion has led to a substantial amount of comparative study (Abramson and Freulich 1972; Berger 2001; Brown 1996; Christianson 1998a; Crüsemann 1979; Fox 1989; Gordis 1955; James 1984; Nichols 1984; Peter 1980; Schwartz 1986; Short 1973), particularly to the work of Albert Camus. Qoheleth indeed shares some distinctive qualities with the existentialists. It seems that it would not be untrue to fix on him A. MacIntyre's designation of the existentialist, 'disappointed rationalist' (1967: 147). The studies highlight numerous shared features, one of the most prominent of which is Qoheleth's penchant for the extreme. Like the dramatists, he has a flair for expressing the absurd in dramatically extreme terms. For example, under Qoheleth's auspices, Solomon's guise took on mythic proportions, and his failure to succeed in Solomon's world (that is, the reliable world of retribution, wisdom and folly – for who is a fool and who is a sage in Qoheleth's eyes?) is a sublime piece of absurdist drama. The Solomonic scenario is Qoheleth's most potent rejection of the easy notion of retribution, and his world is polarized in two extremes: that of the king of wisdom and that of the embittered sage who no longer knows even what wisdom or existence is. (For further development of this comparison, see Christianson 1998a: 259–74, esp. 266 n. 32.)

In this tightly organized opening our protagonist is introduced by the frame narrator (who appears again in 7:27 and 12:8–14) 'Qoheleth, son of David' (1:1). As he is to many simultaneously joyful and miserable, so he is both Solomon and not Solomon, and the playful ascription has cast a peculiar shadow over legion readings. Here also begins his momentous theme of *hebel* (1:2 *et passim*), a word variously translated (e.g. 'vanity', 'futility', 'absurdity'), which if nothing else signifies a gaping negation. In the experiences Qoheleth will go on to relate, *hebel* comes to represent the defiance of all reasonable expectation about the world. This is the 'raw material' for the most voluminous theme in Ecclesiastes' reception history, the refutation and contempt of the vanity of the world. My discussion of these two tremendously important topoi of reading is undertaken in the first two sections that follow.

The remaining portion of the first chapter (which will be taken up in a third, distinct section) begins with a programmatic, rhetorical question about the profit of human endeavour (1:3). This is followed by a brief poem on the circuitous behaviour of the sun, wind and sea (the earth is the only thing that stands still here – v. 4; cf. 3:11), with reflections that seem to beg comparison to human experience (4, 8–11). Qoheleth then undertakes his quest proper to examine what God has done, and indirectly how that activity impacts humanity (12–18). The theme of *hebel* courses all through this passage, even when the word does not appear. It is also here coupled with the 'pursuit of wind' (14), and in the pages that remain nothing now seems certain except instability and uncertainty itself. It is full of the frustratingly unchangeable – what has been, what will be – the irredeemably crooked and the forever forgotten (8–11, 15). And here the Preacher's infeasible credentials are placed on show – a man who is full-to-bursting with life experience and has become more wise than all the sages who preceded him (12, 16). This is neatly coupled to Qoheleth's persuasive and biblically unique epistemological style: 'And so I found . . .' (14 *et passim*) – a style that indelibly stamps the whole book.

This brief and memorable overture expresses futility, sorrow and vexation, but it is also undergirded by the diamond-hard intransigence of Qoheleth's desire to understand, to apply his mind *to know*, even if that knowledge is folly itself, even if in the end it will only bring misery. Already the reader is witness to Qoheleth's peculiar wizardry, his compelling ability to bring into habitation what should not dwell together (wisdom and sorrow), making them disappear and reappear without apology or condition.

Before addressing the two 'momentous themes' of *vanitas* and Solomon, John Trapp, 'M.A. Pastour of Weston upon Avon in Glocester shire', in his *A Commentary or Exposition upon Ecclesiastes, or The Preacher* (1650) offers a suitable note of fanfare to introduce '*The words* of Qoheleth':

> *The words.* Golden words, waighty and worthy of all acceptation, grave and gracious Apophthegmes, or rather Oracles, meet to be well remembered: *Solomon's* Sapientall Sermon of the Soveraigne good, and how to attain to it; *Solomon's* Soliloquie, so some style it; others, his Sacred Retractions; others, his Ethicks, or *Tractate de Summo Bono* [marg. reads '[John] *Serranus*'], of the chiefest good, compiled and composed with such a picked frame of words, with such pithy strength of sentences, with such a thick *series* of demonstrative arguments, that the sharp wit of all the Philosophers compared with this Divine discourse, seems to be utterly cold, and of small account; their elaborate Treatises of *Happinesse* to be *learned dotages*, and *laborious losse of time*. (1650:1–2; in fact, most of the second half of this sentence is derived from the Preface to Serranus 1587)

The Life and Death of Solomon the Author: 1:1 et passim

A. ALIVE AND WELL IN PRE-MODERNITY (–1500)
Of course, the first verse of chapter 1 provides the 'raw materials' for the premise of Solomonic authorship. It is notable, however, that even Qoheleth's first interpreters, the Septuagint translators, who had opportunity to mask the authorial ambiguity to a non-Hebrew-reading public, resisted a clear ascription to Solomon by rendering the first verse as 'The words of Ecclesiastes' (*'rēmata 'Ekklēsiastou*) and not 'of Solomon' (on the tenor and style of the Septuagint's rendering of Ecclesiastes, see Fox 1999: 349). This may be understood in part by an early strand of rabbinic tradition reluctant to acknowledge the inspiration of Solomon in the composition of Ecclesiastes (and, at the time, the Song of Songs; Halperin 1982: 277).

It is widely held that Ecclesiastes was received into the Jewish canon due mainly to its association with Solomon (e.g. Holm-Nielsen 1976: 55; Salters 1974–5: 340–2; Whybray 1989: 3).[1] Debate about the book in general was abundant, with Ecclesiastes and Esther most frequently coming under the erratic microscope of the rabbis. The real issues of those discussions are, however, not always easy to determine (see Christianson 1998a: 148–9). Rather obliquely, discussions gave great weight to a book's ability to 'defile the hands' (see Leiman 1976: 104–20), or to its inspirational status in general (e.g. *b. Yadayim* 2:14; see below). Take, for example, the following (*b. Yadayim* 3:5): 'All the holy writings defile the hands. The Song of Songs defiles the hands, but there is a dispute about Ecclesiastes. R. Jose says: Ecclesiastes does not defile the hands, but there is a dispute about the Song of Songs' (also see *b. Yadayim* 2:14; *b. 'Eduyyoth* 5:3; *b. Megillah* 7a; *Midrash Leviticus* 28.1). *B. Megillah* 7a is similar: as learned 'Rabbi Shimon ben Mennasiah states: Ecclesiastes does not defile the hands since it is the wisdom of Solomon.' Ultimately, defilement of the hands was probably about the degree of ritual effect a book could muster, and may even have been a roundabout measure to keep scrolls from being stored with sacred food, thus leading to mice and rats (see Broyde 1995: 66).

As Leiman suggests, discussions traditionally ascribed to the Council of Jamnia (*c.*100 CE) report that Ecclesiastes was in danger of being *gnz* ('stored away') since it fostered heretical ideas. But the reported debate probably served to confirm its canonical status early on, since only problematic *canonical* books were at risk of being 'stored away' (so Leiman 1976: 79–80, 86, 104–9). In this respect the Solomonic connection faded to the background. In none of the discussions at Jamnia was Solomonic authorship even mentioned, and in the

---

[1] Some of what follows on Solomonic authorship is adapted from Christianson 1998a: 148–54, 165–71.

end no books discussed at Jamnia were withdrawn from canonical use anyway (see Beckwith 1985: 276–7). Contrary to several studies, Ecclesiastes was spared *gnz*, but not because of any association with Solomon (see Christianson 1998a: 150 n. 75).

In an infamous dispute about Ecclesiastes between the Shammaites and the school of Hillel, Solomonic authorship was not mentioned (see above; *b. Yadayim* 3:5; *b. Eduyyoth* 5:3). Indeed, reference to Solomon may not have been effectual anyway, as the early third-century CE tradition of R. Simeon ben Menasya suggests:

> The Song of songs defiles the hands, because it was spoken through Divine inspiration; Ecclesiastes does not defile the hands, because it is [only] Solomon's wisdom. They replied: Did he write this alone? Scripture says, 'He spoke three thousand parables, and his songs were a thousand and five' (1 Kgs 5:12), and 'Do not add to [God's] words, lest He rebuke you and you be found a liar' (Prov. 30:6). (*b. Yadayim* 2:14, with variations; *b. Megillah* 7a; tr. by Halperin, 1982: 277)

Compare Jerome, who in his commentary (388/9), steeped in rabbinic tradition, on 12:13–14 states that

> The Hebrews say that although [Ecclesiastes] used to be among other writings of Solomon in the past, they have not persisted in memory; and this book seems as if it ought to have been omitted [*oblitterandus*], because it asserts that all God's creations are vain and that he thinks everything is done for nothing, and he prefers food and drink and transient pleasures to all things; thus he takes his authority from this one title [Solomon?], so it is now included in the number of divine books, because he argues well and lists many things . . . and he said that his speeches are the easiest to hear, and to understand. (2000: *ad loc.*)

In other words, what really matters about this extraordinary little scroll is that, Solomon or no, it is 'argued well' and that the words bring pleasure to the ear. The significance of Solomon as author will grow almost grotesquely out of proportion before it returns to this meagre size again.

Often debates focused on some of the acknowledged contradictions of the book (even the 'defiling of hands' debate may have had this problem at its centre). *Midrash Qoheleth* 11.9 records what was perhaps the most serious of debates on Ecclesiastes:

> The Sages sought to suppress the Book of Koheleth because they discovered therein words which tend toward heresy. They declared, 'This is the wisdom of Solomon that he said, "Rejoice, O young man, in thy youth!"' (Eccl. 11:9). Now

Moses said, *that ye go not about after your own heart* (Num. 15:39) . . . Is restraint to be abolished? Is there no judgement and no Judge? But since he continued, 'But know thou, that for all these things God will bring thee into judgement', they exclaimed, 'Well has Solomon spoken.'

The first tractate of the Mishnah states the case in general terms. R. Tanhum of Nave says, 'O Solomon, where is your wisdom, where is your intelligence? Not only do your words contradict the words of your father, David, they even contradict themselves' (in *b. Shabbath* 3). Many of the ancient readers are concerned with content and do not seem to be bothered with the much asked modern question, Why is Ecclesiastes in the canon? (See Christianson 1998a: 153–4 for an overview of some modern attempts to answer it.) And tradition-ally the question, Why Solomon?, has been answered with the question, Who else but Solomon could have spoken with such vehement denunciation on the vanity of riches, wealth and even human existence? As R. Eleazar is reputed to have so aptly noted, 'but for Solomon . . . I might have said that this man who had never owned two farthings in his life makes light of the wealth of the world and declares, "*Vanity of vanities*"' (*Midrash Qoheleth* 3.11.1; cf. *Midrash Deu-teronomy* 1.5). Such a view is articulated in the Christian tradition as well. For example, Bonaventure in the Introduction to his commentary (1253–7) notes that

> a poor person with no possessions would not be believed about despising riches since that person *has no experience* and therefore *knows nothing*. So the author of this book had to be a person with experience of all these things, that is, a person who was powerful, rich, voluptuous, and curious or wise. We have not read or heard of anyone who so excelled in all these as Solomon. (2005: 76)

The most substantial biblical narrative about the eventual dispersal of Solomon's kingdom (1 Kgs 11:9–40) is sparse, even ambiguous, and this par-ticular ambiguity may have been the impetus for a number of legends about Solomon (Holm-Nielsen 1976: 71). In those books attributed to him (includ-ing Ecclesiastes) early Jewish tradition sometimes made attempts to under-stand the particular circumstances of Solomon's writing. The most fascinating example is that of Solomon and the demon Asmodai. According to Ginzberg's rendering of the legend, which is known among the talmudim and probably predates them (see Knobel 1991: 22–3), when Solomon gained too many wives for himself and desired too many horses and too much gold, the Book of Deuteronomy (i.e. the Law) stepped before the Lord and requested that Solomon be chastised in the form of dethronement. While Solomon was dethroned, the demon Asmodai assumed his likeness and took his place. During that time Solomon experienced the life of a beggar and consequently returned to his throne in Jerusalem, a repentant king (see Ginzberg 1968: 4. 165ff; cf. *Midrash Numbers* 11.3; *Midrash Song of Songs* 3.7.5). For *Targum Qoheleth* Asmodai was sent because Solomon became too proud. During his dethronement, Solomon travelled the world weeping and saying, 'I am Qoheleth, who was previously named Solomon', and it was then that he wrote Ecclesiastes:

> When King Solomon of Israel was sitting on his royal throne, his heart became very proud because of his wealth, and he transgressed the decree of the Memra [i.e. the 'word', a rabbinic device to 'soften anthropomorphism'] of the Lord; he gathered many horses, chariots, and cavalry; he collected much silver and gold; he married among foreign peoples. Immediately the anger of the Lord grew strong against him. Therefore, He sent Ashmedai king of the demons, against him who drove him from his royal throne and took his signet ring from his hand so that he would wander and go into exile in the world to chastise him. He went about in all the districts and towns of the Land of Israel. He wept, pleaded, and said, 'I am Qohelet, who was previously named Solomon. I was king over Israel in Jerusalem. . . .' (In Knobel 1991: 22)

Targum Qoheleth drives home the notion that Solomon not only wrote Ecclesiastes, but did so by the Holy Spirit: 'When Solomon king of Israel saw through the holy spirit that the kingdom of Rehoboam his son would be divided with Jeroboam the son of Nebat and that Jerusalem and the Temple would be destroyed and the people of the household of Israel would go into exile, he said to himself, "Vanity of vanities . . . of everything for which I and David my father laboured"' (1.1–2, 4). Here we are told to read Ecclesiastes as an exposition of the vanity which is the loss of Solomon's kingdom. The Targum continues (1.13), 'And I set my mind to seek instruction from the Lord at the time when he revealed himself to me at Gibeon' (cf. Eccl. 1:13; 1 Kgs 3:5–9). This link with Solomon is subtle. It is not to support a particular rabbinic argument or (as far as one can tell) to correct some previous misunderstanding of Eccl. 1:13, but rather to underscore the presence of Solomon as the primary narrator/author of these words, a perspective maintained throughout the targum (see e.g. 3.12; 4.15; 7.27; 9.7).

Among Christians, it was Origen who began the tradition of a 'Solomonic corpus', which included Ecclesiastes and provided a scheme of reading that corresponded to spiritual development (see p. 38). From the paraphrase on Ecclesiastes by Gregory Thaumaturgos (*c*.245) onwards the Solomonic context becomes more significant than the formulaic 'Solomon said'. As Gregory's paraphrase begins, we are left in little doubt as to the importance of Solomonic authorship: 'Solomon (the son of the king and prophet David), a king more honoured and a prophet wiser than anyone else, speaks to the whole assembly of God ... (1.1)' (Gregory Thaumaturgos 1990: 7). John Jarick discusses the influence of Solomon throughout the work (ibid. 314–15):

> This presumption of Solomonic authorship gives rise to certain motifs in Gregory's interpretation. One idea referred to throughout ... is that Solomon lost and subsequently regained wisdom – he had received wisdom from God but had afterwards rejected it ... And since Gregory sees Solomon as being ... a prophet, a number of statements are treated as speaking in a somewhat visionary way of the cosmic battle between the forces of good and evil ... this apocalyptic motif reaches its climax in an ingenious paraphrase of the final chapter's 'Allegory of Old Age' as a prophecy of the end of the world.

And Gregory was not alone in finding Solomon's presence worthy of note. In his homilies on Ecclesiastes (*c*.380), Gregory of Nyssa makes frequent reference to the importance of Solomon's experience, such as the following: 'the condemnation of the attitude to life based on enjoyment and emotion comes from the mouth of Solomon, in order to make its rejection convincing to us; for he had absolute freedom to practise a life aimed at pleasure and enjoyment, and utterly repudiates all that seems to be sought after by mankind' (hom. 3, in Gregory of Nyssa 1993: 59; cf. 62).

Augustine, too, finds it relevant that the figure of Solomon, 'the wisest king of Israel, who reigned in Jerusalem, thus commences the book called Ecclesiastes, which the Jews number among their canonical Scriptures: "Vanity of vanities, said Ecclesiastes ..."' (*City of God* 20.3, *c*.410; Augustine 1890: 603). More importantly, however, he rejected Origen's interpretation of Eccl. 1:9–10 (that it suggested the cyclical nature of all things until they returned to their original state): 'At all events, far be it from any true believer to suppose that by these *words of Solomon* those cycles are meant' (*City of God* 12.13 [italics mine], ibid. 338; cf. Origen, *De Principiis* 3.5.3). It may be that the appeal to Solomon here was an attempt to clinch the argument.

Chrysostom (*c*.370) has unusually high praise for the 'words of Solomon' in Ecclesiastes when he says, in the flow of another topic of discussion altogether, '[Solomon] who enjoyed much security ... that very sentiment of Solomon ... so marvellous and pregnant with divine wisdom – "Vanity of vanities"' (*Concerning the Statues*, hom. 15.5, in Chrysostom 1889: 439–40). Jerome, following Origen, grouped Ecclesiastes with Proverbs and the Song of Songs, each representing successive stages of Christian growth. He often used the 'fact' that Solomon wrote Ecclesiastes to make sense of certain texts. Following the rabbis, when Qoheleth laments the bequeathal of the reward from his toil to a fool (2:18–19), the fool becomes Solomon's son.

These examples reflect a secure standing in the early church of both the status of the book (Solomon's words are safe) and the notion of Solomonic

P<small>LATE</small> 6   Solomon preaching to the gathered assembly, the illuminated Naples Bible, fourteenth century

authorship in general. That standing is, on the whole, only assumed and not really exploited, which is most evident where allegorical interpretation held sway. With allegory the character of Solomon eventually became lost among other concerns. Indeed, while midrashic interpreters show concern for 'earthly' matters (e.g. expositing the history of Israel), it was more the habit of the early Christians, with their 'Jesus is the Ecclesiast' approach, to allegorize to the extent that a Solomonic framework was rendered unnecessary (Hirshman 1958: 155–7). For example, Gregory of Nyssa identifies the 'Ecclesiast' with the true king of Israel, Jesus (referring to John 1:49; hom. 2, in Gregory of Nyssa 1993: 34, 48–9).[2] Jewish readers, too, often regarded Solomon's authorship as inconsequential. In *Midrash Qoheleth*, for example, authorship generally is unimportant since the more pressing concern is to create a forum for rabbinic discussion on a vast array of topics. The Solomonic context was only faintly kept.

[2]   Yet another way in which 'Qoheleth as Solomon' impacts Christian tradition is through the *ars praedicandi*, early medieval manuals of preaching that extolled Solomon as the ideal preacher on the 'contempt of the world' (see Eliason 1989: 42).

B. EMBATTLED IN EARLY MODERNITY (1500–1800)
While the relative importance of Solomonic authorship diminished only slightly in the pre-modern period, it is widely held that Martin Luther is the first to challenge the 'fact' itself. In Luther's *Table Talk* he 'said' that 'Solomon himself did not write Ecclesiastes, but it was produced by Sirach at the time of the Maccabees . . . It is a sort of Talmud, compiled from many books, probably from the library of King Ptolemy Euergetes of Egypt.' This is cited by Barton (1959: 21) and was also cited (with slightly different wording) by Ginsburg (1861: 113). It also has been repeated in scholarship since (e.g. J. S. Wright 1946: 19; Bartholomew 1998: 39; Christianson 1998a: 170 [!]). Preston (1845: 12), however, argues that Luther in *Table Talk* was in fact referring to Sirach (indeed, Preston seems to be addressing a misconception in *his* day). It seems likely that either Preston was right or that Luther did not address the problematic question of authorship of either book.[3]

If Luther did not in fact 'discover' non-Solomonic authorship, in 1644 Hugo Grotius certainly did: 'I do not believe it was Solomon, but [Ecclesiastes] was written in the name of this king, as being led by repentance to do it. The proof is that it contains many words which can only be found in Daniel, Esdra [i.e. Chronicles, Ezra, Nehemiah] and the Chaldee paraphrasts [i.e. targumim]' (1644: 1.521; my tr.). But even Grotius was not the first to air the idea. Roughly 1300 years earlier, Didymus the Blind (*c.*313–98) in his commentary on Ecclesiastes suggests that either 'the real author is Solomon, or some [other] wise men have written it. Maybe we should opt for the latter so that nobody may say that the speaker talks about himself' (on 7:9, in J. R. Wright 2005: 192). The Babylonian Talmud (*b. Baba Bathra* 15a) asks, in its usual interrogative style, Who wrote the Scriptures?, and answers that 'Hezekiah and his colleagues wrote . . . Isaiah, Proverbs, the Song of Songs and Ecclesiastes.' The view is

---

[3]   I have been unable to locate anything like the citation in the 1967 critical edition of *Luther's Works*. Ginsburg cites the German of the 'Fösterman and Birdseil' edition, which clearly indicates that Solomon did not write Ecclesiastes ('So hat Salomo selbst das Buch, den Prediger, nicht geschrieben'). As Tappert shows in his introduction to *Table Talk* (in Luther 1967: pp. ix–xxvi), earlier editions suffered from significant revisions, additions and deletions. It is quite possible that the editions available to Ginsburg and Barton were of that ilk. To complicate matters, the 1857 edition (first pub. 1848) of Hazlitt, one of the problematic editions identified by Tappert (1967: p. xv; he makes no mention of Fösterman and Birdseil), reports the following: 'Ecclesiasticus . . . is not the work of Solomon, any more than is the book of Solomon's Proverbs. They are both collections made by other people' (Luther 1857: 11). In Luther's *Notes on Ecclesiastes* (1532) he suggests that '[Solomon spoke these things] after dinner, or even during dinner to some great and prominent men . . . and afterwards what he said was put down and assembled . . . This is then a public sermon which they heard from Solomon' (in 1972: 12; cf. also 22, 28, 38, 144, where Luther appeals to the notion of Solomonic authorship to make sense of what is happening in the text).

repeated in the commentaries of Isaac ibn Ghiyath (1038–89) on Ecclesiastes, David Kimchi (1160–1235) on Proverbs and Samuel ibn Tibbon on Ecclesiastes, *c.*1200 (see Robinson 2001: 87, 125 nn. 46–9). The premise appears to be that, as Tibbon puts it, 'it is . . . impossible that Solomon would not require a great deal of free time to construct [*tiqqun*] the allegories and statements said in proper order . . . It is also possible . . . that Solomon wrote the statements and all the allegories together in confused order or [dispersed] in several different places. Hezekiah and his court scholars then came along and set them down in books' (in Robinson 2001: 104). Neither Tibbon nor Didymus, however, express this view as forcefully as Grotius. As Robinson comments, Tibbon's 'explication of Ecclesiastes is rarely affected by this speculation. He explains the order of chapters and verses and even words as if they were chosen precisely by Solomon himself. Samuel's interest in textual history, nevertheless, is striking' (2001: 87). It is also an intriguing inversion of the premise of source criticism, that words 'in confused order' suggest different sources. Here it is the disparate work of one man that is assumed to have been edited into a coherent whole.

Apart from a few exceptions in the early modern period, therefore, Solomonic authorship was still a given. However, Grotius's work soon made its impact, as is evident in the comments of Jean le Clerc's *Défense des Sentimens de quelques théologiens de Hollande sur l'Histoire critique du Vieux Testament* in 1685 (tr. by John Locke in 1690): '*Grotius* is of Opinion that this Book was not writ by *Solomon* himself, but that it is a Work compos'd under his Name, by one that had been in *Caldea*; because there are divers *Caldean* words in it. If this Conjecture be true, as is not impossible, then this Book will be nothing but a Piece of Wit and Fancy, compos'd by some of those that had been in the Captivity' (1690: 97). Indeed, critical non-Solomonic readings escalated throughout Europe. At least Voltaire could write in the Foreword to his 1759 *Précis* that whether 'Ecclesiastes was, in fact, written by Solomon or whether another inspired author made the wise man speak, this book has always been regarded as a precious monument, and is all the more so because in it is found more philosophy' (in Christianson 2005: 475). Of course, Ecclesiastes scholarship would be no less immune than any other arena to the radical shifts in reading brought on by the Enlightenment. Barton (1959: 21–2) lists five authors from the eighteenth century and reports many more in the nineteenth century, when only a few scholars argued seriously for Solomonic authorship – notably (Hermann?) Wangemann in 1856.

C.   Dead in Modernity – Solomon's Ghost (1800–)

Relatively suddenly commentators were free to speak about the disunity of Ecclesiastes as a manifestation of its non-Solomonic authorship (note Paul

Haupt's words in the Testimonia chapter, p. 4). Many writers of the late nineteenth century, however, clearly struggled with taking the 'non-Solomon' fully on board. After outlining the views of 'modern criticism' against Solomonic authorship, James Bennet in 1870 writes, 'Though there are great difficulties in acknowledging Solomon as the author, we may still, in accordance with ancient Jewish and Christian usage, speak of him as the writer. We would not despoil the great monarch of a crown which we can place only on some vague, imaginary brow. It fits no head so well as that of the wise Solomon' (1870: 4–5). E. J. Dillon, writing 25 years later, is hard on those who would still cling to Solomonic authorship, those 'who admiringly attribute to the Holy Spirit a hopeless confusion of ideas which they would resent as insulting if predicated of themselves' (1895: 89 n. 1). In 1909, James A. Greissinger could say that 'There are some who still believe Solomon wrote it. The linguists are absolutely positive it could not have been written by Solomon. But this question of authorship probably will never be settled' (1909: 734). One hundred years later, and Greissinger is right, though Solomon is out of the critical equation entirely. Elias Bickerman's more recent observation that '[Qohelet is] a scholar turned haranguer' (1967: 143) imagines no royal figure. This general shift in view since Grotius's ground-breaking observation of Ecclesiastes' overall meaning reflects a shift in the 'consensus' perception of the implied author. Of course, there may be much to commend both the new and the old perceptions. One inescapable result, however, is that Qoheleth is no longer sitting comfortably behind any Solomonic mask. That whole conglomerate of protection, criticism and commentary became quite suddenly vacant in readings. Because of the new vision of authorship with which scholars operated (and still operate), the 'remains' of the (oddly unified) author, *as* Solomon *as* Qoheleth, became much more scattered.

Reading 'Solomonically' does make a difference in the pre-modern period. For example, Gregory Thaumaturgos understood Qoheleth's (read Solomon's) quest for wisdom to be motivated by his (Solomon's) historical loss of a wisdom that was once divinely imparted. Qoheleth *did* seek wisdom, and his search was thwarted. If we read Ecclesiastes, like Gregory, with the idea that Qoheleth, as Solomon, *once had* true wisdom and understanding, his consequent need to find it becomes indicative of the divine punishment inflicted on him, instead of becoming an example of, or even metaphor for, the human condition. In a similarly exhortative mode, John Donne, some 1,400 years later, reads the book, as so many before him did, as Solomon's repentance: 'In [Ecclesiastes] he hides none of his owne sins . . . He confesses things there, which none knew but himselfe, nor durst, nor should have published them of him, the King, if they had knowne them. So *Solomon* preaches himself to good purpose, and poures out his owne soule in that Book' (in Bozanich 1975: 270).

It is worthy of reflection that long after the death of Solomon in academia (and even in most churches and synagogues), in fiction and verse he has lived on oblivious. So Melville, fully aware of Solomon's demise in the academy, still writes about that 'unchristian wisdom' of Solomon, 'vanity of vanities' (see p. 128); for Chekhov, dramatically it can only be Solomon who sits alone to deliver his melancholic monologue (see p. 68); Dali represents Qoheleth with a cosmic royal crown (see p. 78). As discussed in the Introduction (p. 72), A. M. Klein appears to be unique among modern literary or artistic interpreters in recognizing Solomon as a rhetorical device, subtly combining his voice with Qoheleth's:

> Koheleth, on his damasked throne, lets weary exhalation follow
> . . .
> The glories of the goblet, yea, these, too, have been a part of me,
> The ecstasies of damosels, these also have been Solomon's,
> (Klein 1974: 20–1; cf. Robert Bridges's 1926
> reference to 'Pseudo-Solomon', below, p. 136)

Solomon's survival (or is it his ghost?) in the arts witnesses to his latent persuasive power on readers, but there is something odd about it. Even though 'Qoheleth' can easily be appropriated by readers because he is only playfully attached to history (he is somewhat contextless), he has not been able to rival the dramatic appeal of Solomon.

Vanitas Vanitatum: *1:2 et passim*

> [Solomon] speaks roundly, that if they read no more, but sleepe all the Sermon after: yet the first sentence shall strike a sting into their heartes, and leaue a sounde behinde to woken them when they are gone, as manie (you know) remember this sentence, which remember no sentence in all this booke beside. Who hath not heard *Vanitie of vanities, &tc.* Though fewe haue conceiued it?
> Henry Smith, 'The Triall of Vanitie', *c.*1590 (in Smith 1592: 832)

Ecclesiastes is a densely thematic text (see Introduction, p. 18). *Hebel* (a word that appears some 38 times and signifies, at the very least, a deficit situation – its translation will be discussed below) is easily the most prominent of its themes, and significantly brackets the book by its appearance in 1:2 and 12:8. Indeed, the recurrence of *hebel* can be somewhat overbearing, as Minos Devine wryly recognized: 'If you can realise what a trial it is to be told forty times that "all is vanity", you may be disposed to exercise some restraint in the repetition of any one idea, however interesting it may be to yourself' (1916: 14). Many readers have subsequently been polarized in their responses, favouring joy or *hebel* (usually the latter) as the defining theme.

There is no other word more firmly connected to Qoheleth's experience than *hebel*. It is used to judge the experience of his narrated (younger) life as a whole, and it is Qoheleth's experience which defines *hebel* for readers. Qoheleth observes the following to be *hebel* in relation to his experience: all that he observes (1:14); the test that he made of wisdom and folly (2:1); all the deeds he has done (2:11, 17); his fate in comparison to the fool (2:14–15); the fate of his inheritance (2:18–19, 21; cf. 2:26; 4:7–8); the days of his life (7:15); and of course, everything (1:2; 3:19; 9:1; 12:8). All that he does is coloured by *hebel*, and there is no better way to encapsulate his story, as the frame narrator recognized in 1:2 and 12:8. As such, *hebel* is more than just a key word. The potential range of meaning is phenomenal. Michael Fox captures the way in which *hebel* renders the multifaceted nature of experience: 'what is fleeting may be precious, what is frustrating may be no illusion, what is futile may endure forever' (1989: 36). As Douglas Miller (2002) has recently shown, *hebel* functions as symbol for all of Qoheleth's narrated experience under the sun. Qoheleth's earliest readers recognized this centrality of *hebel* to his thought. Indeed, for many *hebel* everywhere crushes Qoheleth's lesser themes under its grievous weight. For legion pre-modern readers it provided a way of seeing the world, its trappings a counterfeit jewel, the embodiment of what is worthless and deceptive. For yet other readers *hebel* has given hope, a base counterpoint that makes death shine more brightly and joy a tangible possibility. As is evident in the overview that follows, some readers' view of *hebel* has reflected their whole approach to the book.

The difficulty of translating *hebel* has long been recognized. There have been some provocative proposals. Frank Crüsemann suggests that Qoheleth's 'summation, "all is vanity" or emptiness, a stirring of the air . . . is really not so different from our modern "everything is shit"' (1979: 57; cf. Elsa Tamez, who separately arrives at the same conclusion [2000: 3, 155–56]). F. C. Burkitt offers 'bubble', and hence arrives at a charming, if innocuous, version of 1:2: 'Bubble of bubbles! All things are a Bubble! What is the use of all Man's toil and trouble?' (1936: 9; 'bubble' was a favourite choice of the Elizabethan paraphrasts and commentators). Miller (2002: 2–14) helpfully delineates the way in which *hebel* has forced translators to take three distinctive approaches: abstract (a single, abstract meaning, such as 'incongruous' or 'absurd'), multiple senses (use of multiple terms, depending on context) and single metaphor (a 'live, single metaphor' that has multiple referents). There is at least some consensus on the remarkably broad referentiality of the word, its ability to hold Qoheleth's ideas in tension.

It is indicative of the vagaries of translating *hebel* that in every age interpreters have consistently and explicitly resorted to simile and metaphor to render its inherent complexity. Take, for example, the following from Gregory of Nyssa (*c.*380), who reflects here on *hebel* in the form of the Greek Bible's rendering, *mataiotēs*:

> No substantial object is simultaneously indicated when the term 'futility' [*mataiotēs*] is used, but it is a kind of idle and empty sound, expressed by syllables in the form of a word, striking the ear at random without meaning, the sort of word people make up for a joke, but which means nothing . . . Another sense of 'futility' is the pointlessness of things done earnestly to no purpose, like the sandcastles children build, and shooting arrows at stars, and chasing the winds, and racing against one's own shadow and trying to step on its head . . . 'Futility' is either a meaningless word or an unprofitable activity, or an unrealized plan, or unsuccessful effort, or in general what serves no useful purpose at all. (*Homilies on Ecclesiastes*, hom. 1, in Gregory of Nyssa 1993: 35; he goes on to develop the sand aspect of the metaphor at length, p. 41)

Not only does Gregory note the symbolic meaning to be developed by Miller (one of Miller's key tenets is that, in Gregory's words, *hebel* refers to no 'substantial object', and its referentiality is radically open), but where *hebel* appears to refer to things with no reason or 'point', Gregory develops this with a series of striking images (sandcastles and flung arrows – which, suitably, could in turn cause injury). Karaite commentator Yephet ben 'Ali, *c.*990, also recognized the appropriateness of metaphor to unpack *hebel*: 'It is generally held that [*hebel*] is an appellation for a ray of sunlight in which something like dust becomes visible. You stretch out your hand and grasp at it, but there is nothing in your hand' (in 'Ali 1969: 146). Ramban (1135–1204) offered a comparable notion: *hebel* 'is a noticeable mist, like breath turned to vapour on a cold day, or the polluted, stagnant air trapped at the bottom of a pit. One can see the vapor, feel the heavy air, but both have no substance and swiftly disappear' (in Zlotowitz 1994: pp. xxxvii–xxxviii).

A.   Despising the World through *Vanitas* (–1500)

By far the most influential rendering of *hebel* in all of the book's reading contexts is 'vanity'. Origen's no longer extant commentary is likely to have first exposited the theme. It is there in his Prologue to his Song of Songs commentary in which he articulates a programme of reading:

> Therefore if a person completes the first subject by freeing his habits from faults and keeping the commandments – which is indicated by Proverbs – and if after this, when the vanity of the world has been discovered and the weakness of its perishable things seen clearly [in Ecclesiastes], he comes to the point of renouncing the world and everything in the world, then he will come quite suitably also

to contemplate and to long for the things that are unseen and are eternal. (In Eliason 1989: 49)

As he comments in *de Principiis*, 'Solomon appears to characterize the whole of corporeal nature as a kind of burden which enfeebles the vigour of the soul in the following language: "Vanity of vanities, saith the Preacher; all is vanity . . ." To this vanity, then, is the creature subject . . . subjected to vanity not willingly' (1.4.5, in Roberts and Donaldson 1974a: 264; cf. *Contra Celsus* 7.50 and the Romans citation below). But it is Jerome, on whom Origen had a substantial influence, who pursues the theme programmatically, and sees, as Eliason puts it, 'the goal of contempt of the world . . . as an independent good' (1989: 51).

Jerome's framework for understanding the book is in his articulation of its main theme, of vanity as representative of what is to be despised of the world – *contemptus mundi*. As well as in the introductory words of his Preface concerning 'virtuous Blesilla's book of Ecclesiastes', that he 'taught her to think lightly of her generation and to esteem futile everything that she saw in the world' (see Introduction, p. 26), Jerome makes his own theme clear in his commentary on Qoheleth's first words:

> *Vanity of vanities* [*vanitas vanitatum*] said Ecclesiastes, *Vanity of vanities, all is vanity.* If all things that God made are truly good then how can all things be considered vanity, and not only vanity, but even vanity of vanities? . . . [H]eaven, earth, the seas and all things that are contained within its compass can be said to be good in themselves, but compared to God they are nothing. And if I look at the candle in a lamp and am content with its light, then afterwards when the sun has risen I cannot discern anymore what was once bright; I will also see the light of the stars by the light of the setting sun, so in looking at the world and the multitudinous varieties of nature I am amazed at the greatness of the world, but I also remember that all things will pass away and the world will grow old, and that only God is that which has always been. On account of this realisation I am compelled to say, not once but twice: Vanity of vanities, all is vanity . . . All things are and will be vain, until we find that which is complete and perfect. (Jerome 2000: *ad loc.*)

Here Jerome shows his nuanced development of the *vanitas* theme. It is echoed in a later letter (*c.*394) to Pammachius: 'But if all things are good, as being the handiwork of a good Creator, how comes it that all things are vanity? If the earth is vanity, are the heavens vanity too? – and the angels, the thrones, the dominations, the powers, and the rest of the virtues? No' (letter 49, in Jerome 1954: 73).

This qualified approach to *vanitas*, which ironically mirrors Luther's reasons for rejecting Jerome's reading (see below, p. 106), is found in numerous

PLATE 7   Qoheleth as Solomon, expounding the vanity of worldly riches, thirteenth-century glossed Latin Bible

Christian commentators, such as Augustine (*City of God* 20.3), John Chrysostom (*Homilies on Ephesians* 12) and the later commentary of Gregory of Agrigentum (*c*.600), who 'agrees with Ecclesiastes that all is vanity, but says that nothing can be totally useless, since God made everything. Gregory even says that the ideal person is one who has experienced reality and still chosen the good' (Ettlinger 1985: 320). It also appears, with little modification, in the *Glossa ordinaria* (*c*.1100), Rupert of Deutz (*c*.1110) and Hugh of St Cher (*c*.1230–5; see Eliason 1989: 51–3). Hugh of St Victor (fl. *c*.1118–41), in discussing the idea that *omnia* is *vanitas*, marks out his own approach: 'If everything is vanity, then he himself who says this is vanity. And how can what vanity says concerning vanity not be worthless? Because if it is true that what he says is worthless, he ought not to be heeded, but rather rejected . . . What lives in the flesh is worthless. What lives in God is not worthless, but is true, since it comes from truth' (in Eliason 1989: 53 nn. 30, 31). While most Christian commentators undertake this qualified approach to *vanitas*, others can hate the world through Qoheleth's eyes without condition. So the Arab monastic and theologian John of Damascus (*c*.650–750), in his immensely popular 'romance' *Barlaam and Joseph,* called for the renunciation of the 'corruptible and perishable' world: 'all things are vanity and vexation of spirit, and many are the things that they bring in a moment, for they are slighter than dreams and a shadow, or the breeze that blows in the air. Small and short lived is their charm, that is after all no charm, but illusion and deception of the wickedness of the world; which world we have been taught to love not at all but rather to hate with all our heart' (12:109–10, in J. R. Wright 2005: 203). Now we are closer to the kind of reading which Luther will target (see below).

The most nuanced form of this qualified approach to *vanitas* is found in Bonaventure's commentary (1253–7; see Introduction, pp. 34–5). Bonaventure exemplified an exegetical style distinct from that of his peers, and his handling of the *contemptus mundi* reading (by then well established) is a sterling example. In his Introduction Bonaventure deals explicitly with the purpose (*finis*) of Ecclesiastes and replies to the objection that contempt of the world is by necessity contempt of its creator. His elegant reading is worth citing at length:

> First, about *the purpose*. For it is said that the purpose of the book is *contempt of the world* ...
>
> But against this: ... [T]o despise a work reflects back on the worker. So the person who despises the world, despises God ... Likewise ... [S]omething directed towards its goal [i.e. creation directed towards God] should not be despised, but rather accepted and loved. Therefore, this world, with all that is in it, is to be loved.
>
> I reply: It should be said ... that this world is like a ring given by the bridegroom to the soul itself. Now the bride can love the ring given her by her husband in two ways, namely with *a chaste* or *an adulterous* love. The love is *chaste* when she loves the ring as a memento of her husband and on account of her love for her husband. The love is *adulterous* when the ring is loved more than the husband, and the husband cannot regard such love as good ... Contempt for a ring by treating it as a poor and ugly gift reflects on the husband, but contempt of a ring by regarding it as almost nothing compared to the love of a husband, gives glory to the husband ... It is of such contempt that we are speaking, and so the matter is clear. (2005: 77–9; cf. Smalley's discussion, 1950: 44–5)

Like Donne later (see below), in Bonaventure's hands the *contemptus* reading is transformed. He further develops his reading by noting that while truth exists '*in itself*', vanity can exist 'only by reason of the truth'. That is, 'the person who knows true principles also knows false principles' (2005: 83). Vanity, then, can only be understood in relation to its antithesis, an idea that will, centuries later, be articulated so lucidly by Michael Fox (1989).

The contrast of the most convincing appearance of Qoheleth in the New Testament to Jerome's programmatic reading is worth noting here: 'The creation was subjected to futility [*mataiotēs*], not of its own will but by the will of him who subjected it in hope' (Rom. 8:20; cf. J. R. Wright 2005: p. xxiii for other brief NT parallels). This text appears repeatedly in pre-modern Christian commentaries on Ecclesiastes, all of which equate its vanity to that of Qoheleth.

Jerome himself played a key role in the history of Christian monasticism (Hirshman 1996: 97), and his approach to Ecclesiastes would remain hugely influential until at least the age of reform. Early Christian writers by and large followed the broad contours of the reading with little variation. So for Augustine, vanity represents the world itself, for the Church prays 'that it may be brought out of prison, that is from this world, from under the sun, where all is vanity' (*On the Psalms*, Ps. 142:8; in Augustine 1956: 651). Indeed, in the abbeys of medieval Europe, the reading of Jerome was inescapable. Eric Eliason, in his magnificent survey of medieval *vanitas* readings (in an unpublished thesis from 1989), summarizes the remarkable level of agreement among commentators regarding the *contemptus mundi* theme:

> There was very little disagreement concerning what Solomon taught in Ecclesiastes. His subject was contempt of the world. The opening of Ecclesiastes, with its universal judgment of 'vanity' on everything, and its descriptions of the world in constant but unproductive change suggested to medieval readers very good reasons for withholding one's trust in the *temporalia* which made up the world. As a result, the major enterprise in commenting on Ecclesiastes in the Middle Ages was the effort to distinguish between those things which last and those things which don't. (1989: 51)

For all its popularity, however, one finds significant departures from Jerome (cf. Hirshman 1958: 139).

Jewish authors had their own take on the *vanitas* reading. German rabbi Lipman Mühlhausen, for example, begins his polemical work against Christianity (*c.*1399) as follows: '*Vanity of vanities* . . . Forbid it that such a thought should ever enter into the heart that the works of the blessed God in the creation of the world are vanity! for he has created all things for his glory . . . The meaning is, that all the labour wherewith one labours to acquire and enjoy the things which are under the sun is utterly vain and profitless' (in Ginsburg 1861: 64). This seems to have the Christian *contemptus* reading in its sights (compare Luther's rejection of the reading on similar grounds, below). Earlier Jewish readings seem entirely unaware of Jerome's approach and relate *hebel* particularly to death (and in a sense thereby anticipate seventeenth-century *vanitas* still life painting – see below). So the Talmud (*b. B. Bathra* 100b) notes that 'No less than seven halts and sittings are to be arranged for the dead, corresponding to Vanity of Vanities, saith Koheleth; vanity of vanities, all is vanity.' That is, the mourners were to halt, sit and stand again to provide opportunity to comfort mourners, and the significance of 'seven' is to do with the number of times *hebel* occurs in 1:2 (three in the singular and two in the plural, each of which count as two). Commenting on a popular talmudic passage ('When R. Johanan finished the Book of Job, he said, "The end of the human being is to die, the end of the beast is the slaughter; thus all are doomed to die . . ."'; *b. Berakoth* 17a), Turkish preacher Elijah ha-Kohen of Izmir (*c.*1645–1729) noted that it would have been 'more appropriate for him to say this at the end of the Book of Ecclesiastes, for Kohelet, who reigned in realms above and below [*b. Sanhedrin* 20b], still considered everything vanity, as he said: *Vanity of vanities . . . all is vanity* (Eccles. 1.2). There it would be pertinent to say that the end of the human being is to die, remembering that even Solomon ultimately died, despite his glorious stature' ('Restoring the Soul: Eulogy for Jacob Hagiz', 1674, in Saperstein 1989: 304).

On the whole, Jerome's *vanitas* reading would be adapted, transformed and resisted in various measures through the centuries, but, until relatively recently at least, always reckoned with. (It can still occasionally be found, although not necessarily in Jerome's terms; e.g. see Zlotowitz 1994: p. xxxvii.) Even in the political realm Qoheleth's theme may have had its place. In his *Decline and Fall of the Roman Empire*, Gibbon suggests that Gelimer, the defeated Vandal king, in March of 534 processed in a dignified retreat from Numidia, to which he had fled:

> A long train of the noblest Vandals reluctantly exposed their lofty stature and manly countenance. Gelimer slowly advanced: he was clad in a purple robe, and still maintained the majesty of a king. Not a tear escaped from his eyes, not a sigh was heard; but his pride or piety derived some secret consolation from the words of Solomon, which he repeatedly pronounced, Vanity! Vanity! All is vanity! (Gibbon 1909: 4.314)

The *contemptus mundi* reading had been popularized in the Middle Ages by a proliferation of *De Contemptu Mundi* works, none so popular, however, as Pope Innocent III's *De Contemptu Mundi sive de Miseria Condicionis Humane* (1195; see Introduction, pp. 46–7). Early on (1.10) Ecclesiastes rears its apropos head in order to establish the broad theme:

> There is nothing without labor under the sun, there is nothing without defect under the moon, there is nothing without vanity in time. For time is the period of motion of mutable things. 'Vanity of vanities, says Ecclesiastes, and all is vanity.' O how various are the endeavors of men, how diverse are their efforts! Yet there is one end and the same consequence for all: 'labor and vexation of spirit.' (Innocent III 1978: 108)

In a similar vein, another widely disseminated work fostered the *contemptus mundi* reading in the centuries to come. Thomas à Kempis's *Imitation of Christ* (*c*.1440) pronounces the theme as an overture:

> 'Vanity of vanities, and all is vanity', except to love God and serve Him alone. And this is supreme wisdom – to despise the world, and draw daily nearer the kingdom of heaven. It is vanity to solicit honours, or to raise oneself to high station. It is vanity to be a slave to bodily desires, and to crave for things which bring certain retribution. It is vanity to wish for long life, if you care little for a good life. It is vanity to give thought only to this present life, and to care nothing for the life to come. It is vanity to love things that so swiftly pass away, and not to hasten onwards to that place where everlasting joy abides. Keep constantly in mind the saying, 'The eye is not satisfied with seeing, nor the ear filled with hearing.' [Eccl. 1:8] Strive to withdraw your heart from the love of visible things, and direct your affections to things invisible. For those who follow only their natural inclinations defile their conscience, and lose the grace of God. (Bk 1, ch. 1, in Kempis 1976: 27–8)

Poets, too, often approached the theme, although many would take little liberty with its conception. In the third and final stanza of William Dunbar's (*c*.1460–*c*.1530) 'Of the World's Vanitie' (*c*.1500?), the world reflects the instability of *vanitas*:

> Heir nocht abydis [Here nought remains], heir standis nothing stabill.
> This fals warld ay flittis [always wavers] to and fro:
> Now day up bricht, now nycht als blak as sabill [sable],
> Now eb, now flude, now freynd, now cruell fo,
> Now glaid, now said, now weill, now into wo,
> Now cled in gold, dissolvit now in as [clothed now in ash].
> So dois this warld transitorie go:
> *Vanitas vanitatum et omnia vanitas.*
>
> (poem 11 in Dunbar 2004; cf. William Neville's
The Castell of Pleasure, below)

By the time of reform, this way of understanding *hebel*/*vanitas*, as embodying the world's mutability, and indeed Qoheleth's programme as a whole, was indelibly established.

B.   Renaissance *Vanitas*: Despising Jerome and Suspecting the Sciences (1500–1800)

The sixteenth-century reformers held up *contemptus mundi* as an exemplary target. In his preface to his lectures on Ecclesiastes (1532), Luther addresses the *vanitas* tradition and relates it directly to Jerome. Here he calls 'noxious' the influence of many of the saintly and illustrious theologians in the church, who thought that in this book Solomon was teaching what they call 'the contempt of the world', that is, the contempt of things that have been created and established by God. Among these is St. Jerome, who by writing a commentary on this book urged Blesilla to accept the monastic life. From this source there arose and spread over the entire church, like a flood, that theology of the religious orders or monasteries. It was taught that to be a Christian meant to forsake the household, the political order, or even the episcopal . . . office, to flee to the desert, to isolate oneself from human society, to live in stillness and silence; for it was impossible to serve God in the world. As though Solomon were calling 'vanity' the very marriage, political office, and office of the ministry of the Word which he praises here in such a wonderful way and calls gifts of God! (In Luther 1972: 4; cf. his comments on 2:1–3, ibid., 31–3)

Luther exaggerates the approach of Jerome himself (which is clearly more nuanced) and, of more interest here, regards Jerome's commentary as causing the *contemptus* reading to 'spread over the entire church, like a flood'. Luther's own approach to *vanitas*, which he develops throughout his lectures, is to identify 'the vanity of the human heart, that it is never content with the gifts of God that are present but rather thinks of them as negligible' (1972: 10 *et passim*). The *contemptus* reading is also rejected by two of Luther's Protestant colleagues at roughly the same time: Johannes Brenz (1528) and Philip Melanchthon (1550). This veritable onslaught complemented Luther's own strategy to 'overthrow the principles of monasticism and transform theology out of recognition' (Cameron 2001: 88). Yet the *contemptus* reading did manage to survive, evidence that reading paradigms rarely fall into neat periodization schemes.

Luther and the reformers close to him are neither the only humanist-minded thinkers to be drawn to Qoheleth, nor the only to take issue with the monastic reading (which will continue to be understood in exaggerated terms). Scepticism's champion, Montaigne, engaged frequently with *vanitas* and had numerous citations from Ecclesiastes painted on the support spans of his library, including '*Per omnia vanitas*', 'All is vanity' (Cohen-Bacrie 2000). As Rosin points out, vanity 'is only one of Montaigne's many themes, but it represents an important step in his intellectual odyssey' (1997b: 25). Note Montaigne's opening remarks in one of the longest of his *Essays* (composed between 1580 and 1592), 'On Vanity': 'Perhaps there is no more manifest vanity than writing so vainly about it. That which the Godhead has made so godly manifest should be meditated upon by men of intelligence anxiously and continuously. Anyone can see that I have set out on a road along which I shall travel without toil and without ceasing as long as the world has ink and paper' (1991: 1070). It immediately becomes clear that for Montaigne 'vanity' is largely about the unchecked proliferation of knowledge: 'What can babble produce when the stammering of an untied tongue smothered the world under such a dreadful weight of volumes [as the 'six thousand' books on philology of Didymus]? So many words about nothing but words!' (1991: 1070–1). Indeed, for Montaigne, understanding the true nature of vanity ensures awareness of human limitation and compels one to live *hic et nunc.* Montaigne recognized, suggests Perry, the 'textual absence' of God in Ecclesiastes, an absence of the kind of religious commitment that might impede critical reflection and living in the world. In practical terms this is embodied in scepticism and is set against authoritarian law and religion as represented by the *contemptus mundi* tradition (see Perry 1993a). In a different way to Luther, then, Montaigne has the monastic readings in his sights (further on Montaigne, see the Introduction, pp. 44–6).

Puritan preacher Henry Smith (*c.*1560–91) offered his 'The Triall of Vanitie' in the unmistakable terms of *vanitas* in his hugely popular volume of sermons (which went through 16 editions): 'This booke begins with *All is vanitie*, and endes with *Feare God and keepe his commaundements* . . . That which troubleth us *Salomon* calles *vanitie*; That which is necessarie, hee calles the *Feare of GOD*: from that, to this, should bee everie mans pilgrimage in this worlde; wee begin at *Vanitie*, and never know perfectly that we are vayne, untill wee repent with *Salomon*' (in H. Smith 1592: 819). T. Fuller wrote of the renowned Smith in 1675 that 'he was commonly called the silver-tongued preacher, and that was but one metall below St. Chrysostom [meaning 'golden-mouthed'] himself . . . His Church was so crouded with Auditours, that persons of good quality brought their own pews with them, I mean their legs, to stand thereupon in the alleys' (in Jenkins 2004). Indeed, the rhetorical force with which Smith handles the theme is more impressive than most in the period. He renders the *whole* book in *vanitas* terms, without apology:

> This verse is the summe or contentes of all this booke, and therefore *Salomon* beginnes with it, and ends with it, as if he should saie, First this is the matter which I will prooue, and after, this is the matter which I have proned [proclaimed], now you see whether I tolde you true, that *All is vanitie*. I may call it *Salomons Theame*, or the fardle [bundle] of vanities, which when he hath bound in a bundle, he bids vs caste it into the fire. (in H. Smith 1592: 820)

Like so many others, Smith qualifies the totality of the *vanitas* judgment, for it is the Fall that has caused creation to be vain, and '*Salomon* saith that all are vaine to vs, not vaine of themselves, but because they are not sanctified as they should be' (1592: 827). This gives him grounds to launch his attack on the monastic reading:

> [Solomon] shewes a way how we may make profit of all, and reioyce in our labours and finde a lawfull pleasure in earthly things . . . lest wee should erre as

the Monkes and Eremits haue done before, mistaking these wordes, when he saith that *All is vanity*, they haue forsaken all companie, & gouernement and office and trade, and got themselues into the wildernes amongst beasts, to liue in quiet and silence, saying, that men could not liue in the world, and please God, because *All is vanity*. (in H. Smith 1592: 828)

For Smith, real vanity lies in wilful human production of all manner of learning and other forms of 'ignorance' (cf. the epigraph above, p. 98).

Not long after Smith's popular exposition, the French Calvinist Pierre du Moulin (1568–1658) published his *Heraclitus, or, Mans Looking-Glass and Survey of Life* (*c*.1605; the translator of the 1652 edition informs us that it is '40 years since I translated this piece out of French, and laid it by in loose papers', but there is also a 1609 translation). The work as a whole is a 'Meditation upon the Vanitie and Miserie of Mans Life', which opens with the *vanitas* theme in order to undertake a fairly morbid form of self-examination:

The distracted diversity of the affairs of this World mangles our time in an hundred thousand pieces; every business snatcheth away some part of our life; No time is ours but that which we steal from our selves, robbing some hours to examine our selves apart, and confer with God; there is work enough to be found in these solitary Meditations: But the first work to be considered of is the vanity and misery of our life, not to perplex us for it, but to prepare us to leave it . . . for worldly pleasures nigh at hand dazle & distract the judgement. Now if we would enquire of any that hath trod this path, *Salomon* in the beginning of his *Ecclesiastes* entring into this Meditation cryes out *Vanity of Vanities all is Vanity*. (Moulin 1652: 1–3)

The end goal is soon identified: 'taking the Razour from their hand [i.e. from David and Solomon, who have modelled such reflection], let us Anatomize our selves' (Moulin 1652: 4). Like so many others, du Moulin highlights in the language of Qoheleth the perceived dangers of the pursuit of knowledge:

Now a dayes Vnderstanding consists in the Knowledge of Tongues – the Learned busie themselves to know what the Women of *Rome* spake 2000 years since, what Apparell the *Romans* did wear, in what ceremony Stage-play's were beheld then among the people, and to new furbish over . . . this is to rake a Dunghill with a Scepter, and to make our Vnderstanding . . . a Drudge to a base Occupation . . . *Philosophy* and the *Arts* as they are somewhat higher, so they are somewhat harder . . . so they perplex more; *He that increaseth Knowledge* (saith *Salomon*) *increaseth Sorrow* [1:18]. Ignorance hath some commodity; and when all is done, this Knowledge goes not far: For no Man by *Philosophie* can clearly tell the nature of a Fly, or an Herb, much less of himself; our Spirits travell every where, and yet we are strangers at home, we would know all, but doe nothing, for (to speak properly) our study is no labour, but a curious laziness which tires it self, and goes not forward, like Squirrells in a cage, which turn up and down, and think they goe apace, when they are still where they were; we learn little with great labour, and that little makes us little the better, nay, many times worse; a drop or dram of divine Knowledge is more worth than all humane what-soever ... What are we the better ... by *Astronomy* to learn the motions and influences of the Heavens, and know not how to come thither? ... *This is also Vanity and Vexation of the Spirit* [1:14]. (1652: 26–31)

Here there is a hint of the feature that many later interpreters of Qoheleth will recognize: his exasperation with the circular and existentially frustrating nature of knowledge. Like Henry Smith, du Moulin is at pains to attack what he regards as the unjustified application of *vanitas* to monastic life:

> *This is also Vanity, and a vexatious Corruption.* This makes some men, (when they consider that *Vanity* hath over-spred all Worldly things ...) confine themselves to Deserts and a perpetual solitude, there to remain in extreme silence, and to speak with none but God and themselves ... and when they think to goe out of the World at one door, they come in at another: for griefs of mind, perplexed thoughts, lumpish laziness, windie *Hypochondriacall Melancholy*, despair, presumption ... So St. *Jerome* in the midst of the Wilderness, and in abstinent solitude, yet burnt with incontinent affections, and his mind ran most on dancing with Maids ... what Monk or Cloysterer thinks to goe free? (1652: 33–6)

While the end of the sixteenth century sees a fairly abrupt cessation of the attack on (a caricature of) monastic readings of Ecclesiastes, it is perhaps not an exaggeration to say that readings of the *vanitas* theme between 1500 and 1600 (as well as the examples above, see the discussion of Damião de Góis in the Introduction, p. 46) signify an allegiance for or against the monastic reading and the religious authority it signifies – a sort of political badge of piety (we might note that later Puritan commentators resume Jerome's reading in the mid-seventeenth century; see below).

Scores of poems in the early modern period are framed and, in the manner of William Dunbar's verse (see above, p. 106), often bound by the language of traditional *vanitas* readings. Notable exceptions grow in number in this period, and include the poetry of William Neville, Edmund Spenser, John Donne, Francis Quarles, George Herbert and Anne Bradstreet. Their work marks an engagement with the theme of *vanitas* outside the politicizing context of *contemptus mundi*. William Neville (b. 1497) in his *The Castell of Pleasure* (*c.*1518) reflects on the world's fickle mutability, but in perhaps the most imaginative locale for *vanitas* to date. In Neville's allegorical dream vision, the dreamer,

Desire, is led by Morpheus to the eponymous castle (see Edwards 2004). But now, in the third and penultimate 'movement', Desire is awoken by a 'storme rygorouse' and 'Morpheus vanysshed . . .':

> I entende to wryte the maner herof ryght shortly
> That folkes may consyder this worlde is but straunge
>
> yet to the wyndowe I walked a softe pace
> Ofte syghynge and sobbynge with an heuy herte
> To se where I coude espye of pleasure the palace
> Or of thynhabytauntes [the inhabitants] therof perceyue ony [any] parte
> Eyther conforte or kyndenes whiche made me to smerte
> Fantasy or eloquence whiche dyd desyre forder [further]
>
> . . .
>
> I loked for theyr places where they stode in order
> yf I coude se Credence walkynge in ony broder
> I loked for all these yet I sawe none alas
> Whiche brought to mynde wordes of salomo of wysdome recorder
> Vanitas vanitatu[m] & o[mn]ia mu[n]di vanitas.
>
> Where is Sampson for all his grete strength
> Or where is the sage Salomon for all his prudence
> Dethe hath and wyll deuoure all at lenth
>
> . . .
>
> Where be all the . . . doctours of dyuynyte
> Where is arystotyll for all his phylosophy and logyke.
> Be not all these departed frome this transytory lyfe
> yet theym to dyuers places our creatour dyd name
> With egall Iugement without debate or stryfe
>
> . . .
>
> Be secrete and stedfast without mutabylyte

(Neville 1530: n.p.)

Seeking out comfort, kindness and even Credence itself on its rounds, and finding nothing, sparks for Desire the memory of *vanitas*. Desire, in its moments of disorientation, realizes the levelling power of death, even the deaths of Solomon, Sampson and Aristotle. Like Qoheleth, the Dreamer offers an answer pitched at the level of private understanding, in this case secrecy and steadfastness in the face of the world's mutability.

Edmund Spenser imagines an even more fantastic setting for his exposition of *vanitas*. Spenser (and to a disputed degree, his publisher) oversaw the collection of a group of poems entitled *Complaints: Containing Sundrie Small Poemes of the Worlds Vanitie* (1591; the compositions are probably earlier). His printer suggests the motive: 'finding that [the *Faerie Queene*, 1590] hath found a fauourable passage amongst you; I haue sithence endeuoured by all good meanes (for the better encrease and accomplishment of your delights,) to get into my handes such smale Poemes of the same Authors' (1591: preface, n.p.; the printer, William Ponsonbie, also tantalizingly refers to Spenser's now lost translations of Ecclesiastes and the Song of Songs). The titular theme is broad and ubiquitous, although in his allegorical 'The Ruines of Time' Spenser imagines Qoheleth's theme proper, spoken by a heavenly voice, and witnesses the ruinous destruction of two bears (which may represent the death of the Dudleys, 'Sidney's noble family', d. 1587):

> I saw two Beares, as white as anie milke,
> Lying together in a mightie caue,
>
> . . .
>
> Two fairer beasts might not elswhere be found,
> Although the compast world were sought around.
>
> But what can long abide aboue this ground
> In state of blis, or stedfast happinesse?
> The Caue, in which these Beares lay sleeping sound,
> Was but earth, and with her owne weightinesse
> Vpon them fell, and did vnwares oppresse,
> That for great sorrow of their sudden fate,
> Henceforth all words felicitie I hate.
>
> . . .
>
> And I in minde remained sore agast,
> Distraught twixt feare and pitie [. . .] when at last
> I heard a voyce, which loudly to me called,
> That with the suddein shrill I was appalled.
> Behold (said it) and by ensample see,
> That all is vanitie and griefe of minde,
> Ne other comfort in this world can be,
> But hope of heauen, and heart to God inclinde;
> For all the rest must needs be left behinde:
> (1591: fol. D3)

Here Spenser's 'ensample' of the *vanitas* principle is perfectly couched in the extremity of Qoheleth's thinking – that is, like Qoheleth, he examines the world in a theatre of the absurd, where the pristine bears are crushed by the earth, or where the king, bloated with his own acquisitions, has all that his heart desires but sees nothing but *hebel*.

It may be that in the course of the sixteenth century writers were beginning to draw on the very pervasiveness of the words *vanitas vanitatum et omnia vanitas* in the fabric of public life, which is nicely illustrated by an anecdote regarding Sir Anthony Cooke (d. 1576), consort to King Edward VI (ruled 1547–53):

> A *Sussex* . . . Knight, having spent a great Estate at Court, and brought himself to one Park, and a fine House in it, was yet ambitious to entertain not the Queen, but her Brother at it; and to that purpose had new-painted his Gates with a Coat of Arms, and a Motto overwritten, thus, *OIA VANITAS*, in great Golden Letters: Sir *Anthony Cooke* (and not his Son *Cecil*) offering to read it, desired to know of the Gentleman what he meant by *OIA?* who told him, it stood for *Omnia*. Sir *Anthony* replied, *Sir, I wonder having made your* Omnia *so little as you have, you notwithstanding make your* Vanitas *so large*. (In Lloyd 1670: 385)

Such knowing reference will become far more commonplace in the modern era, and it is difficult to know the degree to which *vanitas* is known in the population at large, although clearly the influential preachers of the day were making use of it, and literacy was gradually on the rise (McKay 2001).

One of the most popular works of verse in the seventeenth century in England was Francis Quarles's *Emblemes* (1635), a series of engravings with accompanying verse. The images are mainly allegorical, in reference to divine love. The relationship between word and image here is subtle and not simply a matter of text 'commenting' on image: 'the emblem was understood to embody a language *in rebus* mutually interchangeable with the language *in verbis* of the accompanying text' (Gilman 1980: 387). *Emblemes* and *Hieroglyphikes* (the 1638 'sequel') appealed to moderate Catholics as well as Protestants because of their concern for the 'general tenets' of the Christian life as opposed to the detail of doctrine (Höltgen 2004). In Embleme VI, *All is vanity and vexation of spirit*, Quarles reflects on a delicate and transitory world, the vastness of which cannot be measured and which provokes human restlessness:

> How is the anxious soule of man befool'd
> > In his desire,
> That thinks a Hectick Fever may be cool'd
> > In flames of fire?
>
> . . .
>
> Whose Gold is double with a carefull hand,
> > His cares are double;
> The Pleasure, Honour, Wealth of Sea and Land
> > Bring but a trouble;
> The world it selfe, and all the worlds command,
> > Is but a Bubble.
>
> . . .

> It [the world] is a vast Circumference, where none
>   Can find a Center.
> Of more than earth, can earth make none possest;
>   And he that least
> Regards this restlesse world, shall in this world find Rest.
>   (Bk 1, Emblem VI, Quarles 1635: 24–6)

The accompanying image shows an angel who, untroubled and serene, holds the world, an orb on an embroidered table, perhaps suggesting how hopeless would be humanity's attempt to do the same.

Clearly writers leading up to the modern period had in place a tradition of *vanitas* to mine for rich reflection on human experience. The struggle of 'earthly learning' remained, as before, a vital theme, as in George Herbert's 'Vanity (I)' (1633):

> The fleet Astronomer can bore,
> And thread the spheres with his quick-piercing mind:
> He views their stations, walks from door to door,
>   Surveys, as if he had designed
> To make a purchase there: he sees their dances,
>   And knoweth long before
> Both their full-eyed aspects, and secret glances.
>
>   . . .
>
>   What hath not man sought out and found,
> But his dear God? who yet his glorious law
> Embosoms in us, mellowing the ground
>   With showers and frosts, with love and awe,
> So that we need not say, Where's this command?
>   Poor man, thou searchest round
> To find out *death*, but missest *life* at hand.
>   (In Rudrum et al. 2001: 135)

Like Herbert, Anne Bradstreet also mines the language of *vanitas* to render human experience broadly conceived. And like Thackeray years later, she manages to capture the theme of vanity as emblematic of the whole book quite brilliantly:

> As he said vanity, so vain say I,
> Oh! vanity, O vain all under sky;
> Where is the man can say, 'Lo, I have found
> On brittle earth a consolation sound'?
>
>   . . .
>
> What is't in flowering youth, or manly age?
> The first is prone to vice, the last to rage.

Where is it then, in wisdom, learning, arts?
Sure if on earth, it must be in those parts;
Yet these the wisest man of men did find
But vanity, vexation of mind.

. . .

This pearl of price, this tree of life, this spring,
Who is possessed of shall reign a king.
Nor change of state nor cares shall ever see,
But wear his crown unto eternity.
This satiates the soul, this stays the mind,
And all the rest, but vanity we find.
('The Vanity of All Worldly Things', 1650,
in Atwan and Wieder 1993: 352–4)

Here Bradstreet conveys Qoheleth's theme of vain and vexatious searching while making it uniquely her own. Indeed, this poem, along with her 'David's Lamentation for Saul and Jonathan', is 'individual and genuine in [its] recapitulation of her own feelings' (further on Bradstreet, see pp. 236–7).[4]

John Donne in his early years turned his attention to Ecclesiastes in sermons and poems, particularly the *Anniversary* series (see below and Introduction, pp. 52–4). In his *Donne's Satyr Containing 1. A Short Map of Mundane Vanity, 2. A Cabinet of Merry Conceits . . . Being Very Useful, Pleasant and Delightful to All, and Offensive to None*, which appears to have been composed in the year of his death (1662), his reflections on *vanitas* are more abrasive. The work begins,

A SHORT MAP OF Mundane Vanity.

Vanitas vanitatum, & omnia vanitas.
Vanity of vanity, and all is vanity.

1. Of Mundane Vanity.
When *Solomon* had tried all variety
Of mundane pleasures, ev'n to full satiety;
And after throughly weigh'd the worlds condition,
And therein mans: concludes with this Position,
All that man can in this wide World inherit,
Is vain, and but vexation of the spirit.

2. Of the World.
The World's much like a fair deceitful Nut,
Whereto when once the knife of truth is put,
And it is open'd, a right judicious eye
Findes nothing in't, but meer vacuity.

4   In 'Bradstreet, Anne', *Encyclopaedia Britannica*, 2004 DVD edn (no author is given).

3. Of the same.
The World's a Book, all Creatures are the Story,
Wherein God reads dumb lectures of his glory.

4. Another of the same.
Earth is the womb from whence all living came,
So is't the tomb, all go unto the same . . .

(Donne 1662: 1–2)

Donne appears to satirize not only the broader *vanitas* tradition in the sheer quaintness of sentiment ('The World's much like a fair deceitful Nut'), but in the structure as well, with uneven stanzas and deliberately mundane headings ('Of the same', 'Another of the same' – and heading no. 5 is the same!). As Peter Kemp (2005) comments, even the projected self-image of satirists of the period in such works may harbour some deliberate parody: 'The satirists popularized a new persona, that of the malcontent who denounces his society not from above but from within, and their continuing attraction resides in their self-contradictory delight in the world they profess to abhor and their evident fascination with the minutiae of life in court and city.' One wonders what Donne is targeting in particular with 'God reads dumb lectures of his glory'. The creatures themselves or the product of their endeavors? If the latter, of science or works that profess to be 'lectures of his glory': namely, treatises of divines?

In his *The Hospitall of Incurable Fooles* (*L'hospidale de' pazzi incurabili*, c.1586), the Venetian humanist Tomaso Garzoni (1549–89, best known for his encyclopedic catalogue of professions, *La piazza universale di tutte le professioni del mundo*, 1585), frames his first section, 'Of Follie in generall: the first discourse', in the terms of *vanitas*:

Considering, I haue taken vpon my selfe this burden, to manifest to the worlde, the prodigious and monstrous kindes of folly . . . with an aspect, and countenaunce more deformed then *Cadmus* his serpent, more vgly then the *Chimera*, fuller of poison then the dragon of *Hesperides* . . . It sufficeth that with the wise man, euerie one may iustly exclayme . . . I haue perused all things done vnder the sunne, and behold all is vanitie, and affliction of minde . . . [1:14] To conclude, all the world is matter from head to foote, and one beateth his braines about one thing, another, about some other: this man feedes himselfe in worldly glorie . . . another ruffleth in his without-booke-Rhetoricke, as though he had no paragon for Latine and Greeke; . . . another stands vpon puntoes [points of behavior] with his drawen sword, like another Gargantua, in that he is exalted to some catchpoale or hangmans office, as if euerie one knewe not, that to put an office into a Fooles hand, is as much as we should set an asse to play on the harpe . . . And thus euerie one sets both good and bad vpon the boord [board], not considering what the wise man saith, that *Vanitas vanitatum, & omnia vanitas*: Vanitie of vanities, and all is vanitie: But because we shall the better know in generall, if we discourse in particular, by little and little, let vs examine Fooles in speciall, for thus shal we attaine to the full and perfect knowledge of Folly, we seeke after. (Garzoni 1600: 1, 5, 7–8)

The delightful rhetoric with which Garzoni inveighs against the world is not unlike that of the Elizabethan satirists that Kemp discusses (above). One of the striking features of this 'first discourse' is that among the marginal notes indicating the sources of Juvenal, Pliny and the like, only Solomon represents Scripture. Of the biblical voices, then, only Solomon can take his rightful place in this invective.

It is intriguing in an era that in some sense rediscovered the ancient languages beloved of scholastics of the Middle Ages, including Hebrew, that relatively little attention is given to the Hebrew 'source' of vanity, *hebel*, but there are some exceptions. Discussing 1:2, John Trapp aptly observes a possible Hebrew wordplay between *hebel* in Ecclesiastes and *hebel* in Genesis 4, namely, Abel: '*Adam is as Abel*, or *Man is like to Vanity*; there is an allusion in the Originall to their two names: yea, *All-Adam is all-Abel*, when he is *best underlaid*, (so the *Hebrew* hath it) every man at his best estate, when he is setled upon his best bottome, is altogether vanity' (1650: 4–5). He goes on to describe the human proclivity towards vanity, in spite of ourselves: 'These outward things are so near to us and so naturall to us, that although wee can say (nay swear) with the Preacher *Vanity of Vanities*, a heap, a nest of vanities, *It is naught, It is naught*, saith the buyer, yet, when gone apart, wee close with them: albeit wee know they are naught and will come to naught' (1650: 5). Similarly, few writers of the period are much concerned to reflect on how *hebel* might best be translated. Edward Hyde, however, gives consideration not only to the Hebrew but also to how Jewish interpreters have treated it:

[David] *Kimchy* in his *Roots* thus expounds . . . *Hebel* Vanity, *Res quae non est quicquam*, A thing which is nothing; and he there tells us that the Jewish Doctors did so call the *Breath* that cometh out of mans *mouth*, for that it is such a thing as presently ceaseth, and cometh to nothing. But in his *Commentaries* upon this place, he saith, *Vanity is that which hath no subsistence; no stability, and will not endure the Touch*, as if you touch a *Bubble* it is gone; wherefore the Ancient Latines properly called man, *Bullam*, a Bubble, That is Vanity, in *Kimchies Gloss*; And *Aben Ezra* goes further saying thus, That *All things are called Vanity, even those which seem most firmly Rooted, and to have the surest subsistence: How much more the Actions of men which are but meer Accidents, and the thoughts of men which are but Accidents of Accidents?* (1657: 11–12)

Also significant here is the use of medieval commentators, which by then represented more reception history than current scholarship.

As remarkable as Hyde's work for its attention to exegetical details is that of Ezekiel Hopkins. His treatise *The Vanity of the World* (1658, reprinted in 1685) promised, his dedication declared, 'to beat down the Price of the World, and to expose its admired Vanities to publick contempt' (1685: n.p.). And still the monastic reading is in the author's sights, although it must have appeared to flog a dead beast: 'We need not shelter ourselves under any Monastick Vow; nor fly to Deserts and Solitudes, to hide us from the Allurements of the World: This is to run away from that Enemy whom we ought to conquer' (1685: n.p.). Hopkins is attuned to the rhetorical features of Qoheleth in a way that marks him out from his contemporaries: 'The whole Verse [1:2] is loaden with Emphases: And it is first observable, That he doth not glide into it, by any smooth connexion of Sence, or sentences; but on a sudden breaks upon us, with a surprising abruptness. *Vanity of vanities*. Which shews a Mind so full of Matter, that it could not attend the Circumstance of a Prologue to usher it in' (1685: 3). He goes on to discuss the significance of the *vanitas* theme expressed in the abstract, so that Qoheleth does not censure all things to be vain, but they are *Vanity* it self' (ibid.).

Hopkins's discussion of the appropriate rendering of *vanitas* as 'bubble' sheds some light on its popularity as an Elizabethan rendering:

> As Bubbles blown into the Air, will represent great variety of Orient and Glitter-ing Colours, not (as some suppose) that there are any such really there, but only they appear so to us, through a false reflexion of Light cast upon them: so truly this World, this Earth on which we live, is nothing else but a great Bubble blown up by the Breath of God . . . It sparkles with ten thousand Glories . . If we come to grasp it, like a thin Film, it breaks, and leaves nothing but Wind and Disap-pointment in our Hands. (1685: 8–9)

From roughly the seventeenth century onwards, 'bubble' signifies that which is 'fragile, unsubstantial, empty, or worthless' (*OED*), and we might add from Hopkins, inherently deceptive, and its extensive application to Ecclesiastes makes perfect sense (as in e.g. Quarles 1635, Hall 1646, Hyde 1657, Wollaston 1691; cf. Anonymous 1765 and Burkitt 1936). William Wollaston's versifica-tion, *The Design of Part of the Book of Ecclesiastes* is typical in this regard:

> UNHAPPY thought! How like a *Bubble's* all
> This *frothy globe* of World, this *empty ball*!
> For look how wide's the *view* of Heaven's *eye*,
> Or compass of its *spangled tapestry*;
> How wide the outmost superfice of Place,

That *coops* us in Imaginary space:
So large is VANITY's deceitful *face*.

(1691: 24)

These are probably the best lines of the lengthy poem, which the popular British moralist offered as a 'few indigested materials, which I had collected among my own thoughts in order to a Poem . . . thrown by and forgotten. In this state of neglect they lay for some years; till lately, tumbling over some other trifles, I found them in the heap, and could not let them pass, *inconsiderable* as they were' (1691: 3–4). He may have regretted his decision to publish his 'heap', for he later sought to suppress it, ashamed of its poor poetic quality (Young 2004). At least he had prepared for readers' judgments in the conclusion of his Preface: 'Reader, I beg your pardon, if I have obtruded any thing upon you offensive to your taste and better Judgment. This I hope *the rather* to obtain, because as I was never troublesome to the World by my Poetry *before*, so in probability *never* shall be *again*' (1691: 22).

Another medium that deals with *vanitas* explicitly in the Renaissance period (flourishing *c.*1530–1650), and which further exposits the scrutiny of human endeavour especially, is the *vanitas* fine art movement. Hans J. Van Miegroet suggests that *vanitas* painting is concerned with human fragility, desires and pleasures in the face of the inevitability and finality of death (1996: 880). Others note the relationship between the words of Qoheleth and the *vanitas* paintings (both still lifes and portraits; see Haak 1984: 125; Cheney 1992: 120; Puyvelde and Puyvelde 1970: 235), but this link is subtle rather than overt. The paintings themselves are largely symbolic representations of a *Zeitgeist*, which, although the themes are present as early as Hans Holbein's celebrated 1533 painting *The Ambassadors* (with its widely acknowledged theme of the futility of human endeavour), is felt most profoundly by the Dutch of the seventeenth century. (That said, several *vanitas* paintings explicitly reference Ecclesiastes and will be discussed below.)

The dangers of an abundance of the good things in life were all too apparent to the Dutch, and to prevent its good citizens from going astray, the teachings known collectively as 'the Wisdom of Solomon' were utilized as corrective guides for moral behaviour. Specially published editions of Proverbs, Ecclesiastes and Sirach were placed in houses of correction, for the edification of those who had gone astray (Schama 1991: 20). It is reasonable to conjecture that the worldly-wise Qoheleth was a particularly appealing guide to a life that could hold great riches and great misery.

Of the *vanitas* paintings that make direct reference to Ecclesiastes I note David Bailly's *Vanitas Still Life with a Portrait of a Young Painter* (1651), Pieter de Ring's *Vanitas Still Life* (1643) and Petrus Schotanus's *Vanitas Still Life* (not

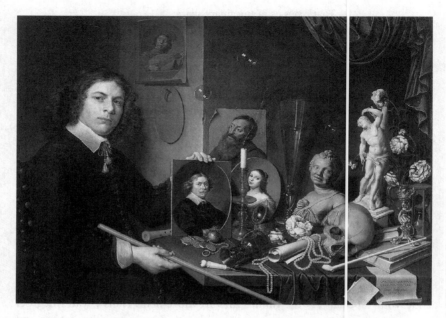

PLATE 8   David Bailly's *Vanitas Still Life with a Portrait of a Young Painter,* 1651

dated; cf. Haak 1984: 126–8). The works by Bailly (plate 8) and de Ring both have slips of paper bearing the Latin *vanitas vanitatum et omnia vanitas* (Bailly's painting actually has *vanitas vanitum et omnia vanitas,* but doubtless refers to Eccl. 1:2), while that of Schotanus shows an open book bearing a paraphrase of Eccl. 9:12, the words appearing beneath the feathery bodies of small dead birds. Bailly's work is a particularly intriguing example that reflects both the narrative structure of Ecclesiastes and the self-examining aspects of Qoheleth's text so often discerned by readers. The young artist himself is seated at a table and holds a portrait of an older man, while *vanitas* symbols fill the table surface. As the artist was 67 years old when he painted this picture, the viewer is faced with the ironic double self-portrait: Bailly as he once was, holding the portrait of Bailly as he actually was (note the accompanying comments on the painting at http://www.wga.hu; cf. Collier's *Still Life with a Volume of Wither's 'Emblemes',* 1696, which also renders Qoheleth's words and is discussed below, pp. 140–1).

Directly from or alongside the *vanitas* painting tradition emerged *vanitas* choral and string music. In a 1995 recording entitled *Vanitas Vanitatum, Tragicomedia,* a group specializing in seventeenth-century music, performs 11 such pieces (Carissimi et al. 2004), all Italian and dated between 1620 and 1677. The sleeve notes, by *Tragicomedia* co-founder Erin Headley, place the works in their context:

Nearly every native and foreign artist looked to Rome for inspiration, and it was the Roman more than any other European who was confronted daily with the *memento mori* of the past. It is no surprise then that Roman poets, painters and composers of the 17th century should have adopted the *vanitas* theme so ardently and so fruitfully . . . Both in the north and in the south of Europe, artists interpreted the *vanitas* theme according to their own temperaments and traditions. In the north it provided painters with an excuse to detail and classify nature, and through what better vehicle than the still life? . . . [M]usic here proves itself to be the ideal medium for symbolising the *vanitas* theme, since it is an art that disappears as soon as it is articulated. (In Carissimi et al. 2004)

The music indeed captures the complexity and inherent incongruity of *vanitas*: haunting melodies set alongside Qoheleth's words (some of the lyrics are direct renditions of chapters 1 and 2 especially, with long choruses of simply *vanitas vanitatum*), or which could have emerged from the mouth of Qoheleth:

> The healthy, the sick
> the brave, the defenceless
> all come to an end:
> you must die.
> (from *Passacalli della
> vita*, 1677, tr. in the
> sleeve notes)

As one reviewer comments: 'Passionate monody, vivid madrigalian wordpainting and lilting *bel canto* airs illustrate both worldly delights and their worthlessness. The colourful *Tragicomedia* continuo – archlute, double harp, keyboard – supports six superbly focused singers and three strings, contemplating the pains of hell in exquisitely sensuous music – delicious irony!'[5]

It is clear that the *vanitas* theme had widespread and enduring appeal. *The Web Gallery of Art* (http://www.wga.hu), for example, which archives *c*.14,500 European fine art works, returns over 35 examples of *vanitas* paintings, and Haak (1984) mentions a dozen more. Cavalli-Björkman (2002) mentions not only Dutch painters but also German, French, Italian and Spanish artists who painted *vanitas*. The impact of the theme continued, with artists such as Van Gogh (*Skull with Burning Cigarette*, 1886/7) and Cézanne (*Nature Morte au Crane* [*Still Life with Skulls*], 1895–1900) producing paintings clearly reminiscent of the *vanitas* still life. In fact, the *vanitas* theme, broadly understood, can still be found in the visual arts. In the summer of 2000, the Virginia Museum of Fine Art held a major exhibition entitled '*Vanitas*: Meditations on Life and Death in Contemporary Art'. The accompanying book (Ravenal 2000) has as

---

[5]   Cited from *BBC Music Magazine*, without issue no. or author indicated, at http://www.jhadden. freeserve.co.uk/cds/vanitas.htm.

its epigraph the opening verses of Ecclesiastes (1:2–4). Ravenal sees the *vanitas* theme as universal and culturally relevant (2000: 13–14). (Also, it is worth noting that a Google or AltaVista image search of 'vanitas' yields some extraordinarily rich and diverse results, ancient and modern; further, see section d below.) The appeal of the *vanitas* painting tradition lies in its successful capture of the subtle balance between transient and joyful modes of living, so vociferously endorsed by Qoheleth.

By all accounts the *contemptus mundi* approach to Ecclesiastes dominated Christian exegesis throughout the Middle Ages (note its influence in Thomas à Kempis's fifteenth-century *Imitation of Christ*, above) and survived the age of reform particularly in moral discourse. As the seventeenth century progressed, the reading faded in poetry but was still typical in the work of pious commentators who closely adapt Jerome's reading as a framework. So in his *A Commentary, upon the Whole Booke of Ecclesiastes* (1639), under the heading 'The generall scope of the Booke', Michael Jermin writes,

> It is a mistake, as some thinke, of the meaning of *Epicurus*, to imagine that he [God] placed the chiefe good of man in a sensuall pleasure; but that he intended the sweet delight of vertue . . . Now much more are they mistaken, who thinke that in this booke a luxurious pleasure is commended to us: seeing it is from a discommendation of worldly things, in respect of the vanitie of them . . . as St. *Hierome* speaketh, that the Preacher laboureth to make us to deny the world. (Jermin 1639: 2; cf. similarly, e.g., Granger 1621 and Mayer 1653)

As well as Jerome, Hugo of St Victor features prominently in such *contemptus mundi* commentaries. However, as I have noted in the case of Bonaventure, in the hands of skilled exegetes, even such a tried and tired mode of reading can be transformed. Take the example of a sermon preached to Whitehall by John Donne, who although known now chiefly for his poetry, was one of the most renowned preachers of his day:

> Solomon shakes the world in pieces, he dissects it, and cuts it up before thee, that so thou mayest the better see how poor a thing, that particular is, whatsoever it be, that thou settest thy love upon in this world. He threads a string of the best stones, of the best jewels in this world . . . and then he shows you an *ire*, a flaw, a cloud in all these stones; he lays this infancy upon them all, vanity, and vexation of spirit. (2 April 1620, with the main text being on 5:13–14; sermon 140, in Donne 1839: 5.507)

(Further on Donne and Ecclesiastes, see the Introduction, pp. 52–4.)

Examples from a range of forms of writing will help to round off *vanitas* readings from the seventeenth century. John Bunyan, in his morality work *The Pilgrim's Progress* (1678), makes iterative use of Qoheleth's theme in the form of his famous site of moral danger: 'the name of that town is Vanity; and at the town there is a fair kept called Vanity-Fair. It is kept all the year long; it beareth the name of Vanity-Fair, because the town where 'tis kept is lighter than vanity; and also, because all that is there sold, or that cometh thither, is Vanity. As is the saying of the wise, *All that cometh is vanity* [11:8]' (in Bunyan 1986: 136). That 'town' would later influence Thackeray (see below), but not in a way that precluded the influence of Ecclesiastes itself (Dooley 1971; further on Bunyan, see chapter 12, p. 229). A more personal encounter with the theme can be discerned in the *Memoirs* of Thomas Boston of Ettrick (1676–1732), which closes with these words:

> And thus have I given some account of the days of my vanity. The world hath all along been a step-dame unto me; and wheresoever I would have attempted to nestle in it, there was a thorn of uneasiness laid for me. Man is born crying, lives complaining, and dies disappointed from that quarter. *All is vanity and vexation of spirit* [1:14]. – *I have waited for Thy salvation, O Lord* [Gen. 49:18]. (In Nicoll and Stoddart 1910: 531)

The tag of Jacob's blessing on the end of Qoheleth's words is intriguing in that Boston leaves himself and his readers still waiting.

Samuel Johnson's *The Vanity of Human Wishes* (1749) in effect takes up Qoheleth's theme of the futility of human desire, as expressed so potently in the *vanitas* tradition in the arts, and applies it to the endeavours of the good and the great of Europe (e.g. Cardinal Thomas Wolsey, Charles XII of Sweden) as well as to broadly conceived types:

> Unnumber'd suppliants croud Preferment's gate,
> Athirst for wealth, and burning to be great;
> Delusive Fortune hears th' incessant call,
> They mount, they shine, evaporate, and fall.
> On ev'ry stage the foes of peace attend,
> Hate dogs their flight, and insult mocks their end.
> Love ends with hope, the sinking statemen's door
> Pours in the morning worshiper no more
>
> . . .
>
> Deign on the passing world to turn thine eyes,
> And pause awhile from letters, to be wise;
> There mark what ills the scholar's life assail,
> Toil, envy, want, the patron, and the jail.
> (ll. 73–80, 157–60, in Johnson 1962: 33, 38)

In *Vanity* Johnson found a way of reflecting on transience and misery without embracing the 'Graveyard School' of poetry so popular in his day (British poetry focusing entirely on death and bereavement). As James Clifford comments, 'Skulls, coffins, epitaphs, and worms were not to his taste . . . [A]nd he remained unmoved by the new literary trends. For him the noblest expression of the old theme of Ecclesiastes – "Vanity of vanities; all is vanity" – could be found elsewhere' (1955: 304). The vanity theme is expressed elsewhere in Johnson, most importantly in a sermon on Eccl. 1:14 (see Introduction, pp. 61–2).

As with Johnson, *vanitas* became a meaningful idea for Voltaire. He makes frequent use of Ecclesiastes in his correspondence, which, suggests Arnold Ages, is 'largely devoid of the cynicism and hostility which Voltaire manifests in his comments on Scripture in his published works' (1966: 51). The first reference to Ecclesiastes comes in May 1756, when Voltaire writes to the Marchioness du Deffand, 'After having previously spoken enough of the pleasures of this world, I now lament its sufferings. I have done as Solomon, without being wise. I have seen that nearly everything was vanity and affliction, and that there is certainly evil on the earth' (in Ages 1966: 51; my tr.). In 1759, dealing with the health of the Marchioness, Voltaire writes of 'his new château at Les Délices and the benefits of country life':

> I see now that the poets are right to eulogize the pastoral life, that the happiness that is attached to the cares of rural life is not an illusion; and I have found even more pleasure in work, in sowing, in planting, in harvesting, than in [writing] tragedies and performing plays. Solomon was certainly right to say that there is nothing better than to live with the one you love, to rejoice in your work, and that all the rest is vanity. (In Ages 1966: 52; my tr.)

Ages notes that the most frequently cited Ecclesiastes passage in all of Voltaire's correspondence with du Deffand (24 times) is 'vanity of vanities': 'Its use is generally a sign of Voltaire's low spirits or declining health' (1966: 52). So in April 1760 he writes, 'After all, it is only about the gentle demise of one's career. All the rest is vanity of vanities, as the other said [*comme dit l'autre*]' (in Ages 1966: 52; my tr.). In March 1761 he writes,

> After having reflected deeply for sixty years on the foolishness that I have seen, and that I have done, I believe I have realized that the world is merely a theatre for a little battle, continuous, cruel and ridiculous, and a heap of vanities that causes heartache, as was very well said by the good Jewish deist who took the name of Solomon in Ecclesiastes, which you have not read. (In Ages 1966: 52; my tr.)

And again, in April 1769 Voltaire returns to his 'easy flippancy': 'All is good, provided that we seize the objective of the day, that we dine and that we sleep; the rest is vanity of vanities, as the other said: but friendship is a true thing' (in Ages 1966: 52; my tr.).

This way of internalizing Qoheleth's thought continued, it seems, well into old age. So in 1770, at the age of 76, he writes to a Madame Necker concerning Pigalle, the sculptor who had come to Ferney to do a bust of him:

> When the people of my village saw Pigalle lay out some of the instruments of his art: 'Why, look', said they, 'he's going to be dissected; that will be curious'. So it is, Madame, as you well know, that any spectacle amuses mankind . . . My statue will make a few philosophers smile, and knit the practiced brows of some villainous hypocrite or some depraved hack: vanity of vanities! But all is not vanity; my fond gratitude for my friends and above all for you, Madame, is not vanity. (In Auerbach 1974: 412)

Qoheleth's main theme here bursts out in a moment of exceptionally witty indignation, calling down his judgment on the world's perception of his burdensome role as 'Voltaire, Innkeeper of Europe'. In what Ages calls 'the most touching use of this verse' ('vanity of vanities'), Voltaire, complaining of his declining health, writes in 1775,

> The infinite number of maladies that kill me is too great, and our life is too brief for us to be able to pass through the plague of war. I will soon finish my career at my corner fire-place; extend your [career], Madame, for as great a length as you can. Enjoy all the pleasures that your sad state will permit. The word of pleasure is very strong . . . All is vanity, said the other; and it pleases God that all that is done is only vanity! but most of the time all is suffering. (In Ages 1966: 52–3; my tr.)

In a way, Voltaire marks the beginning of the 'knowing wink' reference to Ecclesiastes – deeply personalized and brought into public and narrative discourse. (Further on Voltaire and Ecclesiastes, see the Introduction, pp. 62–5, and Christianson 2005.)

C. Literary *Vanitas*: New Points of Reference (1800–)

I have already noted the way in which the literature of this period makes subtle and often short-hand use of Scripture (see pp. 65–6). As for Ecclesiastes, William Makepeace Thackeray (1811–63) was exemplary in this regard. Two passages on the subject from his work are relatively well known. The first is the final paragraph of *Vanity Fair* (1847–8). Its position, set off from what precedes it, lends it the place of commentary on the whole narrative: 'Ah!

Vanitas Vanitatum! Which of us is happy in this world? Which of us has his desire? or, having it, is satisfied? – Come, children, let us shut up the box and the puppets, for our play is played out"[6] (ch. 67, in Thackeray 1963: 699; cf. Dooley 1971: 705; note some of the same language in the later *The Newcomes*, ch. 47, in Thackeray 1962: 2.100; cf. McMaster 1987: 31). Earlier in *Vanity Fair*, Thackeray shows a subtle grasp of the theme in terms of the debates played out by the medieval and Renaissance interpreters of *vanitas*:

> It is all vanity to be sure: but who will not own to liking a little of it? I should like to know what well-constituted mind, merely because it is transitory, dislikes roast-beef? That is a vanity; but may every man who reads this, have a wholesome portion of it through life, I beg: aye, though my readers were five thousand. Sit down, gentlemen, and fall to, with a good hearty appetite . . . Yet, let us eat our fill of the vain thing, and be thankful therefore . . . for these [pleasures] too, like all other mortal delights, were but transitory. (Ch. 51; 1963: 485; cf. Locker-Lampson, below, p. 134)

The second passage is an oft-cited poem (though usually only one verse is cited), *Vanitas Vanitatum*. The collection in which it first appeared was *Ballads and Poems* (Boston, 1855). In her introduction to an 1899 edition, Thackeray's daughter Anne Ritchie describes the collection's origins:

> When my father first published his 'Ballads and Poems', he wrote a preface . . . saying 'These ballads have been written during the past fifteen years, and are now gathered by the author from his own books and the various periodicals in which the pieces appeared originally . . . [The author hopes that the public] may be kindly disposed to his little volume of verses'. (In Thackeray 1899: p. xv)

In an 1885 edition, the poem is headed with a sketch (plate 9), which may be by the author himself (the title-page of that edition simply states, 'with illustrations by the author, Mrs Butler . . . [and six others!]', but does not indicate which are whose).

The poem is a careful reading of Qoheleth's themes and I offer a selection here:

---

[6]   The puppet theme was related to Qoheleth before (see Erasmus, p. 44) and employed later in J. W. Brady Moore's *Koheleth*:

> Age after age a never ending flow
> Of generations come and toil and go –
> But ever Earth remains – a monstrous stage
> Where Human Puppets act their little show.
> (1924: 4)

VANITAS VANITATUM.

Vanitas Vanitatum

How spake of old the Royal Seer?
  (His text is one I love to treat on.)
This life of ours, he said, is sheer
  Mataiotes Mataioteton.

O Student of this gilded Book,
  Declare, while musing on its pages,
If truer words were ever spoke
  By ancient or by modern sages?

. . .

How low men were, and how they rise!
  How high they were, and how they tumble!
O vanity of vanities!
  O laughable, pathetic jumble!

. . .

Oh, vanity of vanities!
   How wayward the decrees of Fate are;
How very weak the very wise,
   How very small the very great are!

. . .

Though thrice a thousand years are past
   Since David's son, the sad and splendid,
The weary King Ecclesiast,
   Upon his awful tablets penned it, –

Methinks the text is never stale,
   And life is every day renewing
Fresh comments on the old old tale
   Of Folly, Fortune, Glory, Ruin.

Hark to the Preacher, preaching still
   He lifts his voice and cries his sermon,
Here at St. Peter's on Cornhill,
   As yonder on the Mount of Hermon
                   (Thackeray 1885: 132–4)

(Further on Thackeray and Ecclesiastes, see the Introduction, p. 67.)

Another oft-cited 'vanity' reference (again usually of only one line) appears in Herman Melville's *Moby Dick* (1851). At this point in the narrative (ch. 96) Ishmael has just lost consciousness at the helm and nearly capsized the ship, which moves him to issue a warning: 'A stark, bewildered feeling, as of death, came over me . . . Look not too long in the face of the fire, O man! Never dream with thy hand on the helm!' (in Melville 1967: 354). The sun will come in the morning, with a truer light:

> The sun hides not the ocean, which is the dark side of this earth, and which is two thirds of this earth. So, therefore, that mortal man who hath more of joy than sorrow in him, that mortal man cannot be true – not true, or undeveloped. With books the same. The truest of all men was the Man of Sorrows, and the truest of all books is Solomon's, and Ecclesiastes is the fine hammered steel of woe. 'All is vanity.' ALL. This wilful world hath not got hold of unchristian Solomon's wisdom yet. But he who dodges hospitals and jails, and walks fast crossing graveyards, and would rather talk of operas than hell; calls Cowper, Young, Pascal, Rousseau, poor devils all of sick men; and throughout a care-free lifetime swears by Rabelais as passing wise, and therefore jolly; – not that man is fitted to sit down on tomb-stones, and break the green damp mould with unfathomably wondrous Solomon.
>
> But even Solomon, he says, 'the man that wandereth out of the way of under-standing shall remain' (*i.e.* even while living) 'in the congregation of the dead.'

[Prov. 21:16] Give not thyself up, then, to fire, lest it invert thee, deaden thee; as for the time it did me. There is a wisdom that is woe; but there is a woe that is madness. (1967: 355)

Here the 'unchristian' wisdom of Ecclesiastes is an illustration of a blistering truth, one that is *willing* to confront the reality of death, 'to sit down on tomb-stones'. Scholars of Melville have suggested not only that this passage is key to Melville's novel, but even that Ecclesiastes is woven into the idea of the whole. So Martin Wank argues that

> Like Ecclesiastes, *Moby Dick* is a summary survey of all human history, with the conclusion that man's efforts have been vain and unworthy, leading to disaster, new trials of human effort, and only new disasters . . . This 'sermon' . . . tended to suggest . . . that the nation . . . was on a vain quest for worldly achievement . . . We need not think that Melville was a simpleton in this (or the Preacher, for that matter). Melville foresaw that America . . . was riding toward a great fall in its drive to dominance, and it was this he hoped to forestall by repeating, for his time, the great wisdom of Ecclesiastes. (1995: 3)

Yet quite apart from *Moby Dick* as allegory, Melville cast a raging epistemological battle, one in which, Elisa New suggests, a Hebraic over-Hellenistic model was prevailing. 'Melville's growing faith in the seasonality, or historicity of truth was only enhanced by his readings in Ecclesiastes, a text he found increasingly compelling' (New 1998: 299). Indeed, in the same year as *Moby Dick* (1851), Melville wrote to Nathaniel Hawthorne of his deepening affection for Solomon's wisdom:

> I have come to regard this matter of Fame as the most transparent of all vanities. I read Solomon more and more, and every time see deeper and deeper and unspeakable meanings in him . . . It seems to me now that Solomon was the truest man that ever spoke, and yet that he a little *managed* the truth with a view to popular conservatism; or else there have been many corruptions and interpolations of the text. (In N. Wright 1949: 96)

Once again, then, *vanitas* provides, in the published work (Wright points to similar Ecclesiastes and vanity themes in *Mardi and a Voyage Thither*, 1849, as well; N. Wright 1949: 98–9), a meaningful language for scrutinizing the enterprise of human inquiry, and, in private, 'unspeakable meanings'.

Appearances of the *vanitas* theme in literature are usually very brief and, more often than not, weighted with memorable significance. So when Prince Andrew at Austerlitz lies wounded in Leo Tolstoy's *War and Peace* (1865–9),

> he saw nothing. Above him there was now nothing but the sky – the lofty sky . . . 'How quiet, peaceful, and solemn, not at all as I ran,' thought Prince

Andrew – '... How was it I did not see that lofty sky before? And how happy I am to have found it at last! Yes! All is vanity, all falsehood, except that infinite sky. There is nothing, nothing, but that ... Thank God!' (Bk 3, ch. 13, in Tolstoy 1942: 300)

Similarly, in *Tess of the d'Urbervilles* (1891) Thomas Hardy compassionately traces the troubled and ultimately tragic arc of 'erring milkmaid' Tess Durbey-field. One night, reflecting on her loneliness, estrangement from her husband and the pain of her life hitherto, she speaks Qoheleth's words:

She thought of her husband in some vague warm clime on the other side of the globe, while she was here in the cold. Was there another such wretched being as she in the world? Tess asked herself; and thinking of her wasted life, said, 'All is vanity.' She repeated the words mechanically, till she reflected that this was a most inadequate thought for modern days. Solomon had thought as far as that more than two thousand years ago; she herself, though not in the van of thinkers, had got much further. If all were only vanity, who would mind it? All was, alas, worse than vanity – injustice, punishment, exaction of death. (Ch. 41, in Hardy 1963: 353)

Qoheleth would not agree and would, of course, include those final items under the judgment of *hebel*. But this is a remarkably personal appropriation of his words, one that mirrors the self-examining aspects of the *vanitas* arts tradition and is not unlike what we will find in *Babette's Feast* (below, p. 141). (Intriguingly, Hardy, a fan of Thackeray's work, attempted in the early 1860s to render Ecclesiastes in Spenserian verse, 'but abandoned this when he found the original unmatchable' [Deacon and Coleman 1966: 29]. Further on Hardy and Ecclesiastes, see the Introduction, pp. 67–8.)

Lord Byron (1788–1824) achieves a comparable feat in 'All is Vanity, Saith the Preacher' (published in his *Hebrew Melodies* collection, 1814):

Fame, wisdom, love, and Power were mine,
     And health and youth possess'd me;
My goblets blush'd from every vine,
     And lovely forms caress'd me;
I sunn'd my heart in beauty's eyes,
     And felt my soul grow tender;
All earth can give, or mortal prize,
     Was mine of regal splendour.

I strive to number o'er what days
     Remembrance can discover,
Which all that life or earth displays
     Would lure me to live over.

There rose no day, there roll'd no hour
  Of pleasure unembitter'd;
And not a trapping deck'd my power
  That gall'd not while it glitter'd.

The serpent of the field, by art
  And spells, is won from harming;
But that which coils around the heart,
  Oh! who hath power of charming?
It will not list to wisdom's lore,
  Nor music's voice can lure it;
But there it stings forever more
  The soul that must endure it.
                    (Byron 1970: 80–1)

One suspects that the voice here, which again captures Qoheleth's sense of poignant failed quest, is Byron's as much as that of his fictive Preacher. Matthew Prior's 'Solomon on the Vanity of the World' (1718) suggests a similar strategy:

Ye Sons of Men, with just Regard attend,
Observe the Preacher, and believe the Friend,
Whose serious Muse inspires him to explain,
That all we Act, and all we Think is Vain.
That in this Pilgrimage of Seventy Years,
Over Rocks of Perils, and thro' Vales of Tears
Destin'd to march, our doubtful Steps we tend,
Tir'd with the Toil, yet fearful of its End.
That from the Womb We take our fatal Shares
Of Follies, Passions, Labors, Tumults, Cares;
And at Approach of Death shall only know
The Truths, which from these pensive Numbers flow,
That We pursue false Joy, and suffer real Woe.
                    (ll. 1–13, in Prior 1905: 264)

Prior excels at (and is unique in) capturing the tension between the vanity to which all are destined and the depth to which endurance of it compels compliance ('Tir'd with the Toil, yet fearful of its End'). In his 'Don Juan' (canto VII, composed in 1822) Byron manages a less indirect engagement with the theme:

Ecclesiastes said, 'that all is vanity' –
  Most modern preachers say the same, or show it
By their examples of true Christianity:
  In short, all know, or very soon may know it;
And in this scene of all confess'd inanity,
  By saint, by sage, by preacher, and by poet,

> Must I restrain me, through the fear of strife,
> From holding up the nothingness of life?
>
> (Canto VII.6; 1970: 744)

'Vanity of vanities' is exceptionally effective (as it is in Ecclesiastes) as a structuring device, such as in critic and poet William Earnest Henley's 'Double Ballade of the Nothingness of Things' (*c*.1877–88):

> The big teetotum twirls,
> And epochs wax and wane
> As chance subsides or swirls;
> But of the loss and gain
> The sum is always plain.
> Read on the mighty pall,
> The weed of funeral
> That covers praise and blame,
> The -isms and the -anities,
> Magnificence and shame: –
> 'O Vanity of Vanities!'
>
> The Fates are subtile girls!
> They give us chaff for grain.
> And Time, the Thunderer, hurls,
> Like bolted death, disdain
> At all that heart and brain
> Conceive, or great or small,
> Upon this earthly ball.
> Would you be knight and dame?
> Or woo the sweet humanities?
> Or illustrate a name?
> O Vanity of vanities!
> . . .
> Burned in one common flame
> Are wisdoms and insanities.
> For this alone we came: –
> 'O Vanity of vanities!'
>   (the first two and part of the
>   sixth of seven stanzas, all of
>   which are similarly framed
>   by Qoheleth's phrase;
>   in Henley 1898: 94–5, 97)

As in Qoheleth's narrative itself, as the incongruous events and ideas are displayed, all the '-isms and the -anities', the *vanitas* refrain becomes increasingly swollen with a host of signifiers. Structurally, other poets have commenced with 'vanity' simply to prompt thinking on a seemingly unrelated subject. So, for example, Robert Browning's 'The Bishop Orders his Tomb at Saint Praxed's Church, Rome, 15__' begins 'Vanity, saith the preacher, vanity! Draw round my bed: is Anselm keeping back? . . .' (Browning 2004).

The vanity theme resonated personally and with clarity for poet Christina Rossetti. Her three most cherished books of the Bible, from which she drew significantly in her poetry, were, in order, the Song of Songs, Ecclesiastes and Revelation. But as for passages,

> Of all the works of Holy Scripture, the passage that Rossetti loved the best and used the most is that which expresses the theme of Ecclesiastes: 'Vanity of vanities: all is vanity'. Not only does she cite this passage more often than any other, but she also quotes other sections from that book, and from others, that stress the same concept: all that makes up life soon vanishes and loses significance. Christina Rossetti is in complete accord with this observation, and like the Koheleth she also pours forth one long drawn out lament of pain and disappointment, for she looks for escape from present misery and finds it not. (Jiménez 1979: p. x)

Like Qoheleth, and indeed the *vanitas* painters, Rossetti was successful at uniting contradictory sides of her nature, and also like Qoheleth, had a strong sense of self-possession and reflection. Note the first half of her 'The One Certainty' (composed 1849):

> Vanity of vanities, the Preacher saith,
> > All things are vanity. The eye and ear
> > Cannot be filled with what they see and hear.
> Like early dew, or like the sudden breath
> Of wind, or like the grass that withereth,
> > Is man, tossed to and fro by hope and fear:
> > So little joy hath he, so little cheer,
> Till all things end in the long dust of death.
> > > > (Rossetti 1979: 72)

'A Testimony' (also composed in 1849) develops the theme at greater length. So, for example:

> > I said of laughter: it is vain.
> > > Of mirth I said: what profits it?
> > > Therefore I found a book, and writ
> > Therein how ease and also pain,
> > How health and sickness, every one
> > Is vanity beneath the sun

. . .

> Therefore the maidens cease to sing,
>> And the young men are very sad;
>> Therefore the sowing is not glad,
> And mournful is the harvesting.
> Of high and low, of great and small,
> Vanity is the lot of all.
>> (first and twelfth of thirteen stanzas,
>> in Rossetti 1979: 77, 79)

With echoes here of chapters 2, 9 and 12, as elsewhere in her work, Rossetti betrays her intimate knowledge of Ecclesiastes. This almost obsessive thematizing of vanity is taken up in at least 13 of Rossetti's published poems, and other Ecclesiastes themes in roughly 10 others (see Jiménez 1979: 30–5). Probably the finest of these is 'Vanity of Vanities' (first published 1847):

> Ah woe is me for pleasure that is vain,
>> Ah woe is me for glory that is past:
>> Pleasure that bringeth sorrow at the last,
> Glory that at the last bringeth no gain!
> So saith the sinking heart; and so again
>> It shall say till the mighty angel-blast
>> Is blown, making the sun and moon aghast,
> And showering down the stars like sudden rain.
> And ever more men shall go fearfully
>> Bending beneath their weight of heaviness;
> And ancient men shall lie down wearily,
>> And strong men shall rise up in weariness;
> Yes, even the young shall answer shiningly,
>> Saying one to another: How vain it is!
>> (Rossetti 1979: 153)

(While this is a subtle exposition, noteworthy too is Rossetti's use of the refrain 'Oh vanity of vanities, desire!' in 'Soeur de la Miséricorde', 1881, in Rossetti 1986: 119–20.)

A notable twist in the literary adaptation of *vanitas* in the late nineteenth century is the manner in which, like other key phrases (e.g. 'nothing new under the sun'), *vanitas* could provide opportunity for witty and light-hearted verse. Frederick Locker-Lampson's 'Vanity Fair' (*c*.1865), which is commenting at least in part on the reception of Thackeray's titular work, is a good example:

'*Vanitas vanitatum*' has rung in the ears
Of gentle and simple for thousands of years;
The wail is still heard, yet its notes never scare
Or simple or gentle from Vanity Fair.

I hear people busy abusing it – yet
There the young go to learn and the old to forget;
The mirth may be feigning, the sheen may be glare,
But the gingerbread's gilded in Vanity Fair.

. . .

Philosophy halts, wisest counsels are vain, –
We go – we repent – we return there again;
To-night you will certainly meet with us there –
Exceedingly merry in Vanity Fair.

(1865: 125–6)

(Compare Frederick Ward's 'Laughing Philosophy', 1890: 'Comes to all the ultimatum,/That snuffs out the Royal gas;/*Vanitas O vanitatum,/Omnia sunt vanitas!/ . . . Therefore laugh and live*'; ll. 37–40, 48; 1890: 787.)

A frequently referenced appearance of Qoheleth's *vanitas* is found in George Bernard Shaw's play *Man and Superman: A Comedy and a Philosophy* (in Shaw 1965: 332–405), composed 1901–3 and first performed in 1905. The third act, the 'Don Juan in Hell' dream sequence, is often performed independently as a distinct piece, and provides opportunity for some philosophical discourse on the futility of endeavour in relation to human progress, and of course it is only appropriate that Qoheleth has his say:

THE DEVIL. Don Juan: shall I be frank with you?

DON JUAN. Were you not so before?

THE DEVIL. As far as I went, yes. But I will now go further, and confess to you that men get tired of everything, of heaven no less than of hell; and that all history is nothing but a record of the oscillations of the world between these two extremes. An epoch is but a swing of the pendulum; and each generation thinks the world is progressing because it is always moving. But when you are as old as I am; when you have a thousand times wearied of heaven, like myself and the Commander, and a thousand times wearied of hell, as you are wearied now, you will no longer imagine that every swing from heaven to hell is an emancipation, every swing from hell to heaven an evolution. Where you now see reform, progress, fulfilment of upward tendency, continual ascent by Man on the stepping stones of his dead selves to higher things, you will see nothing but an infinite comedy of illusion. You will discover the profound truth of the saying of my friend Koheleth, that there is nothing new under the sun. *Vanitas vanitatum* –

DON JUAN [out of all patience]. By Heaven, this is worse than your cant about love and beauty. Clever dolt that you are, is a man no better than a worm, or a dog than a wolf, because he gets tired of everything? Shall he give up eating because he destroys his appetite in the act of gratifying it? . . . Granted that the great Life Force has hit on the device of the clockmaker's pendulum, and uses the earth for its bob; . . . has the colossal mechanism no purpose?

THE DEVIL. None, my friend. You think, because you have a purpose, Nature must have one. You might as well expect it to have fingers and toes because you have them. (Shaw 1965: 387)

For Shaw Qoheleth illustrates well the 'comedy of illusion' that when properly recognized shatters faith in the reliable moral order of the world. A comment a few years earlier, in his preface to *Three Plays for Puritans* (1901), sheds further light on this idea: 'Vanity of vanities, all is vanity! moans the Preacher, when life has at last taught him that Nature will not dance to his moralist-made tunes. Thackeray, scores of centuries later, was still baying the moon in the same terms' (in Shaw 1934: 716). With this and the larger context of this dream sequence, which reflects existentially on the value of human existence stuck against the cyclical futility of 'Nature', Shaw's larger understanding of the theme as it relates to human endeavour becomes clear.

The *vanitas* theme can be seen (re)emerging in some twentieth-century poetry. In his celebrated *The Testament of Beauty* (1929), brought on by the death of his daughter in 1926, Robert Bridges offers a Qoheleth-like stanza that is as bleak as any *vanitas* adaptation:

> . . . surely Nature hath no night
> dark as thatt black darkness that can be felt: no storm
> blind as the fury of Man's self-destructiv passions,
> no pestilence so poisonous as his hideous sins.
>   Thus men in slavery of sorrow imagin ghastly creeds,
> monstrous devilry, abstractions of terror, and wil *look*
> *to death's benumbing opium as their only cure,*
> or, seeking proudly to ennoble melancholy
> by embracement, wil make a last wisdom of woe:
> *They lie in Hell like sheep, death gnaweth upon them;*
> whose prophet sage and preacher is the old Ecclesiast
> pseudo-Solomon, who cryeth in the wilderness,
> calling all to baptism in the Slough of Despond:
> VANITAS VANITATUM, OMNIA VANITAS.
>   (Book II, 'Selfhood', ll. 518–31, in Bridges 1936: 608)

Like Klein (see p. 98), Bridges is one of the very few writers to draw attention to the rhetorical device of Qoheleth's *nom de plume*, 'pseudo-Solomon'. Despite (or because of?) its dark themes, *Testament* was an immediate success. When Oxford University Press published it, 'they were unprepared for its success. Printings could scarcely keep up with demand, and by 1946 it had sold over 70,000 copies' (Phillips 2004).

Few poets of the modern period engaged more comprehensively with the *vanitas* of Ecclesiastes than T. S. Eliot. As Edwards notes,

> *Four Quartets* takes on itself, like 'Prufrock', the burden of Ecclesiastes. As Denis Donoghue has indicated, it is often a meditation on *vanitas vanitatum*. The particular horror of endlessness in the Preacher's lament: 'yet is there no end of all his labour' (4:8), is actually expanded in the Preacher-like dirge of 'Dry Salvages' II, which asks, repetitively, 'Where is there an end of it . . . ?' and replies, 'There is no end, but addition'. The phrase drives one back for a while into the desolation of *The Waste Land* (as also forward to Beckett). There are many further instances, and the most telling are those which show Eliot to have been thinking of Ecclesiastes at the beginning of *Four Quartets*, and at the end of all four of its constituent poems. (Edwards 1990a: 80; cf. T. Wright 2005)

So in 'Dry Salvages', II (1941) of the *Four Quartets* (published 1943), Eliot ruminates,

> Where is there an end of it, the soundless wailing,
> The silent withering of autumn flowers
> Dropping their petals and remaining motionless;
> Where is there an end to the drifting wreckage,
> The prayer of the bone on the beach, the unprayable
> Prayer at the calamitous annunciation?
>
> There is no end, but addition: the trailing
> Consequence of further days and hours
> (In Eliot 1969: 185)

And further on there is something here of Ecclesiastes' sense of the ever-vanishing goal of memory and its consequent meaning (cf. 1:4, 11):

> We had the experience but missed the meaning,
> And approach to the meaning restores the experience
> In a different form, beyond any meaning
>
> . . .
>
> That the past experience revived in the meaning
> Is not the experience of one life only
> But of many generations – not forgetting
> Something that is probably quite ineffable:

> The backward look behind the assurance
> Of recorded history, the backward half-look
> Over the shoulder, towards the primitive terror.
>
> (In Eliot 1969: 186–7)

While, then, the idea of *vanitas* subtly underwrites the whole of *Four Quartets*, it is in part II of 'Little Gidding' (1942) that vanity at last appears:

> Dead water and dead sand
> Contending for the upper hand.
> The parched eviscerate soil
> Gapes at the vanity of toil,
> Laughs without mirth.
> This is the death of earth.
>
> (In Eliot 1969: 193)

(Further on Eliot and Ecclesiastes, see pp. 68–9.)

I have already discussed the rare appearances of Ecclesiastes on film (see pp. 83–4), but I should make mention here of a splendid cinematic *vanitas* reading. *Rembrandt* (1936) follows the artist's life from 1642, a time of his considerable wealth and established reputation to his final years in, as the film has it, relative obscurity (*c.*1668–9). In the closing scenes, Rembrandt (Charles Laughton), who has lost his wife to illness and come to the brink of bankruptcy, wanders the streets of Amsterdam unrecognized and even derided. He falls in with a young bunch of raucous revellers who, charmed by his wit, take him along to a tavern that he might 'sing for his supper, preach a sermon'. Once there, they cheerfully call out toasts: 'To beauty! To woman! To youth! To love! To money! What about you, grandpa? You haven't given us your toast!' 'I can't think of a toast', he replies. The crowd points out that they heard him 'mumble something' into his glass. 'That wasn't a toast, and they weren't my words.' They ask whose words they are, at which point the camera closes in on Laughton's pensive face. 'They were the words of King Solomon. They are the best words I know.' 'Well, let's have them! You can be our King Solomon and teach us wisdom!' With mesmerizing cadence, Laughton delivers Qoheleth's words, and it is not a simple citation, but a medley of thematic verses: 'Vanity of vanities. All is vanity' (1:2b); 'I have seen all the works that are done under the sun. And behold, all is vanity and vexation of spirit' (1:14). This he follows with the King James version of 1:18 and 3:22a, each line followed by the laughter of his tavern audience. Someone enters, however, who recognizes the still highly respected artist. Ashamed, the group seek to make amends, one offering him some money for food, which he promptly uses to purchase fresh pigments. The final scene, then, sees Rembrandt in his makeshift studio,

PLATE 10 Charles Laughton as Rembrandt catches his reflection and is prompted to speak Qoheleth's *vanitas* judgment. *Rembrandt* © London Film Productions, Ltd., 1936

now able to complete his self-portrait (visually recalling his poignant self-portraits of the 1660s), which provides opportunity for the most affective rendering of Qoheleth on film. Regarding himself in his cracked mirror he pauses, transfixed, and speaks the film's final lines: 'Vanity of vanities. All is vanity' (plate 10).[7]

This performance of *vanitas* is richly referential. In terms of social stature, wealth and possessions, Rembrandt in the final scenes is a shadow of his former self, and he has taken on the figure of the disillusioned king (who on the streets of Amsterdam is mockingly referred to as 'his royal highness', and whom the tavern crowd anoint their own 'king') who can now comment on the real worth of the world's wares. Unknowingly perhaps, the film comments on the insights of the *vanitas* tradition in the arts, which could be utilized to great effect in Dutch self-portraits of the period, such as David Bailly's (1651, see above, plate 8). Like Qoheleth, this Rembrandt is commenting on a way of

---

[7] More recently, *Darrow* (1991), which dramatizes the life of the famous socialist lawyer Clarence Darrow (Kevin Spacey), no doubt articulates the sentiment of scores of Ecclesiastes readers when its titular character describes what the Bible means to him: 'Thank God, in our house the good book gathered dust up on the top shelf between Aesop's *Fables* and Bulfinch's *Mythology*. The only thing in the Bible that made sense to me was Ecclesiastes: "Vanity of vanities; all is vanity and a striving after the wind"'.

defining the self (so he adjures the youthful crowd as he departs, 'And remember King Solomon'). It is also empowered by the unique ability of film (or more precisely, the incomparable Charles Laughton) to bring Qoheleth to life through visual empathy with Rembrandt as Solomon/Qoheleth. Indeed, readings in literature and the arts are frequently driven by empathy, empathy with the idea that *vanitas* has come to signify for that performer (which is also clear in the example of the film *Babette's Feast*, below).

D.   THE BREADTH OF *VANITAS*

To summarize, *vanitas* reading can be seen in five stages:

1   *Contemptus mundi* – popularized by Jerome and a host of Christian commentators (Jewish readers generally not interested in the programmatic reading).
2   Anti-*contemptus mundi* – popularized (and politicized) by Martin Luther and other Protestant interpreters, later resumed in Puritan commentaries.
3   Renaissance *vanitas* – a new application, mainly in poetry, fine art and music, commenting on the perceived dangers of the new sciences and on mortality (linked to *memento mori*).
4   Literary *vanitas* – a knowing application that references *contemptus* as well as Renaissance traditions.
5   Contemporary *vanitas* – a rediscovery of Renaissance readings, particularly in the arts.

Such periodization should be regarded as fluid. Readers who targeted *contemptus* (2) also articulated Renaissance scepticism of knowledge with *vanitas* (3). The extent of the unabated influence of *vanitas* (5) is impossible to map accurately. This was brought home to me recently on a visit to the Tate Modern museum in London. It was with some disbelief that I took in the room I had just entered, entitled *Memento Mori*. It began with a late but perfectly classical *vanitas* painting by Edward Collier (a Dutch artist who painted *vanitas* works for the English market, and who anglicized his name from Edwaert Colyer), *Still Life with a Volume of Wither's 'Emblemes'* (1696 – it can at the time of writing be viewed at the Tate's website, http://www.tate.org.uk), the display caption of which read,

> This seventeenth-century work is a typical *vanitas* painting. The skull and hourglass, which symbolise the inevitability of death, are joined by musical instruments, wine and jewels, representing the fleeting pleasures of life. A book by the English poet George Wither is opened at the title page, where a brief poem emphasises the theme of mortality. The Latin inscription in the top left corner

is a celebrated quotation from the Old Testament book of Ecclesiastes, from which the term *vanitas* was derived: 'Vanity of vanities, all is vanity.'

The room had a range of modern work that echoed the themes of mortality inspired by *vanitas*. (I had to assure my wife that our presence there was all very innocent and unplanned!)

In the end comprehending the influence of *vanitas* itself requires imagination. For Renaissance thinkers *vanitas* provided a sceptical line of inquiry weighted with the disquieting authority of Scripture, as well as a polemical language to be voiced against the monastic tradition that had permanently fixed *vanitas* in the intellectual life of Europe. *Vanitas* fired the imagination of artists, musicians and poets from the Renaissance to the present day. Part of the enormous appeal of Qoheleth's theme lies in its radical openness. In Ecclesiastes *hebel* has no reference but itself and the troubled observations that Qoheleth attaches to it, and the superlative construct *hebel* of *hebels* is infamously self-defining (as many exegetes have pointed out, the 'all' of 'all is vanity' also lacks a semantic reference, one that must be provided by readers). These yield meaning only in a discourse that provides their terms of reference, only as poets and moralizers fill them with a host of experientially bound ideas. This non-referential quality also hints at a transgressive power, a power to wrest free from the cultural conditions of its performances. Where it appears to succeed (even if it necessarily fails), *vanitas* often encapsulates the entirety of Qoheleth's story (in a manner not unlike the frame narrative's use of $h^a b\bar{e}l$ $h^a b\bar{a}l\hat{i}m$ to summarize Qoheleth's experience), his sense of failed quest and the yearning of the older Qoheleth to redeem it (see Christianson 1998a: 242–54). I will conclude with one such exceptional example, which *can be seen* to comment on Qoheleth's larger narrative. *Babette's Feast* (dir. Gabriel Axel, 1987) recounts the story of a close-knit and austere Christian sect rattled by the arrival of Babette, a Parisian chef who gradually and metaphorically awakens them. The film climaxes in an extravagant and transformative meal for the community, including old general Lowenhielm. The general, it transpires, made a string of decisions in his youth that led him to military success but away from the woman he loved. Before the meal, at which the general is aware that he will meet his former love, we see intercut scenes of Babette preparing her feast and of the general before a full-length mirror, preparing to attend it. The general's scene begins to take on the qualities of an animated *vanitas* still life. Pausing, he addresses himself: 'Vanity. Vanity of vanities. All is vanity.' Behind him we see a chair in which appears his younger self, arms crossed, proud and defiant. The older turns to address the younger: 'I have achieved all you dreamed of and satisfied your ambition, but to little avail. This evening, you and I shall settle matters.'

The Overture Played Out: 1:3–18

After thousands of words we arrive at last at verse 3 (!), and it is worth noting that, with the possible exception of chapter 12, nothing in Ecclesiastes has engaged interpreters so frequently and comprehensively as the *vanitas* theme just surveyed. Readers should not be surprised, then, to find significantly less space taken up (on a verse to page ratio, as it were) by Qoheleth's remaining chapters.

Qoheleth's dramatic opening lines have provided opportunities for poets to lend gravitas to the commencement of their work. With a little overlap, this will offer an appropriate departure from the *vanitas* section, and a few examples will illustrate the case well. Henry Howard, Earl of Surrey, wrote his *A Paraphrase of Part of the Book of Ecclesiastes* (1–5) on the cusp of his final imprisonment while foreseeing his execution by Henry VIII in 1546 (see p. 47). His opening anticipates the frustration he renders throughout the poem:

> I, Solomon, David's son, King of Jerusalem,
> Chosen by God to teach the Jews, and in his laws lead them,
> Confess, under the Sun that every thing is vain;
> The world is false; man he is frail, and all his pleasures pain.
> Alas! what stable fruit may Adam's children find
> In that, they seek by sweat of brows and travail of their mind.
> We that live on the earth, draw toward our decay;
> Our children fill our place awhile, and then they vade away.
> Such changes make the earth, and doth remove for none;
> But serves us for a place to play our tragedies upon.
> (In Howard 1815: 1.66)

George Sandys in 1632 also began his exquisite paraphrase in vivid terms:

> This Sermon the much-knowing Preacher made:
> King David's Sonne; who Judah's Scepter swai'd
> O restlesse vanitie of Vanities!
> All is but vanitie, the Preacher cries.
> What profit have we by our Labors won,
> Of all beneath the Circuit of the Sun?
> (In Sandys 1638: fol. Aa, 1)

Compare the opening stanza from the anonymous author of the paraphrase *Choheleth* (1765):

O Vain, deluding world! whose largest gifts
Thine emptiness betray, like painted clouds,
Or watry bubbles: as the vapour flies,
Dispers'd by lightest blast, so fleet thy joys,
And leave no trace behind. This serious truth
The Royal Preacher loud proclaims, convinc'd
By sad experience; with a sigh, repeats
The mournful theme, that nothing here below
Can solid comfort yield: 'Tis all a scene
Of vanity, beyond the pow'r of words
T'express, or thought conceive . . .

                              (Anonymous 1765: 1–2)

Like some sort of plot announcements, each of these beginnings sees the poet borrowing freely from the ancient authority of Solomon/Royal Preacher in order to insinuate at least the foundation of Solomon's 'sad experience'. (Compare the openings of A. M. Klein's 'Koheleth', c.1944 [p. 71] and of Thackeray's *Vanitas Vanitatum* [p. 127].)

There are of course other features of 1:1–2 apart from Solomon and *vanitas* that have produced commentary of one kind or another. In the introduction to his sermons of 1649 on Eccl. 8:2–4 in support of King Charles II, Edward Hyde, with typical exegetical flourish, suggests that 'the preacher' does not use a name because he sought to highlight the fact that the words were not his own but were inspired by God. The proof lies, says Hyde, in the use of a feminine title: '. . . [*'Ekklēsiasta*] either [*psychi*, soul] or [*sophia*, wisdom], not a *he* but a *she* Preacher, that is, not a Preaching man, but a *Preaching soul*, or a *Preaching wisedom*'. This directs the reader's attention away from the persona of Qoheleth/Solomon to the purpose of wisdom, which in this book is to exposit 'the publick testimonial of his [Solomon's!] repentance' (Hyde 1662: 12; my transliterations).

The answer to Qoheleth's rhetorical question of 1:3, 'What profit hath a man of all his labour . . . ?', can of course only be 'none', and John Hall in 1646 saw in this observation the illustration of a kind of intellectual *Wanderlust*:

Even as the wandring Traveller doth stray,
       Led from his way
By a false fire, whose Flame to cheated sight
Doth lead aright,

. . .

Another whose conceptions onely dreame
       Monsters of fame,

The vaine applause of other Mad-men buyes
    With his owne sighes,
Yet his enlarged name shall never craule
    Over this Ball,
But soone consume; thus doth a Trumpets sound
Rush bravely on a little, then's not found;

. . .

('What profiteth a Man of all his labour
which he taketh under the Sun?', 1646: 97, 99)

As Hall continues, he suggests that taxonomy also falls under this same curse: 'So a weake Eye in twilight thinkes it sees/New species,/While it sees nought' (1646: 99). Hall extends Qoheleth's idea to apply the notion of 'profit' not just to physical labour but to other ways in which effort is expended.

The opening verses of Ecclesiastes, like its closing elegy, have wrung out from poets not just fine verse but also a tendency, as we have seen in the *vanitas* readings, to relate Qoheleth's words to the broadest forms of human experience. The poetic force of the passage was captured well by T. K. Cheyne, who drew attention to Thomas Carlyle's rendering of 1:4 in his fictionalized autobiography, *Sartor Resartus* (1831):

To me, I confess, the prelude or overture (i. 4–8), though not in rhythmic Hebrew, is the gem of the book . . . [Its] poetry is of elemental force, and appeals to the modern reader in some of his moods more than almost anything else in the Old Testament outside the Book of Job. I cannot help alluding to Carlyle's fine application of its imagery in *Sartor Resartus*, 'Generations are as the Days of toilsome Mankind: Death and Birth are the vesper and the matin bells, that summon mankind to sleep, and to rise refreshed for new advancement.' (1887: 246)

For William Knox Qoheleth's observation on the passing of generations draws comparisons to the natural world beyond the immediate language of the passage. In his 1824 poem 'Mortality', Knox draws on verses 4 and 9–11 (as well as Job 3), extending these to the levelling power of death:

The saint that enjoyed the communion of Heaven,
The sinner that dared to remain unforgiven,
The wise and the foolish, the guilty and just,
Have quietly mingled their bones in the dust.

So the multitude goes – like the flower and the weed
That wither away to let others succeed;
So the multitude comes – even those we behold,
To repeat every tale that hath often been told.

For we are the same things that our fathers have been,
We see the same sights that our fathers have seen

(ll. 25–34, in Knox 2003)

In his poem 'One Generation Passeth Away', Christian mystical poet Jones Very (1818–80), like Knox, related Qoheleth's themes to broad reflection on human experience:

As is the sand upon the ocean's shore,
    So without number seems the human race;
And to that number still are added more,
    As wave on wave each other onward chase.

As are the drops of rain, that countless fall
    Upon the earth, or on the briny sea,
So seem man's generations great and small,
    Those that have been, and those who yet shall be.

. . .

More than the ancient Preacher now we know,
    Though wiser he than all the sons of men;
God through his Son the promise doth bestow,
    That all the sons of earth shall live again.

(In Atwan and Wieder 1993: 351–2)

George Sandys captures the same sense exquisitely in his 1632 paraphrase:

The Earth is fix't, we fleeting: as one Age
Departs, another enters on the Stage.
The setting Sunne resignes his Throne to Night:
Then hastens to restore the morning Light.
The Winde flyes to the South, shifts to the North;
And wheeles about to where it first brake forth.
All Rivers run into th'insatiate Maine;
From thence, to their old Fountaines creepe againe.
Incessantly all toyle. The searching Minde,
The Eye, and Eare, no satisfaction finde.

(In Sandys 1638: 1)

The circuitous activity of 'generations', the Sun and the elements in 1:4–7 has elicited a range of responses. The cosmological debates of the Middle Ages in particular included Eccl. 1:4 and 3:11 in their proof-texting arsenal. Both verses suggest that the Earth itself is not subject to the same mutability or transience as the rest of creation. Moses Maimonides, in his *Guide for the*

Perplexed (*c*.1190), defends 'Solomon' from the idea attributed to him that the world has existed 'from all eternity':

> But as to the existence of the world from eternity, there is no passage [in Ecclesiastes] to indicate that such was his belief, though there is one, it is true, which shews that *he believed that* the world will not perish, but last for ever. Because then they saw that there was a verse proving the stability of the world, they thought erroneously that he believed that the world was not created. Now the verse which speaks of the future eternal duration of the world is this: 'The earth abides for ever.' [1:4] Some have interpreted the expression as [*l*ᵉ*'ôlām*] signifying only for a 'definite' time. But I should like to know what they will make of the passage which we find in David, Ps. x. 4, 5: 'He has founded the earth on its basis that it should not be removed for ever and ever,' [*ôlām wᵉ'ēd*]. But if you should say that the expression [*ôlām wᵉ'ēd*] does not demonstrate its eternal duration, but only its duration for a definite time, you will necessarily say at the same time, that the Creator will only reign for a definite time . . . (2:29; in Preston 1845: 18–19; italics in Preston, my transliterations)[8]

Here Maimonides executes philological exegesis in order to appeal to the plain (if cosmological!) sense of this verse. In a similar vein, medieval commentators on Ecclesiastes related the circuitous waters of the sea in 1:7 to Aristotle's similar notion in *Meteorologica* (2.2): 'Many of these (rivers) form lakes . . . but all of them come round again in a circle to the original source of their flow' (in Smalley 1949: 330). William of Auvergne, *c*.1220, reflected the harmonious agreement between Aristotle and Ecclesiastes, in which 'Aristotle agrees with the Scriptures' (in Smalley 1949: 331). Karlfried Froehlich unpacks the scenario further:

> Hugh of St. Victor treated the verse [1:7] as scientific information, drawing a parallel to the circulation of the body's blood supply. William of Auvergne quoted Aristotle's *Meteorologica* . . . He was cited by the Dominican Postill which added a verse from the poet Lucan . . . It was only when William of Moerbeke's new translation of the *Meteorologica* became available in the 1260s that the matter was clarified. Siger of Brabant pointed out that the real Aristotle did not support, but clearly contradicted the recycling theory of Qoh 1:7. (2000: 531)

This harmonizing approach to philosophy and Scripture would be all but overturned in the early stages of the Renaissance (cf. Cameron 2001: 70).

---

[8]   Note that Ginsburg (1861: 58, 525–8) takes issue with Preston's translation and retranslates this passage, but the implications of his newer translation are not entirely clear.

While many pre- and early modern interpreters triangulate Ecclesiastes to classical philosophy and good doctrine, as in the example just discussed, few before the 1800s make comparative use of writers outside Jewish and Christian tradition for non-doctrinal illumination. However, commenting on 1:5, John Trapp makes his own use of a (pop- or high-?) cultural text:

> For use hereof, hear the Poet [marg. reads 'Catull', i.e. probably the Roman poet Catullus, *c.*84–*c.*54 BCE]:
>
> > The Sunne doth set and rise;
> > But wee contrariwise,
> > Sleep after one short light,
> > An everlasting night.
> >   (1650: 11)

Of commentaries of this period especially, Trapp's strategy is highly unusual for finding 'use hereof' in such material. And the implication of the poem in relation to Ecclesiastes is apt: commentators still struggle over the question of whether he is drawing a sharp contrast between the joyful strength and steadiness of the sun and the elements to the misery of the human condition, or whether he is suggesting that creation, too, can only be miserable (see the classic discussion in Whybray 1988; cf. the discussion of Hemingway's *The Sun Also Rises*, above, p. 69).

Victorian novelist Charles Kingsley, one of the first of the Anglican clergy to support Charles Darwin's theories, recognized in 1:8, in his historical 'prose idyll' *North Devon* (July 1849), a subtle affection for nature.

> Some may call it a pretty conceit. I call it a great world-wide law, which reaches from earth to heaven. Whatever the Preacher may have thought it in a moment of despondency, what is it but a blessing that 'sun, and wind, and rivers, and ocean', as he says, and 'all things, are full of labour – man cannot utter it'. This sea which bears us would rot and poison, did it not sweep in and out here twice a day in swift refreshing current . . . Wonderful ocean-world! (in Kingsley 1880: 269–70)

Kingsley is a good example of readings that seem to emerge so clearly from an ideological momentum, for he writes – as will Robert Louis Stevenson (see p. 252) and as the Renaissance interpreters did not – with an infectious enthusiasm for the discovery of knowledge. There seem to be few moments when the cultural *Zeitgeist* manages to drive such positive assessment of Qoheleth's words.

The 'elemental force' of Qoheleth's opening verses is subtly rendered in Christina Rossetti's 'Subject to Like Passions as We Are' (1892), which like so much of her poetry is liberally and naturally immersed in Qoheleth's imagery (in this case of 1:7–9):

> Experience bows a sweet contented face,
>   Still setting her seal that God is true:
>   Beneath the sun, she knows, is nothing new;
> All things that go return with measured pace,
> Winds, rivers, man's still recommencing race: –
>   While Hope beyond earth's circle strains her view,
>   Past sun and moon, and rain and rainbow too,
> Enamoured of unseen eternal grace.
>
> (In Rossetti 1986: 251)

Rossetti here achieves on a small scale what many see as Qoheleth's achievement: an inexplicable concord between the proving 'seal' of experience (which includes the 'truth' of God) and the ominous distance of hope. It is the Qoheleth-like tension (here at least partially resolved) between these two notions (of burdensome experience and the expectation of something better) that animates a number of Rossetti's *vanitas* poems (see above, pp. 133–4).

As any query to a web search engine will show, the phrase 'there is nothing new under the sun' is still alive and well in the parlance of popular culture (though perhaps less so an awareness of its source). Indeed, the adage is a good example of the quotable Qoheleth, which is not to say that it does not take on different shades of meaning in its variable contexts. In Renaissance readings it often functions as short-hand to underscore the dangers of philosophy (i.e. it is subsumed in that programmatic reading – see Bacon, below). Sixteenth- and seventeenth-century verse exhibits a similar trend (Lok 1597: 'We thinke our world with wisedome doth abound . . . /But ouer-weening thoughts this toy [the world] begits'), which can be seen in the paraphrases of 1:9–11 of Brome, Lok, Quarles and Sandys (see pp. 55–7). Often in post-1800 readings Qoheleth's words do not seem to signify some ominous portent so much as to demonstrate the author's own 'impressive' grasp of an ancient witticism.

For Francis Bacon (see Introduction, pp. 50–1) the truism of 1:9 can only complement the wider Renaissance exposition of the dangers of philosophy. So, in the enlarged version of his *Essays* (*The Essays or Counsels, Civil and Moral*, 1625) Bacon begins his 'Of Vicissitude of Things' (Essay 59): 'Salomon saith, *there is no new thing upon the earth*: So that as *Plato* had an imagination, that all knowledge was but remembrance: so *Solomon* giveth his sentence, *that all novelty is but oblivion*. Whereby you may see, that the river of *Lethe* runneth as well above ground, as below.' He then concludes the essay, 'But it is not good to look too long upon these turning wheels of vicissitude, lest we become giddy. As for the philology of them, that is but a circle of tales, and therefore not fit for this writing' (in Bacon 1730: 3.380, 382). In other words, there is an implicit judgment in Qoheleth's observation that only further serves to underscore the perilous pursuit of knowledge. The poet John Collop makes a similar point some 30 years later in a popular tract on religious tolerance entitled *Medici Catholicon* (1656, repr. in 1658 and 1667 as *Charity Commended*). In his (second) Preface, 'To the Romanist', Collop addresses the circuity of learning, understood in a manner not unlike Bacon's 'circle of tales':

> Error is of a teeming Constitution, this Hydra's heads multiply by amputation, there is no end of writing of Bookes the wisest of men dead said, and the wisest of men living lament. Study is a wearinesss [*sic*] to the flesh, I wish most mens studies were not onely a warines [*sic*] to their own but all flesh ... while there is nothing new under the Sun, not onely bookes but men are transcribed, men are liv'd ore againe: the Pythagorean Metempsychy is verified: the revolution of planets reduce the same constitutions, same errors: hence Learning is in the circle and not in the Progresse: error hath alter'd her modes and garbs with times, someties more gaudy, better painted, trim'd and drest to become more tempting, but still hath carried her old rotten body through all her veils and disguises discoverable to a curious inquirie. (Collop 1667: dedication, n.p.)

Such readings summon the full force of Qoheleth's words to condemn what is new in the realm of the intellect, but they do little to examine the most obvious question: what did Qoheleth mean by 'new'?

Just a few years earlier Patrick Cary grappled more with the inherent incongruity of Qoheleth's observation (as happens so frequently with readings of 12:12) in his *Fallax et Instabilis* (1651), which uses 1:9 as an epigraph:

> 'Tis a strange thing this world,
> Nothing but change I see:
> And yett itt is most true
> That in't there's nothing new,
> Though all seeme new to mee.
>
> . . .
>
> All things below doe change,
> The sea in rest ne'er lyes;
>
> . . .
>
> The sun does thincke nothing of all this strange;
> Since all things here still change.

And this should drive the reader to seek that which does not change:

> Lett none then fix his heart
> Uppon such trifling toyes;
> But seeke some obiect out,
> Whose change hee ne'er may doubt;
>   (In Cary 1820: 53–4)

This reading exposes the tension between the appearance of real change in the world and the potentially frightening reality that there is no such thing as real change, and this prods at the very heart of Qoheleth's thinking (cf. 1:10, 15; 3:14–15).

A more accomplished reading of the same interpretive friction observed by Cary was published by bookseller John Dunton in an eccentric collection of letters splendidly titled *The Art of Living Incognito* (1700). The letters are whimsically semi-autobiographical, and like much of Dunton's writing blur the real and the fantastic (see Hunter 1979: 29, 31). The setting and characters who exchange letters may bear some relation to reality, but the volume is really about Dunton himself, as he suggests in his first letter, 'Of Living Incognito': 'as others Squander away their Time in Publick Hurries, and in rambling from *one Vanity to another*; I chuse rather to retire to a Solitary Village (Blest with a Neighbouring Grove, a Purling-Stream, two Cuckoos, and one Nightingale) and here under the *Covert of a spreading Tree*, I intend to devote the remaining part of my Time, *To study my self*' (1700: 1). In his fourth letter, Dunton devotes nearly 20 pages to proving in quite spectacular fashion that there really is nothing new under the sun. He first relates this to the topics that he is undertaking in his letters and wishes to inform the 'Madam' he is here addressing what he means by intending to write 'uncommon' letters:

> 'tis time now, that I tell ye that by *Uncommon*, I did not mean NEW, but only Subjects that were *Curious*, or very rarely handled. – No Madam, it had been a great Presumption in me to have pretended to any thing *New*, when *Solomon* tells us. – *There is nothing NEW under the Sun*. And Dr. *Winter* adds, *Nor in the Moon neither*, (a Picture of this Mutable World) of whose encrease, tho we have every Year *NEW Ones* a full dozen, Yet all is but the *Old One over and over* . . . The Sun returneth every morning to the same place he came from, with like form, and self-same substance – The *Days and Nights* pass by course, and ever continue of like Essence . . . Nothing is the Object of our Senses, but what is ordinary and familiar: We see nothing strange and New. (1700: 42–3)

And thus he proceeds to list scores of examples that demonstrate his case, from news items that are not really 'new' at all, to the discourse of the coffee house – the never-ending string of happenings can never be new. 'News' may report of an Earl's Cutting his own Throat, and then flinging the Razor out of the Window; – of the penitent Death of some great Lord; – of a Bloody Fight; – of a *Lover hanging himself*; – of a Virgin Ravisht . . . But these '(*tho Real Truths*)' are no *New Things*, but what we have seen over and over. – Not but I must own, if there were a *New Thing* under the Sun, *the Author of the Flying Post* wou'd find it out: But he's an honest Gentleman, and writes nothing but Truth; and *Truth is always the same*; and if his Papers be always the same, what News can there be in them? (1700: 46)

Dunton's overall goal is one of peculiar application: 'when *Solomon*, who was many Hundred Years before St. *Paul*, pronounces of his own Times, That there was not then, nor shou'd ever be, *any New Thing*? How much more then is it true in our Time, being so many years after him? – Thus have I proved there is *Nothing New*' (1700: 50). Indeed, he goes on to apply the judgment to fashion, literature, politics – until with exasperation he claims, 'Madam shall I stop *here*? For you see the further I search, the less hopes I have of finding any *Thing New*?' (1700: 55).

The letter that follows, 'The Lady's Answer', reveals a compliant respondent who has seen her '*Vulgar Error of expecting* new things, *which* Solomon *Affirms the World can never shew, which yet Experience seems to contradict*' (1700: 57). But this is the juncture at which Dunton's extravagant exposition turns mightily insightful, for with this dialogic device he grasps that opposition of desire and reality so key to Ecclesiastes. Dunton now uses the 'Lady's' voice to oppose himself, and in so doing questions, with notable precision, the programmatic reading of resistance to 'new' knowledge:

> But I see not how Solomon *in saying there was* nothing New under the Sun, *could possibly extend it so far as to Arts and Sciences . . . and who could say there was* nothing new, *with respect to Arts and Sciences with less reason then* Solomon, *who sat himself upon* a Throne of so new an Invention . . . *They say, and with great reason too, there are some Inventions so beneficial to the World, that 'tis impossible that being once known, they could ever be lost or laid aside, as* the Invention of Printing, of the Sea Card, Guns and Mills, *which for certain some Ages past the World was Ignorant of, and therefore must be the* new Inventions of later Ages . . . *it binders not but that many things are* thought New, *only for having been so long disus'd that they are out of remembrance.* (1700: 58)

'The Lady' then turns her critique on Dunton's claims about his own project of self-examination:

> Sure Hope has represented to your Fancy *some excessive fine Prospect of learning the Art of Living Incognito, which must be New, for I believe you never was before*

under such an Inchantment; I'll go no farther, therefore, for an Instance then your Self, to find a proof of something new ... there needs no more to convince you of your mistaking the sence of Solomon, I shall add no more, but conclude. (1700: 59–60)

Subsequent readings of 1:9 become increasingly light-hearted. So George Almar, in his play *Pedlar's Acre: Or, The Wife of Seven Husbands* (1831), treats the theme with an obviously comic touch:

> There is nothing new under the sun,
> No no, – ah, no! there's nothing new:
> The skies are as bright as in days of yore,
> The waters beneath are as blue.
>
> . . .
>
> And times have not changed, I do truly believe,
> Since they turned out of Paradise Adam and Eve.
> There is nothing new under the sun, &c.
> (Act I, sc. 2; 1831: 24)

Similarly, in other poetry and drama from the nineteenth century onwards Qoheleth's maxim might best be regarded as a witticism to be nuanced. Matthew Gregory Lewis (who became famous at the age of 19 for his gothic novel *The Monk*, 1796), in the epilogue of his play *Adelmorn, the Outlaw* (1801), provides a good example:

> Since Solomon's time (he who lived with such glee
> In a nest full of wives, like a kind of king-bee)
> To the days of King George, undisputed has run
> This maxim – 'There's nothing new under the sun!' –
> Our Bard (who, no more than myself, as I'm told,
> Likes a foolish thing better because the thing's old)
> Was resolved that this proverb to-night he'd derange,
> And produce something singular, novel, and strange;
> So painted a Wife, who with sentiment true
> Dreads the death of her husband – I'm sure now, that's new.
> But if any dispute it, I beg them to name
> What part of this audience can furnish the same.
> (1801: 99)

Or take the protagonist of Frederick Reynolds's *Begone Dull Care: A Comedy, in Five Acts* (1808), who uses the adage to exposit his 'charming' resistance to married life: 'for the wisest of all men didn't say there was nothing new under the sun, till he had tried a hundred wives. – So, at any rate, I'll try one wife.

– This way, Madam . . .' (Act I, sc. 1; 1808: 7). Or again, take the relatively well-known example from journalist and satirist Ambrose Bierce: 'There is nothing new under the sun, but there are lots of things we don't know yet' (this is often attributed to his *The Devil's Dictionary*, 1911, but I have been unable to locate it in the critical edition, Bierce 2000).

Just as 1:9–10 raises the question of what Qoheleth could have meant by 'new', so 1:11 leaves open the reference of memory. The Karaite commentator Yephet ben 'Ali (*c*.990) reflected on such referentiality in his Ecclesiastes commentary: '*No remembrance* may mean that the people themselves have no remembrance, or it may mean there is no remembrance of them, no vestiges, that is, edifices which are passed on from *generation* to *generation*. The latest is remembered, but the former is always forgotten, and so on' (in 'Ali 1969: 165).

Qoheleth's dramatic introduction at 1:12–13 marks him as a seeker of truth, for he will use his immeasurable wisdom to examine *all that is done*. Given the totality of his scope, it is natural to see Qoheleth as casting his investigation to the farthest possible reaches in order to know what makes it all tick, a sense captured well by Jerome in his commentary (388/9):

> Ecclesiastes therefore set his mind first of all to the acquisition of wisdom, and pursuing this beyond what is allowed, wanted to know the causes and reasoning why children are easily snatched by the Devil; why the righteous and the wicked are equally punished in shipwrecks; and whether these events happen as a result of fate, or by the decree of God. And if by fate, where is providence? If by decree, where is God's justice? With such desire to know these things, he said, I understand the great care and torturing anxiety experienced in many things, which was given to man by God, in order that he might desire to know that which he is not allowed to know. But the cause is inborn first, and God then gives vexation. (2000: *ad loc.*; cf. *Midrash Song of Songs* 1.1.7, which describes Qoheleth/Solomon as an 'explorer of wisdom')

Perhaps surprisingly Jerome does not seek to take the edge off Qoheleth's audacious quest, nor to avoid its theological consequence, the acquisition of forbidden knowledge.

Another early critical note (although much later than Jerome) is sounded by Samuel ibn Tibbon (*c*.1200) regarding the relationship of 1:12 to what precedes (which he regards as a *prooenium*, a prologue): 'That he mentioned his name and his kingdom and the name of his city is proof that this is the beginning of the book. This is the way of those who compose books. Even when they mention their names in the preface of their books, they mention them again at the beginning of the subject ['*inyan*] of the book' (in Robinson 2001: 123 n. 29; cf. Robinson's comments, ibid. 85). He is anticipating such approaches as Edwin Good's on 1:1–11 by some 900 years (Good [1978] sees 1:12 as the real beginning of Qoheleth's thought and the preceding 1:3–10 a pre-emptive, illustrative poetic discourse). (See the Introduction, pp. 31–2, for Yephet's ben 'Ali's strikingly modern observation on 1:12 *c*.990.)

We have seen in the Introduction that 1:17–18 proved popular with Renaissance sceptical thinkers (see pp. 44, 50, for examples). An earlier example is seen in Eudes of Châteauroux (*c*.1190–1273), a 'particularly gifted preacher', and most significantly one who 'as cardinal . . . masterminded the propaganda campaign for Louis IX's first crusade in France' (Maier 2000: 9). In a sermon on the invitation to 'take up the cross', his comments even at this relatively early period paraphrastically relate Socratic scepticism to Qoheleth: 'man knows only this: that he knows nothing, as the Philosopher says' (sermon 4.4, in Maier 2000: 163).

Two typical examples from the Renaissance period will help round out and conclude this whole chapter. In 1576 the poet and 'literary innovator' George Gascoigne closely adapted Pope Innocent III's *De Contemptu Mundi sive de Miseria Condicionis Humane*, which enjoyed huge popularity nearly 400 years previously (1195; see Introduction, p. 46). The adaptation appears as the first section of his *The Droomme of Doomes Day*, 'The View of Worldly Vanities'.

> Let wyse men search narrowly, let them heedely consider the height of the heavens, the breadth of the yearth, and the depth of the Sea . . . and let them always eyther learne or teach, and in so doing, what shall they fynde out of this busie toyle of our life, but traveyle and payne? that knewe he by experience, which sayed: For asmuch as in great wisedome and knowledge there is great disdayne, and he which increaseth knowledge increaseth also payne & travayle [1:18], for although whilest that he sercheth it out, he must sweat many tymes, and watch many nightes with sweat and labor, yet is there scarcely any thing so vyle, or any thing so easy, that man can fully and thorowly understand it, nor that he can clerely comprehende it, unlesse perchaunce that is perfectly knowne, that nothinge is perfectly knowne. (In Gascoigne 1910: 2.223; Gascoigne's translation is very much in agreement with Lewis's critical edition of *De Contemptu*, in Innocent III 1978: 108, 110)

Like Francis Bacon and Pierre du Moulin, Gascoigne, voicing Innocent's much earlier concerns, goes on to develop the thesis of the human failure to grasp the 'reason of Gods workes, yea the more he laboreth to seeke it, so much the lesse shall he fynde it, therefore they faile in the searching, how narrowly so ever they search' (2.223). Paraphrasing 7:29, Gascoigne concludes, 'God first made man, and he hath wrapped him selfe in sundry and infinite questions' (2.224). Not long after, Pierre Charron, a close friend and disciple of Montaigne, in his *Of Wisdome Three Books* (*De la sagesse*, 1601), sets out a lengthy discourse on 'the knowledge of our selves and our humane condition, which is the foundation of Wisdome' (in Charron 1640, unnumbered preface). When discussing the responsibilities of parents to their children in undertaking the proper teaching of science, Charron is reminded of Qoheleth: 'One of the sufficientest men of knowledge that ever was, spake of Science, as of a thing not onely vaine, but hurtfull, painefull, and tedious. To be briefe, Science may make us more humane and courteous, but not more honest . . . The wise man said, that he that increaseth knowledge, increaseth sorrow' (in Charron 1640: 502; similarly, see Moulin, above, p. 109). For Qoheleth's readers in this period it seems that the only way to avoid sorrow is to avoid the 'sciences' altogether – although, with the possible exception of John Dunton, the irony of such sentiments in books that largely drove forward the study of the humanities was entirely lost. As with the observable change of approach to 1:9–10 (from warning to witticism), as the perceived 'danger' of the sciences subsided, so the verse itself faded from public use.

Chapter 2 shows Qoheleth at his most autobiographical (see Christianson 1998a: 40–1), the repetitive use of 'I' lending the passage a solipsistic tone. From the first verse, however, a constructive outcome is envisaged, for this is an exercise in self-reflection, couched in terms of the construction of his self ('I said, *I* in my heart, "Come, I will test you with joy . . ."'). Qoheleth continues to ask programmatic and universal questions about the use of pleasure and the possibility of some profit or advantage in the 'few days' of life (2:2–3). It is here, particularly in verses 4–10, that Qoheleth's persona matches most closely that of King Solomon in 1 Kings 3–11, which describes the immense wealth, wisdom and renown he acquired from Yahweh, but also the means of enhancing his affluence by forced labour and excessive levies (1 Kgs 4:29–34; 5:13–18 [MT 5:9–14, 27–32]). Indeed, his own extravagant palace and grounds (which were laden with gold and took 13 years to build) are contrasted with the less spectacular construction of Yahweh's house (which took Solomon seven years to build; 1 Kgs 6–7; 9:15–21). But the point of Qoheleth's detailed recall is not so much to evoke Solomon's relationship to Yahweh as to ask what happens when there is no restraint on human desire, and to see whether wisdom can alter the outcome. What happens when Qoheleth takes (as Solomon took, or was 'given') *all* that his eyes desired (2:10; cf. 1 Kgs 9:1, 11)? To answer this, Qoheleth extends the traditional narrative of Solomon in his own distinct language. He turns to consider this 'portion', all that *he* had done with his hands, and deems it *hebel* (see above, pp. 98–100) and a pursuit of wind (v. 11). In doing so he questions the worth of wisdom itself and wonders whether the fates of fools and sages are really that different after all (vv. 12–16).

As Qoheleth, Solomon is transformed into a reflective and empirical examiner of experience. But he is also made a morose Solomon, one who in verses 17–23 gives himself over to despair, regret, restlessness and self-loathing, and wonders again at the point of human endeavour. The whole, however, is narrated as completed action from a distinct posture, creating a 'then' (younger Qoheleth) and a 'now' (older, narrating Qoheleth). That is, these are things that Solomon/Qoheleth once experienced and now regards from the vantage point of experience (further, see Christianson 1998a: 210–11, 246–7). So his first note of hope, his first recognition that *something* good comes from God, that God can empower people to enjoy the produce of their toil, is narrated more as a timeless reality ('There is nothing better...', vv. 24–5; a theme to be restated throughout the book). But there is a fly in the ointment. It worries Qoheleth that even these gifts of God are subject to his impenetrable discretion and power. And that, of course, is *hebel* and a pursuit of wind (v. 26).

Wrestling with the Test of Pleasure: 2:1–10

Many readers have seen in chapter 2 a portrait of licentious abandonment and have sought to make clear that Qoheleth is not endorsing such activity. So Gregory of Nyssa, in his homilies on Eccl. 1–3:13 (*c.*380), recognizes here the dangers of encouraging the base inclinations. He paraphrases Qoheleth at 2:1–2 with 'I would say to this servile and mindless merriment, "Why are you doing these things? why do you let womanly softness take over a manly nature? why do you slacken the keenly tuned mind? ... [Why,] I ask you, do you turn murky the clear atmosphere of intelligent ideas ...?"' (hom. 2, in Gregory of Nyssa 1993: 57). As he develops his reading of chapter 2 in homilies 3–5, Gregory relates the 'confession' of the Ecclesiast as a paradigmatic example:

> For Solomon says this quite frankly, making a public statement, and setting up
> for all to see, like a written notice, the confession of the things he has
> done . . . whether he really did these things, or made the story up for our bene-
> fit . . . I cannot say precisely . . . However, whether it is by benevolent design that
> he discusses things which had not happened as if they had, and condemns them
> as though he had experienced them, in order that we might turn away from
> desire for what is condemned . . . or whether he deliberately lowered himself to
> the enjoyment of such things . . . it is for each to decide freely for himself, which-
> ever conjecture he likes to pursue. (Hom. 3, in Gregory of Nyssa 1993: 61)

Here Gregory is acutely aware of what has now become a fine and controver-
sial epistemological distinction between historical and fictional truth, the
world of real and implied authors, and he concludes that the reader's free
decision is in fact paramount. Indeed, Gregory pinpoints an issue that
Qoheleth's readers have frequently confronted: what kind of playful construction is this in which Qoheleth is somehow both himself and Solomon, and
who admonishes his readers through the (seemingly fictional) telling of his
own life?

Gregory also uses chapter 2 to relate one of the most nuanced attacks on
slavery in antiquity. In homily 4, commenting on 2:7 ('I got myself slaves and
slave-girls . . .'), Gregory challenges Qoheleth/Solomon. The humanist and
theological grounds on which he does so are remarkable for their time:

> For what is such a gross example of arrogance . . . as for a human being to think
> himself the master of his own kind? 'I got me slaves and slave-girls', he says, and
> 'homebred slaves were born for me'. Do you notice the enormity of the boast?
> This kind of language is raised up as a challenge to God . . . [W]hen someone
> turns the property of God into his own property and arrogates dominion to his
> own kind, so as to think himself the owner of men and women, what is he doing
> but overstepping his own nature through pride, regarding himself as something
> different from his subordinates? (In Gregory of Nyssa 1993: 73)

Even more remarkably, Gregory continues, seemingly lost in indignation, and
now imaginatively addresses 'Solomon' directly:

> 'I got me slaves and slave-girls'. What do you mean? You condemn man to
> slavery, when his nature is free and possesses free will, and you legislate in com-
> petition with God, overturning his law for the human species . . . For what price,
> tell me? What did you find in existence worth as much as this human nature?
> What price did you put on rationality? How many obols did you reckon the
> equivalent of the likeness of God? . . . To God alone belongs this power; or
> rather, not even to God himself. For *his gracious gifts*, it says, *are irrevocable* (Rom
> 11,29) . . . But if God does not enslave what is free, who is he that sets his own

power above God's? ... Whenever a human being is for sale, therefore, nothing less than the owner of the earth is led into the sale-room ... But has the scrap of paper, and the written contract, and the counting out of obols deceived you into thinking yourself the master of *the image of God*? What folly! ... Your origin is from the same ancestors, your life is of the same kind, sufferings of soul and body prevail alike over you who own him and over the one who is subject to your ownership – pains and pleasures, merriment and distress, sorrows and delights, rages and terrors, sickness and death. Is there any difference in these things between the slave and his owner? Do they not draw in the same air as they breathe? Do they not see the sun in the same way? (In Gregory of Nyssa 1993: 73–5)

Yet another noteworthy feature of Gregory's outburst is that elsewhere in the homilies he shows great deference towards Solomon – for even if he showed foolishness in his youth, Gregory always casts him as the great Repenter. But not here, where he refuses to let Solomon off the hook.

Readers have recognized that Qoheleth's failed 'test' was directed towards an ultimately constructive outcome. So Dionysius of Alexandria (*c.*200–*c.*265) in his commentary on Ecclesiastes writes, 'see how he reckons up a multitude of houses and fields, and the other things which he mentions, and then finds nothing profitable in them. For neither was he any better in soul by reason of these things, nor by their means did he gain friendship with God' (commenting on 2:10, in Coxe 1978: 112). Luther, too, recognizes Qoheleth's struggle for something 'better' and suggests that readers accept God's gifts and not make Qoheleth's mistake of contriving happiness. Commenting on 2:1 in his commentary (1532), he uses an engaging example:

It is as though he were saying: '. . . I shall create ease and tranquility . . .' But this, too, was useless . . . Tranquility is not attainable except from the Word and work of God. Experience itself teaches this. Often dinner parties are arranged to create a happy atmosphere, with foods and entertainment intended to make the guests happy. But usually it comes out just the opposite way, and only seldom does a good party result. Either there are gloomy and solemn faces present, or something else upsets all the arrangements, especially when there is such deliberation and planning about how much fun it will be. By contrast, it often happens that someone happens upon a most joyful dinner party by accident, that is, by the gift of God. (In Luther 1972: 29)

Luther's illustration is fitting, for Qoheleth will also come to the conclusion that joy may come, but only through the 'accidental' gift of God.

Qoheleth's experiment is of course couched in the most extreme, even absurd terms, and this has not been lost on many readers, particularly

Qoheleth's versifiers. The sheer extravagance of his test is impeccably illus-trated in George Sandys's 1632 paraphrase:

> Then sought the cares of Study to decline
> With liberall feasts, and flowing Bowles of Wine.
> With all my wisedome exercis'd, to try
> If she at length with folly could comply:
> And to discover that Beatitude,
> Which Mortals all their lives so much pursu'd.
> Great workes I finish'd; sumptuous Houses built:
> My Cedar roofes with Gold of Ophir guilt.
>
> . . .
>
> For service, and Delight, I purchased
> Both Men and Maides: more in my House were bred.
>
> . . .
>
> Sweet Voices, Musicke of all sorts, invite
> My curious Eares; and sealt with their delight.
> In greater fluencie no Mortall raign'd:
> In height of all, my wisedome I retain'd.
> I had the Beauties which my Eyes admir'd;
> Gave to my Heart what ever it desir'd:
>
> . . .
>
> Then I survey'd all that my hands had done:
> My troublesome delights. Beneath the Sun
> What solid good can mans indeavour finde?
> All is but vanitie, and griefe of Minde.
>   (In Sandys 1638: 2–3)

While rendering in verse has its obvious compromises of sense, at the same time it is an exercise in rethinking the text, and in the hands of Sandys (whom John Dryden described as 'Ingenious and Learned . . . the best Versifier of the former Age'; 1700: unnumbered preface) is something of exceptional worth.

In his 1759 *Précis* of Ecclesiastes, Voltaire also notably conveys the extra-vagance and subsequent palpable frustration of Qoheleth's failed quest:

> What use to me will have been my supreme power,
> which says nothing to the senses, nothing to the heart;
> brilliant opinion, phantom of happiness,
> from which one never, in truth, has enjoyment?
>
> I sought that happiness, which was fleeing from my grasp,
> in my cedar palaces, by a hundred fountains.

I asked for it again to the voice of my Sirens.
It was not within me, I did not find it.

I burdened my mind with too much nourishment.
To satisfy my pleasure I exhausted all my efforts;
but, fleeing from nature, my pleasure was dulled.
True pleasures come only with true needs.

(In Christianson 2005: 476)

As one of Voltaire's few (if not only) empathetic readings of the Bible, this clearly resonates with his own sense of despair over the 'phantom of happiness'. And just as Christina Rossetti would later do, Voltaire adopts Qoheleth's voice as his own (see Introduction, pp. 62–5).

Canadian poet Frederick George Scott, in his 'Solomon' (*c.*1886), is also concerned to convey the full depth of Qoheleth's immersion in pleasure and power:

A double line of columns, white as snow,
And vaulted with mosaics rich in flowers,
Makes square this cypress grove where fountain showers
From golden basins cool the grass below:
While from that archway strains of music flow,
And laughings of fair girls beguile the hours.
But brooding like one held by evil powers,
The great King heeds not, pacing sad and slow.

His heart hath drained earth's pleasures to the lees,
Hath quivered with life's finest ecstasies:
Yet now some power reveals as in a glass
The soul's unrest and death's dark mysteries,
And down the courts the scared slaves watch him pass,
Reiterating, '*Omnia Vanitas!*'

(In Scott 2004)

This imaginative retelling effectively contrasts Qoheleth/Solomon's 'brooding' sense of doom with the airy and musical setting of his palatial grounds, powerless to effect any meaningful change in the great king. Scott's second stanza deftly picks up on the restlessness and futility of Qoheleth's conclusion in 2:20–3 – our cue to look ahead to the next section.

Understanding Wisdom, Folly and God's Gifts: 2:11–24

Qoheleth's deliberate contrast of folly and wisdom in 2:13 ('wisdom excels folly') is taken up in the kabbalistic *Zohar* (*c.*1290), which recognizes its implications and relates it to other parts of Ecclesiastes: 'Wisdom actually derives benefit from folly, because if stupidity did not exist, wisdom's worth would go unrecognized . . . This is the significance of "God has made the one in contrast with the other" [7:14], and it is also written "It is good for you to take hold of the one; and do not withdraw your hand from the other" [7:18]' (in Lachower and Tishby 1989: 3.1352; cf. ch. 10, p. 218). This insight of tensile opposites is not unlike Qoheleth's broader concept of *hebel*, for *hebel* frustrates him precisely because he is driven by a desire to see the world run straight and not crooked (1:15; cf. 7:29), to be able to grasp what principle is at work in what God does (3:11; 8:17 *et passim*) and to become wise (7:23) – in other words, *hebel* exists because Qoheleth can at least imagine a world without it. Elsewhere in the *Zohar*, Qoheleth's development of the comparison is considered: '[Rabbi Simeon] began by quoting: "The wise man, his eyes are in his head" [2:14]. Now, where would a man's eyes be if not in his head? In his body, or in his arm? Is this the way in which the wise man is distinguished from the rest of humanity?' (in Lachower and Tishby 1989: 1.201). The answer lies in an obscure talmudic stipulation, but the import is that the wise man's eyes 'are directed toward Him [i.e. the *Shekinah*, the presence of God] who rests upon his head'. This is more typical of the *Zohar's* tendency to make Scripture provide the language of its mystical discourse.

Ancient Jewish readers recognized in 2:17–19 the voice of Solomon regretting the loss of his kingdom to two foolish sons (Jerome makes reference to this reading but dissents, preferring to see it as the inheritance and squandering of wisdom itself; *Commentary*, 388/9, Jerome 2000: *ad loc.*). This reading becomes so entrenched that Qoheleth's professed hatred of 'life' (*ha-chayyim*) in 2:17 is taken by Rashi (1040–1105) to be 'the living' and therefore prophetically refers to 'the generation of Rehoboam, who were wicked' (in Rosenberg 1992: 26). Oliver Cromwell would read the passage with a more immediate political sense, and with a *pesher*-like application to rival any midrash. In his fourth speech to Parliament of 1655 he addressed the issue of hereditary peerage and found help in Qoheleth's wisdom: 'To have men chosen for their love of God, and to truth and justice; and not to have it hereditary. For as it is in the Ecclesiastes: "Who knoweth whether he may beget a fool or a wise man?" [2:19] Honest or not honest, whatever they be, they must come in, on that plan; because the government is made a patrimony' (in Nicoll and Stoddart 1910: 536).

One of Qoheleth's more prominent themes, enjoying the gifts of God, first occurs in 2:24. Christian and Jewish allegorists fixed this verse squarely to the broken body of Jesus and faithful Torah study respectively (see Introduction, p. 25, and note George Bradley in the Hermeneutical Postscript, p. 260). But readers from both contingents have managed to wrest themselves from that approach. Jewish philosopher Saadia Gaon, in the closing argument of his *Book of Beliefs and Opinions* (933), exegetes what is 'good' in service to God: 'a person should exert himself in his mundane affairs to the extent required for his well-being. He should eat and drink what is permissible in accordance with his need . . . Such a laudable choice represents the net result of the remark made by Solomon . . . in three different places in his book' (in Gaon 1948: 404–5), at which point he cites 2:24, 3:13 and 5:17 (MT). Centuries later, Dietrich Bonhoeffer writes in a spirit akin to Gaon in his *Ethics* (composed in portions from 1940 to 1943, collected and published posthumously in 1949). In a passage on 'The Right to Bodily Life', Bonhoeffer defends a Christian embrace of natural 'bodily joys'. In the course of this argument he pours out a stream of citations from Ecclesiastes, beginning with 2:24 (then 3:12; 9:7–9; 11:9) and concluding with 2:25. These flow naturally into his subsequent point that

> Eating and drinking do not merely serve the purpose of keeping the body in good health, but they afford natural joy in bodily living. Clothing is not intended merely as a mean covering for the body, but also as an adornment of the body. Recreation is not designed solely to increase working efficiency, but it provides the body with its due measure of repose and enjoyment . . . The life of the body assumes its full significance only with the fulfilment of its inherent claim to joy. (In Bonhoeffer 1971: 133)

Of course the 'claim to joy' for readers begins in 2:24 and, as Whybray (1982) so elegantly illustrated, is restated with increasing emphasis (further on the joy theme, see Testimonia, pp. 9–10).

Ecclesiastes 3:1–8

The first verse of this celebrated passage suggests a universal perspective ('For *everything* there is a season . . .'), and the subsequent range of experiences might suggest an attempt to represent exemplary human experience, particularly since the first pair of experiences is the most universal of all: birth and death. Read in the context of Qoheleth's larger narrative, however, the catalogue of times reads something like a list of disconcerting portents. These times are restricted at God's discretion, as Qoheleth is at pains to make clear elsewhere (even immediately following in 3:11) and in this way the poem anticipates the conclusions he will reach in the latter half of the book especially, that the time and purpose of human and divine activity alike are inscrutable (8:5–7, 16–17; 9:1, 12; 10:14; 11:5; cf. 7:17, 24). The 'experiences' themselves can also be understood in relation to Qoheleth's ideas elsewhere. For example, the time to seek (*bqsh*, one of Qoheleth's favourite words) and to lose (*'bd*) of verse 6a in light of 5:14 may be understood as the loss (*'bd*) of profit, which cannot be taken to the grave at any rate (we might note that Qoheleth follows the poem in 3:9 by hinting at the impossibility of lasting profit). And the time of love and of hate (v. 8a) are very tellingly coupled again in 9:1: '. . . the righteous, the wise and their deeds are in the hand of God. Even love! Even hate! No one knows all that awaits them. Everything is alike for all – one fate.'

Of course these instructive parallels to Qoheleth's wider discourse do not prevent the poem proper from being wrested from its context. The passage marks an abrupt change of style, offering a list of merisms (contrasts of opposites to suggest the whole; e.g. 'mountains and valleys' to suggest the whole countryside) quite unlike anything in the Hebrew Bible. It is instantly memorable and it is easy to see why it has managed to stand on its own in the reception history as one of the best-known passages of the Bible in Western culture.

The Totality of Times

I have already touched on one of the cruxes of this passage that continue to tax interpreters, which is the degree of determinism suggested by the pairs of times. Two early examples will demonstrate what I mean. John Cassian (360–432), an influential figure in the development of Western monasticism, saw in Qoheleth's catalogue of activity some freedom in the human capacity to find a suitable time:

> The Divine Wisdom has pointed out in Ecclesiastes that for everything, i.e., for all things happy or those which are considered unfortunate and unhappy, there is a right time: saying: [cites 3:1–8, 17] . . . None therefore of these things does it lay down as always good, but only when any of them are fittingly done and at the right time, so that these very things which at one time, when done at the right moment, turn out well, if they are ventured on at a wrong or unsuitable time, are found to be useless or harmful. (*Conferences* XII, in Cassian 1978: 508)

In other words, as people venture to act out their 'time', there is a chance that they have chosen their moment poorly or, equally, that they will find success. Cassian thereby manages to do justice to the sense of threat I discussed above while preserving the idea of human autonomy. People can therefore inadvertently step outside, as it were, the divine will. Unsurprisingly, Martin Luther (*c.*1532) understands the passage very differently, namely, to endorse the inescapable limitations of the divine will on human activity:

All human works and efforts have a certain and definite time of acting, of beginning, and of ending, beyond human control. Thus this is spoken in opposition to free will. It is not up to us to prescribe the time, the manner, or the effect of the things that are to be done . . . Everything comes and goes at the time that God has appointed. He proves this on the basis of examples of human works whose times lie outside the choice of man. From this he draws the conclusion that it is useless for men to be tormented by their strivings and that they do not accomplish anything, even though they were to burst, unless the proper time and the hour appointed by God has come. (*Notes on Ecclesiastes*; Luther 1972: 49)

Several years before, Luther chose 3:7 to begin the dedicatory letter to Nikolaus von Amsdorf prefixed to his momentous *Appeal to the Christian Nobility of the German Nation* (1520): 'The time for silence is gone, and the time to speak has come, as we read in Ecclesiastes' (in Nicoll and Stoddart 1910: 536). Applying his later exposition, then, Luther saw his moment to speak as divinely appointed.

While this passage has exercised readers for centuries, it has been most culturally influential in the West over the last 50 years or so, being particularly prevalent in the 1960s. It was, for example, read at the televised funeral of John F. Kennedy in 1963 (being apparently one of Kennedy's favourite passages; see Short 1973: 77). Most significantly, *The Byrds* had a major hit with Pete Seeger's song *Turn! Turn! Turn!*, reaching number 1 in the USA in December 1965. It is difficult to establish from the song itself, the lyrics of which are simply a rendition of the Authorized Version of 3:1–8 (apart from the addition of the titular words and the very last line, 'I swear it's not too late'), whether it reflects a determinant reading (one must act in a particular, God-ordained time) or an endorsement of human desire and action free from the constraints of time and space (given the social context, I have always opted for the latter). In his insightful treatment of the song, Tim Connors (1997) recognizes the listener's choice:

> The words . . . could be construed as fatalistic resignation, or criticized as a series of over-simplifications. But the Byrds' version sounded somehow hopeful, and its sentiments were relatively profound for a number one record. The song's ambiguity, and Seeger's editorial embellishment after 'a time for peace', 'I swear it's not too late . . .' allowed the listening public to conclude that the song captured the zeitgeist of late 1965.

Regardless of its reading, the cultural impact of the song is unquestionable. It is the song, for example, and not really the text, that is obliquely referred to by John Updike's narrator in *Rabbit Redux* (1971) in the description of a nightclub singer (this in a scene in which she is playing a range of popular music, from Broadway to the Beatles): 'Into the mike that is there no bigger than a lollipop she begins to sing, sings in a voice that is no woman's voice at all and no man's, is merely human, the words of Ecclesiastes. A time to be born, a time to die. A time to gather up stones, a time to cast stones away. Yes. The Lord's last word. There is no other word, not really' (Updike 1972: 125). Over the years the song has become emblematic of Sixties' counterculture (note, for example, its use in the film *Forrest Gump*, 1994, in a scene set in the late Sixties to represent the sanctity of an individual's 'freedom' to choose a lifestyle). It is odd that few Qoheleth studies have passed comment on the remarkable cultural pervasiveness of the song (the exception seems to be William Brown, who suggests that the 'so-called Baby Boomer generation, cannot hear the first verse without mentally humming the musical version' [2000: 40]).

The poem has featured in other modern musical endeavours. American composer Norman Dello Joio won the 1957 Pulitzer Prize for Music with *Meditations on Ecclesiastes* ('for string orchestra'). The piece was commissioned 'as a ballet score for José Limòn to choreograph for Juilliard's American Music Festival in April, 1956' (Rudy Ennis, in sleeve notes to Dello Joio 1992). Dello Joio comments musically on 3:1–8 with a ten-fold 'theme and variations' treatment (such as 'a time to weep and to mourn' etc.), all, as Ennis suggests, 'readily identifiable, each probing one of the human experiences found in the accompanying biblical text'. The result reflects the title's aim, a musical meditation on Qoheleth's catalogue of human events. British composer Jonathan Wilcocks also set this passage to music in his 'For Every Thing there is a Season', a cantata for baritone, chorus and orchestra. The piece was commissioned by the Portsmouth Choral Union and given its first performance in 1980. It is an uncomplicated rendition of 3:1–9 and is a movement from a larger piece with other movements set to William Blake and Psalm 39 (see Wilcocks 1981).

Some other creative endeavours that mine the poem are worth mentioning. Like chapter 12, chapter 3 seems to bring the best out of poets. For example, Henry Howard's 1546 paraphrase of Ecclesiastes (see Introduction, pp. 47–9) seamlessly progresses from the abstraction of verse 1 to the particularity of verse 2:

> Like to the steerless boat that swerves with every wind,
> The slipper top of worldly wealth, by cruel proof I find.
> Scarce hath the seed (whereof that nature formeth man)
> Received life, when death him yields to earth where he began!
> (Ch. 3, in Howard 1815: 1.70)

Much later, T. S. Eliot seemed not only to hold a special affection for Ecclesiastes, but in particular for this passage (see Edwards 1990a: 79–81 and T. Wright 2005). Eliot's 'The Love Song of J. Alfred Prufrock' (1917) recalls Qoheleth's merisms in its opening lines:

> And indeed there will be a time
> For the yellow smoke that slides along the street
> Rubbing its back along the window-panes;
> There will be a time, there will be a time
> To prepare a face to meet the faces that you meet;
> There will be time to murder and create,
> And time for all the works and days of hands
> That lift and drop a question on your plate;
>   (In Eliot 1969: 13–14)

Like Qoheleth, Eliot intimates universal themes with his reference to 'times', and simultaneously recalls Qoheleth's pervasive style of reflection – 'times', and indeed consideration of 'all works', which 'lift and drop a question on your plate'. The first lines of 'Burnt Norton' (1935), first of *The Four Quartets* (although originally composed as a singular piece), offer an abstraction of 3:11 (and recall 1:9 and 3:15 as well):

> Time present and time past
> Are both perhaps present in time future
> And time future contained in time past.
> If all time is eternally present
> All time is unredeemable.
> What might have been is an abstraction
>
> . . .
>
> What might have been and what has been
> Point to one end, which is always present.
>   (In Eliot 1969: 171)

Eliot concludes 'Burnt Norton' with

> Ridiculous the waste sad time
> Stretching before and after.
>   (In Eliot 1969: 176)

and ends the next *Quartet*, 'East Coker' (1940), with another striking allusion:

There is a time for the evening under starlight,
A time for the evening under lamplight

. . .

The wave cry, the wind cry, the vast waters
Of the petrel and the porpoise. In my end is my beginning.
(In Eliot 1969: 182–3)

As Terence Wright (2005) suggests, 'Burnt Norton' and 'East Coker' especially recall both Qoheleth's language and persona of scepticism throughout. It is with such inventive references to Qoheleth's poem that Eliot structurally frames perhaps his most celebrated poems.

More recently, Sebastian Barker, in his lengthy 'The Time of Ecclesiastes' (1992), seeks to extend Qoheleth's list to an even broader range of human experiences, often observing their inherent irony. The first 10 lines give a good flavour:

For there is a time for living, and there is a time for leaving it alone.
There is a time for making love, and there is a time for love to be unmade.
There is a time for swimming, and there is a time for walking up mountain
    paths to arrive at monastery wells.
There is a time for refraining from striking a match, and there is a time for
    accepting a box of matches from a stranger.
There is a time for turning around and saying, 'Hullo, yes I will', and there is a
    time for turning around and saying, 'No thank you, I'd rather not.'
There is a time for Origin of Species, and there is a time for Consummation of
    Species.
There is a time for the conception of the individual person, and there is a time
    for the astrologer to mark as the turning-point in a calculation.
There is a time for the encasing of new computers in plastic, and there is a
    time for adding up numbers in idle amusement.
There is a time for looks in eyes to give rise to birth, and there is a time for
    birth to give rise to eyes with looks in them.
There is a time for belief in atheism, and there is a time for belief in a belief.
(Barker 1992: 58)

Barker's reading recalls Gregory of Nyssa (c.380), who demonstrates a skill for drawing out the host of experiences that readers can attach to Qoheleth's question in 3:9, 'What profit is there for the worker in their toil?':

. . . he tills the ground, he goes to sea, he endures the hardships of military service, he sells, he buys, he makes a loss, he makes a profit, he goes to court, he fights his case; he loses the case, he wins the verdict; he is pitied, he is congratulated; he stays at home . . . Is it not the case that, as soon as he ceases to live, all things are shrouded in oblivion, and he departs, stripped bare of the things he strove for, taking with him none of his present possessions, but only the conscience about them? (Hom. 8, in Gregory of Nyssa 1993: 141)

On the prose front, in his Expressionistic novel *Berlin Alexanderplatz* (1929), Alfred Döblin utilizes the refrain 'Ein jegliches hat seine Zeit' (3:1: 'For everything there is a season'; see Komar 1981: 322), the wording of the 1912 *Luther Bibel*. *Berlin Alexanderplatz* tells the story of Franz Biberkopf, a Berlin proletarian who tries to rehabilitate himself after his release from jail but undergoes a series of trials, many of them violent and squalid, before he can finally attain a normal life. Kathleen Komar comments on the relevance of Ecclesiastes to the whole narrative:

> In a novel which outlines the progress of a man from naive arrogance and willful pride to the acceptance of his role as a sacrificial victim and his rebirth in the community of men, Ecclesiastes seems a particularly appropriate biblical reference. Beginning with the sentiment 'Vanity of vanities; all is vanity', Ecclesiastes bears directly on Franz's problems and development. (1981: 322; on the use of 4:9–12 in the novel, see below)

In Bible illustration the time poem often receives rich treatment, rendering the merisms in a narrative style (see the examples of Etting 1940 and Vlachos 1995). There is, however, little in the way of gallery-oriented art on the passage, although Philip Ratner is an exception. In 1984, Ratner founded the Israel Bible Museum, in Safad. Included in its permanent collection are a series of paintings representing the time poem. In the example shown in plate 11 (the times for war and peace, v. 8b), as in each of the paintings, the interpretive element is rendered in a circle with the 'opposites' of the verses occupying a kind of yin/yang space. This particular example could of course be seen to be politicized.

Of commentary on the detail of the verses, 3:5, the centre-most 'pair' in the poem, is a good example of the variety of unusual concerns brought to this passage. Early Jewish tradition (represented in *Midrash Qoheleth* 3.5) takes the first line ('A time to cast away stones, and a time to gather stones together') to refer to sexual relations at a time of a woman's ritual purity ('casting away' perhaps implying 'grinding') and refraining from relations (as Fox points out, the implications of 'gathering' in the midrash are not so clear on this point; 2004: 21). In early Christian interpretation the sexual theme was recognized in the next line of verse 5, finding support for abstinence in 'A time to embrace and a time to cease from embracing' (e.g. Jerome, *Letter* 12.19; Augustine, *On Marriage and Concupiscence* 14; *On the Good Marriage* 15; cf. *Testaments of the Twelve Patriarchs*,

PLATE 11   Philip Ratner's *A Time for War – A Time for Peace*, 1998–2002.
© Philip Ratner, reprinted with permission

Naphtali 8). Jerome, who would no doubt have been familiar with the early sexualized readings, addressed his questions differently in his commentary (388/9):

> A time for dispersing stones and a time for collecting stones. I marvel how a learned man could have said this ridiculous note about this passage: 'this passage

speaks about the destruction and killing of Solomon's houses, because men first destroy, then build'. Some amass stones to construct buildings, others destroy those buildings which have been erected, according to Horace's lines 'he demolished, he builds, exchanges squares with wheels, he fluctuates and disagrees with the whole order of life itself' [*Horat. Epist.* 1.1.100, 99]. Whether he is correct in saying this or not I leave up to the reader to decide. Nonetheless we should follow the sequence of the prior explanation – they say it is a time for scattering and collecting stones, similar to what is written in the Gospel: 'God is powerful enough to raise up the sons of Abraham from these stones' [Mt. 3:9]. For there was a time for dispersing the nation and a time for gathering them again into the Church. (2000: *ad loc.*)

Other Jewish traditions (e.g. the eleventh-century *Midrash Lekach Tov* and Rashi) also see the stones as referring in some way to the dispersal of a nation, namely, to the destruction of the Temple and the subsequent ingathering of exiles (see Zlotowitz 1994: 84).

For all the time poem's cultural fame, it is worth noting that cultural readings of this passage are often quaint and platitudinous, gratuitously illustrated by the scores of plates, coffee mugs and so forth that proudly display it. Such 'readings' of the text exhibit an odd and pious compliance with a clichéd reading tradition and testify to the fact that there are few among Qoheleth's readers who have explicitly resisted it – at least none so brilliantly as American novelist Louise Erdrich:

> The book speaks to the audiences of high school choirs throughout the land and the recipients of cards of bereavement, every other one of which compellingly includes the pieties of chapter three: *To everything there is a season . . .* [cites vv. 1–2], a passage that not only states the obvious but that offers no consolation. When bad things happen, what comfort is there in being told it was 'the time' for it to happen? One's response is: Who said so, who determined the time, and how can I get even with the bastard? (1995: 235)

As well as targeting these instances of reception, Erdrich's sparky reading also has Ecclesiastes itself in its sights. In this respect she evokes Yehuda Amichai in his 'A Man in his Life' (1983):

> A man doesn't have time in his life
> to have time for everything.
> He doesn't have seasons enough to have
> a season for every purpose. Ecclesiastes
> Was wrong about that.

A man needs to love and to hate at the same moment,
to laugh and cry with the same eyes,
with the same hands to throw stones and to gather them,
to make love in war and war in love.
And to hate and forgive and remember and forget,
to arrange and confuse, to eat and to digest
what history
takes years and years to do.

A man doesn't have time.
When he loses he seeks, when he finds
he forgets, when he forgets he loves, when he loves
he begins to forget.

. . .

He will die as figs die in autumn,
Shriveled and full of himself and sweet,
the leaves growing dry on the ground,
the bare branches pointing to the place
where there's time for everything.

(In Amichai 2004)

Like Erdrich, although in a different way, Amichai resists Qoheleth. Whereas for Erdrich Qoheleth's words do not make meaningful contact with reality, for Amichai the polarities are too neat. He wonders if people have opportunity at all to meet with profit in their activities, and although he does not proceed to it, he would probably agree with Qoheleth that real 'profit' is unattainable in the end.

Ecclesiastes 3:9–6:12

No matter how diverse the subject matter in these chapters, Qoheleth's own prickly voice is the glue that holds it all together. And the material is not as disparate as it might seem at first sight. These observations are variably concerned with human fate and the totality of human experience. Qoheleth qualifies many of his comments here with the word *all* (used 26 times in this section) – *all* that God has made is fitting; *all* should take pleasure in their toil; *all* of humanity (and even the 'beasts') are subject to the same fatal outcome; *all* times and activities are appointed by God; and so on. Even the 'two are better than one' sayings of 4:9–12 are generalized and inclusive (which is why they appear on the insides of countless wedding rings!).

The themes under scrutiny here cohere well together. It is a crude measure, but a perusal of key words in this section will illustrate the thematic concerns here:

'amal, work/labor: ×12
'aśah, to do: ×9 (of human activity generally)
'akal, to eat/consume (of consuming and enjoying the fruits of labour): ×9
yitron/ytr, profit/gain: ×6
'inyan, business/activity (of God given to humanity): ×4

As this suggests, Qoheleth in these chapters repeatedly turns to the question of profit, of how one is able meaningfully to produce and enjoy it. Even his vignette about the impoverished youth who becomes a lauded king (4:13–16) asks about the nature of success and profit, which in that instance is measured by the memory of his followers. Likewise, the advice on religious conduct (5:1–7[1]) has as its subtext the question of what will advantage those who act wisely in the house of God, and culminates with a return to an explicit concern for profit (5:9–12). Indeed, this whole section is framed by rhetorical questions on the prospect of advantage (3:9 and 6:11). Furthermore, for Qoheleth enjoyment (consumption) of the fruits of labour is inextricably linked to profit (especially in his memorable case studies in 5:13–6:6). Along the way, Qoheleth throws in the occasional conundrum to keep his readers pondering (e.g. 3:15; 5:3, 7; 6:9–10). Even in all of this gloom and perplexity, however, Qoheleth manages to restate his joy theme with increasing solemnity (3:12–13, 22; 5:18–20), and richly complements this by his recognition of what might bring humanity relief from *hebel* (4:1–3; 6:3–5).

On Fate, Knowledge and Anthropology: 3:9–22

As Qoheleth resumes his empirical style in 3:10, he also resumes the topic he had begun to address in earnest, restating his sweeping aims of 1:13, to observe all of the business that God has given people to be busy with. In what many modern commentators regard as one of the book's key verses, he also observes that *everything* that God has made is beautiful in its own time – somehow it 'fits' (another meaning of 'beautiful', *yāpheh*). But once again, for Qoheleth the ointment cannot be fly-free. God has set *'ōlam* (lit. 'the world' or 'eternity', probably meaning 'a sense of timelessness') in the heart of everyone *so that* they cannot discover what he has done from beginning to end (3:11), reminding the reader once again of God's frustrating discretion and suggesting, alarmingly, that God's purposes may be malign.

---

[1] All references to chapter 5 will follow the versification of English translations, which is one verse ahead of the MT (in which the English 5:1 is 4:17).

The earliest interpreters of the verse, however, resist any indictment of God. The Talmud takes 3:11 indirectly to refer to general enjoyment of one's trade, echoing the buzzing activity of the time poem and reflecting the experience of daily life (*b. Berakoth* 43b), and later *Midrash Qoheleth* eradicates the human dimension of the verse altogether: 'He hath made every thing beautiful in its time. R. Abbahu said: "From this [we learn] that the Holy One, blessed be He, kept on constructing worlds and destroying them until he constructed the present one and said, 'This pleases Me, the others did not'"' (3.11.1).

Qoheleth's admission of the inability of human reason to fathom God's works certainly appealed to the Renaissance mind, although not always in a way that discouraged the sciences of knowledge (see Francis Bacon's comments on 3:11 in the Introduction, p. 50). Indeed, in his letter to the Grand Duchess Christina in 1615 on the relationship of science and religion, Galileo appealed to Qoheleth's observation in a remarkably constructive spirit.

> I should think it would be very prudent not to allow anyone to commit and in a way oblige scriptural passages to have to maintain the truth of any physical conclusions whose contrary could ever be proved to us by the senses and demonstrative and necessary reasons. Indeed, who wants the human mind put to death? Who is going to claim that everything in the world which is observable and knowable has already been seen and discovered? . . . Indeed, we also have it from the Holy Spirit that 'God hath delivered the world to their consideration, so that man cannot find out the work which God hath made from the beginning to the end' . . . so one must not, in my opinion, contradict this statement and block the way of freedom of philosophizing about things of the world and of nature, as if they had already been discovered and disclosed with certainty . . . nor should people become indignant if in a dispute about natural phenomena someone disagrees with the opinion they favor, especially in regard to problems which have been controversial for thousands of years among very great philosophers, such as the sun's rest and earth's motion. (In Galileo 1989: 96–7)

The letter, which concerns itself ultimately with squaring Copernican theory with the Bible, argues for careful interpretation of Scripture. In it Galileo appeals to Augustine to suggest that 'all truths always agree with one another' and that Scripture should agree with science, but he will not go so far as to suggest the sacrifice of human reason in doing so. Here Galileo slips outside (presumably with full cognizance) the received tradition. Not only had many Renaissance writers suggested that Qoheleth endorsed scepticism of the new sciences, but Eccl. 1:4–5 was taken (as it long had been) to suggest the immovability of the Earth and movement of the Sun, thereby refuting Copernicus. Galileo mentions that this ancient view is supported by the Bible, but counters by boldly suggesting that 'in many places Scripture is open to interpretations far removed from the literal meaning of the words' (1989: 96), and goes on to cite Ecclesiastes against itself.

God's 'gift' of 'the world' ('ōlam) to the human heart in 3:11 (a notion unique to Qoheleth) has elicited other notable readings. George Sandys's paraphrase (1632) brilliantly evokes the simultaneously hopeful and sullen senses of the verse:

> He in their times all beautiful hath made;
> The world into our narrow hearts convay'd:
> Yet cannot they the causes apprehend
> Of his great workes; the Originall, nor End.
>   (In Sandys 1638: 4)

Focusing almost entirely on the imparting of 'the world', Matthew Arnold, in the conclusion to his attack on literalist and dogmatic approaches to the Bible and religion, *Literature and Dogma* (1873), appeals to 3:11 to reflect on the relationship between conduct (which is Hebraic and the embodiment of a moral imperative) and culture (art and science, of which religion is in fact the highest expression):

> Only it certainly appears . . . that conduct comes to have relations of a very close kind with culture. And the reason seems to be given by some words of our Bible, which though they may not be exactly the right rendering of the original in that place, yet in themselves they explain the connexion of culture with conduct very well. 'I have seen the travail', says the Preacher, 'which God hath given to the sons of men to be exercised in it; he hath made everything beautiful in his time, also he hath set the world in their heart.' *He hath set the world in their heart!* – that is why art and science, and what we call culture, are necessary. They may be only one-fourth of man's life, but they are *there*, as well as the three-fourths which conduct occupies. 'He hath set *the world* in their heart.' And, really, the reason which we hence gather for the close connexion between culture and conduct, is so simple and natural that we are almost ashamed to give it. (In Arnold 1968: 408)

Arnold thus takes 'the world' to refer to a God-given sense of culture to which people can aspire. In a not dissimilar vein, in his autobiography (*Praeterita*, 1885–9), John Ruskin suggests that 3:11 describes God forming a bond between the human and divine realms:

> The woods, which I had only looked on as wilderness, fulfilled, I then saw, in their beauty the same laws which guided the clouds, divided the light, and balanced the wave. 'He hath made everything beautiful in His time', became for me

thenceforward the interpretation of the bond between the human mind and all visible things. (In Nicoll and Stoddart 1910: 538)

Qoheleth's remarkably anthropological ideas in 3:18–21 yield yet another example of the quotable Qoheleth in the pervasive funerary words, 'Ashes to ashes, dust to dust' (a composite of Eccl. 3:20, 'all are of the dust, and all turn to dust again', 12:7 and Gen. 2:7; 3:19). The passage has, since at least Augustine (in e.g. *Letters, On the Soul and its Origin* 4.37 and *City of God* 13), attracted discussion of the ontology of animals and humans. Gregory the Great passed his own judgment on the matter in a hugely influential passage from his *Dialogues* (*c.*593; see Introduction, p. 28), in which Gregory envisages Solomon addressing 'the weak' (who represent Qoheleth's unorthodox views):

> [W]hen [Solomon] speaks from the minds of the infirm, our preacher voices an opinion based on suspicion. 'For the lot of man and of beast', he says, 'is one lot; the one dies as well as the other. Both have the same life-breath, and man has no advantage over the beast' [3:19]. Later, however, he presents conclusions drawn from reason and says, 'What has the wise man more than the fool? and what the poor man, but to go where there is life?' [cf. 6:8] So ... he again specifies that the wise man has an advantage not only over the beast, but also over the foolish man, namely, his ability to go 'where there is life'. With these words he points out ... that man's true life is not found here on earth, for he claims that it is found elsewhere. (In Gregory the Great 1959: 195)

Gregory goes on to appeal to 9:10 ('whatever your hand finds to do ...') to argue that the activities listed there ('work, reason, knowledge, wisdom') belong solely to the provenance of human beings, and therefore it is only human beings who live on after death. The voice of 3:18–21, then, belongs to one of the 'minds of the infirm', whom Solomon corrects throughout his book.

Nowhere, however, were the issues surrounding this passage more acutely and publicly felt than in the trial of Anne Hutchinson in New England, 1637–8. A successful advocate of home Bible study and prayer meetings, Hutchinson drew the suspicions of the Puritan authorities of the Massachusetts Bay Colony. These eventually accused her of antinomianism, the doctrine that Christians are not bound by law, which Hutchinson suggested was a consequence of the believer's possession of the Holy Spirit. During her lengthy trials in 1637 she acquitted herself confidently in exegetical debate. She was nonetheless convicted for 'traducing the ministers'. Hutchinson was imprisoned over the winter of 1637–8, during which she had ample time to pursue her scriptural studies. 'In this dark hour a cruel irony led her to that compendium of disillusion, the Book of Ecclesiastes' (Battis 1962: 234). In Eccl. 3:18–21 Anne recognized the possibility that humans are born with a (merely) mortal soul, and therefore only the soul we receive on regeneration of the spirit makes us immortal. Therefore, all grace is from regeneration and is not born in us, and here she might find further grounds for her case. The ministers who visited her in this period listened intently to her 'anguished doubts' and concluded that they could 'collate and classify into a formal ecclesiastical indictment the numerous errors they had heard from her own lips during these past weeks' (Battis 1962: 235). Of the points raised against her, the first set the tenor of the debate. Her accusers accounted her 'a verye dayngerous Woman to sowe her corrupt opinions to the infection of many . . . [and they laboured] to reduce her from her Errors and to bare witness agayst them'. Anne responded: 'I did not howld divers of these Things [that she had spoken in her imprisonment] I am accused of, but did only ask a Question. Eccl. 3.18–21.' Minister Shephard replied, revealingly, that 'the vilest Errors that ever was [sic] brought into the Church was brought in by way of Questions' (in Adams 1894: 290). Anne's own minister, John Cotton, then engaged in the following exchange with her:

> Mr Cotton. Yo[ur] first opinion layd to yo[ur] charge is *That the Soules of all Men by nature are mortall & die* like Beastes. [A]nd for that you alledge Eccl. 3.18–21.
>
> Mrs Hutchinson. I desire that place might be answered; the spirit that God gives returns.
>
> Mr Cotton. That place speaketh that the spirit ascends upwards, soe Eccles. 12.7. Mans spirit doth not returne to Dust as mans body doth but to God. The soul of man is immortall.
>
> Mrs Hutchinson. Every Man consists of Soul & Body . . . Soe than *the Spirit that God gives man, returnes to God indeed, but the Soule dyes.* & That is the spirit Eccles. speakes of, & not of the Soule. Luk. 19.10.
>
> (In Adams 1894: 290–1)

And so they continued, matching scripture for scripture. Towards the end of her trial Anne made the fatal mistake of claiming special revelation for her views. She was subsequently commanded 'in the name of Ch[rist] Je[sus] and of this Church *as a Leper to withdraw your selfe out of the Congregation*' (in Adams 1894: 336). (Anne might have found solace in the much later views of Paul Tillich, who said of this passage that 'the modern naturalist would need to change nothing in the words of Ecclesiastes'; 1963: 73.)

On Oppression and the Value of Companionship: 4:1–12

Qoheleth's sentiments in 4:1–3 are an oft-cited example of his lack of concern for real justice, for here he seems to present himself as a detached observer not directly advocating action. (See the 'Qoheleth and Justice' section of the Testimonia chapter, where many of the comments come in the context of a discussion of this passage.) Many earlier readers have not always seen it so. *Midrash Qoheleth*, for example, uses the text to correct a misunderstanding about a marginalized social group:

> 'They had no comforter'. Daniel, the tailor, applied this to bastards – to bastards themselves and not to their fathers. A man has been unchaste, and has begotten a bastard. But how has the bastard sinned, and what concern is it of *his*? R. Judah b. Pazzi said: Even the bastard will enter the life to come; for God says, 'In this world they are regarded as unclean, but in the world to come I look at them as all gold'. (4.1.1)

Portuguese commentator Damião de Góis, known for his concerns for social justice, in his *Ecclesiastes de Salamam* (1538) recognizes similar concerns here, and draws them out in his liberal translation of the Vulgate: 'I came to care for all the others, and I saw done all the evils, tyrannies, and oppressions under the sun, and I saw tears of the innocents whom no one consoled, nor could the poor, abandoned of all help, resist the forces of their tyrants and oppressors' (in Earle 2001: 60, tr. A. Dawson). Where the Vulgate simply offered *calumnias*, Góis translates 'evils, tyrannies, and oppressions' ('maldades, tyranias, e oppressões'), serving to foreground Qoheleth's sense of moral outrage.

In his 1546 paraphrase, Henry Howard, Earl of Surrey, was moved by Qoheleth's observations here as well, perhaps because he was at the time anticipating his unjust execution (see pp. 47–8):

> When I bethought me well, under the restless Sun
> By folk of power what cruel works unchastised were done;
>   I saw where stood a herd by power of such opprest,
> Out of whose eyes ran floods of tears, that bayned [bathed] all their breast;
>   Devoid of comfort clean, in terrors and distress;
> In whose defence none would arise such rigor to repress.
>   Then thought I thus; 'Oh Lord! the dead whose fatal hour
> 'Is clean run out more happy are; whom that the worms devour:
>   'And happiest is the seed that never did conceive;
>   'That never felt the wailful wrongs that mortal folk receive.'
>   (Ch. 4, in Howard 1815: 1.73)

Even a seventeenth-century book of advice for kings cites approvingly the example of 'Solomon' in 4:1–3, so that it might be known 'how a King ought to carry himselfe towards those that finde themselues iniuryed and aggrieued' (Juan de Santa María, *Policie Unveiled*, 1632: 150–1). Many years later, E. H. Plumptre is so impressed with Qoheleth's ethical stance in this passage that he writes:

> It may be noted that the tone is that of a deeper compassion than before. He sees the tears of the oppressed and sighs at their hopelessness . . . We can see in this new element of despair, that which was the beginning of a better life. The man was passing, to use modern terms, from egoism to altruism, thinking more of the misery of others than of his own enjoyment. (1881: 138)

More modern commentators have been less willing to let Qoheleth off the hook, and theologian Francis Watson is particularly clear on the matter:

> . . . despite Qoheleth's reputation for fearless integrity and realism, this analysis of oppression [in 4:1–3] as part of the tragedy of the human condition subtly evades and distorts the experience of oppression. The tears of the oppressed do not express a longing to escape from the troubles of existence by returning to the peace and rest of non-being. The oppressed desire not their own non-existence but the non-existence of oppression . . . For all his gentle compassion, he will not lift a finger to help the oppressed in their desperate plight, even if his own eyes are filled with tears as he passes by on the other side. (1994: 283–4)

Watson's view is echoed in contemporary India in the commentary of E. G. Singgih, *Living under the Shadows of Death: An Interpretation of the Book of Ecclesiastes* (2001), which suggests that the force of 4:1 is that even God does not comfort the oppressed (see Drewes 2005: 131).

In observing the plight of the oppressed, Qoheleth takes opportunity to praise the dead, and even more, those 'who have not been', for these have escaped a worse fate (cf. 9:4–5). While his comments have not proved as awkward as one might think, Christian commentators sometimes make reference to other ideas to perhaps blunt the implications. So it is with reference to the Resurrection that Ambrose in 379 comments,

> Not to be born is . . . by far the best, according to Solomon's sentence. For they also who have seemed to themselves to excel most in philosophy have followed him. For he, before these philosophers in time, but later than many of our writers, spoke thus in Ecclesiastes [cites 4:2–4] . . . But Solomon was not the only person who felt this, though he alone gave expression to it. He had read the words of holy Job: 'Let the day perish wherein I was born.' [Job 3:3] Job had

recognized that to be born is the beginning of all woes . . . and wished that the day of his birth might perish that he might receive the day of resurrection. (*On the Belief in the Resurrection* 2.30, 32, in Ambrose 1955: 178)

In his commentary, Jerome (388/9) accounts for Qoheleth's view by reference to Origen:

> Some people in fact understand this passage in this way: they say they are better, who have died, than those who are living, it is permitted to them before they were sinners [cf. Origen's *peri Archon* 1.5.5; Hieronymus, *Epist.* 124.3]. For until now the living were in battle and were held back as if closed in by the prison of the body; but those who have opposed death are already without cares and have stopped sinning . . . For our souls mingle among the gods, before descending to these bodies and are blessed so long as the heavenly ones are held in Jerusalem and in the choir of angels. (Jerome 2000: *ad loc.*)

The medieval exegete Hugh of St Cher, *c.*1230–5, directly refuted this view, arguing that, according to Ecclesiastes, the 'unborn are said to have seen no evil; hence it cannot refer to their previous existence with the angels in heaven'. As Smalley suggests, 'Hugh proves at length that life, with all its attendant evils, is better than non-existence' (1949: 353). (See the discussion of this text's use at the funeral of Queen Mary I, pp. 208–10, where it proves awkward for political reasons!)

The subject now shifts in chapter 4 from the plight of the oppressed to observations on work and the value of companionship (vv. 4–12). For G. C. Martin in the 1908 Century Bible, Qoheleth's disapproval of human rivalry had a contemporary ring: 'It is curious to find how very modern this conception is. It would make a splendid motto for a Socialist address against the evils of competition' (in Cohen 1952: 132). More personally, Henry Howard, Earl of Surrey, feels the reality of Qoheleth's words in 4:9–12 when, alone and betrayed by friends (see above, pp. 47–8), he writes in his 1546 paraphrase,

> For as the tender friend appeaseth every grief,
> So, if he fall that lives alone, who shall be his relief?
>   The friendly feeres [companions] lie warm in arms embraced fast;
> Who sleeps alone, at every turn doth feel the winter blast.
>   What can he do but yield, that must resist alone:
> If there be twain, one may defend the t'other overthrown.
>   The single twined cords may no such stress endure
> As cables braided threefold may, together wreathed sure.
>   (Ch. 4, in Howard 1815: 1.74)

Centuries later, Alfred Döblin in his 1929 novel *Berlin Alexanderplatz* (on which, see p. 170), also draws resourcefully on the language of 4:9–12, here to reflect on the nature of human fate. As Kathleen Komar suggests, protagonist Franz Biberkopf ultimately finds 'salvation'

> through incorporation into the community, an ending which has seemed so contrived to many critics and troublesome even to Döblin himself, receives a certain logic of imagery in its echoing of Ecclesiastes 4.9–12 . . . Shortly before Franz's triumphant march with the masses, he thinks: [my tr.: Much misfortune comes when one goes it alone. Where there are several, it is certainly different. One must get accustomed to listen to others, because what others say also concerns me. Thereby I notice who I am and what I can decide to do . . . What is fate? One person is stronger than me. When we are two, it is more difficult to be stronger than me. When we are ten, yet more difficult. And when we are one thousand and a million, then it is entirely difficult. But it is also more enjoyable and preferable to be with others.] (In Komar 1981: 322–3)

Early Jewish interpretation of the 'threefold cord' is typically diverse. According to the Mishnah, the cord consists of 'knowledge of Scripture and Mishnah and right conduct' (*Qiddushin* 1.10 [Talmud: *b. Qiddushin* 40b]). True to form, however, the Talmud can apply the verse more freely, in praise of three generations of scholars all living at the same time, a reference to 'R. Oshaia, son of R. Chama, son of Bisa' (*b. Ketuboth* 62b; repeated nearly verbatim in *b. Baba Bathra* 59a), or to the 'absolute security against sinning' when one enacts the threefold cord by wearing the *tefillim* on the arm, the *zizith* on the garment and placing the *mezuzah* on the doorpost (*b. Menahoth* 43b).

On Conducting Oneself in the House of God: 5:1–8

It is not uncommon in the early modern period to apply Qoheleth's concern for care in synagogue worship to the context of Christian worship. '*To take heed unto our feete when as we goe unto the house of God*, is to worship god with a pure and sound mind, or, to carrie a pure & sound mind in worshipping of god, in which kind of speech . . . [is] to lead our life as is meete and agreeable unto the Gospell' (Serranus 1585: 243–4). John Trapp, in his 1650 commentary, draws on (his own peculiar construct of!) Pythagoras to make his point about the care one must exercise in the house of God.

> Shooes we have all upon our feet, that is (to speake in St. *James* his phrase) *filthinesse and superfluity of naughtinesse* in our hearts, that must be put off at Gods Schoole-doore, as God taught *Moses* and *Joshua*. And *Pythagoras* (having

read *Moses* belike) taught his scholars as much, when he saith . . . Put off thy shooes when thou sacrificest, and worshippest. His followers the *Pythagoreans* expounded his meaning, when they would not have men . . . worship God carelesly, or by the way; but prepare themselves at home beforehand. (1650: 50)

In a section that has garnered little attention in reception history, Qoheleth continues to offer observations on proper religious conduct and implicitly reflects on the advantage of wisdom (on the talmudic reading of 5:5, see p. 29). Jerome, in his commentary (388/9), relates Qoheleth's obscure words at 5:7 to earlier observations in order to supply a referent:

> *In spite of all dreams, futility and idle chatter, rather: Fear God!* The Hebrews explain this passage in great detail, and in the following way: and you should not do the things detailed above, about which he has already spoken, lest you believe too readily in dreams. For when you see different things, your mind will be troubled by many fears throughout your night's rest, or aroused by promises, you despise those things that are dream-like. You should only fear God. For he who believes in dreams gives himself over to vanities and nonsense. (2000: *ad loc.*)

Other 'Hebrews' relate the same dreams to the mercurial activity of interpreting dreams: 'R. Chanan said: Even if the master of dreams [i.e. an interpreter of dreams, such as Joseph or Daniel] says to a man that on the morrow he will die, he should not desist from prayer, for so it says. *For in the multitude of dreams are vanities and also many words, but fear thou God*' (*b. Berakoth* 10b).

In 5:8 Qoheleth again expresses something like resignation in the face of injustice (cf. 4:1–3), although now he pitches squarely at the macro-level of experience, the 'higher' political authorities. For someone so attuned to the injustices of authority of any kind, it is notable that Martin Luther, in his *Notes* (1532), here sees a call to readers to find peace in their worldly affairs: 'For it is impossible that everything be done rightly and without injustice. Therefore this book teaches you to have a quiet and peaceful heart in the affairs of this life, so that when you hear or see evil, you do not become indignant but say: "Such is the trouble in the course of the world. There is no other way here"' (in Luther 1972: 84).

On the Possibility of Profit and Relief from hebel: 5:10–6:12

Again profit is the dominant theme as Qoheleth offers observations on human labour, and again Henry Howard reflects elegantly on Qoheleth's words

(5:12) in his 1546 paraphrase, relating them to the wider theme of justice
at work:

> The sweet and quiet sleeps that wearied limbs oppress,
> Beguile the night [of] diet thin, and feasts of none excess:
> But waker lie the rich; whose lively heat with rest
> Their charged bulks with change of meats cannot so soon digest.
> (Ch. 5, in Howard 1815: 1.76)

Norman Whybray (1982) has drawn attention to the development and
prominence of the joy theme in Ecclesiastes in such key texts as 5:18–20, and
he is well anticipated by Martin Luther, commenting on 5:20 in his *Notes*
(1532): 'This is the conclusion of this entire book or argument, which was
stated earlier in chapters two and three ... This statement is the interpreter of
the entire book: Solomon intends to forbid vain anxieties, so that we may
happily enjoy the things that are present ... In this way he has joy in his toil
here, and here in the midst of evils he enters into Paradise' (in Luther 1972:
93). Even closer to the view that Whybray will so forcefully state, however, is
the anonymous author of *Choheleth*: 'This advice to live chearfully ... is
repeated at proper intervals; and the reader can scarce avoid taking notice how
judiciously it always comes in, after some sad and melancholy subject' (Anonymous 1765: 52; cf. his comments on the joy theme *re* ch. 9, p. 211).

Around the same time as *Choheleth*, Voltaire suggests a remarkably balanced reading of the passage in his *Précis* of Ecclesiastes (1759, here versifying
3:22 and 5:18–19):

> Of time which ceaselessly perishes,
> let us seize the moments.
> Let us possess wisely,
> let us enjoy, without excess,
> the riches that the indulgent heavens
> grant to our youth.
>
> May the pleasures of the dinner table,
> amusing conversations,
> make time last longer for us,
> and may a pleasant companion
> inspire in me a durable love
> without ruling too much over my senses.
>
> Mortal, that is your share,
> granted by destiny.
> On this wealth, on your use of it,
> is founded all your happiness.

> May the wise man own it,
> without being possessed by it.
>
> Use but do not abuse; do not be prey
> to unbridled desires, tumult or error.
> Vain outbursts of joy, you have caused me distress;
> your noise disturbs me, and laughter is a deceiver.
>
> (in Christianson 2005: 480)

As I have shown elsewhere (Christianson 2005), Voltaire appropriates Qoheleth's concerns as his own, and expresses the kind of pragmatic solution to human misery that he proposes in *Candide*.

In a moving vignette, Qoheleth envisages a man who has produced spectacular wealth, but tragically God does not *enable* him to enjoy it (6:1–4). Perhaps concerned that readers might see cruelty in God's decision to withhold enjoyment, Jerome (388/9) suggests an odd compassion at work:

> Nor does he say this in exaggeration, for even if he produced an hundred books and lived longer than Adam, that is almost one thousand years, but lived two thousand years, he would rot his mind with desire and avarice. He is born prematurely in a worse state that dies, as soon as he seems born. For he did not see evil things or good things; but although he used to possess good things, he was tormented by thoughts and sadness, and having been born prematurely he has more rest than a greedy man who is old. But both however are seized by the same fate, while both the first and the last are taken away by the same death. (2000: *ad loc.*)

Qoheleth is unclear about exactly *why* the aborted birth that travels into *hebel* and into darkness is better off. From the context it seems that lack of any sort of knowledge is more desirable than knowledge of a miserable fate, something that Rashbam (*c*.1080–*c*.1160) draws out well in his typically literal approach: 'although the abortion did not see anything and did not know anything it is better off than he; for the abortion saw neither good nor evil, whereas this man saw nothing but evil all day' (in Rashbam 1985: 144, 146).

In some of the best verses of the poet's paraphrase (1632), George Sandys renders the poignancy of the still born in this passage:

> This, as a Common Misery, have I
> With sorrow seene beneath the ambient Sky:
> God Riches and Renowne to men imparts;
> Even all they wish: and yet narrow hearts
> Cannot so great a fluency receive;
> But their fruition to a Stranger leave.
> What falser vanitie, or worse disease,

Could ever on the life of Mortals seaze?

. . .

Enveloped with shrouds of endlesse Night;
Who never saw the Sunne display his Light,
Nor Good or Evill knew: he is more blest;
And soon descends to his perpetuall Rest.

(In Sandys 1638: 7–8)

Sandys shows no restraint in seeking to expose the full force of this example of *hebel*, as well as the bold solution of rest that Qoheleth endorses.

Around the same time as Sandys, John Donne comments on the way in which Qoheleth's exposition of desire in this passage is emblematic of his overall quest:

> That which the Vulgat reads, Eccles. 6.9. *Desiderare quod nescias, To desire to know that which thou knowest not yet*, our Translation cals, *The wandring of the desire*, and in the Originall it is, *The walking, the pilgrimage of the Soule*; the restlesnesse, and irresolution of the Soule. And when man is taught that which he desired to know, then the Soule is brought home, and laid to rest. Desire is the travaile, knowledge is the Inne; desire is the wheele, knowledge is the bed of the Soule. (Sermon in Bozanich 1975: 272)

Bozanich suggests that here Donne indicates a source for the title of his *The Second Anniversary* ('Of the Progres of the Soule', 1612), as well as its marginal note on the soul's 'ignorance in this life and knowledge in the next' (1975: 272). Typically, the Talmud imagines a more pragmatic and sensual context: 'Resh Lakish said: Better is the pleasure of looking at a woman than the act itself as it is said: "*Better is the seeing of the eyes than the wandering of the desire*"' (*b. Yoma* 74b).

Once again Qoheleth returns to his favourite theme of profit, but he is now more concerned with the personal gain of a wise demeanour than with material wealth. He also continues to develop the theme of death, so poignantly contemplated in chapter 6. In the first four verses of chapter 7 he refers to it in some way four times (the day of death, the house of mourning [twice], the end of 'everyone') and even champions vexation and sadness in doing so. In each case he suggests that there is something 'better' about these realms of experience (subtly restated in his praise of the 'end of a thing' over its beginning in v. 8). In his remaining proverbial observations (vv. 5–9) Qoheleth reflects on the value of wise conduct, endorsing the more traditional values of humility (vv. 5–6), integrity (v. 7), patience (vv. 8–9), acceptance of fate (v. 10) and wisdom itself (vv. 11–12).

Verse 13 marks the resumption of an earlier theme (e.g. 1:15; 3:11–14; 6:12), the inscrutability of the work of God. As elsewhere, conundrums and incongruities occur to Qoheleth without the benefit of resolution (v. 15; cf. 8:10–14). Like Job, he is clearly unhappy about the erratic pattern of reward and punishment at work in the world, and offers a not very satisfactory *via media* (vv. 14, 16–18). After reminding us once again of the advantage of wisdom and wise conduct (vv. 19–22), he settles down to his most penetrating interrogation of the whole enterprise of wisdom (vv. 23–9). Here he wonders if becoming truly wise is at all possible and figuratively suggests in the most personal language he can muster that wisdom is distant from him (vv. 23–4). In a passage that is all about losing and finding, many have seen an underlying correspondence with Genesis 2–3 (see Christianson 1998b: 116–17). Here Qoheleth implicitly restates a goal made more explicit elsewhere: to become wise (even in a philosophized sense), and specifically to *understand* wisdom (cf. 1:13, 16–17; 8:16–17; 9:1; see Christianson 1998a: 208–9, 230). In one sense this sets Qoheleth apart from the wider biblical wisdom tradition in which the attainment of Wisdom *herself* is the implicit goal (cf. Prov. 1:20–33; 8:1–8, 17–21; Wis. 6:12–21; Sir. 4:11–16). In his quest to find it, he implicates the figure of woman, interpreted, as we shall see, with great variety.

Chapter 8 further broadens the portrait of wisdom by relating it to the task of interpretation and suggests that wisdom can even change one's appearance (vv. 1–2). The observations that follow (vv. 3–9) reflect again on proper conduct, this time in relation to the royal court and to the limits of power and authority. Even in these realms, in which Qoheleth/Solomon boasts the highest qualifications, he admits to the impossibility of avoiding misery (v. 6), of comprehending what will be (v. 7) and of even hoping to alter the outcome (death and war) when authority is foolishly wielded (vv. 8–9). Again he observes insoluble incongruities in the realms of the righteous and the wicked (vv. 10–14) and concludes by resuming two favourite themes: the call to joy (v. 15) and the inscrutability of what God does, stating for the first time that even the sage, though he claim otherwise, cannot know it (vv. 16–17).

The Curious Values of Wisdom: 7:1–12

The paronomasia of 7:1a (*tob shem mishemen tob*) is notoriously difficult to capture, but H. Odeberg's 'Better is name than nard' (1929: 110) is appealing. The second line, like other proverbs in this passage (vv. 2–4, 8), seems to run contrary to common sense. Why should death be better than birth? To make sense of it, *Midrash Qoheleth* narrates a compelling exegesis by analogy:

When a person is born all rejoice; when he dies all weep. It should not be so; but when a person is born there should be no rejoicing over him, because it is not known in what class he will stand by reason of his actions, whether righteous or wicked, good or bad. When he dies, however, there is cause for rejoicing if he departs with a good name and leaves the world in peace. It is as if there were two ocean-going ships, one leaving the harbor and the other entering it. As the one sailed out of the harbor all rejoiced, but none displayed any joy over the one which was entering the harbor. A shrewd man was there and he said to the people, 'I take the opposite view to you. There is no cause to rejoice over the ship which is leaving the harbor because nobody knows what will be its plight, what seas and storms it may encounter; but when it enters the harbor all have occasion to rejoice since it has come in safely.' Similarly, when a person dies all should rejoice and offer thanks that he departed from the world with a good name and in peace. (7.1.4; cf. *Midrash Exodus* 48.1 and Jerome's *Commentary*, which seems to have been influenced by the first part of this reading)

The illustration fits well with Qoheleth's pervasive frustration with the unknown and his advice to cope with it – there is little point in rejoicing at birth, for too much remains unknown (as Qoheleth puts it in 4:3, the one who has not yet been is better off than the living and the dead, since it will not see the evil activity that is done under the sun).

The same verse features briefly in Patricia Cornwell's novel *The Last Precinct* (2000). At a crime scene, the protagonist, forensic specialist Kay Scarpetta, notices something odd:

I move over to the dresser and look at the Bible. It is open to the sixth and seventh chapters of Ecclesiastes, and the exposed pages are sooty, the area of the dresser under the Bible spared, indicating that this was the position the Bible was in when the fire started. The question is whether the Bible was open like this before the victim checked in, or does it even belong with the room, for that matter? My eyes wander down lines and stop at the first verse of the seventh chapter. 'A good name is better than precious ointment; and the day of death than the day of one's birth.' I read it to Marino. I tell him that this section of Ecclesiastes is about vanity. (Cornwell 2000: 337)

Qoheleth's words are apropos here in that Kay is throughout the story being falsely accused – it is her good name that is at stake.

Qoheleth continues in verses 2–4 to defy common sense by now suggesting that the house of mourning is somehow to be preferred to that of feasting and pleasure (seemingly contrary to his own advice to enjoy eating). Jerome (388/9), however, sees here what the *memento mori* and *vanitas* traditions will endorse as so cathartic: 'It is more useful to go to the rites of a funeral than to the house where there is a party, since at the house of mourning we are warned of our creator and of our mortality on account of seeing the dead body. But in the happiness of a party, even if we seem to have any fear, we lose it' (2000: *ad loc.*; cf. similar traditional Jewish views in Cohen 1952: 149). Such an assumption about the thrust of Qoheleth's words is easily granted given the way in which he uses the idea of death to make, as Crüsemann puts it, life shine more brightly (1979: 67). This can also be seen as an attempt to capture the balance of pleasure and misery so frequently encountered in life, which Percy Shelley conveys in his *Defence of Poetry* (1821):

> Sorrow, terror, anguish, despair itself, are often the chosen expressions of an approximation to the highest good. Our sympathy in tragic fiction depends on this principle; tragedy delights by affording a shadow of the pleasure which exists in pain. This is the source also of the melancholy which is inseparable from the sweetest melody. The pleasure that is in sorrow is sweeter than the pleasure of pleasure itself. And hence the saying, *It is better to go the house of mourning than to the house of mirth.* (Part First, in Nicoll and Stoddart 1910: 540–1)

Qoheleth resumes with cryptic remarks on the value of wise behaviour. In his paraphrase of 7:6 (1801), John Hookham Frere, known for his satirical verse, aptly recognizes and enlarges the insubstantiality of the 'cracking thorns' of the fire:

> The mirth of fools, somewhere the preacher says,
> Is like the cracking thorns when in a blaze;
> So unsubstantial are their liveliest joys,
> Made up of thoughtless levity and noise:
> Tho' at the first the mantling flame looks bright,
> 'Tis but a momentary glare of light,
> With nothing solid to sustain the fire,
> It quickly sinks, and all their joys expire.
> (In Hookham 1872: 2.496)

This evokes well Qoheleth's notion of 'mirth', here the antithesis of a wise rebuke, which is contrasted throughout verses 2–6 with the more grave and substantial engagement with mourning and even sorrow.

Rabbinic views on 7:8 were not unlike those on 7:1 (see above). So Rashi (1040–1105) says, 'at the beginning of the thing we do not know what will be at its end; but when its end is good, it is concluded with good' (in Cohen 1952: 151). Phoebe Hesketh's hushed poem 'After Ecclesiastes' (1989) also takes up the question of the preferability of endings:

And the end of a party is better than the beginning.
Quietness gathers the voices and laughter
into one cup –
we drink peace.

Crumpled cushions are smoothed as our souls
and silence comes into the room
like a stranger bearing gifts
we had not imagined,
could not have known
without such comings
and such departures.

(In Hesketh 1994: 94)

(On the latter half of 7:8, see the charming illustration of 'patience' in *Midrash Qoheleth*, above, pp. 29–30.)

Qoheleth's words on the value of wisdom in relation to money (7:12) elicit a range of rabbinic readings. Money and wisdom are comparable in that if one gives money to a scholar, then blessing will come in heaven (*b. Pesachim* 53b)! And the notion that wisdom preserves the life of its owner can be demonstrated by a variety of experiences. Thus, when one thinks rightly in a dangerous situation, thereby possibly saving one's own life, the principle of this verse is followed. This could be: sating one's ravenous hunger by choosing to eat from the more fruitful (eastern) side of the fig tree (*b. Yoma* 83b); stripping off one's clothes and running after being 'rubbed against' by a mad dog (*b. Yoma* 84a); cooling oneself from fever by sitting in water (*b. Chullin* 59a); and, infamously, avoiding the fate of the 59 scholars who became impotent by not relieving themselves during the long-winded discourses of R. Chuna. And how to avoid that? As R. Acha b. Jacob cryptically put it, by following 'the principle, *Wisdom preserveth the life of him that hath it*' (*b. Yebamoth* 64b; it seems that he managed to pee behind the college cedar tree). Other Jewish tradition continues the theme, with the story of R. Meir escaping from the Roman authorities by deceiving them into thinking that he ate swine's blood in their presence, thereby successfully concealing his identity (*Midrash Qoheleth* 7.12.1).

The Incongruity of Experience and the Inaccessibility of Wisdom: 7:13–29

Qoheleth's fatalistic remark on the unchangeable crookedness of what God has made (cf. 1:15) is used provocatively as the opening graphic in the film *Gattaca* (1997), which tells the story of a genetically imperfect man living in a future world in which genetic faults are not tolerated. He dreams of travelling to space and adopts the identity of another person in order to achieve his goal. As Larry Kreitzer suggests, 'The verse sets up an interesting exploration of eugenics and the moral implications of decisions being made on the basis of genetic information' (personal correspondence; cf. George Sandys's rendering of 7:13–14, Introduction, p. 54).

Again Qoheleth seems to defy reason by suggesting that one can be too righteous, on which the Talmud offers its own unique reflection. Over-righteousness is suggested of Saul when he 'lay in wait' for the Amalekites (and thus chooses not to slay all of them, 1 Sam. 15:5–9; *b. Yoma* 22b), and over-wickedness when he slays the priests at Nob (1 Sam. 22:17–19; cf. the equation of over-wickedness with bad breath in *b. Shabbath* 31b). A pretty ingenious way around the idea is offered by renowned Elizabethan preacher Edward Stillingfleet, and in his audience's terms: '*Be not Righteous overmuch.* Can there be the least Danger of that, in such a corrupt and degenerate Age as we live in?' (sermon 13, preached at Worcester, 17 August 1690; Stillingfleet 1698: 490). After exploring a range of senses in which righteousness might be understood (as wisdom and virtue particularly), Stillingfleet concludes in terms that resonate with recent approaches to understanding Qoheleth's persona (e.g. Brown 1996; Christianson 1998a):

Avoid a needless Scrupulosity of Conscience, as a thing which kepps our Minds always uneasie. A Scrupulous Man is always in the dark, and therefore full of Fears and Melancholy apprehensions; he that gives way to Scruples, is the greatest Enemy to his own Peace. But then let not the fear of Scrupulosity make you afraid, of keeping a good Conscience; for that is the wisest, and best, and safest Companion in the World. (1698: 530)

Scott Langston explores in detail a remarkable debate on the question of 'over-righteousness' in 7:16–17. The exchange took place between two British clerics of the mid-eighteenth century, Joseph Trapp and George Whitefield. Langston describes the scenario at length:

In 1739 . . . Joseph Trapp preached and published a series of four sermons entitled *The Nature, Folly, Sin, and Danger of being Righteous over-much; With a particular View to the Doctrines and Practices Of certain Modern Enthusiasts.* Taking Eccl. 7:16 as his text, Trapp proceeded to challenge and refute systematically George Whitefield's brand of 'enthusiastic' religion. Whitefield then responded by preaching and publishing two sermons on the same verse, but coming to a different interpretation than Trapp. The first was entitled, 'The Folly and Danger of Being Not Righteous Enough', and the second, 'A Preservative Against Unsettled Notions and Want of Principles in Regard to Righteousness and Christian Perfection; Being a More Particular Answer to Dr. Trapp's Four Sermons Upon the Same Text.' Subsequently, several pamphlets were written by others either defending or attacking the two opposing views. (1998)

Langston sketches the historical context of the debate, suggesting that Britain in the eighteenth century was experiencing previously unparalleled material consumption and enjoyment. In the best of all possible worlds, this little passage makes for difficult reading. In an economic revolution in which the Church is developing its stance towards personal piety in relation to the growth of individual wealth, reading gets even more complex. For Whitefield, Qoheleth was preaching a Puritan life of restraint and piety, a message that had particular relevance to a newly materialist British culture. Trapp, on the other hand, saw in Qoheleth's words a call to moderation, which 'allowed his parishioners to participate in the consumer boon . . . without feeling pangs of guilt' (Langston 1998). As Langston suggests, the whole episode is a fine example of opposing interpretations, each legitimated by the particular socio-religious views of its proponent.

Not long after Whitefield and Trapp's debate, Robert Burns versifies the same text to commence his 1786 'Address to the Unco Guid, or the Rigidly Righteous':

> My Son, these maxims make a rule,
>   An' lump them aye thegither;
> The Rigid Righteous is a fool,
>   The Rigid Wise anither:
> The cleanest corn that ere was dight [before was winnowed]
>   May hae some pyles o' caff in;
> So ne'er a fellow-creature slight
>   For random fits o' daffin [frolicking].
>   Solomon. – Eccles. ch. vii. verse 16.

The 'unco guid', or 'uncommonly good', refers to those who Burns regarded, in perfect keeping with Qoheleth here, to be 'professedly strict in matters of morals and religion' (*OED*), and as he continues, he takes opportunity to reflect on hypocritical judgment of one's neighbour:

> Hear me, ye venerable core,
>   As counsel for poor mortals
> That frequent pass douce [prudent] Wisdom's door
>   For glaikit [foolish] Folly's portals:
> I, for their thoughtless, careless sakes,
>   Would here propone defences –

Their donsie [dreary] tricks, their black mistakes,
  Their failings and mischances.

    . . .

Who made the heart, 'tis He alone
  Decidedly can try us;
He knows each chord, its various tone,
  Each spring, its various bias:
Then at the balance let's be mute,
  We never can adjust it;
What's done we partly may compute,
  But know not what's resisted.

                              (In Burns 2005)

Qoheleth goes on to modify his theme of uncommon righteousness in 7:20 (there is 'no one' righteous) and his twist proves very popular among early Christian commentators, particularly Augustine (see the selection in J. R. Wright 2005: 254–5).

The 'all this' of 7:23 has been taken variously to refer to one of three things: (1) to the previous passage (vv. 15–22 or 1–22), (2) to *everything* Qoheleth has considered up until this point or (3) to what follows (vv. 25–9, esp. v. 28). *Targum Qoheleth*, evidently aware of the ambiguity, opts for the second of these: 'All that I said I have tried by wisdom.'

In verse 24 Qoheleth elaborates on the extraordinary inaccessibility of wisdom by using terms of geographical distance (see Fox and Porten 1978: 37), and his views recall those of Job: 'The Deep says "It is not in me" and the sea says "It is not with me"' (Job 28:14). In a remarkable passage in his commentary (388/9), Jerome deftly teases out the gist of Qoheleth's singular claim to become wise (note that this is the only instance in the Hebrew Bible where the verb *chakam*, 'to be wise', relates reflexively to the speaker – Qoheleth uniquely seeks to *be* wise, to *become* wise; cf. 2:15, 19):

he says that he sought wisdom more than other men, and tried to reach the pinnacle, but the more he sought, the less he found, and in the midst of his confusion, he was surrounded by the darkness of ignorance. But at another time, regarding him who was learned in the Scriptures – the more he wanted to know, the more a greater obscurity arose each day for him. Another meaning of this is: he seems to mean that contemplation of wisdom in this life is like looking in a mirror or at a picture; therefore if I look at my face in the mirror in the future I'll think back to the way it used to be, and then in the liquid pool I'll recognise that I differ greatly from the way I used to be. (2000: *ad loc.*; cf. Rupert of Deutz's comments in Testimonia, p. 10)

Jerome intimates, as Qoheleth, a philosophized sense of becoming here, a becoming that is far off and deep. Wisdom herself, however, according to Gregory of Nazianzus (*c.*380), is the elusive object: 'I said, I will be wise, says Solomon, but she was far from me beyond what is . . . For the joy of what we have discovered is no greater than the pain of what escapes us; a pain, I imagine, like that felt by those who are dragged, while yet thirsty, from the water . . . or are suddenly left in the dark by a flash of lightning' (*In Defence of his Flight to Pontus* 2.75, in Browne et al. 1983: 220). George Sandys would convey a similar idea in his 1632 paraphrase:

> All this by wisedome try'd, I seemed wise:
> But shee from humane apprehension flyes.
> Can that which is so farre remov'd, and drown'd
> In such profundities, by Man be found?
> Yet in her search I exercis'd my Mind;
> Of things the Causes, and Effects to find:
> (In Sandys 1638: 10)

(The identification is also made in Coverdale's 1539–40 Bible and will find restatement in Krüger 1993.)

A more general application of 7:24 to the human endeavour to understand 'the subject of God', and one that anticipates the themes of Renaissance readings of Ecclesiastes generally, can be found again in the work of Gregory of Nazianzus: 'Solomon, who was the wisest of all . . . to whom God gave breadth of heart, and a flood of contemplation, more abundant than the sand, even he, the more he entered into profundities, the more dizzy he became. And he declared the furthest point of wisdom to be the discovery of how very far away wisdom was from him' (*On Theology, Theological Oration* [*c.*380] 2.21, in J. R. Wright 2005: 255). Basil the Great (*c.*329–79) is even more emphatic:

> Even if all minds . . . should combine their researches and all tongues would concur in their utterance, never . . . could anyone achieve a worthy result in this manner. Solomon, the wisest of all, presents this thought clearly to us when he says [cites 7:23] . . . wisdom appears unattainable particularly to those to whom knowledge has been given in an exceptionally high degree by the grace of God. (*Concerning Faith*, in J. R. Wright 2005: 255)

The rabbis understood such dissonant cognitive distance to refer to the unattainability of a perfect understanding of Torah (*Midrash Qoheleth* 7.23). Rashbam (*c.*1080–*c.*1160) reflects more the sense of gnostic, mystical wisdom when he writes of 7:24, 'That which is, is far off: profound (wisdom), which is of the past, as for example the "Merkaba Mysticism" and the "Book of

Creation"; it is far from me in that I cannot cope with it; and deep, very deep is the quality of this superior wisdom, and who is that man who, by his great wisdom, can find it out?' (in Rashbam 1985: 162). Indeed, with its mystical edge, the *Zohar* (*c.*1290) relates this verse to the perception of God himself: 'All thoughts weary themselves when thinking of Him; and even Solomon, of whom it is said "he was wiser than all men" (1 Kings 5:11), sought to perceive Him in thought, but could not; and so he said, "I said: I will get wisdom; but it was far from me"' ('*En-Sof* and the World of Emanation' 7, in Lachower and Tishby 1989: 1.268; similarly, 3.1124). In his 'In Ecclesiastes I Read' (1987), American poet J. P. White relates the elusive object to inconstant human understanding of the Earth:

> In Ecclesiastes I read,
> 'That which is far off and exceeding deep,
> Who can find it out?'
> Who can tell the earth's tale of wearing down,
> building up, erosion, creation,
> a swirl of embers breathing amethyst and tourmaline,
> a suffering bounded by the four baleful rivers of Hell
> and a sun that will one day collapse,
> engulfing it in one long dragon breath of dying out?
>
> . . .
>
> Most of us worried there will be too little time
> to light the lamps of our fingers
> and walk the narrow path in the rain.
> But what of the earth? Who can find it out –
> embrace its drifting continents,
> who can love it as it is – unfinished,
> smudged with the dust of rare constellations,
> flickering on and off like a rain-drenched fire in the woods?
>
> (In Atwan and Wieder 1993: 362–3)

Perhaps unwittingly, with references to creation, precious stones and paths, White's reading echoes wisdom's enigmatic bond with creation in Proverbs 8 and Job 28.

The passage that follows (vv. 25–9) is Qoheleth's most conspicuous discussion of women, who are mentioned in passing in only two other places (2:8; 9:9). Readers have differed starkly on whether Qoheleth is misogynistic or simply misunderstood, and modern commentators in particular have gone to some length to suggest that Qoheleth's misogyny is only apparent. Often the issue has turned on whether the woman is understood as a type, a specific person, Woman Folly or 'women in general'. The Talmud strikes an intriguing balance in the following discussion:

> Rab Judah taught his son R. Isaac: Only with one's first wife does one find pleasure, as it is said: *Let thy fountain be blessed and have joy of the wife of thy youth* [Prov. 5:18]. 'Of what kind of woman do you speak?' he asked him – 'Of such as your mother', was the reply. But is this true? Had not Rab Judah taught his son R. Isaac, the verse: *And I found more bitter than death the woman whose heart is snares and nets* [Eccl. 7:26], and he [the son] asked him: 'What kind of woman?' He answered, 'Such as your mother'? – True, she was a quick-tempered woman but nevertheless easily appeased with a word. (*b. Sanhedrin* 22a–b)

This reading is grounded in personal experience. The woman is understood as a type that the reader has encountered – in this case one's own mother! – and, more importantly, the text is seen to reflect, like a *pesher*, the daily life of the community who reads it. Here our verse is deemed an adequate descriptor of a bad-tempered woman (cf. *b. Yebamoth* 63a–b in which the same verse is used several times as a euphemism for a bad or 'baleful' wife). *Midrash Qoheleth* associates the woman with death itself. After listing 14 examples of 'things that are stronger one than the other', R. Judah said, 'Illness is strong, but the Angel of Death dominates it and takes it away. Stronger [i.e. worse] than them all, however, is a bad woman' (7.26.2; the only direct connection of 'woman' to death in later biblical tradition also makes the connection: 'From a woman sin had its beginning, and because of her we all die'; Sir. 25:24; cf. 26:22). *Targum Qoheleth* understands the woman of verse 26 as she who 'causes her husband many sorrows' (lit. 'sorrowful deeds', in Knobel 1991: 41; see Fontaine's discussion [1998: 155–7] of the targum's reading). Perhaps unsurprisingly, early Christian writers see this woman as embodying a type that will draw a man away from God, and with whom 'consecrated men' should exercise caution (e.g. Clement [died *c.*215], *Two Epistles concerning Virginity* 10, in Roberts and Donaldson 1974b: 64). Eudes of Châteauroux (*c.*1190–1273), a 'gifted preacher', in part avoids the issue by ingeniously aligning the woman with the *contemptus mundi* reading tradition (see above, pp. 100–10):

> And when they think that they are filled with happiness and joy they are [in fact] filled with bitterness and sadness, according to the testimony of Solomon who says in Ecclesiastes: *I found more bitter than death.* On the whole a man finds more pleasure in a woman than in wine or food and wealth or honour. So if he finds *a woman*, who is considered to be the sweetest thing, *more bitter than death*, which is more bitter than anything else, what about other [pleasures]? (Sermon 4.3, in Maier 2000: 163)

In other words, Qoheleth's contempt for 'a woman' only directs one to contempt of all worldly pleasure.

In a wonderfully caustic anecdote, novelist Louise Erdrich pushes the referential power of 'woman' here all the way to the other gender (1995). Retrieving a misaddressed package from 'a small ranch-style house by a nameless river', Erdrich met with a 'grim . . . sour-mouthed hostess'. She noticed post-its 'adhering to walls, to lampshades, television, doors', all inscribed with verses from Ecclesiastes. She was intrigued.

> I begged her, with as much diffidence as seemed appropriate, for a tour.
>
> 'Ecclesiastes is my favorite book', I explained, intent on seeing what quotes decorated the bathroom medicine cabinet, the bedroom, the rest of the house.
>
> Her answer to me was a shrug of refusal, a hand waved at the walls. She lit a cigarette and tapped a bit of tobacco off her tongue. 'I don't know the first thing about the Book', she said, 'My sister put this shit up to get me in the right mind-set.' She gestured at the crucifix.
>
> I tend not to look very closely at the faces on crucifixes, so I hadn't noticed that over the features of the suffering Christ a man's clean-jowled photo obviously cut from a studio portrait had been pasted . . . Over his head the misogynistic verse of the seventh chapter, altered for the gender blamed in this particular instance, was printed in bold. *And I find more bitter than death the man whose heart is snares and nets.* (Erdrich 1995: 234–5)

The image of searching in this passage serves to illustrate Qoheleth's entire intellectual struggle. He is unable to find the sum of what should be *like* the answer to a simple mathematical problem: 1 + 1. As with the rest of his searching, the answer eludes him (see Christianson 1998a: 230–1). He also fails to discover even one woman among a thousand, and the very intensity of his search raises the question of value. The fact that Qoheleth found a man among a thousand, but among the same number of people he found no woman, is presented as evidence of human integrity (see Brenner 1995: 59). Qoheleth's words appear to convey antagonism in that the failure to discover, regardless of the object, is elsewhere a cause of his perpetual vexation. Rachel Speght, in her proto-feminist tract *A Mouzell for Melastomus* (1617), takes issue with Solomon's failure to find. After drawing attention to the tradition of 700 wives and 300 concubines, Speght argues that in this 'enigmaticall Sentence', 'Hee saith not, that among a thousand women neuer any man found one worthy of commendation, but speakes in the first person singularly, *I haue not found*, meaning in his owne experience: for this assertion is to be holden a part of the confession of his former follies, and no otherwise, his repentance being the intended drift of *Ecclesiastes*' (1617: 8–9). Not only is this remarkable as the earliest example of taking the 'blame' reading to task, but it is one of the few early modern examples of exegesis to make reference to the rhetorical signifi-cance of the first-person style (cf. 'Ali, above, p. 31). The 'learned Dr Gill' (whom Ginsburg estimates to be not very learned at all) clearly was unfamiliar with (or unpersuaded by) Speght's reading: '*But a woman among all those have I not found*: that is, among all the harlots and adulterous women I ever knew or heard of, I never knew nor heard of one that was ever reclaimed from her evil ways, and reformed or became a chaste and virtuous woman' (1748; in Ginsburg 1861: 174–5). The Doctor goes on to point out that Solomon did not mean women in general but those who were his downfall, his unhappiness, and of whom 'he lamented and repented'.

While Qoheleth's misogyny is disputed, the passage has found its way into real instances of social misogyny. Making cryptic reference to the unusual use of the participle of 'to find' at 7:26 (*wmwts' 'ny*) a Western Jewish tradition developed of men asking each other whether they were happy in their marriage by saying *mts' 'w mwts'*, meaning 'Happy or not?' (*b. Berakoth* 8a; cf. *b. Yebamoth* 63b – see the discussion in Fontaine 1998: 153–5). Much later, and more seriously, the imagery of Qoheleth's 'bitter' woman was used to detail the identification of witches in the fifteenth-century Inquisitor's witch-hunting manual *Malleus Maleficarum* (*Hammer of Witches*; for the full citation, see above, p. 40). The author of *Malleus* had the easy task of adapting a ready-made language for its purpose (cf. the Talmud's linking of 7:28b to witchcraft in *b. Gittin* 45a). Indeed, one might legitimately question the degree to which texts such as this and Proverbs 7 have fuelled the Western myth of the evil adul-teress who lies in wait to trap a clearly 'innocent' man (as in Prov. 7 [esp. vv. 22–3], the man in our text [7:26b] is simply 'trapped' by her). It is a myth frequently restated in popular culture (see Newsom 1989: 157–9).

In modern scholarship Qoheleth's misogyny is rarely understood without qualification (Fox and Porten are typical: 'the wisdom teachers were certainly aware that not every woman was a blessing', 1978: 32). Earlier readers were not so uncomfortable with 'outing' Qoheleth. David Friedländer (1788), a student of Moses Mendelssohn, realizes Qoheleth's potential slur and observes that folly 'is here personified as a harlot, and, by the way, an attack is made upon the whole female sex' (in Ginsburg 1861: 82). Ginsburg himself follows this view, suggesting that men making women the embodiment of wickedness 'in all ages' has been 'to the detriment of themselves, the female sex, and society at large' (1861: 387). In 1898 Elizabeth Cady Stanton suggested that women have not always felt compelled to read Qoheleth's abrasive words at anything less than face value: 'The commentators vouchsafe the opinion that there are more good women than men. It is very kind . . . of the commentators to give us a word of praise now and then; but from the general tone of the learned fabulists, one would think that the Jezebels and the Jaels predominated. In fact, Solomon says that he has not found one wise woman in a thousand' (in Cady Stanton 1985: 2.100). Cady Stanton's remarks reflect a recurring trend in feminist approaches to the Bible of critiquing the practice of 'redeeming' often implacably androcentric texts such as Eccl. 7:26–9. She might even have endorsed the views of Louise Erdrich, which are refreshingly unforgiving and suggest the potentially destructive cultural impact of Qoheleth's words:

> There is misery in Koheleth's enjoyment of everything, but an inability to love or at least respect the opposite gender is an embarrassment to any complex intelligence. Somebody told this guy what, or he was jilted, let down royally. He used that as an excuse to write three self-righteous, arrogant, and mean little verses of diatribe. Men are made by God, he concludes, but there's not one good woman in a thousand. [cites 7:26, 'I find more bitter than death . . .'] . . . These words have stood through time in thought, no doubt been spoken from pulpits, used to punish uppity and opinionated women, been cited as God's actual credo on the female subject. These are words that have done historical harm, and yet they were probably written in the same short-sighted spirit that any gender uses in complaining about the other. That barstool spleen taken as divine revelation casts a sick pall upon the acquired wisdom of Koheleth, just as it did in my strange encounter [see above, p. 199]. (1995: 237)

About Wisdom, Power and Authority: 8:1–17

Regarding Qoheleth's penetrating question at 8:1, 'Who knows the interpretation of a thing?', Arthur Kirsch suggests that, 'As in *King Lear*, which also poses this question insistently, there is no satisfying answer, and certainly no consoling one. But again like *Lear*, Ecclesiastes does offer a characteristic perception of human existence in the face of death, if not an interpretation of it' (1988: 158). Although Qoheleth never features in Shakespeare's politically charged work, his comments in verses 2–9 on wise conduct in the royal court have consistently been related to political contexts. So, for example, in his attempt to win Queen Elizabeth I's favour with his dedicatory sonnets on Ecclesiastes, Henry Lok took advantage in particular of the content of this passage. As Doelman comments, 'the Geneva Bible reads: "Where the word of the king is, there is power, and who shall say unto him, what dost thou?" [8:4], but in Lok's paraphrase, the monarch appears more majestic and divine':

> Who dare unto account his soveraigne call,
> Who to no power in earth inferiour is?
> Who will not at his feet all prostrate fall,

Who hath the power to punish his amis?
As deputies to God, on earth they raigne,
And by his sword of Justice state maintaine.
(Doelman 1993: 4; text in Lok 1597: 75;
ch. 8, ll. 47–52; see above, p. 52,
for his treatment of 8:1–2)

An even more explicit political application is found in the sermons of Edward Hyde, who in 1649, following the execution of Charles I and against strong opposition from republicans, preached on Eccl. 8:2–4 in support of the king's succession by his son, Charles II. The sermons had the express purpose that readers and hearers would be 'true and faithfull to the [new] King' (in Hyde 1662: 26). Hyde goes on to specify the exegetical detail of his argument:

> in these words, *To keep the Kings Commandment* . . . to observe argues an act of loving, honouring and obeying . . . here, *to observe the mouth or command of the King*, is, to love, honour, and obey his commands, with an unwearied diligence, with an undisturbed patience . . . [The] Preacher here bids us so observe the Kings Commands as to be sure not to leave them undone, for then our observation will but make us guilty of the greater contempt: the wise Historian sets those down for little better then a mutinous rabble, of whom he saith, *Interpretari magìs quàm exequi*, they were more ready to interpret then to execute all commands. (In Hyde 1662: 27–8)

More in keeping with Qoheleth's subversive spirit is a later Jewish application, which inverts the location of power. In the midst of a controversy over the question of Jewish obedience to the British state, Jewish preacher Hirschel Levin in 1757/8 made appeal to verse 2:

> This appears to me to be the meaning of the verse from Ecclesiastes [8:2] . . . According to Rashi's commentary, these words apply to the community of Israel . . . Now it is obvious that we are always obliged to pray for the welfare and prosperity of our kings. Even if we are not specifically commanded by the king to do this, we should take the initiative ourselves. For how else can we serve the king under whose protection we live? If we were to suggest that we serve him by fighting in his armies, 'what are we, how significant is our power?' [citing from the liturgy] ('Sermon on *Be-Ha'aloteka*', London; in Saperstein 1989: 351)

As Saperstein points out, the 'question of the Jews' capacity to live as obedient subjects of the king had been forcefully raised during the controversy over the "Jew-Bill" of 1753 . . . Anti-Jewish tracts . . . accused Jews of high treason because of their continued justification of the Crucifixion' (1989: 351 n. 3).

Qoheleth again turns to what is incongruous, this time that the wicked are honoured with a good burial while the righteous are neglected (8:10; cf. 1:11; 2:16; 9:5). Jerome in his commentary (388/9) recognizes the truth of the observation in his own experience:

> We can see how this evidence pertains to certain bishops, who come to power in the Church, and speak ill of those who had taught and had urged them to follow better pursuits. These men are very often praised after death in the Church, and blessed for those things, which they in all likelihood did not even do, or openly are warned by their successors or the congregation. And even this is vanity, since while they live they do not heed advice and are not immediately visited for their sins (since none dares accuse his superior), besides they act as if holy and blessed, and as if they are walking in the precepts of the Lord, and they increase their sins one on top of another. Such an accusation of a bishop is difficult. For you see, if he has sinned, it is not believed, and if he is accused, he is not punished. (2000: *ad loc.*)

Johannes Brenz, in his commentary on Ecclesiastes (1528), relates the verse to a more politicized context. Brenz suggests that Qoheleth's words in 8:10 are a salient reminder for rulers in the context of reform. As Robert Rosin puts it,

> In supporting the Reformation and moving more rapidly, the rulers ought to worry only about how God will view their conduct and efforts, not about what others in the world think. Brenz cites Ecclesiastes 8:10 . . . as a reminder that there is no lasting fame in the eyes of the world. Those who depart from what God wishes in an effort to make a name for themselves in the eyes of others are pursuing an illusion, falling victim to vanity, as Brenz sees things. (Rosin 1997b: 208)

Many readers have seen in 8:16–17 admonitions about the excesses of human inquiry, regarding Qoheleth as a living anti-exemplar. Jerome's commentary (388/9) exegetes the notion in memorable terms:

> He searches for the causes and understanding of the world, why this or that is done, and for what reason the world is steered by good or bad turns of events; why one is born blind and frail, another born healthy and with sight; why one is poor, another rich; why one is of high birth, another inglorious. Nothing else is of use, unless he is tortured in his search, and has an argument instead of anguish, but he does not find what he is looking for. And when he says that he knows, then he has the beginning of ignorance in him, and starts to sink into deeper madness. (2000: *ad loc.*)

In a different vein the admonition is echoed in the mortality lyrics of the fourteenth century (see Introduction, pp. 37–8). This is particularly well expressed in the following passage from 'This World Passes like a Dream' (*c.*1325–50):

> It is an idle boast to flourish as a
> A master of divinity.
> Remember we live lowly here on earth
> And God lives on high in majesty;
> We concern ourselves with material mortality
> And not of other power.
> The more we trace the Trinity,
> the more we fall into delusion.
> (ll. 89–96, in Brown and Smithers
> 1952: 163; my tr.)

The Renaissance sees these concerns reappearing, as in Agrippa von Nettesheim's influential *Of the Vanitie and Uncertaintie of Artes and Sciences* (1530; see Introduction, p. 47), where he links his own enterprise to Ecclesiastes:

> The knowledge of all Sciences, is so difficulte (I will not say impossible) that all mans life will faile, before one small iote of learning maie perfitely be founde out: which thing it seemeth vnto me, that *Ecclesiastes* affirmeth, when he saieth . . . [cites 8:17]. Nothing can chaunce vnto man more pestilente, than knowledge: this is the very pestilence, that putteth all mankinde to ruine, the which chaseth awaie all Innocencie, and hath made vs subiecte to so many kindes of sinne, and to death also: which hath extinguished the light of Faith, castinge our Soules into blinde darkeness: Which condemning the truth, hath placed errours in the hiest throne. (In Agrippa 1974: 15–16)

This is Agrippa's most sustained encounter with Qoheleth and it is not an insignificant one. Commenting on the same verse, Theodore Beza in his *Ecclesiastes* (1588) found his way to critique the 'scrutiny' of providence, an activity he judged to be on the rise and riddled with futility:

> I found that the reason of that order & providence, wherby almightie God governeth all and every thing, doth so farre passe all capacitie and understanding of men, that though the wisest man that ever was, use never so great cunning and diligence to find them out, and make his boast that he hath attained this knowledge: yet he is not able to reach unto no not the knowledge of one of Gods workes. (In Beza 1593: fol. C.8; cf. the very similar frustration expressed in Gascoigne's 1576 translation of Pope Innocent III's *De Contemptu Mundi*, above, p. 154)

Finally, Mendelssohn, commenting on these verses in his 1770 commentary, also understands Qoheleth to be outlining the limits of human inquiry:

> If I wish to understand something of the ways of God's providence, it is necessary to become acquainted with all of God's works, with what was and what will be, in this world and the world to come. For no one can grasp any aspect of the way of superior [i.e. divine] wisdom by considering only the actions taken in this world. This would be like a dream without an interpretation, a question without an answer. (In Sorkin 1996: 36)

Mendelssohn's description of this-worldly scientific enterprise as a 'dream without interpretation' is a fitting description of what vexes Qoheleth. Dreams often simply display the incongruous without explanation, and that is the reality Qoheleth has resolved to live with, and to deem *hebel*.

Again Qoheleth marks the beginning of a passage with a note of universality: *all this* I set to heart (v. 1; cf. 3:1; 7:23), and the verses that follow are concerned with a remarkable gamut of human experience. Indeed, while in verse 2 he delineates a religious realm of experience, he ends the passage (v. 11 especially) by suggesting a much wider realm, and concludes that everyone is susceptible to a time of calamity. Humanity's inescapable fate is evil (v. 3), and although Qoheleth does not judge this *hebel*, even in his call to joy he reckons all of their days *hebel* (v. 9). And where Qoheleth finds himself getting carried away here with the theme of hope, he soon quells it with death. A cursory reading, then, may lead to the notion that Qoheleth, even when clearly enamoured of life's most compelling joys, is incapable of breaking free from his infamous misery.

Here again, however, Qoheleth demonstrates a startling wizardry. Each reflection on death sheds some light on what he values most about life. People's hearts are full of misery and folly, all the way to the grave (v. 3), but if they are merely joined to the land of the living, there is hope (v. 4). The traits of the dead are morbidly catalogued. They have no knowledge, no wages, no memory, no emotion (love, hate, envy) and no portion (vv. 5–6). But this is another way of pinpointing what should matter most to the living. Even the jubilant portions of bread and wine, love and celebration that readers should seize (vv. 7–9) only become meaningful for Qoheleth cast against the locale of Sheol, where there is no activity, reasoning, knowledge or wisdom (v. 10). So while he has rendered the dimensions of Sheol in more detail than perhaps anywhere else in the Hebrew Bible, he has done so with a very specific purpose: to make clear what is most vital about the land of the living. Thus one can understand that odd comment in verse 5, that it is somehow hopeful for the living to 'know that they will die'. It is hopeful because the living know that in death, love and hate will perish, and there will be nothing for the body or for the mind, no lasting reward or meaningful occupation. For Qoheleth such an awareness can only drive people to experience life with meaning. His conclusion, then, which reminds the living of their fragile and constant exposure to impending death (vv. 11–12), is ultimately life-affirming.

The Wisdom of Death and Life

Qoheleth's brief categorization of the fate of all, in which the 'types' are pretty clear, has not drawn much attention in reception history. It is whom he means by 'the living' and 'the dead' that has perplexed the most. *Midrash Qoheleth* (9.5.1) relates these to a traditional and familiar grouping:

> On a certain occasion R. Jonathan repeated this verse [9:4] to R. Chiyya. 'My son . . . you know the Scriptures, but not their interpretation. "The living", these are the righteous, for even after their death they are called living; "the dead", these are the wicked, for even in their lifetime they are called dead' . . . Then said R. Jonathan, 'Blessed be he who has taught me the interpretation', and he kissed him.

It seems that it was not enough for the midrashic authors to see advantage in mere existence, and Qoheleth's simple observation lacks the immediately apparent moral force that has here been added. For the midrash the living are only made alive through recognition of their righteousness. Luther also relates these to the ethical category of good works:

> You must understand all of this in an active sense . . . that all the good deeds [the dead] did by loving, obeying, etc., are handed over to oblivion . . . Therefore [Solomon] wants us to use life as much as is permitted and to work as much as we can. For we are forced to relinquish the larger part of the world to Satan and can scarcely gain a thousandth part of it for God. And so if your lion dies, you had better not kill your dog. (*Notes*, c.1532, in Luther 1972: 148)

Luther's notion of good deeds being most relevant to the living is perhaps in keeping with Qoheleth's regard for survival.

Qoheleth's distinction between the most despised and the most lauded animals of the ancient world is blunt enough. Its subtlety lies in the suggestion that, by the simple fact of living with others, those who lie at the bottom of the social heap are more fortunate than any of the dead, even the most noble. That makes this text perhaps not the most suitable for exposition at a royal funeral. However, at the funeral of Queen Mary I, 4 December 1558, John White, the Catholic bishop of Winchester, put caution to the wind and preached what monarchical historian David Starkey calls an 'explosive sermon' (2000: 258). In order, presumably, to provoke in the congregation some sympathy with his own pro-Mary and anti-Elizabeth (and anti-Protestant) sentiment, White introduced his sermon as follows:

> THESE be the words of Solomon . . . : *I can commend the state of the dead above the state of the living; but happier than any of them both is he that was never born.* [Eccl. 4:2–3a]
>
> The first part containeth a doctrin incredible in the judgment of man: for al men commonly measureth the matter after another sort, coveting rather to live than to dy, rather to have a being in this world than no being. (in Strype 1822: 536)

After explaining that the latter part of the verse (3b) was 'tending to paganity' and therefore to be disregarded, White then introduced the more 'explosive' element:

> The words of Solomon, *Laudavi mortuos magis* [I commend the dead more than], &c. seemeth rather to compare the estate of the living and the dead, both being in the favour of God. And altho' of itself there be no doubt nor question herein among the faithful, yet the love that we have toward this present life . . . hath made a question: and so much the more, because Solomon in the book of Proverbs [*sic*!] hath other words . . . clean contrary, *Melius est canis vivus, quam leo mortuus* [A living dog is much better than a dead lion; Eccl. 9:4b]: which is a perillous place, not only preferring the living before the dead, but preferring the living in a vile and base estate before the dead, being a far more worthy creature in man's judgment. For what beast is more vile than a dog, more

worthy than a lion? For such is the sense of the letter; but far from the meaning
of the writer. Wherefore let us seek the right meaning. (in Strype 1822: 543)

White seems to be aware of the potential offence in both texts, for in the first
he translates *laudavi mortuos* as 'I commend *the state* of the dead', not simply
'the dead' – in other words, here was a little something to soften his dangerous
commendation of Mary over Elizabeth (who was forced to attend the funeral);
it was only her state of death, not her (the dead) itself that was being praised.
Also, after citing 9:4b, White was at pains to argue that dogs are good, really
('of all beasts the most familiar and faithful to man', p. 543), and dead lions
are not so good (pp. 544–5). Nevertheless, Starkey is of the view that White
was taking risks:

> [The choice of texts] was probably a mistake. Before him was a congregation
> of all of the old English establishment and much of the new. As one, their jaws
> must have hit the floor. The bishop was saying, [implying, really] wasn't he, that
> 'a dead Mary was [somehow] better than a living Elizabeth'? He was even
> saying, wasn't he, that 'Elizabeth was a living dog and Mary a dead lion'? (2000:
> 258–9)

Starkey further suggests that 'his English translations and the heat of the
moment had done the damage' (2000: 259). Although Kenneth Carleton
expresses reserve about the sermon's anti-Elizabeth sentiment (though he does
not state why he doubts such a reading), he provides some details regarding
'the damage':

> In the course of his sermon he made either the biggest *faux pas* of his career, or
> was subject to the most unfortunate misunderstanding . . . This [citation of
> Eccl.] was taken, perhaps unjustly, as a comparison between the new queen
> Elizabeth and her recently departed half-sister, and as a result White was placed
> under house arrest [he was admonished and released a month later]. John Jewel,
> later bishop of Salisbury, described the sermon . . . as mad and very seditious.
> (Carleton 2004)

One of the most remarkable facets of that story is the manner in which the
bishop may have carefully placed an effective ideological barb in a text which
seems to carry no obvious political overtones. As White masked his own sentiments with the words of the Preacher, he provided enough distance to invite
the listener to consider the possibility that he was a mere vassal for the authority of the Bible itself. That is, for White this is calling the situation as the Bible
sees it. This is very clear in the first example of commending Mary above
Elizabeth. He is far more subtle, however, in his use of the lion and dog text.

If Elizabeth is 'better' in any sense, it is only in the one qualitative difference between her and Mary: she is alive. This allowed White to deliver his barb to Elizabeth in a thin veneer of praise. (An intriguing footnote to this story is the publication of Henry Lok's dedicatory sonnets on Ecclesiastes to Queen Elizabeth in 1597 – see p. 52.)

The contrast of fates so elegantly expressed throughout chapter 9 is neatly captured in Louis Untermeyer's 1928 poem 'Koheleth' (cf. the preceding lines cited in the Introduction, p. 70):

> I started to teach
> Life cannot be bettered:
>
> That the warrior fails
> Whatever his weapon,
> And nothing avails
> While time and chance happen.
>
> That fools who assure men
> With lies are respected,
> While the vision of pure men
> Is scorned and rejected.
>
> That a wise man goes grieving
> Even in Zion,
> While any dog living
> Outroars a dead lion.
> (Untermeyer 1928: 242)

Untermeyer opposes any of the hope of the passage, opting to pass over the subtle hope of 9:4 as well as the overt strains of joy.

Charles Schultz also passes over such themes, but for a different reason: to reflect on the dog's perspective (plate 12). This is a marvellous comment not only on the ability of this book to confound, but of the experience of many

PLATE 12   Peanuts strip. © United Feature Syndicate, reprinted with permission

who read it and have a sense of empathy with Qoheleth while not knowing exactly why.

Few have commented so sharply on the luminous literary shift from seeming despondency to joy that takes place between verses 6 and 7 than the anonymous author of *Choheleth* in 1765:

> . . . nothing can be more striking than that beautiful passage in the ninth chapter, where, after having most emphatically described the land of darkness, where all things are forgotten [cf. v. 5], in order to remove the doleful impression which so sad a subject must naturally raise, he breaks out, all on a sudden, into such a strain of gayety, as can scarce escape the most cursory reader's observation. (Anonymous 1765: pp. xii–xiii)

In *Midrash Qoheleth* (9.7.1) that joyous 'strain' is related to a liturgical setting: 'R. Huna b. Acha said: When children leave school, a heavenly voice [*bat qōl*] calls out, "Eat thy bread with joy"; the breath of your lips is received before me as a sweet savour. And when the Israelites leave their Synagogues and Houses of Study, a heavenly voice declares, "Eat your bread with joy"; your prayers have been heard before me as a sweet savour.' Traditionally the verse is read out at the end of Yom Kippur, when the time has come for celebrating, and is a divine imperative to be 'festive' that derives from another midrash about the voice of heaven (*bat qōl*) declaring this ruling to be of Abraham (Nulman 1996: 202; cf. *Midrash Leviticus* 20.2; *Midrash Numbers* 17.2). The Talmud relates the verse to a story about Bar Hedya, an interpreter of dreams who accepted money for his services. To those who paid him he gave a favourable interpretation, to those who did not he gave an unfavourable one. Abaye and Raba had the same dream in which they were made to read certain verses of Scripture. Abaye paid Bar Hedya, Raba did not: 'We were made to read in our dream the verse *Go thy way, eat thy bread with joy, etc.* To Abaye he said: Your business will prosper, and you will eat and drink, and recite this verse out of the joy of your heart. To Raba he said: Your business will fail, you will slaughter [cattle] and not eat or drink and you will read Scripture to allay your anxiety' (*b. Berakoth* 56a). The two ways of reading Scripture touched on in this passage provide an insight into the ideal rabbinic method. The first reflects a state of blessing in which one is enabled to read *out of the joy of the heart*, the other a state of curse in which one reads *to allay anxiety*.

Cyril of Jerusalem, *c.*347, in the fourth of his influential *Mystagogical Catacheses* (4:1–9, 'On the Eucharistic Food'), like the midrash, relates the passage to a liturgical context, but with allegory:

> Therefore Solomon also, pointing at this grace, says in Ecclesiastes, *Come hither, eat thy bread with joy,* (that is, the spiritual bread; *Come hither,* calling with words

of salvation and blessing,) *and drink thy wine with a merry heart*; (that is, the spiritual wine;) *and let thy head lack no ointment*, (thou seest he alludes even to the mystic Chrism;) *and let thy garments be always white, for God now accepteth thy works*; for before thou camest to Baptism, thy works were *vanity of vanities*. But now, having put off thy old garments, and put on those which are spiritually white, thou must be continually robed in white. (In Petry 1962: 132)

Jerome, about 40 years later, applies this text more pragmatically as he mourns the death of Blesilla (for whom he composed his commentary) in a letter to St Paula (389): 'Be at peace, dear Blaesilla, in full assurance your garments are always white' (letter 39, in Jerome 1954: 49). In Jewish tradition the same endorsement of glad garments is read as a moral. In *b. Shabbath* (153a) the verse is likened to a parable of a king who invited his servants to a banquet without appointing a time. The wise servants prepared by adorning themselves with appropriate attire while the foolish prepared themselves only when the banquet was under way. They were then made to stand and watch the wise enjoy themselves (cf. a not dissimilar story in *Midrash Qoheleth* 9.8.1).

With a direct sequestering of Qoheleth's voice, Theodore Beza (1588) gently commends readers to take up Qoheleth's advice, and sees the garments as a joyful provision that transcends what is merely necessary in life:

And yet I do not discommend something above that which even for bare neces-sity mans life cannot be without, for as much as God hath for mans sake created not onely things necessarie, but many things also to serve for ornament, and honest delight. Therefore let even thy garments shine, and I forbid thee not to sprinckle thine heade with sweete oyntments, seeing God of his liberalitie hath graunted them also unto thee. (In Beza 1593: fol. D.1)

Not long after, George Sandys, in his marvellous 1632 paraphrase, also appro-priates Qoheleth's voice in direct counsel:

> Then take my Counsell; eate thy Bread with joy:
> Let wine the Sorrowes of thy heart destroy.
> Why should unfruitfull Cares our Soules molest?
> Please thou thy God, and in his favour rest.
> Be thy Apparell ever fresh, and faire;
> Powre breathing Odors, on thy shining haire:
> (In Sandys 1638: 12)

The woman with whom Qoheleth suggests the 'young man' (i.e. the narratee) should enjoy life (9:9) is variously understood as a 'wife' or (any) 'woman' (for examples see Christianson 1998b: 124–5). The endorsement is often taken to ameliorate Qoheleth's earlier attitude towards women in chapter 7. So for the anonymous author of *Choheleth*, 'These words . . . are a sufficient proof, that the bitter sarcasm Solomon had before cast on Women, was not intended as a satyr on the whole sex' (1765: 82).

Of course in the first part of Qoheleth's call to joy in verses 7–10, he reflects on the *product* of one's labour (food, wine and clothing) and only then moves on to human labour proper. Not surprisingly, readers have identified with the zeal for work and, like Thomas Carlyle (1795–1881), related it to a broader concern for living: 'Here on earth we are as soldiers, fighting in a foreign land, that understand not the plan of the campaign, and have no need to understand it; seeing well what is at our hand to be done. Let us do it like soldiers, with submission, with courage, with a heroic joy. *Whatever thy hand findeth to do, do it with all thy might*' (in Nicoll and Stoddart 1910: 548). In retrospect (such as Qoheleth's own narratival aspect), the passage can prompt regret, as Thomas Edward Brown (1830–97) relates in a moving letter to a friend on the death of Brown's son: 'The pain of separation from those we love is so intense that I will *not love* . . . He and I might have been intertwined a great deal more, and that we were not appears to me now a great loss. In this, as in everything else, I accept the words of the Ecclesiast – "What thine hand findeth to do, do it with thy might; for" – you know the rest' (in Nicoll and Stoddart 1910: 548). John Ruskin, in a lecture entitled 'The Mystery of Life and its Arts' (1868), uses verse 10 to reflect on the nature of 'true work' in the artistic guilds, as distinct from the futility of most human endeavour:

> Ask the labourer in the field, at the forge, or in the mine; ask the patient, delicate-fingered artisan, or the strong-armed, fiery-hearted worker in bronze . . . and none of these, who are true workmen, will ever tell you, that they have found the law of heaven an unkind one – that in the sweat of their face they should eat bread, till they return to the ground; nor that they ever found it an unrewarded obedience, if, indeed, it was rendered faithfully to the command – 'Whatsoever thy hand findeth to do – do it with thy might.' (Ruskin 1868: n.p.; see the note on this item in the Bibliography, p. 273)

From here he reflects further on a 'great and constant' lesson,

> a sadder one, which they [the laborers] cannot teach us, which we must read on their tombstones. 'Do it with thy might.' There have been myriads of human creatures who have obeyed this law – who have put every breath and nerve of their being into its toil . . . who have bequeathed their unaccomplished thoughts at death . . . And, at last, what has all this might of humanity accomplished, in six thousand years of labour and sorrow? (1868: n.p.)

Ruskin goes on to discuss the human failure to produce materials of lasting worth, yet one senses that he does not fully realize that in his own terms (of doubting the static truth of the proverb) Qoheleth would certainly have agreed.

As Jewish tradition has it (e.g. *Midrash Qoheleth*, Rashi and Rashbam), Qoheleth's memorable observations in 9:11 are about exceptions to the rule. The swift normally do win, but sometimes they do not, such as the runner Asahel (2 Sam. 2:18–32), who died on account of his swiftness (in Rosenberg 1992: 122–4; cf. Fox 2004: 64). Two modern literary figures offer very different takes. In his 'Race and Battle', D. H. Lawrence (1885–1930) sees more of a reversal than an exception to the rule:

> The race is not to the swift
> but to those that can sit still
> and let the waves go over them.
>
> The battle is not to the strong
> but to the frail, who know best
> how to efface themselves
> to save the streaked pansy of the heart from being trampled to mud.
> (In Atwan and Wieder 1993: 365)

George Orwell's brief encounter with 9:11 is, at the least, perceptive and witty. In a 1946 essay entitled 'Politics and the English Language' (in Orwell 1968: 127–40), Orwell turned his attention to the verse for, as we shall see, very particular issues of linguistic style. Although his example is not concerned with interpreting the verse *per se*, it is a fascinating aside in Ecclesiastes' cultural history (note his description of the verse as 'well known'). Furthermore, not only is it an apt exposition of the universal and concrete language that has made Ecclesiastes such an accessible text to so many, it shows Orwell producing an affectionate parody of Ecclesiastes.

After offering examples of poor modern writing (always in a parodic vein), Orwell turns to the exemplary writing of the Authorized Version:

> Now that I have made this catalogue of swindles and perversions, let me give another example of the kind of writing that they lead to. This time it must of its nature be an imaginary one. I am going to translate a passage of good English into modern English of the worst sort. Here is a well-known verse from *Ecclesiastes*:
>
> > I returned, and saw under the sun, that the race is not to the swift, nor the battle to the strong, neither yet bread to the wise, nor yet riches to men of understanding, nor yet favour to men of skill; but time and chance happeneth to them all. [9:11]

Here it is in modern English:

> Objective consideration of contemporary phenomena compels the con-
> clusion that success or failure in competitive activities exhibits no ten-
> dency to be commensurate with innate capacity, but that a considerable
> element of the unpredictable must invariably be taken into account.

This is a parody, but not a very gross one . . . It will be seen that I have not
made a full translation. The beginning and ending of the sentence follow the
original meaning fairly closely, but in the middle the concrete illustrations – race,
battle, bread – dissolve into the vague phrase 'success or failure in competitive
activities' . . . Now analyse these two sentences a little more closely. The first
contains 49 words but only 60 syllables, and all its words are those of everyday
life. The second contains 38 words of 90 syllables . . . The first sentence contains
six vivid images, and only one phrase ('time and chance') that could be called
vague. The second contains not a single fresh, arresting phrase, and in spite of
its 90 syllables it gives only a shortened version of the meaning contained in the
first . . . Still, if you or I were told to write a few lines on the uncertainty of human
fortunes, we should probably come much nearer to my imaginary sentence than
to the one from *Ecclesiastes*. (In Orwell 1968: 133–4)

In an article on the disconcerting rise of 'doublespeak' in public discourse,
Terence Moran comments rather depressingly on Orwell's example:

> Both passages have been given to students in English class from high school
> through college to graduate school. Sad to report, there is an increase in the
> percentage of students who find the modern version 'clearer and more informa-
> tive' as the level of schooling is raised. In other words, the more schooling the
> better the chances that the student will pick the less concrete and more abstract
> passage. (Moran 1974: 192)

The ominous tenor of 9:12 comes nicely to life in the film *Final Destination*
(2000), in which a group of friends begin to die in horrific circumstances that
are entirely unexpected and unpredictable. The mayhem gains momentum
after the group misses a flight because one of them has a premonition. Of
course the plane crashes, and at a memorial for the victims the speaker reflects:
'As each day passes without a determining cause for the accident, we ask ourselves why. Ecclesiastes tells us: "Man no more knows his own time than fish
taken in a fatal net, or birds trapped in the snare. Like these, the children of
men caught when the time falls suddenly upon them."'

Qoheleth begins this section with a vignette on the value of wisdom (9:13–16) not dissimilar to that of 4:13–16. It is cast in extravagant terms (the 'poor man' somehow delivers the city against a mighty army by wisdom alone) and demonstrates that even when wisdom so clearly triumphs, it will not necessarily be duly recognized. This sets the stage for a series of observations on the wise and the foolish. In just a few verses (9:17–10:6, 12–15), Hebrew words for fools and folly (from *ksl* and *skl*) appear ten times, usually in contrast to wise behaviour. The fool is typified by anger, disquiet (9:17; 10:4; cf. 7:5–6), a lack of restraint and discretion (10:2–3), a loose tongue (10:12–14a) and ignorance (10:15). Folly is also recognized by its ability to have a destructive impact greater than its appearance would suggest (9:18; 10:1). Of course the wise can countenance the foolish by being calm, quiet, discrete and just. But folly, as in the opening vignette, is at work in the realms of political power as well. Qoheleth is indignant about those who would transgress royal protocol and irate that power does not lie in the proper hands (10:5–7, 16–18; cf. 10:20). Such behaviour is aligned to that of the fool, for the ruler can share the fool's proclivity for hotheadedness, ignorance and laziness. Again wisdom can offer protection, in this case against the ruler's foolish anger (10:4). Typically, however, Qoheleth would not have us trust in wisdom to achieve meaningful success in life, because the weightier theme here, not disconnected to that of folly, is uncertainty.

Qoheleth turns to the realm of the hard labourer to suggest endeavours wrought with volatility (10:8–11: pit digging, demolition, quarrying stones, chopping trees – though he concludes with the more obscure example of snake charming). Uncertainty characterizes each of these examples and one can only hope to escape harm through technical skill, grounded in wisdom. That this is no guarantee is subtly reinforced a few verses later with the resumption of an earlier theme, one that by now is perhaps the book's keynote: humanity's ignorance of what will happen (10:14). Chapter 11, too, subtly takes this up in its first six verses. Acts of generosity (11:1–2), the behaviour of the natural world (11:3), and the farmer's futile attempt to predict the weather (11:4) are all obscured by a veil of ignorance with regard to the works of God (11:5). Every activity, then, should be undertaken with this solemn awareness (11:6).

Just as Qoheleth's earlier call to joy (9:7–10) was tempered by the surrounding theme of calamitous uncertainty, so it is here, and the juxtaposition is no less rhetorically effective. The reader is ready for good news, and the final command to rejoice is the most emphatic so far (11:7–10). With its compelling contrasts (sweet light//oppressive darkness; youthful abandon//divine accountability), Qoheleth sets the tone perfectly for his most memorable passage (12:1–7).

Wise Conduct in the Light of Uncertainty: 9:13–11:6

The material between 9:13 and 10:20 has garnered little in the way of distinctive comment in reception history.

For Jerome (388/9), Qoheleth's vignette about the value of wisdom calls to mind a concurrent state of affairs:

> I see even the greatest wisdom in this verse, because it happens repeatedly that there is a small township with only a few inhabitants, and it is surrounded by an army of a very powerful enemy, and the people inside are killed by the siege and

by hunger. And suddenly and unexpectedly a poor man is found, who has more wisdom than all the rich men, than all those powerful and pompous men who are in danger, and who fear the siege. And he thinks, seeks and finds an answer as to how the town might be saved from the oppressors. But O ungrateful oblivion of men, after they were freed from bondage and released from captivity, and the freedom was given back to the fatherland, no one remembers that wise old man, no one gives thanks for their salvation, but all show honour to the rich, who were able to do nothing to help when in time of danger. (2000: *ad loc.*)

Jerome's recollection shows early readers relating to what is today largely a lost referential world, in this case of armies laying siege to autonomous townships. As such, it is one of Qoheleth's less accessible passages (which may account for the almost total lack of interest in this vignette and that of 4:13–16 outside the comprehensive discourse of commentaries).

Qoheleth's observation that a fly in the ointment gives off a foul odour (10:1a) is of course a good example of the Bible's lasting impact on popular discourse. That a little folly outweighs wisdom and honour (10:1b) is taken up in the *Zohar* (*c.*1290), which, while ignoring the controlling sense of the first line of the verse, captures well the inverse relationship of wisdom and folly in Ecclesiastes: 'Rabbi Jose said ... what constitutes the glory and beauty of wisdom, and the glory of honor? The answer is "a little folly". A little folly serves more than anything else to demonstrate and reveal the glory of wisdom and honor in the world above. "A light has an advantage from darkness." [Eccl. 2:13] The benefit of light comes only from the existence of darkness' (in Lachower and Tishby 1989: 3.1352).

In Qoheleth's reflections on the dangers of everyday chores (10:8–11; see Fox 2004: 69), Jewish tradition has seen a moral lesson: do not seek to harm others, or harm may befall you. In other words, digging a pit is read as setting a trap, like a hunter would for prey (so *Midrash Qoheleth* and Rashi, who comments, 'sometimes you have someone plotting evil and it ultimately returns upon him in the end'; in Rosenberg 1992: 133). Ginsburg follows this tradition in a similar vein, reading, for example, the demolition of the wall as a metaphor for 'attempting to destroy the fabric of despotism' (1861: 429–30). Rashbam (*c.*1080–*c.*1160) departs from this mode with his typically literal approach and offers an insightful analysis of what underlies Qoheleth's list of odd uncertainties:

If the iron is blunt [10:10]: even if iron swords are blunt and their edge and point have struck (against something) and are impaired, and one does not sharpen or whet their blades ... yet strength is increased; for the sword supplies courage and strength to increase power and success in battle. Thus is the merit of weapons even if they are not sharpened. Yet there is more advantage and merit in the skill of wisdom than in these. This verse is parallel to ... 'Wisdom is better than weapons of war' (9:18). (In Rashbam 1985: 192)

In other words, even those who possess a remarkable command of technology have no advantage over those who possess skill with wisdom.

Qoheleth's anger at the inappropriate placement of royal power (10:16–20) may have limited relevance to modern readers, but for a culture for which the 'workings' of royalty had more practical and immediate relevance, this text had particular significance, as is evident in George Sandys's 1632 paraphrase:

> Woe to that Land, that miserable Land,
> Which gaspes beneath a Childes unstai'd Command:
> Whose Nobles rise betimes to perpetrate
> Their Luxuries; the ruine of the State.
> Happy that Land, whose King is Nobly Borne:
> Whose Lords with Temperance his Court adorne.
> By Sloths supine neglects the building falls:
> The hands of Idlenesse pull downe her walls.
> Feasts are for Laughter made, Wine cheares our hearts:
> But soveraigne Mony all to all imparts.
> Curse not thy Rulers though with vices fraught;
> Not in thy Bed-Chamber, nor in thy thought:
> For Birds will beare thy whisperings on their wings,
> To the wide eares of Death-inflicting Kings.
>
> (In Sandys 1638: 13)

In his commentary (388/9), Jerome made a more figurative connection to the 'king' of 10:20:

> ... This is to be understood as an exaggeration, just as we are accustomed to saying, 'walls have ears to hear those things, which we think are said in private'. But it is better to hear a teaching in this way, so that we know that we have a commandment to follow, not only that nothing should be spoken rashly against Christ, but also in the secret places of our heart, however we are troubled by our many problems, nothing should be blasphemed, nothing thought which is impious. (2000: *ad loc.*)

The call to 'cast thy bread upon the waters' (11:1) represents one of Qoheleth's most unfettered instances of concern for others. Certainly the classical rabbis think so, as is particularly evident in *Midrash Qoheleth* on 11:1, which relates several example stories regarding the benefits of charity. Christians also respond to Qoheleth's endorsement of giving. So Isaac of Nineveh (d. *c.*700), in one of his many *Ascetical Homilies* adjures,

> When you give, give generously, with a joyous countenance, and give more than
> you are asked for, since it is said, 'Send forth your morsel of bread toward the
> face of the poor man, and soon you will find your recompense.' Do not separate
> the rich from the poor or try to discriminate the worthy from the unworthy, but
> let all persons be equal in your eyes for a good deed. (Hom. 4, in J. R. Wright
> 2005: 274)

Much later novelist Louise Erdrich recognizes the passage's implicit and poetic
urging of generosity:

> If I were to choose a passage most valuable to me from Ecclesiastes, I wouldn't
> choose the face-to-the-wall, sulking *all is weariness, the soul cannot utter it, and
> there is nothing new under the sun*. I'd choose the line that has something to do
> with trusting an instinct for generosity, *Cast thy bread upon the waters*. For the
> image of a man or a woman standing in a boat or on the shore and throwing
> bread at the waves makes no sense and yet speaks volumes, as does the best
> poetry. (1995: 237)

Perhaps unsurprisingly, Christian exegetes have often spiritualized the
sowing of 11:4, 6. Alcuin, in a letter *Extolling Christian Learning* (795, *Epist.*
121) relates it to his own sense of mission:

> Meanwhile, I shall, within the limits of my own modest ability, not be dilatory
> in sowing the seeds of wisdom among your servants in this area [the 'research
> for knowledge . . . through wisdom']. In so doing I shall have in mind the
> passage: 'In the morning sow your seed and in the evening withhold not your
> hand.' In the morning, during a period of flourishing studies I sowed the seed
> in Britain. Now, in the evening as it were, and with the cooling blood of age, I
> do not cease to sow seed in France. (In Petry 1962: 391)

In some 2,500 sermons, C. H. Spurgeon only made use of Ecclesiastes (or
referred to it in passing) seven times. The most significant example was
preached in July 1890, 'Sowing the Wind; Reaping under Clouds'. Like Alcuin,
he sees sowing as a kind of evangelism, but he touches on other activities as
well: 'Take the case of the sailor. If he regards winds and clouds, will he ever
put to sea? Can you give him a promise that the wind will be favourable in any
of his voyages, or that he will reach his desired haven without a tempest? He
that observeth the winds will not sail; and he that regardeth the clouds will
never cross the mighty deep' (in Spurgeon 1892: 326).

The times of morning and evening in 11:6 are taken in Jewish tradition
to refer to youth and old age respectively. The Talmud reads the verse as a
warning: R. Joshua says that if a man had children in his youth, he should also

have them in his old age, just in case anything happens to them. R. Akiba, on the other hand, takes it to refer to the acquisition of disciples in both youth and old age (*b. Yebamoth* 62b; cf. *Midrash Qoheleth* 11.6.1).

The Final Call to Joy: 11:7–10

George Sandys's paraphrase (1632) offers a suitably energetic rendering of this climactic expression of joy, one particularly attuned to the weighty contrast between days of light and of darkness:

> How sweet is Light! how pleasant to behold,
> The mounted Sun discend in beames of Gold!
> Yet, though a Man live long; long in delight:
> Let him remember that approching Night
> Which shall in endlesse darknesse close his Eyes:
> Then will he all, as vanitie, despise.
>
> (In Sandys 1638: 14)

Ecclesiastes 11:9 has proved troublesome from the earliest times, particularly Qoheleth's proposal that the young man he is addressing walk 'in the way of your heart' (which Num. 15:39 forbids, in precisely the same language; see Salters's survey of readings, 1998: 50–7). Some manuscripts of the Septuagint, for example, add 'innocently' after 'your heart' (Fox 2004: 75). Rashi suggests that the advice is 'like a man who says to his slave or to his son, "Sin, sin, for one time you will suffer for all"' (in Rosenberg 1992: 151). In his influential commentary (1253–7), Bonaventure sought to alleviate the perceived tension by modifying the ancient strategy of competing voices, which understands Qoheleth to employ a different *style* of speaking: 'he says some things *plainly*, others he says *ironically*... An ironic statement occurs in Ecclesiastes 11:9 ... *Rejoice therefore, O young man, in your youth*. That this statement is ironic is clear from what shortly follows in 11:9: *And know that for all these God will bring you into judgment*' (2005: 233; cf. Stillingfleet's reading, below). While he is perhaps indirectly addressing the same concerns, Luther takes a more liberal view on the verse:

> ... Young people should avoid sadness and loneliness. Joy is as necessary for youth as food and drink, for the body is invigorated by a happy spirit. Education should not begin with the body but with the spirit, so that this is not over-looked ... Therefore one must be indulgent with youth, and must let them be happy and do everything with a happy spirit. Yet one must see to it that they are not corrupted by the desires of the flesh. For carousals, drinking-bouts, and love

affairs are not the happiness of the heart of which he is speaking here but rather make the spirit sad. (*c*.1532, in Luther 1972: 177)

Such concerns about the passage remained in religious discourse for many years, which makes the inventive departure of Francis Quarles remarkable. His immensely popular *Hieroglyphikes* (1638), a sequel to his *Emblemes* (1635), is a series of engravings accompanied by his own verse (see the discussion above, p. 113). Here Quarles places Qoheleth's words in the context of transitoriness, time and fate:

> *Rejoyce O young man, and let thy heart cheare thee, but know, &c*
> Ecclesiastes XI.9

> How flux! how alterable is the date
>   Of transitory things!
> How hurry'd on the clipping wings
>   Of Time, and driv'n upon the wheeles of Fate!
> How one Condition brings
>   The leading Prologue to an other State!
> No transitory thing can last:
>   Change waits on Time; and Time is wing'd with hast;
> Time present's but the Ruins of Time past.
>
>   . . .
>
>   Consume thy golden daies
> In slavish freedome; Let thy waies
>   Take best avantage of thy frolick mirth;
> Thy Stock of Time decaies;
>   And lavish plenty still foreruns a Dearth:
> The bird that's flowne may turne at last;
>   And painefull labour may repaire a wast;
> But paines nor price can call thy minits past.
>   (Hieroglyph 11, Quarles 1638: 42–4)

In the final stanza Quarles restates Qoheleth's endorsement, commending a youthful embrace of 'slavish freedome' and 'frolick'. Repentance of some sort may occur and 'repaire a wast' (a woe or waste?). The accompanying image – an impossible arrangement of a candle, an orb, a floating goat, a vine, a bow and quiver of arrows – is a perfect example of what Ernest Gilman describes as the embleme's tendency to 'jumble' allegorical pictures with 'devils, souls, cupids, globes, wheels of fortune, candles, and bowling balls' (1980: 397). For Gilman, this is the spiritual innovation of the emblemes (to be resumed with Blake), which 'refocus our sight telescopically from the image before us . . . to the "latter end" of spiritual insight, an object of thought and meditation beyond the pictorial surface. Their vanishing point is not in the depths of the image but in the soul of the viewer' (ibid.).

A notably literary reading of 11:9, undertaken with fluent reference to the context of the whole book, is offered by the renowned Elizabethan preacher and theologian Edward Stillingfleet, bishop of Worcester. In a sermon preached to the King and Queen at Whitehall, 23 March 1689/90 [*sic*], Stillingfleet carefully builds his reading by suggesting that Solomon, by the admonition to 'let thy heart cheer thee in the days of thy youth, and walk in the ways of thine heart, and in the sight of thine eyes' (AV), seems 'to give a Permission to young Men in the time of Youth to indulge themselves in their Mirth and Vanity' (1698: 134). Stillingfleet's resolution is alive to the rhetorical features of the passage:

> Some think that the wise Man only derides and exposes them for their Folly in so doing [i.e. in following the 'ways of thine heart']; but that seems not agreeable with the grave and serious Advice that follows. And we find nothing like *Irony* or *Sarcasm* in any Part of the foregoing Book; for he begins it with a Tragical Exclamation against the Vanities of humane Life; *Vanity of Vanities, saith the Preacher, Vanity of Vanities: all is Vanity.* (1698: 134)

A little further on Stillingfleet argues from the *experience* of Qoheleth, so central to Qoheleth's epistemology and advice:

> And he pursues his Argument by a particular Induction of the most tempting and pleasing Vanities of Life; and particularly all sorts of sensual Delights . . . But what a melancholy Reflection doth he make on all these Pleasures of Life? . . . [2:11 is cited] What incouragement then could the wise Man, after so much Experience of the World, give to young Men here in the Text, to *rejoyce in the days of their Youth, and to walk in the way of their hearts, and in the sight of their eyes?* i.e. to pursue *Vanity,* and to lay the Foundation for greater Vexation of Spirit, when they come to reflect on their own Follies. (1698: 134–5)

Although Stillingfleet represents a sophisticated version of it, the strategy is typical of the period, with whole publications given over to the adjuration of wayward youths. Indeed, the entry for 11:9 in James Darling's *Cyclopaedia Bibliographica* catalogues 29 sermons, more than for any other Ecclesiastes text, most with titles along the lines of 'An exhortation to youth to prepare for judgment' (1859: 2. cols 572–3). We might note the examples of Daniel Williams's *The Vanity of Childhood & Youth Wherein the Depraved Nature of Young People is Represented and Means for their Reformation Proposed* (1691), or the anonymous *The Young Man's Alarum* [alarm] . . . *a Discourse upon the 9th. Verse of the 11th. Chapter of Ecclesiastes* (1680). The latter is little more than a list of examples of those who would 'wilfully run headlong into misery, and so carefully to provide for [themselves] eternal Torment' (1680: 3). The author is duly scandalized by the only perceivable outcome, which is to 'see Men hurry on by so many several ways to Death and Diseases, the only two Bugbears thought of humane Nature' (1680: 8). A few years later, John Edwards takes a similar line by acutely expressing his fear over 'misunderstanding' the verse. In a tract subtly entitled, *The Judgments that Attend Sinners*, Edwards cites 11:9 as his epigraph and continues:

> Upon which Words I imagine I hear the voluptuous and prophane Person make this most cursed Comment: Ay, this is good Doctrine indeed, I like *Solomon's* Council very well; now (if ever) he speaks like a *wise Man* . . . Religion is a dull and dismal Thing, 'tis good for nothing but to make folks melancholy mopish . . . Thus the brutish Epicure and sensual worldling makes this Interpretation of these Words, to fit his own carnal and debauched Appetite. (Edwards 1726: 617–18)

So sure is Edwards of the implied curbing of that same 'Appetite' in the latter part of the verse that he proclaims, 'You may feel the very Flames of Hell in every Word' (1726: 618).

Other readings manage to reflect Qoheleth's ambiguity regarding God's judgment on the joyful 'young man'. In his *A Speech at Eton* (1879), Matthew Arnold, in a spirit akin to Luther's reading (above), resists the traditional reading of moral admonition (with which he was most likely familiar) and succeeds in capturing Qoheleth's programmatic concern with the best way to live. After citing the verse to the young men gathered, he continued, 'In other words: Your enjoyment of life, your freedom from restraint, your clear and bold reason, your flexibility, are natural and excellent; but on condition that you know how to live with them, that you make a real success with them' (in Arnold 1973: 31). Oliver Stone's *Platoon* (1986) departs entirely from the moralistic reading (though probably not consciously). The film opens simply with the text, '"Rejoice young man in the days of thy youth" – Ecclesiastes', accompanied by Samuel Barber's Adagio for Strings. The scene which immediately follows has a young soldier (Charlie Sheen) arriving by helicopter in the middle of Vietnam. Fresh-faced, his naivety contrasts with the battle-hardened young men already there. As he and the other newcomers disembark, other soldiers are loading the helicopter with body bags. The epigraph prefigures the loss of the young man's youth and joy that the film will chronicle. As A. C. Beck points out, Stone does not complete the verse and thereby excises the perspective of God's judgment altogether, steering 'viewers away from expecting a story structured by moral absolutes. In the end, this silence has the effect of misleading viewers, for the film, in fact, retells the battle between good and evil, between the risen Christ and the beast' (1995: 45).

The referential world of this poem is notoriously obscure, which has perhaps encouraged the excessive allegorizing to which these words have been subjected. The poem is structured by time, by the moment of remembering (or better, 'being alive to' or 'cognizant of') 'your' creator in youth. Such times are marked by demise, first, of personal delight in life (v. 1), which Qoheleth has just finished endorsing in emphatic fashion (11:7–10). The shift to apocalyptic imagery, of the darkening of the sun and stars and the coming of clouds (v. 2), is startling and unexpected. This is the language of the day of Yahweh's judgment, 'a day of darkness and gloom, a day of clouds and thick darkness', in which 'the sun and moon are darkened, and stars withdraw their brightness' (Joel 2:2a, 10b; cf. Ezek. 30:3; 32:7–8; Isa. 13:9–10; Amos 5:18, 20; Zeph. 1:15). To bring to bear so abruptly such an other-worldly perspective on this, the most intensely self-oriented book of the Bible, is part of the poem's brilliance.

But the context of Qoheleth's own words is even more compelling. The sun here recalls what the dead cannot see or experience (6:5), and so its darkening is an apt image for the diminishment of youthful living – an existence that is a few lines earlier described as the sight of the sun (11:7; cf. 7:11).

Qoheleth renders a distinctly domestic realm in the images that follow, a portrait of a village in mourning. He describes the haunting effects of death on the home (v. 3), the workplace (at the mill, vv. 3, 5) and the street (vv. 4 and 5). Death has brought ceremonial recognition (the shutting doors of v. 4) and even fear in the byways (v. 5). The people are shaken, made silent and brought to an eerie standstill (v. 3). Only the mourners on the street show movement, made all the more conspicuous by the cessation of the mill, of the singers and of the now inaudible songbirds (vv. 4–5). The only other movement is figurative, of humanity going to their eternal home (v. 5) and the dust and spirit returning to their rightful places (v. 7). This lifeless rupture is thrown into sharp relief by the abundant life of the blossoming almond tree, the ripening berries and the locust swollen from feasting (v. 5). Like the littered landscape of a *vanitas* still life, the broken objects of verse 6 recall the collapse of an established society. The silver and golden furnishings eventually wear out, and the technology for living (the pitcher, the wheel in the pit) breaks down and will be replaced, along with any meaning it once held for its users.

Qoheleth has already hinted at the poignancy of loss, particularly in his lament over the stillborn who comes in *hebel*, whose name remains covered in darkness and who will never see the sun (6:3–5). Such loss is narrated to make his young reader seize the life that is before him, but any reader can easily identify with the 'you' of Qoheleth's discourse (see Christianson 1998a: 245–7). In 12:1–7 we can also make Qoheleth's deathly rumination very much our own (as Fox so memorably puts it, 'when we peer through the murk of the images . . . we realize with a shudder that we are descrying our own obliteration'; 2004: 77). That ubiquitous self-perspective is reinforced by the recurring time-markers ('before', 'in the day') that govern the moment of 'your' divine cognizance in every line, but it is also tempered by the communal aspect and the return to God at the poem's end (v. 7).

As a meditation on any of the hard themes that have gone before, Qoheleth has here surpassed himself. And that is why these seven verses have received more distinct attention than any other passage in Ecclesiastes' reception history. Whether they have here seen their own demise or that of the world, readers have long recognized the brilliance of these exquisite lines.[1]

---

[1]   I have organized the commentary section here differently from anywhere else. Since the reception material for this passage falls generally into allegorical and non-allegorical readings, these are the contours along which I have arranged the commentary. As always, it is not an entirely foolproof categorization, as will become clear.

The Rule of Allegory

As Jerome testifies, this text has, from at least his own day, generated a remarkably diverse range of readings:

> In this chapter there were many explanations of all things and almost as many opinions as men themselves. It would take too long however to recount all the opinions of everyone and their arguments in which they want to prove their opinions, the matter would require a volume to itself. But it is enough for wise men to have shown what they feel, and like in a small picture, to have depicted the thirst of the earth, the waste of the whole earth, and the belt of the ocean, and to have shown them in such a small collection. (2000: *ad loc.*)

(Jerome proceeds to a lengthy allegorical reading that he attributes to 'the Hebrews': the 'you' is Israel, who should enjoy the days of her youth before the harsh days of Babylonian captivity come. He then offers what will become a familiar Christian allegorical reading.) It is also clear that whatever the details of this passage ultimately refer to, it is about the end *of something*. 'The end of what?' is the interpretive question that resounds down the ages.

Allegory forces, through a process of codification, reference to another reality, a substitution of one realm's attributes by those of another. Countless interpreters, suggests John Jarick, 'have exercised considerable imagination in breaking open the supposed allegory' (1995: 311). In Jewish tradition the allegory appears in four sources: *Targum Qoheleth*, *Midrash Qoheleth*, b. *Shabbath* 151a–153a and *Midrash Leviticus* (for an analysis of the complex source relationship between these, see Kraus 1999–2000: 202). Kraus offers, in two helpful appendices, tables that compare the allegorical approaches. In the first he compares *Midrash Qoheleth* and Jerome. In the second he compares all four classical Jewish sources and Jerome. Here is one example from the second appendix (1999–2000: 225):

Targ. Q.	Midr. Q.	Midr. Lev. 18	b. Shab. 151a–153a	Jerome
[MT:] *the moon*				
beauty of your cheeks	the forehead	the nose	soul	ears?

(Knobel offers a similar, briefer table, though without Jerome; 1991: 53, 55.) Of these sources we can take the Talmud (b. *Shabbath* 151a–153a) as illustrative, not least because it indirectly influenced the Christian allegorical approach (Kraus argues that a 'fixed form' of the passage heavily influenced Jerome's allegorical reading, therefore placing it before 388 CE; 1999–2000: 24 *et passim*). The Talmud takes most of the figures to refer to concrete experiences of old age. For example, '. . . "*and the stars*" – these are the cheeks; "*and the clouds return after the rain*" – this is the light of man's eyes [his eyesight], which is lost after weeping. Samuel said: For tears, until the age of forty there is a recovery, but thenceforth there is no recovery' (*b. Shabbath* 151b). The allegory is total. In brief: the trembling keepers of the house are the deteriorating ribs, the ceasing grinders the teeth, those looking through the darkened windows the eyes (v. 3), the snapping of the silver cord the spinal cord, the broken pitcher the stomach (v. 6). As with any reading that attempts total cohesion, there are bound to be unconvincing elements. In this case, the darkening sun, light and moon (v. 2) are the head, nose and soul respectively. Jewish interpreters have by and large followed this particular allegorical code, although the kabbalistic *Zohar* (*c*.1290) marks a notable departure. In the flow of a discourse on the subject of good days and evil days, the bodily code is explicitly replaced with a mystical cryptogram:

> What are these evil days? You might think that they are the days of old age, but it is not so, for if you have children and grandchildren the days of old age are good days . . . They are as it has been explained, for it is written 'Remember your Creator in the days of your youth, before the evil days come' . . . These are not the days of old age, but the secret of the matter is as follows. When the Holy One, blessed be He, created the world, He created it with the letters of the Torah, and every letter came into His presence, until all the letters stood by the letter *bet* [i.e. the first letter of Torah], and all those thousand letters *bet*, around which the [other] letters revolved, were ready to help in the creation of the world. (In Lachower and Tishby 1989: 2. 526)

Christian readings tend to conflate the allegory of an individual old man with that of the decline of the Church (and with it individual piety) and the end of the world. In this scheme, for example, as Jerome would have it (2000: *ad loc.*), 'the brightness of the moon (that is of the Church) will be taken away, and the stars will die, about which is written, "in which you shine like the lights in the world having reason of life" (Phil. 2:15)'. This is developed in varying degrees by Alcuin (730–804), Rupert of Deutz (*c*.1110), Nicholas of Lyra (*c*.1270–1349) and Hugh of St Cher (*c*.1230–5; see Eliason 1989: 61–7; the apocalyptic aspect is present in Talmud as well; *b. Shabbath* 151b, 152b). Bonaventure (1253–7), who is representative of the medieval interpreters, offers a very detailed allegory of the body (of which even Dr Smith would be envious – see below). The crushed pitcher, for example, is about the collapse of the bladder (also a receptacle for water) in old age, but even that is ultimately about the inability of the spiritual man to live in purity. The items equally relate to the final judgment, so the 'keepers of the house' represent 'the final state of the Church' trembling before the judgment of Christ (in Bonaventure 2005: 399–421 [411–12]). Even Luther (*c.*1532), who valiantly resists allegory throughout his commentary, cannot resist *likening* the figures of the passage to an old man. So of the grasshopper of verse 5 he says, 'that is, "such an old man is like a grasshopper, for his whole body is nothing but skin and bone." His bones stick out, and his body is exhausted. He is nothing but a sort of image of death' (1972: 181). The codification of the allegory to death itself continued with Puritans of the seventeenth century, such as in the closing episode of John Bunyan's *The Pilgrim's Progress* (1678), through which Qoheleth's final poem runs like a refrain as tokens are delivered to those who, having died, await their entry to the Celestial City. The tokens, which are lines from Ecclesiastes 12, confirm the hearers' deaths and entry to the City. For example, 'it was noised abroad that Mr Valiant-for-Truth was taken with a summons . . . and had this for a token that the summons was true, *That his pitcher was broken at the fountain*' (in Bunyan 1986: 382). In a way, this is an application of the allegory to the whole Christian struggle in which Bunyan's characters engage. In Christian discourse, as in Jewish, there are only occasional departures. John Donne, for example, took the imperative to remember at 12:1 as a call to repentance, 'to repent the not remembering him till now' (a theme he develops at length in his sermon at Lincoln's Inn, 18 April 1619; in Donne 1839: 6. 17–33 [18]).

The allegorical approach reaches dizzy heights in *The Pourtract of Old Age* (1676) by John Smith, 'M.D. of the College of Physicians', which seeks to relate every item in 12:1–6 to a particular bodily function or specific corpuscle, as such relate to old age. So, for example, even the fear of what is 'high' and 'in the road' (v. 5) relates to the 'powers and faculties of the mind, as they are weakened in Age . . . In these words is notified unto us, that most remarkable change that is made upon the affects and passions of the mind in the same condition' (1676: 152). Discussing the shutting doors of verse 4, Smith declares,

> And hence it is, that the Orbicular Muscles, which make the substance of the lips, (being therefore called the *Calves of the lips*,) and have the power of the keys to shut and open them, are called *Oris Pylori* . . . And therefore those former Interpreters that have applied these words to the Lips, have done exceeding well; the report they have given hath been true. (1676: 120)

But this detail is not enough, and the reader will not be spared the more potentially objectionable, indeed 'extream', locations of the human anatomy.

For beside these doors, there are other extream doors also, *viz.* the back doors, which serve only for the carrying out of the Excrements. And although the Ears, the Nostrils, and the Eyes, and all the *Emunctories* of the body may be here included, yet those which are principally intended, are those eminent Posterns, which so long as Man lives in strength are alwayes ready for their work, which is to give pass to those ... Excrements which we daily avoid. (1676: 120–1)

And so Doctor Smith continues, page upon page. As C. H. Spurgeon (2004) said of the work in 1876, we 'mention it because of its singularity'. To lesser degrees this approach would continue to be found. For example, Moses Mendelssohn's 1770 commentary also renders the anatomical symbolism in detail: 'It is apparent that the circulation of the blood ... was known to King Solomon [as 'described' in 12:6] ... [and] this theory was hidden to the sages of all the ancient nations and was not made known until a century ago by experiments [i.e. William Harvey's theories of 1628]' (in Sorkin 1996: 43).

Rigorous allegorical reading of 12:1–7 extends beyond Jewish and Christian discourse. In 'The Picture of Old Age' (1761), noted classicist and translator Francis Fawkes renders it with a subtle rhetorical strategy. In its first half Fawkes takes on the voice of Qoheleth to speak to his 'son', and in the second abstracts the figure of demise into 'he':

> My son, attentive hear the voice of truth;
> Remember thy Creator in thy youth,
> Ere days of pale adversity appear,
> And age and sorrow fill the gloomy year,
>
> . . .
>
> Ere the bright soul's enlighten'd pow'rs wax frail,
> Ere reason, memory, and fancy fail,
>
> . . .
>
> Ere yet the grinding of the teeth is o'er,
> And the dim eyes behold the sun no more;
> Ere yet the pallid lips forget to speak,
> The gums are toothless, and the voice is weak;
>
> Restless he rises when the lark he hears
> Yet sweetest music fails to charm his ears.
>
> . . .
>
> Ere broke the golden bowl that holds the brain,
> Ere broke the pitcher at the fountful heart,
> Or life's wheel shiver'd, and the soul depart.
> Then shall the dust to native earth be given,
> The soul shall soar sublime, and wing its way to heaven.
>
> (In Fawkes 2004)

The influence of the totalizing allegory of the Talmud is clear, as is that of *Targum Qoheleth*, from which he follows the coding for the golden bowl as a skull. Even the theist Voltaire, in his article 'Emblème', for the *Questions sur l'Encyclopédie* (1771), claims that 'One of the most stunning emblems ['Un des plus beaux emblèmes'] among the Jewish books is this passage from Ecclesiastes' (in Voltaire 1877: 18. 522). He was most certainly referring to its allegorical attributes, which reflected the concurrent sense of 'emblème' (he goes on to cite his own reading of 12:3–6 as an allegory of old age, though in his 1759 *Précis* his reading only vaguely hints at allegory).

The sheer volume of allegorical readings prompted Charles Taylor's 1874 study *The Dirge of Coheleth*. Taylor's systematic dissatisfaction with allegory – what he terms the 'anatomical reading' – is unusual for the period (although he is preceded by Ginsburg 1861: 457–69). Taylor argues at length that 12:1–5 describes 'the state of a household or community on an occasion of death and mourning' (1874: pp. iii–iv; it is worth noting that the extensive Talmud allegory follows on from Mishnaic instructions regarding the preparation of a body for funeral; *b. Shabbath* 151a).[2] Taylor's study offers useful summaries of the various literal and figurative approaches to the passage. Of the anatomical readings he concludes that 'the great contrariety of opinion amongst the commentators seems to shew at any rate that no particular anatomical combination has been approximately made out, and to suggest grave doubt as to whether it is possible to combine the details harmoniously in any way whatever' (1874: 56).

As John Sawyer has shown, the allegorical approach fails to account for textual details, details which for Sawyer suggest 'a man's pessimism in face of the tyranny of time and the illogicality of events' (1975: 531). To borrow philosopher Jacques Ellul's phrase (see below), 12:1–7 is a song of the end, and of course it has been applied to more than one end – to a strange conglomeration of the end of a life, a community or the world. Ultimately the appeal to allegory can, as Ellul argues, be understood as a resistance to this passage's manifest poetry:

> everyone reads this passage like an enigma from which we must find the allegorical meaning of each term ... I think the poem is too vast for this, and too 'polysemous' ... It is *first of all* a poem! In other words, it is not at all a problem to solve ... First of all we must let the beauty of the text grip us, as we listen to

---

[2]   Understandably, Qoheleth's poem continues to be used as a funeral dirge. It was read, e.g., by the Bishop of York at the televised funeral of the Queen Mother in September 2002. Ps. 121 was sung and Eccl. 12:1–8 was then read 'over' the casket, draped in royal robes.

it in silence, like music. We should let the poem strike our emotions first, and allow our sensitivity and imagination to speak before we try to analyze and 'understand' it. (1990: 285)

To put it another way, when the motionless women at the mill are merely a code for useless teeth, and the reader has accepted the new (and far less 'polysemous') referent, the primary imagery of an industry made silent by grief is sapped of its power to evoke.[3] Allegory strictly applied also diminishes the ability of readers to inhabit the space of Qoheleth's implied reader, and in this regard we might note novelist Doris Lessing's reflections on the poem:

> From the very first verse of Ecclesiastes you are carried along on a running tide of sound, incantatory, almost hypnotic, and it is easy to imagine yourself sitting among this man's pupils, listening to – for instance, 'Remember now thy creator in the days of thy youth, while the evil days come not, nor the years draw nigh, when thou shalt say, I have no pleasure in them.' Your ears are entranced but at the same time you are very much alert. You have to be old to understand that verse [at the time of publishing this, Lessing was 79], to see your whole life from early heedlessness to present regret for heedlessness; you find yourself drifting off into speculation. Was this particular admonition addressed to young people, to remind them that old age will come to them too? Or reserved for grey heads who would hear it with the ears of experience? Or flung out in an assembly, to be caught by anyone who could – who had the ears to hear, as Jesus put it. (1998: p. x)

Taylor, Sawyer and Ellul are just a small sample of the many interpreters, particularly those whose audience is conceived as beyond (while perhaps still including) Jewish and Christian readers, who have expressed their dissatisfaction with the allegorical reading, sometimes implicitly by merely constructing a different approach.

Beyond Allegory

There were only rare exceptions to allegory in early Jewish and Christian quarters. John Jarick draws attention to the resolutely literal approach of Theodore

---

[3]   Ellul's own reading would be difficult to construct under the sway of allegory: the poem 'calls to mind all declines, all breaches, closures, and endings. Not just the decline of an individual nearing death, not just human destiny, but everything: the end of any work which is no longer done, which disappears because no one is present to do it anymore . . . the end of a village or community . . . the end of a love replaced by fear; the end of an art, its works shattered, unless they die in our museums . . . It is the song of the End' (1990: 285–6; Fisch's evocative reading is similar, 1988: 178).

of Mopsuestia (*c.*350–428) in his Ecclesiastes commentary. For example, Theodore says of the 'ceasing' women at the mill (v. 3) that 'those who perform duties in your house cease their accustomed duties because your possessions have diminished' (in Jarick 1995: 312), and that is because evil days have fallen on this estate ('your house'). The whole reading is a compelling portrait of a house in disrepair, one which reminds readers not to rely on wealth and its attendant pleasures, which can fall to ruin at any time (see Jarick 1995: 313–14). It is a portrait that anticipates much later readings of the passage that relate these verses to the demise of communal life.

Rebecca Beal has drawn attention to an early and nuanced appropriation of the passage (in particular 11:9–12:1, 8) in Geoffrey Chaucer's *Troilus and Criseyde* (*c.*1385), a long narrative poem in 'vernacular', relating the doomed love affair of the titular couple in the city of Troy during the Trojan war. The ending, she argues, 'contains two important . . . allusions to the conclusion of Ecclesiastes . . . and each occurs at a crucial moment in the conclusion, the first when Troilus dies, rises above the world, and calls everything below him "vanitie"' (1982: 243):

> And down from thennes faste he gan avyse [. . . from that dense place he did
>   surmise]
> This litel spot of erthe that with the se[a]
> Embraced is, and fully gan [did] despise
> This wrecched world, and held al vanitie
> To respect of the pleyn felicitie [With respect to the perfect felicity]
> That is in hevene above; and at the laste,
> Ther he was slayn his lokyng down he caste, [. . . his gaze he cast down,]
>   (5.1814–20, in Chaucer 1988: 584)

This epiphanic moment mirrors the influential view of Hugh of St Victor (*c.*1118–41) that Qoheleth/Solomon's insight of *vanitas* was one of rapture: 'In this light, therefore, being rapt in spirit above all transient and perishable things, this man perceived that among all this is, there is nothing that lasts, and, as if stricken with fear at this new and unfamiliar sight exclaimed, "Vanity of vanities, and all is vanity"' (on 1:2, in Beal 1982: 248).

The second allusion occurs as Chaucer admonishes his youthful audience to turn from 'worldly vanitie':

> O yonge, fresshe folkes, he or she,
> In which that love up groweth with youre age,
> Repeyreth hom fro [Return to home from] worldly vanitie,
> And of youre herte up casteth the visage
> To thilke God [To that same God] that after his ymage

> Yow made, and thynketh al nys but a faire [. . . all is nought but an
>   amusement],
> This world that passeth soone as floures [flourish] faire.
>
> (5.1835–41, in Chaucer 1988: 584)

Here Chaucer's advice, broadly directed to 'he or she', presumes a necessary
detachment from the world (a living *contemptus mundi*). Beal regards the
references as a very deliberate alignment of Troilus's experience to the medieval understanding of the mutability of vanity in Ecclesiastes. For Troilus is a
character 'beset by mutability', whose love affair is set against the doomed city
of Troy, the Trojan war negating 'the possibility of any happy ending' (1982:
246, 254).

Douglas Bush, in his study of English literature in the seventeenth century,
calls Qoheleth's closing poem 'one of the greatest of meditations on mortality'
(1948: 69). To illustrate the rhetorical development that takes place from the
Great Bible of 1539–40 (Coverdale) through to the 'noblest monument of
English prose', the King James Bible of 1611, Bush samples Eccl. 12:1–8, which
is especially instructive. Here, for example, is how verses 1–3 are developed (in
Bush 1948: 69–71):

The Great Bible (1539–40, published without poetic line breaks)
Remembre thy maker in thy youth, or ever the dayes of adversytie come, and or
the yeares drawe nye, when thou shalt saye: I have not pleasure in them: before
the sunne, the lyght, the moone and starres be darckened, and or the cloudes
turne agayne after the rayne, when the kepers of the house shall tremble, and
when the stronge men shal bowe them selves: when the myllers stande styll,
because they be so few, and when the syght of the windowes shall waxe
dymme:

The Geneva version (1560)
   Remember now thy Creator in the daies of thy youth, whiles the evil daies
come not, nor the yeres approche, wherein thou shalt say, I have no pleasure in
them:
   Whiles the sunne is not darke, nor the light, nor the moone, nor the starres,
nor the cloudes returne after the raine:
   When the kepers of the house shal tremble, and the strong men shal bowe
them selves, and the grinders shal cease, because thei are fewe, and they waxe
darke that loke out by the windowes:

King James (1611)
   Remember now thy Creatour in the dayes of thy youth, while the evil daies
come not, nor the yeeres drawe nigh, when thou shalt say, I have no pleasure
in them:

> While the Sunne, or the light, or the Moone, or the Starres bee not darkened,
> nor the cloudes returne after the raine:
>
> In the day when the keepers of the house shall tremble, and the strong men
> shall bowe themselves, and the grinders cease, because they are fewe, and those
> that looke out of the windowes be darkened:

Bush finds that, on the whole, 'the Jacobean revisers, while eclectic, may be
said ... to have carried Coverdale's refinement and elevation of phrase and
rhythm to its consummation without losing the plain strength of Tyndale'
(1948: 68).

Bush's illustration helps us to understand the Elizabethan poets' attraction
to the book, particularly to its most sonorous passages. Like chapter 3,
chapter 12 is a magnet for poets, a pull no doubt sustained by the deliberate
ambiguity of Qoheleth's mournful imagery. But for poets this can only be a
very mixed blessing, for the poem presents a daunting prospect for versifica-
tion. The anonymous author of the paraphrase *Choheleth* (1765), with its
often exquisite lines (see above, pp. 59–60), comments on the task of rendering a poem of such elegance in verse: 'Nothing can be more concise or expres-
sive, insomuch that the greater part of force and beauty [of these verses], if not
entirely lost, must be considerably diminished, by a paraphrase, or circumlocu-
tion of words, which was almost unavoidable in a work of this nature' (1765:
110).

In the Introduction (see pp. 54–7) I have provided examples of verse from
Henry Lok (1597), John Donne (1610s and 1620s), George Sandys (1632),
Francis Quarles (*c.*1645) and Alexander Brome (*c.*1648), so will here only offer
one representative example, from the incomparable Sandys:

> Man must at length to his long home descend:
> Behold, the Mourners at his gates attend.
> Advise, before the Silver Cord growes slacke;
> Before the golden Boule asunder crack:
> Before the Pitcher at the fountaine leake;
> Or wasted Wheele besides the Cisterne breake.
> Man, made of Earth, resolves into the same:
> His Soule ascends to God, from whom it came.
> O Restlesse Vanitie of Vanities!
>
> (In Sandys 1638: 15)

As with most of the versifications of the period, there is little if any hint of
allegory. Instead, Sandys is remarkably attentive to the immediate sense of the
language: 'Behold', he says, 'the Mourners at his [i.e. any person's] gates' – for
countless readers allegory had likely obscured their presence.

Another outstanding example comes from Anne Bradstreet's 'The Four Ages of Man' (1650, though probably composed a few years earlier), which in the fifth section, on Old Age, uses Qoheleth to frame her verse:

> In every Age I've found much vanity.
> An end of all perfection now I see.
> It's not my valour, honour, nor my gold,
> My ruin'd house, now falling can uphold;
>
> . . .
>
> My Almond-tree (gray hairs) doth flourish now,
> And back, once straight, begins apace to bow.
> My grinders now are few, my sight doth fail,
> My skin is wrinkled, and my cheeks are pale.
> No more rejoice, at music's pleasant noise,
> But do awake at the cock's clanging voice.
> I cannot scent savours of pleasant meat,
> Nor sapors find in what I drink or eat.
> My hands and arms, once strong, have lost their might.
> I cannot labour, nor I cannot fight:
> My comely legs, as nimble as the Roe,
> Now stiff and numb, can hardly creep or go.
> My heart sometimes as fierce, as Lion bold,
> Now trembling, and fearful, sad, and cold.
> My golden Bowl and silver Cord, e're long,
> Shall both be broke, by wracking death so strong.
>
> . . .
>
> From King to beggar, all degrees shall find
> But vanity, vexation of the mind.
> Yea, knowing much, the pleasant'st life of all
> Hath yet amongst that sweet, some bitter gall.
> Though reading others' Works doth much refresh,
> Yet studying much brings weariness to th' flesh.
> My studies, labours, readings all are done,
> And my last period can e'en elmost run.
> (ll. 9–12, 67–82, 89–96, in Bradstreet 2004;
> see also above, p. 114)

Bradstreet emigrated to New England in 1630, where she published this poem in her *The Tenth Muse Lately Sprung Up in America*, which quickly won her wide acclaim. From that publication she may lay claim to be 'the first female poet and the first colonial poet in English, and a radical figure' (Keeble 2004). Here she is ground-breaking as probably the first poet to relate, even if in semi-allegorical mode, Qoheleth's poem inventively to her own imagined demise (note that several poets will follow in this, including Christina Rossetti some two centuries later).

An Collins (whose biographical details are virtually unknown – 'An' could even refer to 'Anthony'; see Howard 2005) in her 'Verses on the Twelvth Chapter of Ecclesiastes' (1653), reflects on the passage in a somewhat less personal vein than Bradstreet:

> All Earthly Glories to theyr periods post,
> As those that do possesse them may behold,
> Who therfore should not be at too much cost
> With that which fades so soon, dies & growes old
> > But rather minde him in their youthfull dayes,
> > Who can give glory which shall last always.
>
> Ere Light of Sun or Moon or Stars expire,
> Before the outward sence eclipsed be,
> Which doth direct the heart for to admire
> These works of God which obvious are to see,
> > The Fabrick of the Earth, the Heavens high,
> > Are to the mind discoverd by the eye.

In a mode now similar to Bradstreet, Collins develops the imagery to refer to the demise of any individual. For example,

> The Almond Tree shall blossoms [*sic*] then declare,
> Gray hairs presage to them the end is nigh,
> Naturall heat having no more repaire,
> Desires fayle, as flames wanting fuell, dy,
> > Nothing remayning wherby strength's suppli'd
> > The marrow wasted, and the moysture dri'd.

Unusually, Collins proceeds to include Ecclesiastes' orthodox conclusion:

> All here is vanity the Preacher sayes,
> Yea use of many books are wearisome,
> If cheifly don for self-respect or prayse
> It doubtlesse will to such a snare become:
> > Of all the matter, then the End let's hear,
> > Keep Gods commandements with son-like fear.
> > > (In Collins 2004)

With this Collins perhaps has shifted (as Qoheleth's epilogist) the reader's focus from the 'marrow wasted' to a redemption from bodily misery made possible by the fear of God.

Sometimes the passage's influence on poets is more subtle than overt. In Samuel Johnson's *The Vanity of Human Wishes* (1749), a poem that draws on Qoheleth's theme of the futility of human desire (see above, pp. 123–4), Johnson offers the following reflection on old age:

> Enlarge my life with multitude of days,
> In health, in sickness, thus the suppliant prays;
> Hides from himself his state, and shuns to know,
> That life protracted is protracted woe.
> Time hovers o'er, impatient to destroy,
> And shuts up all the passages of joy:
> In vain their gifts the bounteous seasons pour,
> The fruit autumnal, and the vernal flow'r,
> With listless eyes the dotard views the store,
> He views, and wonders that they please no more;
> Now pall the tasteless meats, and joyless wines,
> And Luxury with sighs her slave resigns.
>
> (ll. 255–66, in Johnson 1962: 43)

This reading resounds well with the clear timbre of Qoheleth's poem, that the joys of youth with soon wither into 'tasteless meats, and joyless wines', and it is the fool who will not see this. A few years later Voltaire would express this personal understanding with remarkable similitude in his versified *Précis* of 12:3 and 5 (1759):

> Thus all is corrupted, all is destroyed, everything passes.
> Soon my ears will be deaf to concerts,
> the heat of my blood will turn to ice,
> my eyes will be covered by a thick cloud.
>
> The nourishing sap of the wines of Mont-Liban
> will no longer be able to delight my listless appetite.
> Bent over, scarcely dragging myself along in a heavy walk,
> I will approach the end that we all reach.
>
> I will never see you again, Beauty, whose tenderness
> consoled my sorrows and delighted my happy days.
> O charm of life! O precious intoxication!
> You flee far from me, you flee forever.

Of time which ceaselessly perishes,
let us seize the moments.
Let us possess wisely,

. . .

May the pleasures of the dinner table,
amusing conversations,
make time last longer for us
(In Christianson 2005: 479–80)

Like Voltaire, Christina Rossetti (see ch. 1, p. 133) personalizes her reading, suggesting that the golden bowl figures as the lifeless body of a friend:

Strike the bells solemnly,
    Ding dong deep:
My friend is passing to his bed,
    Fast asleep;

    . . .

There is no music more for him:
    His lights are out, his feast is done;
His bowl that sparkled to the brim
Is drained, is broken, cannot hold;
My blood is chill, his blood is cold;
    His death is full, and mine begun.
(The second of two stanzas
of "A Peal of Bells", 7 July 1857;
in Rossetti 1979: 49)

This personal funerary context will be repeated a few years later by Thomas Woolner, a member of the Pre-Raphaelite Brotherhood, who manoeuvres the imagery in much the same way in his lament *For My Beautiful Lady* (1861):

She passed like summer flowers away.
    Her aspect and her voice
    Will never more rejoice,
For both lie hushed in cold decay.
    Broken the golden bowl
    Which held her vital soul
(In Woolner 1863: 90)[4]

[4] Unsurprisingly, the funerary context continues to be relevant, such as in John White's 'Also like him' (2005):

The slow tramp to the Kirk, the laying down
Is done now. Folk drift down October lanes.

cont. on p. 240

One week before she composed 'A Peal of Bells', in 'A Better Resurrection' Rossetti applied the same imagery to her own inner life:

> My life is like a broken bowl,
>   A broken bowl that cannot hold
> One drop of water for my soul
>   Or cordial in the searching cold;
> Cast in the fire the perished thing,
>   Melt and remould it, till it be
> A royal cup for Him my King:
>   O Jesus, drink of me.
>
> (Third of three stanzas,
> in Rossetti 1979: 68)

If there is a hint of allegory in these readings, it is applied to the poets themselves. Voltaire, for example, reads the darkened clouds as the cataracts in his own eyes, and in the men of strength and the locust he envisages his own future (or perhaps his present), 'bent over, scarcely dragging myself along'. These poets follow in the steps of Bradstreet in making Qoheleth's voice their own, and their reflections on old age are only mildly influenced by the allegorical traditions. It is likely that they are more substantially and directly informed by the poem's time structure, which asks readers to look with Qoheleth's young man into the future, to a time when the world will be lifeless in their eyes.

Gradually, if imperceptibly, poets would wrest themselves entirely from allegory to a simpler form of allusion. William Wordsworth, who made only rare use of the Bible in his poetry, perhaps held what Avni calls a 'skeptical affinity' with Qoheleth, particularly in the terms of the imagery of chapter 12.

The book says *man goeth to his long home* –
A dark-eyed house with heavy-lidded panes.
That spirit-quickening psalm of yesterday
Ignited even my raw stuttering breath;
Now clacking crows cloaked in a parody
Of mourning fill the expanding emptiness.
This 'emptiness', the door shut to the street,
Is habit-forming, soon solidifies,
Or so I reckon, raking leaves, back straight
And (also like him) smiling with widening eyes.
Next door an engine revs up – labour of love.
A boy is playing 'Chopsticks' up above.

(White 2005: 6)

There are only three poems where Avni reckons this takes place: 'An Evening Walk', 'Descriptive Sketches' (both 1793) and 'The Excursion' (1814). In 'An Evening Walk', a grieving mother remembers her son and

> bids her soldier come her woes to share,
> Asleep on Bunker's charnel hill afar;
> For hope's deserted well why wistful look?
> Chok'd is the pathway, and the pitcher broke.
>> (ll. 253–6, in Avni 1981b: 67)[5]

The subtle reference to the broken pitcher and 'well' of verse 6 serves to abstract Wordsworth's reflection on death and loss (Avni even suggests that the 'chok'd' pathway may refer to the shut doors of v. 4). In 'Descriptive Sketches', Wordsworth avows his commitment to France:

> And thou! fair favoured region! which my soul
> Shall love, 'til Life has broken her golden bowl
> Till Death's cold touch her cistern-wheel assail
> and vain regret and vain desire shall fail.
>> (ll. 740–3, in Avni 1981b: 67)

In the third poem, 'The Excursion', Avni suggests a broader affinity with Ecclesiastes in which Wordsworth may have recognized a comparable spirit of inquiry, as well as of the obscurity of knowledge, the fruitless pursuit of science and philosophy (1981b: 68–70).

In prose, too, the poem has like so much biblical content slipped almost imperceptibly into literature. The mortality by which that remembrance is so starkly defined is illustrated with remarkable clarity in Charles Kingsley's 'prose idyll' *North Devon* (July 1849). Kingsley relates the wreck of a ship as it veered towards shore, and subsequently what he discovered on board:

> And well I recollect the sad records of the log-book which was left on board the deserted ship; how she had been waterlogged for weeks and weeks . . . the crew clinging in the tops, and crawling down, when they dared, for putrid biscuit-dust and drops of water, till the water was washed overboard and gone; and then notice after notice, 'On this day such an one died', 'On this day such an one was washed away' – the log kept up to the last . . . [and told] how at last, when there was neither food nor water, the strong man's heart seemed to have quailed, or

---

5   I should note here that I consulted three separate versions of Wordsworth's poetical works and was unable to match this text (as well as the lines cited from 'Descriptive Sketches') with the edition that Avni cites (which is *Wordsworth: Poetical Works*, ed. T. Hutchinson [OUP, 1969]).

perhaps risen, into a prayer, jotted down in the log – 'The Lord have mercy on us!' – and then a blank of several pages, and, scribbled with a famine-shaken hand, 'Remember thy Creator in the days of thy youth;' – and so the log and the ship were left to the rats, which covered the deck when our men boarded her. (In Kingsley 1880: 293–4)

In its assumption of biblical literacy, this short-hand reference has a function analogous to poetic allusion, and its very brevity allows this text's latent piety to interact with a new set of circumstances and ideas. In other words, the narrative context creates a vivid space for performance, which is both entirely new and memorable.

The entrenched and short-hand allusion found in poetry, particularly to the silver cord and golden bowl, is well illuminated in T. R. Henn's study of the Bible as literature:

There are . . . many interpretations of the 'silver lace' [12:6] – later 'silver cord' – and of the 'golden bowl'. These all involve culminating death images: the golden lamp-bowl (light and oil imagery combined with the 'gold' of value) suspended by the tenuous thing, as in the perennial thread metaphors. Of this kind are Milton's

> 'Comes the blind Fury with th'abhorrèd shears,
> And slits the thin spun life.' [*Lycidas*, 1637]

and Sir Thomas Browne's:

'But I, that have examined the parts of man, and know upon what tender filaments that fabrick hangs . . .' [*Religio Medici*, i.44, *c*.1635] (Henn 1970: 53)

We might add to these references Oliver Wendell Holmes's *The Iron Gate*, 'Read at the Breakfast given in honor of Dr. Holmes's Seventieth Birthday by the publishers of the *Atlantic Monthly*, Boston, December 3, 1879':

> Old age, the graybeard! Well, indeed, I know him, –
> Shrunk, tottering, bent, of aches and ills the prey;
> In sermon, story, fable, picture, poem,
> Oft have I met him from my earliest day
>
> . . .
>
> And sad 'Ecclesiastes, or the Preacher,' –
> Has he not stamped the image on my soul,
> In that last chapter, where the worn-out Teacher
> Sighs o'er the loosened cord, the broken bowl?
>
> (Holmes 1893)

And we may also note Jewish Canadian poet A. M. Klein, who finds in Qoheleth's 'golden bowl' an image of knowledge frustrated:

> O cirque of the Cabbalist! O proud skull!
> Of alchemy O crucible!
> *Sanctum sanctorum*; grottoed hermitage
> Where sits the bearded sage!
> O golden bowl of Koheleth! and of fate
> O hourglass within the pate!
> Circling, O planet in the occiput!
> O Macrocosm, sinew-shut!
>> ('Out of the Pulver and the
>> Polished Lens', *c*.1944; in Klein 2004)

Harold Fisch, commenting on the significance of Henry James's title *The Golden Bowl* (1904), deftly suggests the aptness of its use in literature:

> It was with a fine insight that Henry James made of this golden bowl of Ecclesiastes an emblem of art's perfection and also of its vulnerability and treachery. Art measures itself against death as in the pastoral elegy, taking away all its horror, all its abruptness . . . Death becomes a magic sequence of images, the beauty of a golden sunset. But Qohelet does not allow us to indulge ourselves in that beauty. He does not say to us, 'That strain again; it had a dying fall.' The requiem has to be savored, but it has to be resisted as well. (Fisch 1988: 178)

Victor Gustave Plarr's paraphrase of the passage, published in his *In the Dorian Mood* (1896), flirts with allegory while finding a personal voice. It begins by observing the sad figure of Solomon from an unaffected, youthful perspective:

> He hath a few more days to live, and we
> Go to the festal, dight with robes and flowers,
> And all is goodly in this world of ours,
> And 'All is Vanity,' saith he.
>
> For him the sun, and moon, and stars are dark:
> After the rain the clouds return for him.
> The keepers of his soul's house quake in limb,
> The strong men bow themselves adown, and hark!
>
> . . .
>
> For him sweet Musick's daughters are brought low:
> He careth not at all for dance or cup,

Plarr's shift to the first person in the lines that follow is barely noticeable, and reflects once again the subtle rhetoric of self-reflection in Qoheleth's poem:

> Because to-day man seeketh his long home,
> And mourners go about the vacant streets:
> Oh, little day of life; oh, bitter sweets!
> Whence have I come, and what shall I become?
>
> Or ever the silver cord be loosen'd, or
> The golden bowl be broken on the wall,
> Or the full pitcher at the fountain fall,
> Or ever the cistern-wheel can turn no more,
>
> Then shall the dust return unto the earth
> Even whence it came – it trod, and shall be trod, –
> And the thin spirit shall go back to God
> Of Whom we know not, and who gave it birth.
> (Plarr 1896: 63–5)

As with Bradstreet, Johnson, Voltaire and others, the allegory is only faintly kept (it is pretty well abandoned in the closing stanzas), giving the whole a very different tone to Jewish and Christian allegorical readings.

An even more subtle reading is offered by Francis Thompson (1859–1907), best known for his poem 'The Hound of Heaven'. In his 'Past Thinking of Solomon' (first published posthumously in 1913), Thompson refuses to look beyond the first two verses of chapter 12, and fuses their imagery with Qoheleth's most brooding and discouraging themes:

> Wise-Unto-Hell Ecclesiast,
> Who siev'dst life to the gritted last!
>
> This is thy sting, thy darkness, Mage –
> Cloud upon sun, upon youth age?
>
> Now is come a darker thing,
> And is come a colder sting,
>
> Unto us, who find the womb
> Opes on the courtyard of the tomb.

Thompson sees age as an approaching gloom, cold with decrepitude. From here he proceeds to render the fading lights of verse 2 in terms of his own environment.

> Now in this fuliginous
> City of flesh our sires for us

> Darkly built, the sun at prime
> Is hidden, and betwixt the time
>
> Of day and night is variance none,
> Who know not altern moon and sun;
>
> Whose deposed heaven through dungeon-bars
> Looks down blinded of its stars.
>
> Yea, in the days of youth, God wot,
> Now we say: They please me not.
> (In Thompson 1946: 156)

The deathly curse that he envisages reaches from Qoheleth's village to his own darkened city, and allows all readers to say that such a predicament, imagined or no, cannot please. With such extended imagery of urban misery, this reading, free in all ways from allegory, comes as close as any to a romantic sensibility.

I have noted elsewhere in the commentary the bearing of Ecclesiastes on the work of T. S. Eliot. As Michael Edwards notes, chapter 12 seems to have had a particularly comprehensive influence:

> Later poems remember in particular the twelfth and last chapter. It leads one into and out of *The Waste Land*, with far more allusions than the single one which Eliot indicates in the Notes, and is audible in *Ash-Wednesday*, *Murder in the Cathedral*, and *The Family Reunion*. That it should have exercised Eliot in work after work is especially interesting when one realises the significance of one of its unquoted phrases: 'of making many books there is no end' . . . The phrase is equally relevant to *Four Quartets*, which also returns to that last chapter . . . In the very passage where Eliot seeks to repel his earlier distress at the 'making of many books', he actually returns to Ecclesiastes, to hear the Preacher's deeper distress, as voiced in the just preceding verses, about age and end. (1990a: 80, 83)

Edwards may be overstating the mimeticality of the detail, but Qoheleth's influence on *Four Quartets* (1943) is worth noting. Edwards sees, for example, in the description in 'Little Gidding', II, of 'the gifts reserved for age' – 'First, the cold friction of expiring sense' (in Eliot 1969: 194) – an echo of 'desire shall fail' (v. 5). And the next gift recalls enjoyment of youth before the days come when there is no pleasure in them (12:1):

> Second, the conscious impotence of rage
> At human folly, and the laceration
> Of laughter at what ceases to amuse.
> (Ibid.)

The potent brew of open-ended imagery in this passage still divides modern commentators, who often see a deliberate authorial mix of allegorical and literal reference (see Seow 1997: 372–4 for a useful overview). It is perhaps not surprising, then, that the passage has been so inventively and incessantly allegorized. Even if the evocative descriptions of a village in mourning are straightforwardly understood, such a scenario is entirely new to the book, making these seven verses the proverbial sore thumb. In that sense the lines are hard to contextualize, and allegory offers a neat solution. As interpreters moved beyond that reading scheme, however, they allowed themselves to be enchanted by what Fox describes as a 'dark and broken landscape through which we must find our way with few guideposts' (2004: 77). No doubt the potential of this imagery for use in poetry will continue to be recognized, as has been the case more than with any other passage in this frequently lyrical book. And I am certain that in its peerless way, Qoheleth's text will continue to remind us of our mortality.

The final section begins by completing the Bible's most elegant and effective inclusio: '"Vanity of vanities", said Qoheleth. "All is vanity"' (v. 8; cf. 1:2). The brief biographical introduction in 1:1–2, the even briefer interjection at 7:27 ('said Qoheleth'), and the evaluation of the main character in this epilogue all conform to the ancient Near Eastern genre of frame narration (other clear biblical examples are Deuteronomy and Job). The rhetorical power of this interpretive position is not to be underestimated. It is comparable to the commanding influence of the picture frame on its bordered image (see the discussion at the end of this chapter).

The incisive comments about Qoheleth in verses 9–10 are often passed over by interpreters. It is only here that Qoheleth is identified as a sage, and without disclaimers. Qoheleth everywhere is concerned with what is 'good' or 'profitable' for humanity, a programmatic concern of Proverbs. However, being truly wise is a goal he reckoned beyond reach (7:23–4 *et passim*), and wisdom does not hold for Qoheleth the theological meaning it does elsewhere (cf. Exod. 36:1–8; Deut. 1:13–15; Prov. 1:7; 15:33). That Qoheleth taught knowledge, listened, studied and composed proverbs fills gaps in the narrative, but also chimes well with biblical constructs of the sage. That he found elegant words to write, that they were written with integrity (*yashar*, which refers to the kind of moral uprightness Job was made of) and were 'true' are views undoubtedly shared by countless readers. These say little, however, about Qoheleth's character (particularly in terms of piety, as one sees in the frames of Deuteronomy and Job), and the more probing questions are left for readers to engage.

With such oblique phrases as 'words of sages', 'collected sayings', 'one shepherd' and especially 'beyond *these*' (the 'collected sayings'? Qoheleth's words?), the next two verses read like the jargon of a closed community. Here wisdom is like the shepherd's goad, a sharp stick that compels intellectual obligation. The linguistic product of that wisdom is immovable, a semantic bulwark, and likewise bears a likeness to the shepherd's directorial tools. As his favourite refrain suggests, for Qoheleth the language of shepherding is suited to a contrary purpose: 'Everything is *hebel* and a pursuit [*r'ût*, which some suggest derives from *r'h*, 'to shepherd', 'herd'] of wind'. Getting wisdom – let alone understanding its enterprise – is as feasible as rounding up the wind and resembles a kind of comic, futile shepherding (1:17; cf. 1:14; 2:17). As a sage, Qoheleth models the wisdom endeavour by experience, by explicit (as opposed to tacit) and risky engagement with the world. The frame narrator recognizes that risk and sees something wearisome in it (Qoheleth would call it *hebel*). He is clear that if his 'son' (i.e. his student) emulates it, he will only pollute the world with more published words.

The final words here (vv. 13–14) are perhaps the least ambiguous in the whole book. They are blunt, reminiscent of the language of covenant, and lay claim to the whole of humanity. Where the frame narrator declares that *everything* for *everyone* can be boiled down to fearful obedience of God's command, he forces evaluation of (and in a sense competes with) Qoheleth's claim that all is *hebel*. That God will bring every deed into judgment recalls Qoheleth's similarly constructed directive in 11:9. The telling difference is that in this case Qoheleth's reminder is not a universal declaration, but functions to temper his invitation to joy (11:9 can also be seen to comment on the Torah with which it plays havoc, Num. 15:39). As we shall see, whether it was written for such a purpose or not, in its clarion style the epilogue has always 'competed' for the commitment of Ecclesiastes' readers.

The Final Word

Rashbam (*c*.1080–*c*.1160) is rightly credited with being the first to identify the presence of an edited frame in Ecclesiastes. Commenting on 1:1–2, he says, 'These two verses "the words of Qoheleth" "Vanity of vanities" . . . were not said by Qoheleth but by the person who edited the words as they stand.' On 12:8 Rashbam points out that 'the book is completed; those who edited it speak from now on' (in Rashbam 1985: 34). Japhet and Salters draw attention to the consequence of his insight.

> In these extremely important critical remarks Rashbam is both grasping the literary setting of the book and recognizing its present form as the result of 'editing'. Moreover, 'those who edited it' did more than give the book its present form. In their short statements at the beginning and end, they summarized the message of the book, thus revealing the principle of the book's editing and becoming its interpreters. (In Rashbam 1985: 34–5)

Rashbam is the first to recognize that the epilogue can be understood as the first commentary on Ecclesiastes. (James Armstrong would later paint the scenario more cynically: 'Even Ecclesiastes was not spared the impact of the reviser's pen' [1983: 19].)

Classical rabbinic literature is rich and diverse on the epilogue, particularly in relating it to the *process* of interpretation. The most sustained discussion appears in *Midrash Numbers*, a lengthy and fascinating discourse on each phrase of 12:11–12. For example:

> Why were the words of the Torah likened to a goad? To tell you that as a goad directs the cow along the furrows, in order to bring life to the world, so the words of the Torah direct the heart of those who study them away from the paths of death and along the paths of life . . . More than of the words of the Torah be careful of the words of the Scribes. In the same strain it says, *For thy beloved ones are better than wine* [Song 1:2], which means: The words of the beloved ones (the Sages) are better than the wine of the Torah. Why? . . . From the words of the Sages . . . one can derive the proper law, because they explain the Torah. And the reason why the words of the Sages are compared to goads is because they cause understanding to dwell in men. (*Midrash Numbers* 14.4)

The description of Qoheleth's activity in the epilogue is taken by the Talmud as preservative and restrictive. So on verse 9, 'Ulla said in the name of R. Eleazar, "Before Solomon appeared, the Torah was like a basket without handles; when Solomon came he affixed handles to it"' (*b. Yebamoth* 21a;

cf. *b. 'Erubin* 21b). In other words, that Qoheleth (read Solomon) 'listened' (or 'pondered', *'zn*) is taken to mean he 'made handles' (rabbinic Heb. of *'zn*) – he made the Torah something that could be controlled. That control can be understood somewhat loosely:

> R. Berechiah said: What is the meaning of 'like goads' [*kedorbonot*]? It means *Kaddur Banot*, a girl's ball, which maidens toss in sport from one to another, one hither, one thither. So it is when the sages enter the house of study, and are occupied with the Law. One says its meaning is this, and another says its meaning is that. One gives such an opinion, his fellow a different one. But they all were 'given from one shepherd' – that is, from Moses, who received the teaching from Him who is One and unique in the world. (*Pesikta Rabbati* 8a, in Montefiore and Loewe 1974: 163; it appears in similar form in *Midrash Numbers* 14.4 and *Midrash Qoheleth* 12.11.1; cf. *Midrash Numbers* 15.22)

Such commentary, as Gerald Bruns suggests, reflects a pragmatic concern:

> In the midrashic texts themselves . . . [there is] a relentless preoccupation with the *force* of interpretation . . . – 'The Words of the wise are like goads', and so on – is a favourite of the rabbis because it concerns the point of midrash, its practical as against purely academic context . . . The words of the wise are *situated*; their meaning is embedded in their situation . . . The relation between Torah and sage, text and interpretation, is one of *appropriation*. (1990: 203–5)

The rabbinic 'appropriation' is perfectly in keeping with the force of the shepherding metaphors,[1] and it is entirely understandable that the same terms are not applied to Qoheleth's less categorizable approach to wisdom.

Eighteenth-century Polish Jewish preacher Joseph ben Dov Baer, in a sermon based on the portrait of Qoheleth in the epilogue, finds in the same shepherding imagery encouragement for effective moral instruction. Preachers should perform their task with innovation and, in a spirit akin to recent narrative approaches to homiletics, should avoid

> telling the people what to do and what not to do . . . In this way, fine parables are enjoyable, so sweet to hear that everyone loves them. After the parable, they will also hear its meaning, which is the essence of ethical instruction and piety.

---

[1] Another reading alive to the metaphorical force is offered by prolific seventeenth-century author Thomas Fuller (1608–61): 'Give me such solid reasons whereon I may rest and rely . . . [he cites 12:11] A nail is firm, and will hold driving in, and will hold driven in. Send me such arguments' (in Nicoll and Stoddart 1910: 555).

That is why the words of the sages, which teach the people ethical standards and piety, are compared to the cow's goad, the yoke of the plow (Eccles. 12:11). Without this goad, the cow would not walk in the furrows at all; it would go wherever it wanted. The goad makes it walk and plow in the furrows, keeping it in the path intended by the person plowing. The same is true when a scholar instructs people in the proper moral path. Without the parable, the thoughts of those standing around him would wander, and they would think of other things. His fine words would never be heard, for their minds would be occupied elsewhere. But through the parable, he captures the attention, so that people will hear what he says. This way they also hear the essence of his ethical message, the meaning of the parable. (In Saperstein 1989: 428)

Dov Baer strikes an intriguing balance by drawing on the imagery's inherent forcefulness (the goads will keep the oxen/students on the 'proper path') while managing to encourage the rhetorician to engage the imagination and, to perhaps a lesser extent, to trust the hearer.

Qoheleth's famous dictum regarding the 'making of many books' graces the opening page of (too!) many academic monographs,[2] and most commentators have taken the words at face value. Few, however, have wrestled with its implications with such gravity as Origen in the preface to his *Commentary on John* (*c.*235):

I, for my part, am inclined to shrink from toil, and to avoid that danger which threatens from God those who give themselves to writing on divinity; thus I would take my shelter in Scripture in refraining from making many books. For Solomon says in Ecclesiastes [cites 12:12] . . . For we . . . have directly transgressed the injunction, we have not guarded ourselves against making many books . . . And . . . the Sacred History seems to agree with the text in question, inasmuch as none of the saints composed several works, or set forth his views in a number of books. I will take up this point: when I proceed to write a number of books, the critic will remind me that even such a one as Moses left behind him only five books. (In Menzies 1974: 346)

With similar indignation, Basil the Great (*c.*329–79) condemns Apollinarius, who 'is a cause of sorrow to the Churches. With his facility of writing, and a tongue ready to argue on any subject, he has filled the world with his works, in disregard of the advice of him who said, "Beware of making many

---

[2]   The epigraphic placement of the verse of course draws attention to its inherent irony. Ibn Ezra (1092/3–1167) is perhaps the first author to apply that irony to the academic enterprise: 'The end of the matter is – to midrashic interpretation there is no end' (from the introduction to his commentary on Torah; in Yarchin 2004: p. xxii).

books." . . . How is it possible to avoid sin in a multitude of words?' (cf. Eccl. 5:7; in *Letters*, Basil 1955: 302). In his 1770 commentary Mendelssohn takes a slightly different angle on the aphorism, suggesting 'action rather than commentary, study, or reading is the essence. Action is the goal, foundation, and essence of all' (in Sorkin 1996: 36). Later commentators continued to recognize its applicability. So G. C. Martin, in the 1908 Century Bible, suggests that 'If the words had force then, they have undoubtedly much more force to-day, when we are easily tempted to dissipate our energies in either the reading or writing of useless books, and when we might with profit lay to heart not only this counsel, but that of the Stoic emperor [Marcus Aurelius] that we should free ourselves from the thirst for books' (in Cohen 1952: 190). Michael Edwards also aligns himself with the epilogist's cynicism and recognizes 'a writer's sadness here, before the plethora of writings, the redundance of the world – an unlimited anxiety of influence – to which writers like Montaigne and Eliot seem to have responded and which they knew in their own work' (1990b: 186–7).

In complete and refreshing contrast to all of these, Robert Louis Stevenson, in his 1878 essay 'El Dorado', sees Qoheleth's warning as apropriate to his reflections on humanity's ever 'onward-looking' quests, and his comments teem with the intoxication of discovery that marked his times:

> 'Of making books there is no end', complained the Preacher; and did not perceive how highly he was praising letters as an occupation. There is no end, indeed, to making books or experiments, or to travel, or to gathering wealth. Problem gives rise to problem. We may study for ever, and we are never as learned as we would. We have never made a statue worthy of our dreams. And when we have discovered a continent, or crossed a chain of mountains, it is only to find another ocean, or another plain upon the further side. In the infinite universe there is room for our swiftest diligence and to spare. It is not like the works of Carlyle, which can be read to an end. Even in a corner of it, in a private park, or in the neighbourhood of a single hamlet, the weather and the seasons keep so deftly changing that although we walk there for a lifetime there will be always something new to startle and delight us. (In Stevenson 1904: 176–7; cf. Francis Bacon, who in some way anticipates this spirit in his *Advancement of Learning* [1605], above, p. 50)

The religiously cautious closing verses (13–14), which in various ways obscure Qoheleth's more probing wisdom, have had an enormous influence on overall conceptions of the book (cf. Murphy 1992: 126). Some, however, have read the verses quite apart from their relationship to the book. Christopher Smart, for example, concludes his delightful *Hymns for the Amusement of Children* (1770) with 'The Conclusion of the Matter':

> Fear God – obey his just decrees,
> And do it hand, and heart, and knees;
> For after all our utmost care
> There's nought like penitence and prayer.
>
> Then weigh the balance in your mind,
> Look forward, not one glance behind;
> Let no foul fiend retard your pace,
> Hosanna! Thou hast won the race.
>
> (In Smart 1949: 2.1001)

But such examples are rare. For the most part, the final verses (13–14) have proved a terrifically strong post on which to hang the conservatizing sentiments of many orators and commentators, Christian and Jewish, who often confuse the epilogist's views with those of Qoheleth.

Bonaventure, in the introduction to his commentary (1253–7), related the epilogue to a corrective persona in the book:

> Ecclesiastes continues with his argument until the end of the book where he gives his solution when he says in 12:13–14: *Let us all together hear the conclusion of the discourse. Fear God . . . and know that God will bring you to judgment for every error . . .* In this conclusion Ecclesiastes condemns every opinion of the foolish, the carnal, and the worldly. So in this last statement he is speaking in his own name, but what he rejects is spoken in the name of others. Hence the book cannot be understood without paying attention to all of it. (2005: 85)

This misconstrual of authorship (which Rashbam long ago paved the way to avoid) persists in modernity. Because of the ending, J. S. Wright feels able to say of the *book*, 'To summarize its contents, the book constitutes an exhortation to live a God-fearing life, realizing that one day account must be rendered to him' (1982: 296; see Christianson 1998a: 115–16 for other modern examples). A similar, though far more eloquently expressed, version of ideological alignment comes from Bishop Wordsworth:[3]

> These two sentences at the end of Ecclesiastes [vv. 13–14] afford the best guidance for its right interpretation. They are like the rudder by which the whole book is steered. Sometimes the sacred vessel of this marvellous composition may seem to the eye of a cursory reader to be tossed about by winds of doubt; sometimes to be even plunging and floundering in the depths of despondency and

---

[3] As Scott offers no details, I have been unable to determine which Bishop Wordsworth he has cited (the *Oxford Dictionary of National Biography* lists three, all of whom flourished in the latter half of the nineteenth century).

despair; but this is an optical illusion. The ship is riding safely on the billows, and it goes down into the bosom of the abyss in order to ride more gloriously to the crest of the wave, and to ride buoyantly and joyfully like a bright and divine thing in the midst of the storm; for the eye of the pilot is fixed on the stars above, and his hand is firmly grasping the helm; and on his heart are inscribed the words, 'Fear God, and keep His commandments, for this is the whole man. For God shall bring every work into judgment, whether it be good, or whether it be evil.' (In Scott 1929: 89)

This reading derives not from an authorial conflation of Qoheleth and the frame narrator, but rather readerly choice. Wordsworth recognizes the frame narrator's position as commentator ('guidance for its right interpretation') and illustrates the choice facing all readers at the end of Ecclesiastes.

In their own ways each of these readings is responding to the hermeneutical force of the epilogue. Partly that is enabled by the frame's simple position as border – there is no other way to see Qoheleth except through this lens. Equally, however, the psychological consequence of endings cannot be underestimated (Hollywood is a sterling example of a whole industry that has grasped this reality and cynically manufactured its product to exploit it). As James Crenshaw points out, the Masoretic scribes repeated verse 13 after verse 14, ending with the duty of humanity to keep God's commands instead of with God's wrath poured out on the secrets of the heart. 'Few people', suggests Crenshaw, 'can endure words of relentless wrath. Or the conclusion that life is utterly futile' (1988: 192). In a manner similar to the book of Job, the ending of Ecclesiastes provides what is for many an irresistibly secure (fixed, pious) vantage point. As Fox contends, the author 'blunts objections to the book as a whole by implying through use of a frame narrator that he is just reporting what Qohelet said, without actually rejecting the latter's ideas. The epilogist thus allows the more conservative reader to align himself with him, so that a reader need not reject the *book*, even if he does reject the views of Qohelet' (1977: 103–4).

The frame narrative's obstinate presence remains something of a conundrum. Despite its obvious conservatism, there is no conclusive evidence that the epilogue contributed to Ecclesiastes' acceptance into the canon, and it is impossible to say what the book's reading history would look like without it.[4] And whether the frame narrator is a character created by the same author(s) who penned the inner material or a later editor(s) who thought Qoheleth's words worthy of presentation is still disputed. However these questions are

---

[4]   See Christianson 1998a: 148–54. The remainder of this chapter is adapted in part from ibid. 121–5.

answered, there is little doubt about the frame's capacity to raise compelling questions about our interpretation of the whole, and the analogy of the picture frame is exceptionally helpful here.

Frames can encourage us to query the image they contain as well as our own viewing habits (such as by caricaturing traditional exhibition practices). They can raise the question of what is real, making it difficult for viewers to commit to any one ideology or viewpoint. If we assume that the author(s) of Ecclesiastes *intended* to raise questions about the relationship of the frame to the words of Qoheleth, the epilogue could be read as irony, or as an attempt to trouble in some way the enterprise of traditional wisdom (this reading is well represented in recent scholarship). The artifice of the whole would then intend to teach us a truth that does not rest on the surface of the words either of Qoheleth or of the frame narrator. Thus we could grant that a hyper-self-conscious author wrote the entire text, manipulating the literary conventions of the frame with remarkable acumen. When frames are unintentionally mismatched, however, they tend to focus attention on themselves at the expense of the picture. If this is analogous to the composition of Ecclesiastes, we have seen such ideological imposition at work with conservative readings, based on the frame, as it were, and not the picture. In such a scenario the book might not come from one author but at least two, of Qoheleth's words and of the frame, each driven by wholly different conceptions of wisdom. One might ask further if the frame was produced simply to grant Qoheleth's words the least problematic admission to the 'public' domain of Scripture (comparable to the widespread nineteenth-century use of elaborate gilded frames to 'legitimize' reception). For whatever reason, many readers have expressed their preference for the more 'legitimate' view on offer in Ecclesiastes.

Understanding the Pervasive Appeal of Qoheleth

The frame narrator of Ecclesiastes is of course the first to interpret Qoheleth's whole narrative, to reduce it to a phrase, presenting us with *hebel hᵃbālîm* (1:2; 12:8) – what would most commonly be translated 'vanity of vanities'. By doing so, 'he' pointed the way to reading the book merely in the terms of *vanitas*. But apart from the *vanitas* theme (which at times seems to have been wrested only from the surface of Qoheleth's discourse), readers have not 'received' a coherent idea from Qoheleth. What they have received, in abundance, is the spirit of his persona, the whole distilled essence of his brooding presence. Qoheleth the man, therefore, has had greater impact than any one passage of Ecclesiastes. Even in the most influential lines, chapter 12's poem of the end, the spirit of Qoheleth stubbornly haunts readers.

Those readings attached firmly to Qoheleth's persona are exceptionally diverse. As such, while many readings may lack exegetical nuance, they witness to the extraordinary elasticity of Ecclesiastes as a performative, open text. Conversely, the diversity of reception may witness to the equally elastic skill of readers, many of whom are resistant. Indeed, one of the most arresting features of Ecclesiastes' reception is the way in which writers slip in and out of the provenance of established readings. So when Galileo in 1615 appeals to Eccl. 3:11 in order to legitimize human inquiry (see p. 176), he is set against a host of readers who more commonly exercised caution in such matters and saw Qoheleth as a model of how to avoid the misery of intellectual pursuit. But Galileo sees in Qoheleth a call to epistemological joy. In a similar vein, Robert Louis Stevenson sees in the warning against making many books an encouragement to engage more actively in the world around (see p. 252), thereby flouting the admonition of scores of readers – mainly theologians.

Such examples hint at Qoheleth's literary and psychological appeal. It is bordering on a commonplace to suggest that Qoheleth speaks to people in all ages, or as Robert Gordis put it 50 years ago, 'speaks to the modern age across an interval of two thousand years with the immediacy of contact of a contemporary' (1955: p. vii). Why have countless authors seen something of themselves so forcefully reflected in Qoheleth's words? Donne, Voltaire, Johnson and Thackeray all at least found in Qoheleth an empathetic sparring partner. As I have argued elsewhere (1998a: 243–7), the rhetorically open structure is one factor that allows readers to inhabit the space occupied by the implied reader. More significantly, however, all of those readers experienced an intangible empathy, which I will address below.

The cultural pervasiveness and appeal of the Preacher is captured well by Paul Tillich: 'The spirit of the Preacher is strong today in our minds. His mood fills our philosophy and poetry. The vanity of human existence is described powerfully by those who call themselves philosophers or poets of existence. They are all children of the Preacher, this great existentialist of his period' (1955: 168). The many citations in the 'True to life' section of the Testimonia chapter of this book testify to the long history of this phenomenon. Indeed, Paul Marcus, in the most rigorous engagement from a cross-disciplinary perspective to date, argues that Ecclesiastes has insights for psychoanalysis precisely due to its ability to connect to human experience, broadly conceived:

> Ecclesiastes not only identifies with startling brilliance and poetic insight some
> of the central problematics of the human condition . . . but offers what is in
> many ways a reasonable and feasible attitude toward contemporary life. More-
> over, Ecclesiastes' way of looking at life is similar to certain life attitudes and
> values embodied implicitly in the Freudian world view, but also suggests what

psychoanalysis might in part appropriate or further explore and develop as it tries to enhance itself as a narrative of the human condition . . . In other words, Ecclesiastes provides us with some of the most illuminating and insightful reflections on modern existence and our sense of what, for many, ultimately matters in life. (Marcus 2000: 228)

Marcus goes on to argue that the accessible and relevant dimensions of Qoheleth's narrative are made possible by his unflinching acceptance of ambiguity and uncertainty: 'For Ecclesiastes, the experience of life cannot be reduced to a system by means of moral principles because they collapse amidst the anomalies of experience, just as the attempt to reduce life to a system of theoretical ideas collapses as it tries to resolve the antinomies and paradoxes of existence' (2000: 239).

There is a discernible connection in the scattered examples of this book between empathy and experience, a recognition of readerly solace with Qoheleth. So it is in his imprisonment, foreseeing his execution by Henry VIII, that Henry Howard, Earl of Surrey, composes one of the finest versifications of Ecclesiastes that any age has seen. It is under the threat of persecution, at a moment of profound disillusionment with religion and the created order, that Voltaire produces a starkly sympathetic reading of Qoheleth. It is just as Melville comes to the realization of the vacuity of fame that he sees in Ecclesiastes 'deeper and deeper and unspeakable meanings'. Michael Edwards states the existential appeal this way:

> The power of Ecclesiastes is surely that, while everywhere acknowledging a just, bountiful and transcendent God, it describes a fallen world and leaves one in it. It says, unswervingly, what the facts are, and so it can be taken by the Christian for a hard and truthful look at the *miseria* of the world, which remains and is not to be simply spirited away by faith; and by the atheist, the agnostic, after the ablation of some of its parts, as saying what he too thinks in the starkest way possible. (1990a: 79)

Edwards's insightful description requires, I think, some qualification. One must go farther than imply that 'there is something here for everyone' (or worse, which Edwards does not do, suggest this is only ideological timidity). The real artistry of this brilliant little scroll lies in its thematic assembly. *Hebel* leads in the end to joy, and yet all of the most fulfilling experiences are tinged with vexation and grief. Unless readers have employed allegory, or dissolved the borders between Qoheleth's words and the epilogue, Ecclesiastes has compelled them to work out for themselves how the realities of *hebel* and joy must coexist. In other words, any careful reader is invariably made to ask the hard questions.

The Exegetical 'Fidelity' of Ecclesiastes' Reception History

One of the more intriguing questions raised by this commentary is how, with our own bag of exegetical tools, we might in some way assess Ecclesiastes' reception history. For example, we might ask whether Ecclesiastes is in fact a clarion call to repudiate the world's vanity, or if it really is an overture to humanist scepticism. In other words, how do these particular readings 'measure up' in contemporary exegetical terms? With regard to the former example, when Luther dismisses a sea of interpretation in describing the destructive 'flood' of the *contemptus mundi* reading of Ecclesiastes (see p. 107), he is indirectly addressing the tendency to reduce the book to one unforgiving motto. And if nothing else, the reading he refutes is rigid. Anthony Perry regards with suspicion the tendency to relegate Ecclesiastes to its 'englobing' single lament, 'All is vanity'. 'Why readers have succumbed to the enticing violence of the pseudoconclusion is worthy of reflection' (1993b: 4). Summarizing, as the frame narrator does, the whole of Qoheleth's narrative as *hebel* obscures its other dimensions, particularly that of joy. Furthermore, when Qoheleth breaks out with joy, it is almost exclusively narrated in a 'now' aspect to the reader (usually as a command, such as 'eat your bread with joy'; 9:7). If readers lose their grasp of that narrative structure, they are in danger of getting lost in the 'then' of Qoheleth's most pessimistic reflection.

We might also reflect on the humanist take. Is Ecclesiastes, as Renaissance reception suggests, and as Harold Fisch more recently put it, 'the nearest thing to humanism that the Bible has to offer, even a radical humanism' (1988: 158–9)? And what exactly does that entail? Menachem Fisch has argued that Qoheleth shares something with humanism, but is not committed to what he regards as its crippling implications: 'For *Qohelet*, quite unlike . . . early modern European philosophy, truth and justice, the desired goals of wisdom, are ultimately regarded as regulative concepts rather than obtainable objectives. Progress . . . is attainable only by insistently treating our present conclusions, norms, plans and strategies critically, and by being willing to modify them accordingly' (1995: 185). I would suggest, however, that this constructive scepticism is precisely what the early modern Europeans identified with in Ecclesiastes. Again, empathy was at work here. Renaissance thinkers were faced with the challenge of testing that whole scientific and rational approach to the world's phenomena in a way that clarified the relationship between deed and consequence, and queried what intellectual artefacts could be known. In Qoheleth they recognized a figure who achieves the same feat, with the kind of spirit they could respect and understand: epistemological inquiry that took seriously the realm of the divine and held sacrosanct the integrity of the individual.

Qoheleth provides that most rare and cherished Renaissance ideal: sacred scepticism.

To put our 'measuring' question another way, is Graham White right to call Luther's approach to Ecclesiastes 'exegetical rape' (1987: 181)? Or what of J. N. D. Kelly's suggestion that for 'the modern student . . . Jerome's commentary is worse than useless' (1975: 152)? Or C. D. Ginsburg's damning comment on the 'monotony of patristic exposition' (1861: 105)? Is George Bradley, in his *Lectures on Ecclesiastes: Delivered in Westminster Abbey* (1898), hitting the nail on the head when he launches an extraordinary attack on Jewish and Christian readings (such as understanding Qoheleth's call to 'eat and drink' as 'to hide something very different', the 'Sacred Communion'), which have 'effectually disposed of' all the 'difficulties, all the problems, which the book stirs' (1898: 46)? All 'the real interest', suggests Bradley,

> as well as all the real difficulty, of the book evaporates under such treatment. This moody soliloquy, these heart-stirring confessions, these riddling utterances . . . wearing at one time the guise of earnest but troubled prose, where we seem to see language struggling to convey thoughts too big for its framework, at another rising to the sad heights of the poetry of despair; this book . . . becomes merely a storehouse of well-contrived riddles, where homely truths . . . lose their force by being wrapped up in meaningless conundrums. The book becomes no longer a serious study for earnest men, but a pastime for grown-up children, a playground for trifling pedants. (1898: 47)

In the Introduction I take the assessments of Ginsburg and Kelly to task, for one need not look too hard to find remarkably subtle and insightful exceptions. These are, however, still exceptions, and I think Bradley is pretty much right. Qoheleth, like so much of the Bible, has for centuries borne the weight of unwieldy doctrine on his broad shoulders.

Having said as much, it also remains clear that no reading bears lightly on Qoheleth's shoulders. As A. V. Desvoeux recognized nearly 250 years ago, even where some find in Ecclesiastes nothing but what is agreeable to 'revealed Doctrine', others 'spy out Monsters' (1760: 6), unable or uninterested to reconcile the book to any doctrinal scheme. Roland Murphy's more recent question as to whether we are simply 'locked up in [our] own crippling presuppositions' is particularly apt, if inevitable (1982: 336). From the often 'aware' vantage point of the academy, there are numerous ways in which we all champion an often blind-sighted agenda: in the choice of text in which we choose to specialize, in the application of an ideological method that sheds 'new light' or in our drive to meet the next research assessment exercise. Although we are all too aware of the myth of impartiality, in judging the readings of the past with our own interested forms of exegesis, we betray a prejudice.

But there is something wrong-headed about the very question of fidelity to our own exegesis, and some readings easily expose its inadequacy. Writers can come to Ecclesiastes with little or no commitment to its detail, or even to its spirit, 'borrowing' its authority without apology. So Jean Baudrillard begins what is perhaps his most influential work, *Simulacra and Simulation* (published in French in 1981), with a tantalizing epigraph:

> The simulacrum is never what hides the truth – it is truth that hides the fact that there is none.
>   The simulation is true.
>   – Ecclesiastes
> (Baudrillard 1994: 1)

The copy I have before me from my university library bears an enthusiastic hand-drawn star with a squiggly line in the margin. I wonder what informed this moment of recognition. Was it the insight of truth's malice? Was it being struck by the irony (or enjoyable synch?) of Baudrillard's postmodern treatise being overturned by an ancient biblical manifesto? And I wonder how many cultural studies undergraduate essays on Baudrillard have somewhere put forth, 'according to Ecclesiastes . . .' Not even in his most abstracted observations does Qoheleth come close to the epigraph. But Baudrillard's strategy materializes as he writes. He goes on to discuss the 'Borges fable' in which the simulated beauty of an ageing map of Empire, matching the deterioration of the real, 'possesses nothing but the discrete charm of second-order simulacra' (1994: 1). His own 'epigraph' is a failed simulacrum, one that he later confessed to be a 'Borges-like' fabrication (see R. G. Smith 2005, n. 4). Baudrillard *uses* Ecclesiastes, but in a way that simply cannot chime with modern exegesis.

How Might This Reception History Inform the Discipline?

A couple of salient points first, to offer a reflective pause. The first is that the practice of assaying Qoheleth's currency in culture has a longer history than we might suspect. Reading his nineteenth-century commentators (e.g. Cheyne, Haupt, Plumptre) and those of the first half of the twentieth century (e.g. Greissinger, Jastrow, Wright), one is struck by the natural flow of references to literary works on which Qoheleth has had an impact. Early modern interpreters often resourced their reading of Ecclesiastes with all kinds of literature (e.g. Trapp 1650; Anonymous 1765). We might further note the regular appearance of reception histories of Ecclesiastes through the centuries (see pp. 19–22).

The second point is that, with the possible exception of Voltaire, the examples of empathy discussed above should cause us to blur our often rigid classification of reception as 'in the church/synagogue' or 'in culture'. It is a hard distinction to avoid, and this commentary sometimes operates with it, usually for the sake of convenience (particularly in the arrangement of bibliographical material). Of course the church and the synagogue have never existed in some cultural vacuum, and some of the most provocative readers are those who inhabit what we perceive as the realms of religion and of culture. It is a sermon of Samuel Johnson, for example, that unlocks the vision of *vanitas* that underscores his 'Vanity of Human Wishes' and *Rasselas* (see p. 61). Similarly, many readings of Ecclesiastes in nineteenth-century literature adapt the *vanitas* theme from its established use in monastic life, transforming its meaning and knowingly reworking its system of referents (Thackeray is perhaps the chief example).

There are some compelling metaphors on offer for reflecting on the complex activity of reception. Mary Callaway (2004) has recently suggested that reception history can 'send us back to the text with a new perspective that allows us to see something that our own horizon concealed. It can keep us alert to the limitations of our own readings, and especially to the moral consequences of absolutizing our own horizon.' Applied to Ecclesiastes, we might suggest that each reading re-imagines the disposition of Qoheleth, re-situates him for us in new and strange contexts and allows us to hear his voice among those we might not have imagined to place him. In her splendid study of Jonah's reception in culture, Yvonne Sherwood imagines a feast at which Jonah is served. Like his grotesque fish, we devour the remarkably endurable remains of his narrative, and Jonah is likewise kept alive by this consumption (2000: 2). Qoheleth, too, is sustained by the discourse he nudges into being. He feeds on and survives by the piqued interest of so many novelists, poets and painters. He even receives some paltry sustenance from those who feed so gluttonously on him: biblical critics. Finally, Rachel Nicholls (2005) has suggested that the discipline of reception history shares a number of qualities with *parkour*, or 'freerunning', which she describes as 'the art of crossing an urban landscape in original, daring and elegant ways, using jumps, leaps and turns to scale walls, cross rooftops and even move around fences and bollards.' Nicholls suggests that the qualities that make for good *parkour* – personal commitment, acting wisely within limitations, aiming for disciplined results without 'showboating' – may be asked of interpretation. This means that there is a need to engage with the historically conditioned contexts of interpretation with intellectual energy and creativity, and with a combined spirit of boldness and modesty. In the case of

Ecclesiastes, Nicholls finds herself in the good company of Gregory of Nyssa (*c*.380), who was certain of the agility required by Qoheleth's words, as interpreters 'fight for a foothold for their thoughts, using their skill as athletes so that they may not find their argument overthrown, but in every intellectual encounter keep the mind on its feet to the end through the truth' (see above, p. 1).

Each of these metaphors offers a measure of insight, and each must accommodate a staggering quantity of interpretive inquiry. Each is seeking to reflect on the nature of reading and its perpetual reformulation, and the reading history of Ecclesiastes, like any book, presents unique questions. What exactly enables that intangible moment of empathy with Qoheleth to take place? Even from the whole morass of readings he manages to emerge as a compelling paradigmatic figure, offering for emulation his ability to hold die-hard scepticism and fierce *joie de vivre* in tandem. Or why is it that where poets have merged their narrating 'I' with Qoheleth's voice, they have (it seems exclusively) done so in order to relate not his joyful but his bleakest themes? Furthermore, in what ways can we account for the breadth of Qoheleth's appeal? This book has drawn readers from religion's critics as much as from its defenders. It has a magnetism that cannot be accounted for merely by its status as Scripture (although it is that very status that makes its dissonant charm possible). Whatever the answers, I am certain that the raw material for the questions will continue to materialize.

Bibliography

Note: because the Bibliography is arranged in numerous sections, readers are referred to the name index, which includes coverage of the Bibliography.

ANF = *Ante-Nicene Fathers*. Grand Rapids, Mich.: William B. Eerdmans.

N&PNF, 1st ser. = Philip Schaff, ed., *Nicene and Post-Nicene Fathers*, 14 vols. Grand Rapids, Mich.: William B. Eerdmans.

N&PNF, 2nd ser. = Philip Schaff and Henry Wace, eds, *Nicene and Post-Nicene Fathers*, 14 vols. Grand Rapids, Mich.: William B. Eerdmans.

References to the Babylonian Talmud are from Isidore Epstein ed. 1961. *The Babylonian Talmud*, 35 vols. London: Soncino Press.

References to the *Midrashim* are from Harry Freedman ed. 1939. *Midrash Rabbah*, 10 vols. London: Soncino Press.

PRIMARY SOURCES

1. PRE-1500

'Ali, Yephet ben. 1969. 'The Arabic Commentary of Yephet ben 'Ali on the Book of Ecclesiastes, Chapters 1–6', tr. with introduction and commentary by Richard Murray Bland. 'Authorized facsimile' of PhD thesis at University of California, Berkeley. Ann Arbor, MI: University Microfilms. [A noteworthy Karaite biblical commentary, c.990 CE.]

Ambrose. 1955. *Select Works and Letters [of] St Ambrose*, tr. H. de Romestin. N&PNF, 2nd ser. 10. [Orig. pub. 1896.]

Augustine. 1890. *St. Augustine's City of God and Christian Doctrine*, ed. P. Schaff. N&PNF, 2. New York: Christian Literature Publishing Company.

—— 1956. *Exposition on the Book of Psalms, by St Augustin*, ed. P. Schaff. N&PNF, 1st ser. 8.

Basil the Great. 1955. *The Treatise De Spiritu Sancto: The Nine Homilies of the Hexaemeron and the Letters of Saint Basil the Great, Archibishop of Caesarea*, tr. with notes by Blomfield Jackson. N&PNF, 2nd ser. 8. [Orig. pub. 1895.]

Bettenson, Henry, ed. 1963. *Documents of the Christian Church*. London: Oxford University Press.

Bonaventure. 2005. *Works of St. Bonaventure: Commentary on Ecclesiastes*, tr. and notes by Campion Murray and Robert J. Karris. In *Works*, 7. Bonaventure, NY: Franciscan Institute Publications. [Hugely influential commentary, written 1253–7.]

Brown, C., and G. V. Smithers, eds. 1952. *Religious Lyrics of the XIVth Century*, 2nd edn. Oxford: Oxford University Press. [Includes Ecclesiastes-themed mortality lyrics from the Vernon MS; cf. Matsuda 1989.]

Browne, C. G., et al., eds. 1955. *The Catechetical Lectures of St Cyril, Archbishop of Jerusalem; Select Orations of Saint Gregory Nazianzen, Sometime Archbishop of Constantinople*. N&PNF, 2nd ser. 7. [Orig. pub. 1894.]

Cassian, John. 1978. *Sulpitius Serverus, Vincent of Lérins, John Cassian*, tr. E. C. S. Gibson, ed. P. Schaff. N&PNF, 1st ser. 11.

Chaucer, Geoffrey. 1988. *The Riverside Chaucer*, ed. L. D. Benson, 3rd edn. Oxford: Oxford University Press.

Chrysostom, John. 1889. *Concerning the Statues*. N&PNF, 1st ser. 9. New York: Christian Literature Co.

Coxe, A. Cleveland, ed. 1978. *Gregory Thaumaturgus, Dionysius the Great, Julius Africanus, Anatolius and Minor Writers, Methodius, Arnobius*. ANF 6.

Dunbar, William. 2004. *William Dunbar: The Complete Works*, ed. J. Conlee. Kalamazoo, Mich.: Western Michigan University. [Full text at http://www.lib.rochester.edu/camelot/teams/dunfrm1.htm.]

Gaon, Saadia. 1948. *The Book of Beliefs and Opinions*, tr. S. Rosenblatt. New Haven: Yale University Press.

Gregory of Nyssa. 1993. *Gregory of Nyssa: Homilies on Ecclesiastes*, ed. S. G. Hall. Berlin: Walter de Gruyter. [Full English translation of the eight homilies (*c.*380) as well as accompanying studies of each.]

Gregory Thaumaturgos. 1990. *Gregory Thaumaturgos' Paraphrase of Ecclesiastes*, tr. and notes by John Jarick. SBL Septuagint and Cognate Studies, 29. Atlanta: Scholars Press. [Translation and commentary on the oldest complete work (*c.*245) on Ecclesiastes.]

Gregory the Great. 1959. *Saint Gregory the Great: Dialogues*, tr. O. J. Zimmerman. Fathers of the Church, 39. Washington, D.C.: Catholic University of America Press.

Innocent III, Pope. 1910. *De Contemptu Mundi*. In *Works*, 2, ed. and tr. G. Gascoigne. Cambridge: J. W. Cunliffe.

—— 1978. *Lotario dei Segni (Pope Innocent III): De Miseria Condicionis Humane*, ed. and tr. R. E. Lewis. The Chaucer Library. Athens, Ga.: University of Georgia Press.

Irblich, Eva, and Gabriel Bise, eds. 1979. *The Illuminated Naples Bible (Old Testament)*. Productions Liber SA. [Plates with commentary from a fourteenth-century MS.]

Jerome. 1954. *St. Jerome: Letters and Select Works*, tr. W. H. Fremantle. N&PNF, 1st ser. 6. Grand Rapids, Mich.: Eerdmans. [Orig. pub. 1893.]

——2000. *Commentary on Ecclesiastes*. Unpublished translation by Robin MacGregor Lane. [Frequently insightful and easily the most influential work in the entire reception history.]

Kempis, Thomas à. 1976. *The Imitation of Christ*, tr. and introduction by Leo Sherley-Price. London: Penguin Books. [Full text of Kempis's influential *c.*1440 work also available at http://www.ccel.org.]

Knobel, P. S., ed. and tr. 1991. *The Targum of Qohelet*. The Aramaic Bible, 15. Edinburgh: T. & T. Clark.

Lachower, F., and I. Tishby, eds. 1989. *The Wisdom of the Zohar: An Anthology of Texts*, tr. D. Goldstein, 3 vols. Oxford: Oxford University Press.

Maier, Christoph T. 2000. *Crusade Propaganda and Ideology: Model Sermons for the Preaching of the Cross*. Cambridge: Cambridge University Press.

Manns, Frédéric, ed. and tr. 1992. *Le Targum de Qohelet*. http://198.62.75.1/www1/ofm/sbf/Books/LA42/42145FM.pdf.

Martínez, F.G., and E. J. C. Tigchelaar, eds. 1997. *The Dead Sea Scrolls Study Edition*, vol. 1: *1Q1–4Q273*. Grand Rapids, Mich.: Eerdmans.

Menzies, Allan, ed. 1974. *Original Supplement to the American Edition*. ANF, 10.

Montefiore, C. G., and H. Loewe, eds. 1974. *A Rabbinic Anthology*. London: MacMillan and Co.

Patrick. 1955. *The Writings of Bishop Patrick, 1074–1084*, ed. Aubrey Gwynn. Dublin: Dublin Institute for Advanced Studies.

Petry, Ray C, ed. 1962. *A History of Christianity: Readings in the History of the Early and Medieval Church*. London: Prentice-Hall International.

Rashbam. 1985. *The Commentary of R. Samuel ben Meir Rashbam on Qoheleth*, ed. and tr. S. Japhet and R. Salters. Jerusalem: Magnes Press; Leiden: E. J. Brill. [Full study, with Hebrew and English trans. of the commentary of the celebrated French rabbi (*c.*1080–*c.*1160) and grandson of Rashi.]

Roberts, A., and J. Donaldson, eds. 1974a. *Tertullian Part Fourth, Minucius Felix, Commodian, Origen – Parts First and Second.* ANF, 4.

——1974b. *The Twelve Patriachs . . . the Clementina, Apocrypha, Decretals, Memoirs of Edessa and Syriac Documents, Remains of the First Ages.* ANF, 8.

Romano, Tim. 1998. 'The Wanderer.' http://www.aimsdata.com/tim/anhaga/edition. htm. [A critical edition of the facsimile and translation of the Old English poem, *c.*975.]

Saperstein, M, ed. 1989. *Jewish Preaching, 1200–1800: An Anthology.* New Haven: Yale University Press.

Sprenger, Jakob, and Heinrich Institoris. 1928. *Malleus Maleficarum*, ed. and tr. Montague Summers. Suffolk: John Rodker. [Orig. pub. in successive editions, 1430–1505. Also available in subsequent editions published by Pushkin Press.]

Vajda, G. 1971. *Deux commentaires Karaïtes sur l'Ecclésiaste.* Etudes sur le Judaïsme Médiévale, 4. Leiden: Brill. [Translation of the tenth-century commentaries of Salmon ben Jeruhim and Yephet ben 'Ali.]

2. 1500–1800

Adams, C. F., ed. 1894. *Antinomiansim in the Colony of Massachusetts Bay, 1636–1638.* Boston. [Includes the report of the trial of Anne Hutchinson.]

Agrippa von Nettesheim, Henry. 1974. *Of the Vanitie and Uncertaintie of Artes and Sciences by Henry Cornelius Agrippa*, ed. Catherine M. Dunn. Northridge, Calif.: California State University. [An influential early scepticism work of 1530.]

Alshich, Moshe. 1992. *The Book of Koheleth . . . In Pursuit of Perfection: The Commentary of Rabbi Moshe Alshich on Megillath Koheleth/Ecclesiastes*, tr. Ravi Shahar. Jerusalem: Feldheim. [Translation of a pious and cautious commentary published in 1606 by a rabbi who exercised particular influence on later Hasidic Judaism.]

Anonymous. 1680. *The Young Man's Alarum . . . a Discourse upon the 9th. Verse of the 11th. Chapter of Ecclesiastes.* London: William Thackery.

Anonymous. 1765. *Choheleth, or the Royal Preacher: A Poem Most Humbly Inscribed to the King.* London: W. Johnston. [A remarkable introduction and lengthy and frequently delightful poem, often attributed to Walter Bradick, or Brodick.]

Bacon, Francis. 1730. *Francisci Baconi . . . Opera Omnia, Quatuor Voluminibus, Comprehensa*, 4 vols. London: R. Gosling.

Beza, Theodore. 1593. *Ecclesiastes, or the Preacher: Solomons Sermon Made to the People . . .* Cambridge: John Legatt. [Orig. pub. 1588.]

Bradstreet, Anne. 2004. 'The Four Ages of Man', ed. Ian Lancashire. In *Representative Poetry Online.* http://rpo.library.utoronto.ca. [Orig. pub. 1650.]

Brome, Alexander. 1982. *Poems: Alexander Brome*, ed. Roman R. Dubinski, 2 vols. Toronto: University of Toronto Press. [Elizabethan poet whose decasyllabic paraphrase of Eccl. 1 can be found in 1.335–7, with commentary and notes in 2.120.]

Broughton, Hugh. 1605. *A Comment upon Coheleth or Ecclesiastes: Framed for the Instruction of Prince Henri our Hope*. London: W. White. [An unremarkable work of piety, frequently cited in later works.]

Bunyan, John. 1986. *The Pilgrim's Progress*. London: Penguin Books. [Orig. pub. 1678.]

Burns, Robert. 2005. 'Address to the Unco Guid, or the Rigidly Righteous.' http://www.robertburns.org. [Orig. pub. 1786.]

Byron, Lord. 1970. *Byron: Poetical Works 1788–1824*, ed. Frederick Page. Oxford: Oxford University Press.

Carissimi, Giacomo, et al. 2004. *Vanitas Vanitatum: Rome 1650 – Tragicomedia*. Apex. Warner Classics. [Recording of 11 seventeenth-century choral and string pieces based on *vanitas*, often with direct reference to Ecclesiastes.]

Cary, Patrick. 1820. *Trivial Poems, and Triolets: Written in Obedience to Mrs. Tomkin's Commands*. London: John Murray. [Orig. pub. 1651.]

Charron, Pierre. 1640. *Of Wisdome Three Books*, tr. S. Lennard. London: Richard Badger. [Orig. pub. 1601.]

Collins, An. 2004. 'Verses on the Twelvth Chapter of Ecclesiastes.' In *Divine Songs and Meditacions. Literature Online*. http://lion.chadwyck.com. [Orig. pub. 1653, pp. 93–6.]

Collop, John. 1667. *Charity Commended, or, A Catholick Christian Soberly Instructed*. London. [Orig. pub. 1656.]

Desvoeux, A. V. 1760. *A Philosophical and Critical Essay on Ecclesiastes*. London: G. Hawkins, Milton's Head. [A remarkable study, 'not the result of a sudden sally of imagination, but the product of serious and often revised reflexions', which engages with a wide range of scholarship of the day (and much earlier), and with a richly detailed philological analysis comprising the last 234 pp.]

Donne, John. 1662. *Donne's Satyr Containing 1. A Short Map of Mundane Vanity, 2. A Cabinet of Merry Conceits, 3. Certain Pleasant Propositions and Questions with their Merry Solutions and Answers: Being Very Useful, Pleasant and Delightful to All, and Offensive to None*. London: Printed by R. W. for M. Wright.

—— 1839. *The Works of John Donne DD, Dean of Saint Paul's 1621–1631, with a Memoir of his Life*, ed. Henry Alford, 6 vols. London: John W. Parker.

Dryden, John. 1700. *Fables Ancient and Modern Translated into Verse from Homer, Ovid, Boccace, & Chaucer, with Original Poems, by Mr. Dryden*. London: Printed for Jacob Tonson . . .

Dunton, John. 1700. *The Art of Living Incognito*. London: A. Baldwin.

Edwards, John. 1726. *Discourses on Those Graces and Duties which Are Purely Evangelical . . .* London: T. Cox at The Lamb.

Erasmus, Desiderius. 1989. *The Praise of Folly and Other Writings*, ed. Robert Adams. New York: W. W. Norton & Co.

Fawkes, Francis. 2004. 'The Picture of Old-Age: Paraphrased from the Seven First Verses of the 12th Chapter of Ecclesiastes.' In *Original Poems and Translations. Literature Online*. http://lion.chadwyck.com. [Orig. pub. 1761, pp. 90–1.]

Galileo (Galileo Galilei). 1989. *The Galileo Affair: A Documentary History*, ed. and tr. M. A. Finocchiaro. Berkeley: University of California Press.

Garzoni, Tomaso. 1600. *The Hospitall of Incurable Fooles: Erected in English, as Neer the First Italian Modell and Platforme, as the Vnskilfull Hand of an Ignorant Architect Could Deuise.* London: Edm. Bollifant. [Orig. pub. *c.*1586.]

Gascoigne, George. 1910. *The Complete Works of George Gascoigne,* ed. J. W. Cunliffe, 2 vols. Cambridge: Cambridge University Press.

Goldsmith, Oliver. 2003. 'The Deserted Village, A Poem,' ed. Ian Lancashire. In *Representative Poetry Online.* http://rpo.library.utoronto.ca. [Orig. pub. 1770.]

Granger, Thomas. 1621. *A Familiar Exposition or Commentarie on Ecclesiastes.* London: T. S. for T. Pavier.

Greville, Fulke. 1633. *Certaine Learned and Elegant Workes of the Right Honorable Fvlke Lord Brooke . . .* London: E. P. (for Henry Seyle). [Includes his 'Treatie of Humane Learning'.]

Grotius, Hugo. 1644. *Annotata ad Vetus Testamentum,* 3 vols. Paris. ['Ad Ecclesiasten' appears in 1.521–40.]

Hall, John. 1646. *Poems* [followed by] *The Seconde Booke of Divine Poems.* Cambridge. [The *Second Booke* bears the imprint 'London, 1647'.]

Hall, Joseph. 1635. *The Character of Man Laid Forth in a Sermon Preach't at the Court, March, 10. 1634. By the L. Bishop of Exceter.* London: Printed by M. Flesher, for Nat: Butter.

Hopkins, Ezekiel. 1685. *The Vanity of the World.* London: King's Arms and Golden Lion. [Orig. pub. 1668.]

Howard, Henry. 1815. *The Works of Henry Howard, Earl of Surrey and of Sir Thomas Wyatt the Elder,* ed. G. F. Nott. 2 vols. London: T. Bensley. [Includes Howard's remarkable 1546 paraphrase of Eccl. 1–5, in 1.66–77.]

Hyde, Edward. 1657. *A Christian Legacy Consisting of Two Parts: I. A Preparation for Death. II. A Consolation against Death . . .* London: Printed by R[obert?] W[hite?] for Rich. Davis in Oxon.

—— 1662. *Allegiance and Conscience Not Fled out of England . . . in Several Sermons Anno 1649 on the Words of the Ecclesiastes . . .* Cambridge: John Field. [Sermons on Eccl. 8:2–4 in support of King Charles II.]

Jermin, Michael. 1639. *A Commentary, upon the Whole Booke of Ecclesiastes.* London: R. Hodgkinsonne.

Johnson, Samuel. 1823. *The Works of Samuel Johnson,* ed. A. Murphy, 12 vols. London: Thomas Tegg et al.

—— 1962. *The Poems of Samuel Johnson,* ed. D. N. Smith and E. L. McAdam. Oxford: Clarendon Press.

—— 1978. *The Yale Edition of the Works of Samuel Johnson,* vol. 14: *Sermons,* ed. J. Hagstrum and J. Gray. New Haven: Yale University Press.

Laud, William. 1857. *The Works of the Most Reverend Father in God, William Laud, D.D., Sometime Lord Archbishop of Canterbury,* ed. William Scott, 7 vols. Oxford: John Henry Parker.

Le Clerc, Jean. 1690. *Five Letters concerning the Inspiration of the Holy Scriptures Translated out of French.* 'S.L.' [A translation traditionally attributed to John Locke.]

Lloyd, David. 1670. *State-Worthies, or, The States-Men and Favourites of England Since the Reformation . . .* London: Printed by Thomas Milbourne for Samuel Speed.

Lok, Henry. 1597. *Ecclesiastes, Otherwise Called the Preacher* . . . London: R. Field. [Available at *Literature Online*, http://lion.chadwyck.com.]

Lowth, Robert. 1995. *Lectures on the Sacred Poetry of the Hebrews*, 2 vols. London: Routledge. [Orig. pub. 1787.]

Luther, Martin. 1857. *The Table Talk of Martin Luther*, ed. and tr. W. Hazlitt. London: H. G. Bohn.

——1956. *The Reformation Writings of Martin Luther*, 2, ed. and tr. B. L. Woolf. London: Lutterworth Press.

——1967. *Table Talk*, tr. T. G. Tappert. In *Luther's Works*, Philadelphia: Fortress Press, vol. 54.

——1972. *Notes on Ecclesiastes*, tr. J. Pelikan. In *Luther's Works*, St Louis: Concordia Publishing, 15. 1–187. [Orig. pub. 1532.]

Mayer, John. 1653. *A Commentary upon the Holy Writings of Job, David, and Salomon*. London.

Montaigne, Michel de. 1991. *Montaigne: The Complete Essays*, ed. and tr. with introduction by M. A. Screech. London: Penguin.

Moulin, Pierre du. 1652. *Heraclitus, or, Mans Looking-Glass and Survey of Life*, tr. H. L'Estr. London: Henry Seile. [The translator writes that it is '40 years since I translaed this piece out of French, and laid it by in loose papers'.]

Neville, William. 1530. *The Castell of Pleasure* . . . London: In the Fletestrete at the sygne of the Sonne by Wynkyn de worde. [Orig. pub. *c*.1518.]

Paine, Thomas. 1896. *The Writings of Thomas Paine*, ed. M. D. Conway, 4 vols. London: G. P. Putnam's Sons.

Prior, Matthew. 1905. *Poems on Several Occasions*, ed. A. R. Waller. Cambridge: Cambridge University Press. [Contains his influential 1718 poem 'Solomon on the Vanity of the World.']

Quarles, Francis. 1635. *Emblemes*. London: Printed by G[eorge] M[iller] and sold at Iohn Marriots shope . . .

——1638. *Hieroglyphikes of the Life of Man*. London: Printed by M. Flesher, for Iohn Marriot.

——1739. *Solomon's Recantation*. London: L. Hinde. [Contains his lengthy paraphrase, *c*.1644, dedicated to Elizabeth. Full text available at *Literature Online*, http://lion. chadwyck.com.]

Rollins, H. E., ed. 1927. *The Paradise of Dainty Devices (1576–1606)*. Cambridge: Cambridge University Press.

Rudrum, Alan, Joseph Black and Holly Faith Nelson, eds. 2001. *The Broadview Anthology of Seventeenth-Century Verse and Prose*. Letchworth: Broadview Press.

Sandys, George. 1638. *A Paraphrase upon the Divine Poems*. London: John Legatt. [Includes his stunning paraphrase of Ecclesiastes, orig. pub. 1632.]

Santa María, Juan de. 1632. *Policie Unveiled Wherein May Be Learned, The Order Of True Policie in Kingdomes* . . . , tr. 'I. M. of Magdalen Hall'. London: Thomas Harper.

Serranus, John. 1585. *A Godlie and Learned Commentarie upon the Excellent Book of Solomon, Commonly Called Ecclesiastes, or the Preacher*. London: John Windet. [The author is also known as Jean de Serres.]

Smart, Christopher. 1949. *The Collected Poems of Christopher Smart*, ed. with introduction by N. Callan, 2 vols. London: Routledge & Kegan Paul.

Smith, Henry. 1592. *The Sermons of Master Henrie Smith, Gathered into One Volume*. London: Thomas Orwin.

Smith, John. 1676. *The Pourtract of Old Age: Wherein is Contained a Sacred Anatomy Both of Soul and Body, and a Perfect Account of the Infirmities of Age Incident to Them Both. Being a Paraphrase upon the Six Former Verses of the xiith Chapter of Ecclesiastes*. London.

Speght, Rachel. 1617. *A Mouzell for Melastomus: The Cynicall Bayter of, and Foule Mouthed Barker against Evahs Sex* . . . London: Nicholas Okes.

Spenser, Edmund. 1591. *Complaints: Containing Sundrie Small Poemes of the Worlds Vanitie*. London: William Ponsonbie.

Stillingfleet, Edward. 1698. *Thirteen Sermons Preached on Several Occasions* . . . *The Third Volume*. London: Printed by J. H. for Henry Mortlock. [Sermons 4 and 13 are sterling examples of Elizabethan preaching on Ecclesiastes.]

Strype, J., ed. 1822. *Ecclesiastical Memorials*. Oxford: Clarendon Press. ['A Sermon Preached at the Funerals of Queen Mary: by the Bishop of Winchester', John White, appears in 3. 2.536–50.]

Temple, William. 1690. *Miscellanea: In Four Essays*. London: J. R. for . . . Simpson.

Trapp, John. 1650. *A Commentary or Exposition upon Ecclesiastes, or The Preacher*. London: T. R. and E. M. for John Bellamie.

Voltaire. 1759. *Précis de l'Ecclésiaste*. Paris: Louvre. [For a detailed study and full English translation, see Christianson 2005.]

—— 1877. *Oeuvres complètes de Voltaire*. Paris: Garnier Frères. [The Louis Moland edition, published 1877–85 in 52 vols.]

—— 1991. *Candide or Optimism: A Norton Critical Edition*, ed. and tr. Robert Adams. 2nd edn. New York: W. W. Norton & Company. [Orig. pub. 1759.]

Wollaston, William. 1691. *The Design of Part of the Book of Ecclesiastes* . . . *Represented in an English Poem*. London: For James Knapton, at the Crown.

3. Post-1800

Almar, George. 1831. *Pedlar's Acre: Or, The Wife of Seven Husbands: A Drama*. London.

Amichai, Yehuda. 2004. 'A Man in his Life.' http://oldpoetry.com.

Arnold, Matthew. 1968. *Dissent and Dogma*, ed. R. H. Super. Ann Arbor: University of Michigan Press.

—— 1973. *English Literature and Irish Politics*, ed. R. H. Super. Ann Arbor: University of Michigan Press.

Bantock, Granville. 1913. *The Vanity of Vanities: A Choral Symphony for Unaccompanied Voices*. London: J. Curwen. [Score.]

—— 1996. *Granville Bantock: Two Choral Symphonies – Atalanta in Calydon and Vanity of Vanities*. BBC Singers Conducted by Simon Joly. Albany Records.

Barker, Sebastian. 1992. *Guarding the Border: Selected Poems.* London: Enitharmon.

Baudrillard, Jean. 1994. *Simulacra and Simulation*, tr. S. F. Glaser. Ann Arbor: University of Michigan Press. [Orig. pub. 1981.]

Bierce, Ambrose. 2000. *The Unabridged Devil's Dictionary*, ed. D. E. Schultz and S. T. Joshi. Athens, Ga.: University of Georgia Press. [Orig. pub. 1911.]

Bonhoeffer, Dietrich. 1971. *Ethics*, ed. E. Bethge, tr. N. H. Smith. London: SCM Press. [Orig. pub. 1949.]

Bradbury, Ray. 1984. 'Long after Ecclesiastes.' In J. N. Williamson, ed., *Masques*, London: Futura, 245–51.

—— 1993. *Fahrenheit 451.* London: Flamingo. [Orig. pub. 1953.]

Brahms, Johannes. 1992. *Schubert and Brahms: Leider, Kleinman, London, Serkin, Fleisher.* SBK. Sony Classical. [Recording of *Vier ernste Gesänge*, 'Four Serious Songs', of 1897, two of which are based on Ecclesiastes. With detailed sleeve notes by R. Wehner.]

Bridges, Robert Seymour. 1936. *Poetical Works of Robert Bridges with The Testament of Beauty but Excluding the Eight Dramas.* Oxford: Oxford University Press.

Browning, Robert. 2004. 'The Bishop Orders his Tomb at Saint Praxed's Church, Rome, 15__', ed. Ian Lancashire. In *Representative Poetry Online.* http://rpo.library.utoronto.ca. [Orig. pub. in *Hood's Magazine*, 1845.]

Chesterton, G. K. 1927. *The Collected Poems of Gilbert Keith Chesterton.* London: Cecil Palmer. ['Ecclesiastes' is on p. 299.]

Cornwell, Patricia. 2000. *The Last Precinct.* London: Warner Books.

Dali, Salvador. 2002. *Bible Illustrations: Blatt Nr. 49, Vanitas Vanitatum Liber Ecclesiates 1.12, 13.* http://daliland.com/bible10.html. [Scans from Dali's rare illustrated *The Holy Bible*, 1964–7.]

Dello Joio, Norman. 1956. *Meditations on Ecclesiastes: For String Orchestra.* New York: C. Fischer. [Score.]

—— 1992. *Menotti, Apocalypse. Dello Joio, Meditations on Ecclesiastes.* Oregon Symphony, James DePriest, Conductor. International Classics. Westbury, N.Y.: Koch. [Recording with detailed sleeve notes by Rudy Ennis.]

Dick, Philip K. 2001. *The Man in the High Castle*, with introduction by Eric Brown. London: Penguin Books. [Orig. pub. 1962.]

Eliot, T. S. 1969. *The Complete Poems and Plays of T. S. Eliot.* London: Faber & Faber. [*Four Quartets* also available at http://www.tristan.icom43.net/quartets.]

Ellis, Havelock. 1926. *The New Spirit*, 4th edn. London: Constable & Company. [Orig. pub. 1890.]

Hardy, Thomas. 1963. *Tess of the D'Urbervilles: A Pure Woman.* London: MacMillan and Co. [Orig. pub. 1891.]

—— 2000. *Far from the Madding Crowd*, ed. with introduction by R. Morgan. London: Penguin Books. [Orig. pub. 1874.]

Henley, William Ernest. 1898. *Poems.* London: David Nutt.

Hesketh, Phoebe. 1994. 'After Ecclesiastes.' In *The Leave Train: New and Selected Poems.* London: Enitharmon, 94. [Available at *Literature Online*, http://lion.chadwyck.com.]

Holmes, Oliver Wendell. 1893. *The Poetical Works of Oliver Wendell Holmes*, 3 vols. [Full text at http://www.gutenberg.org.]

Hookham, John (Frere). 1872. *The Works of John Hookham Frere in Verse and Prose*, ed. W. E. and B. Frere, 2 vols. London: Pickering. [Includes Hookham's (1769–1846) brief paraphrase of Eccl. 7:6 in 2.496.]

Housman, A. E. 1936. *More Poems*. London: Jonathan Cape. [Full text available at http://www.kalliope.org.]

Kingsley, Charles. 1880. *The Works of Charles Kingsley*, vol. 15: *Prose Idylls*. London: MacMillan and Co.

Klein, A. M. 1974. *The Collected Poems of A. M. Klein: Compiled and with an Introduction by Miriam Waddington*. Toronto: McGraw-Hill Ryerson. [Includes 'Koheleth'.]

——2004. 'Out of the Pulver and the Polished Lens.' In *Canadian Poets*. http://www.library.utoronto.ca/canpoetry.

Knox, William. 2003. 'Mortality', ed. Ian Lancashire. In *Representative Poetry Online*. http://rpo.library.utoronto.ca. [Orig. pub. 1824.]

Lewis, Matthew Gregory. 1801. *Adelmorn, The Outlaw: A Romantic Drama, in Three Acts/As Originally Written by M. G. Lewis. First Performed at Drury Lane Theatre on Monday, May 4, 1801*. London: Printed for J. Bell, by Wilks and Taylor.

Locker-Lampson, Frederick. 1865. *A Selection from the Works of Frederick Locker*. London.

Mahon, Derek. 1999. 'Ecclesiastes.' In *Collected Poems*. Loughcrew: Gallery Press. [Available at *Literature Online*, http://lion.chadwyck.com.]

Melville, Herman. 1967. *Moby Dick*. London: W. W. Norton. [Ch. 96 specifically engages with Qoheleth. Available at http://www.gutenberg.org. Orig. pub. 1851.]

Orwell, George. 1968. *The Collected Essays, Journalism and Letters of George Orwell*, vol. 4: *In Front of your Nose, 1945–1950*, ed. S. Orwell and I. Angus. London: Secker & Warburg.

Plarr, Gustave. 1896. *In the Dorian Mood*. London. [Available at *Literature Online*, http://lion.chadwyck.com.]

Ratner, Philip. 2002. 'The Virtual Israel Bible Museum: Ecclesiastes Virtual Gallery.' http://israelbiblemuseum.com. [Scans of Ratner's paintings of Eccl. 3.]

Renan, Ernest. 1873. *L'Antéchrist*. Paris: Michel Lévy Frères.

Reynolds, Frederick. 1808. *Begone Dull Care: A Comedy, in Five Acts. As performed at the Theatre-Royal, Covent-Garden*. London: Printed for Longman, Hurst, Rees, and Orme [etc.].

Rossetti, Christina. 1979. *The Complete Poems of Christina Rossetti*, 1, ed. with notes and introduction by R. W. Crump. Baton Rouge, La.: Louisiana State University Press.

——1986. *The Complete Poems of Christina Rossetti*, 2, ed. with notes and introduction by R. W. Crump. Baton Rouge, La.: Louisiana State University Press.

Ruskin, John. 1868. *Mystery of Life and its Arts*. London: Henry Frowde. [This is the third lecture of his influential 'Sesame and Lilies' series, which does not appear in all editions of that work. This edition has no page numbers.]

Scott, Frederick George. 2004. 'Solomon.' In *The Gates of Time and Other Poems. Literature Online.* http://lion.chadwyck.com. [Orig. pub. *c.*1886.]

Shaw, George Bernard. 1934. *Prefaces.* London: Constable.

—— 1965. *The Complete Plays of Bernard Shaw.* London: Paul Hamlyn. ['Man and Superman: A Comedy and a Philosophy,' performed in 1905, appears on pp. 332–405. The full text is available at http://www.gutenberg.org.]

Shelley, Percy. 1880. *The Prose Works of Percy Bysshe Shelley,* ed. H. B. Forman, 4 vols. London: Reeves and Turner.

—— 1887. *The Poetical Works of Percy Bysshe Shelley,* ed. H. B. Forman, 4 vols. London: Reeves and Turner.

Spurgeon, C. H. 1892. *The Metropolitan Tabernacle Pulpit: Sermons Preached by C. H. Spurgeon,* vol. 38. London: Passmore and Alabaster.

Stevenson, Robert Louis. 1904. *Virginibus Puerisque and Other Papers,* 26th edn. London: Chatto & Windus.

Thackeray, William M. 1885. *The Works of William Makepeace Thackeray in Twenty-Six Volumes,* vol. 21: *Ballads and The Rose and the Ring.* London: Smith, Elder, & Co.

—— 1899. *The Works of William Makepeace Thackeray with Biographical Introductions by his Daughter, Anne Ritchie, in Thirteen Volumes,* vol. 13: *Ballads and Miscellanies.* London: Smith, Elder, & Co. [Includes his *Vanitas Vanitatum.*]

—— 1962. *The Newcomes, in Two Volumes.* London: J. M. Dent & Sons.

—— 1963. *Vanity Fair.* London: J. M. Dent & Sons.

[NOTE: all of the above works by Thackeray can be accessed at http://www.gutenberg. org.]

Thompson, Francis. 1946. *The Poems of Francis Thompson.* London: Hollis and Charter.

Tillich, Paul. 1963. *The Shaking of the Foundations.* Harmondsworth: Penguin.

Tolstoy, Leo. 1942. *War and Peace,* tr. L. and A. Maude. London: Macmillan. [Orig. pub. 1865–9.]

Untermeyer, Louis. 1928. 'Koheleth.' *The Nation* 126.3269, 242. [Repr. in Atwan and Wieder, 1993. 363–4.]

Updike, John. 1972. *Rabbit Redux.* London: André Deutsch. [Orig. pub. 1971.]

Ward, Frederick. 1890. '*Twixt Kiss and Lip; or, Under the Sword, by the Author of 'Women Must Weep'* (F. Harald Williams). London.

White, John. 2005. 'Also Like him.' *Oxford Magazine* 236: 6.

Whittier, John Greenleaf. 1889. *The Writings of John Greenleaf Whittier in Seven Volumes.* London: MacMillan and Co. [The poem, *My Summer with Dr Singletary,* appears in vol. 5 and is also available at http://www.gutenberg.org.]

Wilcocks, Jonathan. 1981. *Voices of Time: A Cantata for Baritone, Chorus and Orchestra.* London: Oxford University Press. [Score. Includes a movement based on Eccl. 3 entitled 'For Every Thing There is a Season'.]

Wolfe, Thomas. 1968. *You Can't Go Home Again.* London: Heinemann. [Orig. pub. posthumously in 1940.]

Woolner, Thomas. 1863. *My Beautiful Lady.* London: Macmillan and Co.

Zelazny, Roger. 1963. 'A Rose for Ecclesiastes.' *The Magazine of Fantasy and Science Fiction* 25.5: 5–35. [The first appearance of the cult 'novelet', which has appeared in various anthologies since.]

Reception Histories of Ecclesiastes

Studies that explore the influence or use of Ecclesiastes in particular works, figures, movements or periods.

1. Jewish and Christian (*some of these studies also include overviews of academic approaches of the nineteenth and twentieth centuries – for more on which, see section 2*)

Backhaus, F. J. 1993. 'Qohelet und Sirach.' *Biblische Notizen* 69: 32–55. [A useful discussion of an old question which argues that there is no evidence of a direct literary relationship between the two works.]

Bartholomew, Craig G. 1998. *Reading Ecclesiastes: Old Testament Exegesis and Hermeneutical Theory.* Analecta Biblica, 139. Rome: Pontifical Biblical Institute. [In particular, 'How Ecclesiastes Has Been Read: The History of Interpretation of Ecclesiastes', 31–51.]

Barton, G. A. 1959. *The Book of Ecclesiastes.* International Critical Commentary. Edinburgh: T. & T. Clark. [Orig. pub. 1908; his History of Interpretation section (pp. 18–31) seeks to bring Ginsburg 1861 up to date.]

Beal, Rebecca S. 1982. 'The Medieval Tradition of the *Libri Salomonis* in Dante's *Comedia* and Chaucer's *Troilus and Criseyde.*' Unpublished PhD thesis, University of Texas at Austin. [Ch. 1 outlines medieval approaches to Proverbs, Ecclesiastes and the Song of Songs in Christian works. Cf. Eliason 1989 below.]

Berndt, R. 1994. 'Skizze zur Auslegungsgeschichte der Bücher "Proverbia" und "Ecclesiastes" in der abendländischen Kirche.' *Sacris erudiri* 34: 5–32.

Blank, Sheldon H. 1970. 'Prolegomenon.' In Ginsburg 1861 [repr.]: pp. ix–xliv. [Brings Ginsburg's survey up to date.]

Broyde, Michael J. 1995. 'Defilement of the Hands, Canonization of the Bible, and the Special Status of Esther, Ecclesiastes, and the Song of Songs.' *Judaism* 44.1: 65–79.

Bruns, G. 1990. 'The Hermeneutics of Midrash.' In *The Book and the Text*, ed. R. Schwartz, 189–213. Oxford: Blackwell.

Christianson, Eric S. 1998b. 'Qoheleth the "Old Boy" and Qoheleth the "New Man": Misogynism, the Womb and a Paradox in Ecclesiastes.' In *Wisdom and Psalms: A Feminist Companion to the Bible*, 2nd ser., ed. A. Brenner and C. Fontaine, 109–36. Sheffield: Sheffield Academic Press. [Surveys traditional approaches to Qoheleth's texts about women, particularly 7:23–8:1.]

Cohen, A., ed. 1952. *The Five Megilloth: Hebrew Text, English Translation and Commentary*, 2nd edn. London: Soncino Press. [Offers access to a range of traditional Jewish commentary. Orig. pub. 1946. Cf. Rosenberg 1992.]

Darling, James. 1859. *Cyclopaedia Bibliographica: A Library Manual of Theological and General Literature . . .* London. [Extensive lists of commentaries and sermons, with the Ecclesiastes entry at vol. 2. cols 555–76.]

Dell, K. J. 1994. 'Ecclesiastes as Wisdom: Consulting Early Interpreters.' *Vetus Testamentum* 44: 301–29.

Diego Sánchez, Manuel. 1990. 'El "Comentario al Ecclesiastés" de Didimo Alejandrino.' *Teresianum* 41: 231–42.

Drewes, B. F. 2005. 'Reading the Bible in Context: An Indonesian and a Mexican Commentary on Ecclesiastes: Contextual Interpretations.' *Exchange* 34.2: 120–33.

Earle, T. F. 2001. '*Ecclesiastes de Salamam*: An Unknown Biblical Translation by Damião de Góis.' *Portugese Studies* 17: 42–63. [Discusses the recent discovery of the only known translation of a book of the Bible into Portugese in the Renaissance.]

Ehrhart, Margaret J. 1980. 'Machaut's *Jugement dou roy de Navarre* and the Book of Ecclesiastes.' *Neuphilologische Mitteilungen* 81.3: 318–25.

Eliason, Eric J. 1989. '*Vanitas Vanitatum*: "Piers Plowman", Ecclesiastes, and Contempt of the World.' Unpublished PhD thesis, University of Virginia. [Ch. 2 is a magnificent survey of *vanitas* readings from Origen to the medieval monastic scholars. Cf. Beal 1982 above.]

Ettlinger, Gerard H. 1985. 'The Form and Method of the Commentary on Ecclesiastes by Gregory of Agrigentum.' In *Papers of the Ninth International Conference on Patristic Studies: Oxford 1983*, ed. E. A. Livingstone, Studia Patristica, 19, 317–20. Leuven: Peeters.

Flesher, P. V. M. 1990. 'The Wisdom of the Sages: Rabbinic Rewriting of Qohelet.' Conference paper, Society of Biblical Literature Annual Meeting. [Abstract available in *AAR/SBL Abstracts*, 390. Atlanta: Scholars Press, 1990.]

Fontaine, Carole R. 1998. '"Many Devices" (Qoheleth 7.23–8.1): Qoheleth, Misogyny and the *Malleus Maleficarum*.' In *Wisdom and Psalms: A Feminist Companion to the Bible*, (2nd ser.), ed. A. Brenner and C. Fontaine, 137–68. Sheffield: Sheffield Academic Press. [An extensive and provocative survey of the use of the ch. 7 passage in rabbinic literature and in the *Malleus*. Cf. Noonan 1998.]

Fox, M. V. 1999. 'Qohelet.' In *Dictionary of Biblical Interpretation*, ed. J. H. Hayes, 2 vols., 2. 346–54. Nashville: Abingdon Press.

——2004. *Ecclesiastes*/קהלת, JPS Bible Commentary. Philadelphia: Jewish Publication Society. [A general survey of Jewish approaches features in the introduction and informs the commentary.]

Geitmann, G. 2004. 'Ecclesiastes.' In *The Online Catholic Encyclopedia*. http://www.newadvent.org/cathen. [Orig. pub. 1909.]

Ginsburg, C. D. 1861. *Coheleth (Commonly Called the Book of Ecclesiastes)*. London: Longman (repr. New York: KTAV, 1970). [Invaluable, and perhaps the most exhaustive survey of Ecclesiastes reading up to his time. Cf. Preston 1845, which covers some similar material though to a far lesser depth.]

Ginzberg, Louis. 1933. 'Die Haggada bei den Kirchenvätern: V. Der Kommentar des Hieronymus zu Kohelet.' In *Abhandlugen zur Erinnerung an Hirsch Perez Chajes*, 22–50. Vienna: The Alexander Kohut Memorial Foundation. [Identifies in detail the rabbinic traditions that inform Jerome's commentary on Ecclesiastes.]

Gregory of Nyssa. 1993 (details in Primary Sources section). [As well as the full translation of Gregory of Nyssa's eight homilies on Ecclesiastes, includes some useful studies of the homilies and at least one on early Christian uses of Ecclesiastes (cf. Starowieyski 1993).]

Gregory Thaumaturgos. 1990 (details in Primary Sources section). [Includes John Jarick's commentary on the paraphrase as well as discussion of Qoheleth in other early Christian writers and rabbinic sources.]

Hirshman, M. 1958. 'The Greek Fathers and the Aggada on Ecclesiastes: Formats of Exegesis in Late Antiquity.' *Hebrew Union College Annual* 59: 137–65. [Assesses the exegetical method of four early Christian works on Ecclesiastes and insightfully compares them to *Midrash Qoheleth*.]

—— 1996. 'The Midrash on Ecclesiastes and Jerome's Commentary.' In *idem, A Rivalry of Genius: Jewish and Christian Biblical Interpretation*, 95–108. Albany, NY: SUNY Press.

Holmes, Jeremy. 2003. 'Bonaventure on Ecclesiastes.' In *St Paul Center for Biblical Theology*. http://www.salvationhistory.com. [Offers a detailed discussion of the context and content of Bonaventure's commentary on Ecclesiastes (1253–7).]

Holm-Nielsen, S. 1974. 'On the Interpretation of Qoheleth in Early Christianity.' *Vetus Testamentum* 24: 168–77.

—— 1976. 'The Book of Ecclesiastes and the Interpretation of it in Jewish and Christian Theology.' *Annual of the Swedish Theological Institute in Jerusalem* 10: 38–96.

Jarick, John. 1995. 'Theodore of Mopsuestia and the Interpretation of Ecclesiastes.' In *The Bible in Human Society: Essays in Honor of John Rogerson*, ed. Daniel Carroll R. et al., Journal for the Study of the Old Testament Supplement Series, 200, 306–16. Sheffield: Sheffield Academic Press.

—— 1997. 'The Bible's "Festival Scrolls" among the Dead Sea Scrolls.' In *The Scrolls and the Scriptures: Qumran Fifty Years After*, ed. Stanley E. Porter and Craig A. Evans, Journal for the Study of the Pseudepigrapha Supplements, 26; Roehampton Institute London Papers, 3, 170–82. Sheffield: Sheffield Academic Press.

Kallas, E. 1979. 'Ecclesiastes: *Traditum et Fides Evangelica*. The Ecclesiastes Commentaries of Martin Luther, Philip Melanchthon, and Johannes Brenz Considered within the History of Interpretation.' Unpublished PhD thesis, Graduate Theological Union, Berkeley.

Kraus, Matthew. 1999–2000. 'Christians, Jews, and Pagans in Dialogue: Jerome on Ecclesiastes 12:1–7.' *Hebrew Union College Annual* 70–1: 183–231. [One of the most thorough studies of the context and sources of Jerome's commentary on Ecclesiastes.]

Krüger, Thomas. 2004. *Qoheleth*, Hermeneia. Minneapolis: Augsburg Fortress. [The overview, pp. 27–34, and the bibliographical material, pp. 244–51, are particularly useful.]

Langston, Scott. 1998. 'Ecclesiastes 7:16 in the Sermons of George Whitefield and Joseph Trapp: Societal Influences in Biblical Interpretation.' Conference paper, Society of Biblical Literature Annual Meeting.

Leanza, Sandro. 1978. 'Eccl. 12,1–7: L'interpretazione excatologica dei Patri e degli esegeti medievali.' *Augustinianum* 18: 191–207.

—— 1986. 'Sulle fonti del *commentario all'Ecclesiaste* di Girolamo.' *Annali di storia dell'esegesi* 3: 173–99. [Isolates the influence of Origen on Jerome's commentary on Ecclesiastes.]

Lehmann, R. G. 1989. 'Bibliographie zu Qohelet.' In *Untersuchungen zur Eigenart des Buches Qohelet* by Michel Diethelm, Beihefte zur Zeitschrift für die alttestamentliche Wissenschaft, 152: 290–322. Berlin: de Gruyter. [An extensive bibliography that focuses 'zur Rezeptions- und Wirkungsgeschichte.']

Lubac, Henri de. 1960: *Exégèse médiévale: les quatre sens de l'ecriture*, 4 vols. Paris: Aubier.

Miller, Douglas B. 2000. 'What the Preacher Forgot: The Rhetoric of Ecclesiastes.' *Catholic Biblical Quarterly* 62: 215–35. [Summarizes five approaches to reading Ecclesiastes through history.]

—— 2002. *Symbol and Rhetoric in Ecclesiastes: The Place of Hebel in Qohelet's Work*, Academia Biblica 2. Atlanta, GA: Society of Biblical Literature.

Monti, D. 1979. 'Bonaventure's Interpretation of Scripture in his Exegetical Works.' Unpublished PhD thesis, University of Chicago. [Ch. 2 places Bonaventure's work on Ecclesiastes in the context of his academic career.]

Murphy, R. E. 1979. 'Qoheleth's "Quarrel" with the Fathers.' In *From Faith to Faith*, ed. D. Y. Hadidian, 235–45. Pittsburgh: Pickwick.

—— 1982. 'Qohelet Interpreted: The Bearing of the Past on the Present.' *Vetus Testamentum* 32: 331–7. [An influential survey, described by Murphy as a 'few *jalons* into the history of the interpretation of Ecclesiastes'.]

—— 1992. *Ecclesiastes*, Word Biblical Commentary, 23a. Dallas: Word. [The History of Interpretation section, pp. xlviii–lvi, is one of the best to be found in modern commentaries.]

Nicoll, W. R., and J. T. Stoddart, eds. 1910. *The Expositor's Dictionary of Texts*, vol. 1: *Genesis to Mark*. London: Hodder & Stoughton. [The Ecclesiastes entry has numerous items from Christian homiletic interpretation as well as literary readings.]

Noakes, K. W. 1984. 'The Metaphrase on Ecclesiastes of Gregory Thaumaturgus.' *Studia Patristica* 128: 196–9.

Noonan, Brian B. 1998. 'Wisdom Literature among the Witchmongers.' In *Wisdom and Psalms: A Feminist Companion to the Bible*, 2nd ser, ed. A. Brenner and C. Fontaine, FCB, 2: 169–74. Sheffield: Sheffield Academic Press. [Cf. Fontaine 1998.]

Paulson, Gail Nord. 1998. 'The Use of Qoheleth in Bonhoeffer's *Ethics*.' *Word & World* 18.3: 307–13.

Penna, Angelo. 1950. *Principi e crattere dell'esegesi di San Gerolamo*. Rome: Pontifical Biblical Institute.

Philippe, E. 1926. 'Ecclésiaste (le livre de).' In *Dictionnaire de la Bible*, ed. F. Vigouroux, 5 vols. 2. 1533–43. Paris: Librarie Letouzey et ané. [Orig. pub. 1895–1912.]

Poole, Matthew. 1684–6: *Synopsis Criticorum*, 5 vols. Ultrajecti. [An exhaustive catena in Latin, orig. pub. 1669–76. The Ecclesiastes entry in this edition appears in 2. 1810–1962.]

Preston, Theodore P. 1845. *The Hebrew Text, and a Latin Version of the Book of Solomon Called Ecclesiastes; with Original Notes, Philological and Exegetical, and a Translation of the Commentary of Mendlessohn* [*sic*] *from the Rabbinic Hebrew; Also a Newly Arranged English Version of Ecclesiastes*...London: John W. Parker. [Includes a translation of Mendelssohn's commentary and various other portions of rabbinic and Christian commentaries, such as Isaac Aramah's preface to his 1492 commentary.]

Rayez, A. 1932. 'Ecclésiaste: 3, Commentateurs.' In *Dictionnaire de Spiritualité*, ed. M. Viller et al., 4. 47–52. Paris: Beauchesne.

Robinson, James. 2001. 'Samuel Ibn Tibbon's Commentary on Ecclesiastes and the Philosopher's Prooemium.' In *Studies in Medieval Jewish History and Literature*, ed. Isadore Twersky, 3 vols, 3. 83–146. Cambridge, Mass.: Harvard University Press.

——forthcoming. *Philosophy and Exegesis on Samuel Ibn Tibbon's Commentary on Ecclesiastes*. London: Kegan Paul. [Ibn Tibbon's (*c*.1165–1232) 'ideas and explications', which are illustrated with a selection of passages in translation and set in the broader cultural and historical context.]

Rosenberg, A. J. 1992. *The Five Megilloth*, vol. 2: *Lamentations, Ecclesiastes*. New York: Judaica Press. [Contains 'a new English translation of text, Rashi and other commentaries'. Cf. Cohen 1952. Note that the complete translated text of Rashi on Ecclesiastes is available at http://www.chabad.org/library.]

Rosin, Robert. 1997a. 'Melanchthon and "The Preacher": A Theology for Life.' *Concordia Journal* 23: 295–308.

——1997b. *Reformers, the Preacher and Skepticism: Luther, Brenz, Melanchthon, and Ecclesiastes*. Mainz: Philipp von Zabern. [An in-depth survey of the reformers' complex relationship to Renaissance scepticism, assessed through their commentaries on Ecclesiastes.]

Salters, R. B. 1974–5. 'Qoheleth and the Canon.' *Expository Times* 86: 339–42. [Cf. Salters 1978 and 1979 below, both of which include surveys of Jewish and Christian approaches.]

——1988. 'Exegetical Problems in Qoheleth.' *Irish Biblical Studies* 10: 44–59.

Sandberg, R. 1999. *Rabbinic Views of Qoheleth*. Lampeter: Mellen Biblical Press. [Includes selections from *Qoheleth Rabbah* and the commentary of Rabbi Samuel ben Meir (Rashbam) on the book of Ecclesiastes.]

Smalley, B. 1949, 1950. 'Some Thirteenth-Century Commentaries on the Sapiential Books.' *Dominican Studies* 2: 318–55; 3: 41–77, 236–74. [These three consecutive articles amount essentially to a mini-monograph, and while the focus is also on Job and Proverbs, it is Ecclesiastes that is singled out for special attention. Reprinted in 1986, below.]

——1952. *The Study of the Bible in the Middle Ages*, 2nd edn. Oxford: Basil Blackwell. [Very useful material on Hugh and Andrew of St Victor (including a translation of Hugh's preface to his homilies on Ecclesiastes) and on Bonaventure.]

——1986. *Medieval Exegesis of Wisdom Literature: Essays by Beryl Smalley*, ed. R.E. Murphy. Atlanta: Scholars Press. [Three articles are reprinted from Smalley 1949, 1950 (above) and a fourth, also from 1950, which deals almost entirely with Proverbs.]

Sorkin, David. 1996. *Moses Mendelssohn and the Religious Enlightenment*. Berkeley: University of California Press. [Discusses Mendelssohn's 1770 commentary on Ecclesiastes in depth.]

Spurgeon, C. H. 2004. *Commenting upon Commentaries*. http://www.theologybooks. com/commentaries. [Orig. pub. 1876, Spurgeon offers frequently withering and often insightful remarks on key works on, among other books, Ecclesiastes from the 1600s until his own time.]

Starowieyski, Marek. 1993. 'Le Livre de l'Ecclésiaste dans l'antiquité chrétienne.' In Gregory of Nyssa 1993: 405–40. [An exhaustive survey of Ecclesiastes in early Christian literature, with an accompanying bibliographical list of 187 Christian (and some Jewish) works on Ecclesiastes up to the Middle ages.]

Vajda, G. 1967. 'Quelques observations en marge du commentaire d'Isaac ibn Ghiyāth sur l'Ecclésiastes.' *Jewish Quarterly Review*, 75th anniversary volume, 518–27.

——1982. 'Ecclésiastes XII, 2–7 interprété par un auteur juif d'Andalousie du XIe siècle.' *Journal of Semitic Studies* 27: 33–46.

White, Graham. 1987. 'Luther on Ecclesiastes and the Limits of Human Ability.' *Neue Zeitschrift für Systematische Theologie und Religionsphilosophie* 29: 180–94.

Wölfel, E. 1958. *Luther und die Skepsis: Eine Studie zur Kohelet-Exegese Luthers*. Munich: Kaiser.

Wright, J. R., ed. 2005. *Ancient Christian Commentary on Scripture. Old Testament*, vol. 9: *Proverbs, Ecclesiastes, Song of Solomon*. Downers Grove, Ill.: InterVarsity Press. [A splendid compilation of early Christian commentators in translation with some helpful introductory comment and extensive bibliographies.]

Zlotowitz, Meir. 1994: *Koheles: Ecclesiastes/A New Translation with a Commentary Anthologized from Talmudic, Midrashic and Rabbinic Sources*, 2nd edn, Artscroll Tanach Series. New York: Mesorah Publications. [Makes reference, from a strictly Orthodox perspective, to a large number of traditional Jewish exegetes – e.g. Rashi, Rashbam, Ibn Ezra, Saadia Gaon – with a helpful biographical supplement.]

2. SURVEYS OF ACADEMIC APPROACHES (*unlike section 1, these studies focus almost entirely on academic approaches*)

Breton, Santiago. 1973. 'Qoheleth Studies.' *Biblical Theology Bulletin* 3: 22–50.

——1980. 'Qoheleth: Recent Studies.' *Theology Digest* 28.2: 147–51.

Crenshaw, J. 1983. 'Qoheleth in Current Research.' *Hebrew Annual Review* 7: 41–56.

Elbourne, Don A. 2002. 'Ecclesiastes Bibliography.' http://elbourne.org/biblicalstudies. [A comprehensive bibliography of 81 pages, though often lacking detail.]

Galling, K. 1932. 'Kohelet-Studien.' *Zeitschrift für die alttestamentliche Wissenschaft* 50: 276–99.

——1934. 'Stand und Aufgabe der Kohelet-Forschung.' *Theologische Rundschau* 6: 355–73.

Murphy, R. E. 1990. *The Tree of Life: An Exploration of Biblical Wisdom Literature.* Grand Rapids, Mich.: Eerdmans. [With surveys of critical approaches updated in supplements in subsequent editions in 1996, 2001.]

——1993. 'Recent Research on Proverbs and Qoheleth.' *Currents in Research: Biblical Studies* 1: 119–40.

Newsom, Carol A. 1995. 'Job and Ecclesiastes.' In *Old Testament Interpretation: Past, Present, and Future*, ed. J. Mays, D. Petersen and K. Richards, Festschrift G. Tucker, 177–94. Nashville: Abingdon Press.

Salters, R. B. 1978. 'Notes on the History of the Interpretation of Koh 5,5.' *Zeitschrift für die alttestamentliche Wissenschaft* 90: 95–101.

——1979. 'Notes on the Interpretation of Qoh 6,2.' *Zeitschrift für die alttestamentliche Wissenschaft* 91: 282–9.

Spangenberg, I. J. J. 1998. 'A Century of Wrestling with Qohelet: The Research History of the Book Illustrated with Discussion of Qoh 4,17–5,6.' In *Qohelet in the Context of Wisdom*, ed. A. Schoors, Bibliotheca ephemeridum theologicarum lovaniensium, 136: 61–91. Leuven: Peeters.

Washington, Harold. forthcoming. 'Recent Research on Ecclesiastes/Qoheleth.' *Currents in Research: Biblical Studies.*

Wright, J. S. 1946. 'The Interpretation of Ecclesiastes.' *Evangelical Quarterly* 18: 18–34.

3. Literature

Ages, Arnold. 1966. 'Voltaire, The Marchioness of Deffand and Ecclesiastes.' *Romance Notes* 8: 51–4.

Anselment, Raymond A. 1984. 'Alexander Brome and the Search for the "Safe Estate".' *Renaissance and Reformation* 8.20.1: 39–51. [Examines Ecclesiastes' relevance to Brome's political and satirical verse.]

Atwan, Robert, and L. Wieder, eds. 1993. *Chapters into Verse*, vol. 1: *Genesis to Malachi.* Oxford: Oxford University Press. [The entry for Ecclesiastes is fairly extensive in this anthology of biblically inspired poetry.]

Avni, Abraham. 1981a. 'Coleridge and Ecclesiastes: A Wary Response.' *The Wordsworth Circle* 12.2: 127–9.

——1981b. 'Wordsworth and Ecclesiastes: A "Skeptical Affinity".' *Research Studies* 49.1: 66–71.

Beal 1982 (details in section 1). [Traces Ecclesiastes' influence on Dante and Chaucer through medieval Christian commentaries.]

Bozanich, Robert. 1975. 'Donne and Ecclesiastes.' *Proceedings of the Modern Language Association* 90: 270–6. [Argues that 'Ecclesiastes exerted a profound and lifelong influence on Donne'.]

Bush, Douglas. 1948. *English Literature in the Early Seventeenth Century 1600–1660.* Oxford: Clarendon Press.

Campbell, James L. 1975. 'The Book of Ecclesiastes and Eighteenth-Century Literature.' Unpublished PhD thesis, University of Virginia. [Examines the use of and attitudes towards Ecclesiastes in the works of Joseph Addison, Jonathan Swift and Samuel Johnson.]

Christianson, Eric S. 2005. 'Voltaire's *Précis* of Ecclesiastes: A Case Study in the Bible's Afterlife.' *Journal for the Study of the Old Testament* 29.4: 455–84.

Cochran, Robert W. 1968. 'Circularity in *The Sun Also Rises.' Modern Fiction Studies* 14: 297–305.

Cowan, S. A. 1983. 'Robert Cohn, The Fool of Ecclesiastes in The Sun Also Rises.' *Dalhousie Review* 63.1: 98–106.

Doelman, James. 1993. 'Seeking "The Fruit of Favour": The Dedicatory Sonnets of Henry Lok's Ecclesiastes.' *English Literary History* 60.1: 1–15.

Dooley, D. J. 1971. 'Thackeray's Use of Vanity Fair.' *Studies in English Literature, 1500–1900* 11.4: 701–13.

Edwards, Michael 1990a. 'Rewriting "The Waste Land".' In *European Literature and Theology in the Twentieth Century: Ends of Time,* ed. David Jasper and Colin Crowder, 70–85. Basingstoke: Macmillan. [Surveys the presence and influence of Ecclesiastes throughout T. S. Eliot's work.]

Hattaway, Michael. 1968. 'Paradoxes of Solomon: Learning in the English Renaissance.' *Journal of the History of Ideas* 29.4: 499–530. [A wide-ranging and invaluable survey of Renaissance texts that in some way employed Solomon – as the Preacher – as a paradigmatic 'symbol of valor' and even sceptic, and Ecclesiastes as a philosophical polemic.]

Henn, T. R. 1970. *The Bible as Literature.* London: Lutterworth Press. [Includes some stimulating examples of the more subtle influences of Ecclesiastes in English literature.]

Jeffrey, D. L. ed. 1992. *A Dictionary of Biblical Tradition in English Literature.* Grand Rapids, Mich. Eerdmans. [See entries for Qoheleth, Solomon and Vanity of vanities. Cf. Nicoll and Stoddart (1910) above for another compilation of literary and Christian references.]

Jiménez, Nilda. 1979. *The Bible and the Poetry of Christina Rossetti: A Concordance.* Westport, Conn. Greenwood Press. [Ecclesiastes features quite heavily, as it was a favorite text of the Pre-Raphaelite poet.]

Komar, Kathleen. 1981. 'Technique and Structure in Döblin's *Berlin Alexanderplatz.' German Quarterly* 54.3: 318–34. [Suggests that Döblin's novel (1929) found the inspiration for its tone and themes partly in Ecclesiastes.]

Lacy, Paul de. 1998. 'Thematic and Structural Affinities: *The Wanderer* and Ecclesiastes.' *Neophilologus* 82: 125–37. [Suggests that the difficult structure and thematic disparity of the Old English poem 'The Wanderer' is best accounted for by Ecclesiastes being a 'primary influence' on the poet.]

Levine, Étan. 1981. 'Ecclesiastes in New England.' *Journal of Reform Judaism* 28: 60–4. [Suggests that Robert Frost deliberately adapts the 'voice of Qoheleth' in his poetry.]

Matsuda, Takami. 1989. 'Death and Transience in the Vernon Refrain Series.'

English Studies 70.3: 193–205. [Explores how Middle English 'mortality lyrics' of the Vernon ms make fundamental use of Ecclesiastes. Cf. Sitwell 1950.]

McCrea, B. 2000. 'Lemuel Gulliver's "Treacherous Religion": Swift's Redaction of Ecclesiastes.' *Christianity and Literature* 49.4: 465–84.

McMaster, R. D. 1987. 'The Pygmalion Motif in "The Newcomes".' In *William Makepeace Thackeray, Modern Critical Views*, ed. Harold Bloom, 21–36. New York: Chelsea House. [Traces the manner in which Ecclesiastes 'hovers' over Thackeray's *The Newcomes*.]

New, Elisa. 1998. 'Bible Leaves! Bible Leaves! Hellenism and Hebraism in Melville's *Moby Dick*.' *Poetics Today* 19.2: 281–303.

Norton, D. 1993. *A History of the Bible as Literature*, 2 vols. Cambridge: Cambridge University Press. [Includes Ecclesiastes references and a particularly useful discussion of Thomas Paine's approach to Scripture in *Age of Reason*.]

Peck, Russell A. 1985. 'Ecclesiastes as a Pivotal Biblical and Literary Text.' *ADE Bulletin* 81: 43–8.

Perry, T. A. 1993a. 'Montaigne y Kohelet sobre las vanidades de este mundo: hacia una filosofía sefardí.' In *Actas del Simposio Internacional sobre Literatura*, 263–78. Barcelona: Universidad de Barcelona.

Quinney, Laura. 1990. 'Skepticism and Grimness in Shelley.' *Colloquium Helveticum* 11.12: 169–82.

Ross, Morton L. 1972–3. 'Bill Gorton, the Preacher in *The Sun Also Rises*.' *Modern Fiction Studies* 18: 517–27.

Rossbacher, Peter. 1968. 'Čexov's Fragment "Solomon".' *The Slavic and East European Journal* 12.1: 27–34. [Discusses (and includes a translation of) Anton Chekhov's intriguing notebook fragment from *c*.1892 entitled 'Solomon', the germinal idea for a play based on Ecclesiastes.]

Sitwell, Gerard. 1950. 'A Fourteenth-Century English Poem on Ecclesiastes.' *Dominican Studies* 3: 285–90.

Smith, Paul. 1982. 'Almost All Is Vanity: A Note on Nine Rejected Titles for *A Farewell to Arms*.' *Hemingway Review* 2: 74–6.

Stock, R. D. 1985. 'Johnson Ecclesiastes.' *Christianity and Literature* 34.4: 15–24. [Examines the 'Ecclesiastes theme' in Johnson's main works, as well as in Boethius and Pascal.]

Wank, Martin. 1995. 'Melville and Wolfe: The Wisdom of Ecclesiastes.' *The Thomas Wolfe Review* 19.2: 1–20.

Wills, Jack C. 1973. 'The Deserted Village, Ecclesiastes, and the Enlightenment.' *Enlightenment Essays* 4.3–4: 15–19.

Wright, Nathalia. 1949. *Melville's Use of the Bible*. Durham, NC: Duke University Press.

Wright, Terence. 2005. 'The Wisdom of Age: Four Quartets and Ecclesiastes.' Conference paper, 'T. S. Eliot and the Bible.' University of Oxford.

SPECIALIST COMPARATIVE STUDIES

Studies that suggest comparative themes between Ecclesiastes and other works (usually from literature)

Aichele, G. forthcoming. 'Local Heroes.' In *That We May See and Believe: Cinema and the Spectacle of Scripture*, ed. D. Shepherd, Semeia Studies. Atlanta: SBL. [An 'intertextual play' between Bill Forsythe's 1983 movie and Eccl. 9:14–16, and other texts.]

Carasik, Michael. 2004. 'Transcending the Boundary of Death: Ecclesiastes through a Nabokovian Lens.' Conference paper, Society of Biblical Literature Annual Meeting.

Christianson 1998a (details below): 235–42, 259–74. ['Gustave Flaubert's *Bouvard et Pécuchet*: A Comparison' and the Postscript on Ecclesiastes and Holocaust reflection literature.]

Deacy, Christopher. 2001. *Screen Christologies: Redemption and the Medium of Film*. Cardiff: University of Wales Press. [Compares Ecclesiastes to themes raised in classic *film noir*.]

Friedman, Barton R. 1988. 'Antihistory: Dickens's "A Tale of Two Cities".' In *idem*, *Fabricating History: English Writers on the French Revolution*, 145–71. Princeton: Princeton University Press. [Gives brief notice of some shared epistemological themes in the two works.]

Goodrum, William D. 1963. '*Ecclesiastes* in Goethe's *Faust*.' *McNeese Review* 14: 74–9.

James, K.W. 1984. 'Ecclesiastes: Precursor of Existentialists.' *The Bible Today* 22: 85–90.

Jarick, John. 2000. 'The Hebrew Book of Changes: Reflections on *hakkōl hebel* and *lakkōl zᵉmān* in Ecclesiastes.' *Journal for the Study of the Old Testament* 90: 79–99.

Johnston, Robert K. 2004. *Useless Beauty: Ecclesiastes through the Lens of Contemporary Film*. Grand Rapids, Mich.: Baker Academic.

Kirsch, Arthur. 1988. 'The Emotional Landscape of *King Lear*.' *Shakespeare Quarterly* 39.2: 154–70. [A stimulating survey of shared themes with Ecclesiastes, particularly regarding the significance of death and the extremes of existential experience.]

Kreitzer, L. 1994. '*A Farewell to Arms*: "A Time to Give Birth and a Time to Die".' In *idem*, *The Old Testament in Fiction and Film*, The Biblical Seminar, 24, 170–221. Sheffield: Sheffield Academic Press.

Murphy, R. E. 1955. 'The *Pensées* of Coheleth.' *Catholic Biblical Quarterly* 17: 304–12.

Nichols, F. W. 1984. 'Samuel Beckett and Ecclesiastes: On the Borders of Belief.' *Encounter* 45: 11–22.

Peter, C. B. 1980. 'In Defence of Existence: A Comparison between Ecclesiastes and Albert Camus.' *Bangalore Theological Forum* 12: 26–43.

Pierce, D. L. T. 1992. 'Echoes of the Past in Flaubert's "L'Education Sentimentale", "Bouvard et Pécuchet" and "Salambo".' Unpublished PhD thesis, Louisiana State University and Agricultural and Mechanical College. [The chapter on *Bouvard et Pécuchet* offers an extensive comparison to Ecclesiastes.]

Plumptre 1881 (details below). [Appendices on Ecclesiastes and Shakespeare, Tennyson and twelfth-century Persian poet Omar Khayyam.]

Roe, George. 1912. *Koheleth: A Metrical Paraphrase of the Canonical Book of Ecclesiastes . . . with an Introduction and Many Notes, Comparing the Philosophy of Koheleth, the Hebrew, with that of Omar Khayyam, the Astronomer-Poet of Persia*. New York.

Ruthenberg, Myriam. 1998. 'Kohelet/Ecclesiastes: Erri De Luca's Wasteland of Writing.' Conference paper, 18th Annual Conference of the American Association of Italian Studies.

Schwartz, Matthew J. 1986. 'Koheleth and Camus: Two Views of Achievement.' *Judaism* 35.1: 29–34.

Stockhammer, M. 1960. 'Kohelets Pessimismus.' *Schopenhauer-Jahrbuch* 41: 52–78. [A comparison between Qoheleth and Schopenhauer, the 'philosopher of pessimism'.]

Templeton, Douglas A. 1992. 'A "Farced Epistol" to a Sinking Sun of David: *Ecclesiastes* and *Finnegans Wake*: The Sinoptic View.' In *Text as Pretext: Essays in Honour of Robert Davidson*, ed. R. P. Carroll, Journal for the Study of the Old Testament Supplement Series, 138: 282–90. Sheffield: Sheffield Academic Press. [An intriguing reflection on parody as interpretation that reflects, however indirectly, on Qoheleth and Joyce.]

ECCLESIASTES GENERAL SECONDARY SOURCES

Abramson, J., and R. Freulich. 1972. *The Faces of Israel: A Photographic Commentary on the Words of Koheleth*. New York: T. Yoseloff. [The text accompanied by photos by Abramson's father. Includes a reflective introduction on Ecclesiastes and existentialism by Abramson.]

Armstrong, James F. 1983. 'Ecclesiastes in Old Testament Theology.' *Princeton Seminary Bulletin* 94: 16–25.

Barton, J. 1984. 'Ecclesiastes: An Example.' In *idem, Reading the Old Testament*, 61–76. London: SCM Press.

Belaïs, Abraham. 1850. *The Dust of the World: A Commentary on Ecclesiastes*. London. [A fairly unremarkable conservative commentary, but notable for being perhaps the earliest distinct Jewish reading from a British perspective.]

Bennet, James. 1870. *The Wisdom of the King: Studies in Ecclesiastes*. Edinburgh: William Oliphant and Co.

Berger, Benjamin Lyle. 2001. 'Qohelet and the Exigencies of the Absurd.' *Biblical Interpretation* 9.2: 141–79.

Bickerman, E. 1967. 'Koheleth (Ecclesiastes) *or* The Philosophy of an Acquisitive Society.' In *idem, Four Strange Books of the Bible*, 139–67. New York: Schocken Books.

Blumenthal, J. designer. 1965. *Ecclesiastes, or The Preacher*. New York: Spiral Press. [Series of wood engravings.]

Bradley, George G. 1898. *Lectures on Ecclesiastes: Delivered in Westminster Abbey*. Oxford: Clarendon Press.

Brenner, A. 1995. 'Some Observations on the Figurations of Woman in Wisdom Literature.' In *idem* (ed.), *A Feminist Companion to Wisdom Literature*. Feminist Companion to the Bible, 9: 50–66. Sheffield: Sheffield Academic Press.

Brown, W. P. 1996. 'Character Reconstructed: Ecclesiastes.' In *idem, Character in Crisis*, 120–50. Grand Rapids, Mich.: Eerdmans.

——2000. *Ecclesiastes*. Interpretation. Louisville, Ky.: John Knox Press.

Buchanan, Alastair. 1904. *The Essence of Ecclesiastes in the Metre of Omar Khayyam*. London: Elliot Stock.

Burkitt, F. C. 1936. *Ecclesiastes: Rendered into English Verse by F. Crawford Burkitt*. London: Macmillan.

Burns, J. E. 1963. 'Some Reflections on Coheleth and John.' *Catholic Biblical Quarterly* 25: 414–16.

Burrows, Millar. 1927. 'Kuhn and Koheleth.' *Journal of Biblical Literature* 46: 90–7.

Ceresko, A. R. 1982. 'The Function of *Antanaclasis* (*ms'* "to Find"//*ms'* "to Reach, Overtake, Grasp") in Hebrew Poetry, Especially in the Book of Qoheleth.' *Catholic Biblical Quarterly* 44: 551–69.

Cheyne, T. K. 1887. *Job and Solomon, or The Wisdom of the Old Testament*. London: Kegan Paul, Trench & Co.

Christianson, Eric S. 1998a. *A Time to Tell: Narrative Strategies in Ecclesiastes*. Journal for the Study of the Old Testament Supplement Series, 280. Sheffield: Sheffield Academic Press.

Cox, Samuel. 1896. *The Book of Ecclesiastes*. The Expositor's Bible. London: Hodder & Stoughton.

Crenshaw, J. 1986. 'Youth and Old Age in Qoheleth.' *Hebrew Annual Review* 10: 1–13.

——1988. *Ecclesiastes*. Old Testament Library. London: SCM Press.

Crüsemann, F. 1979. 'The Unchangeable World: The "Crisis of Wisdom" in Koheleth.' In *God of the Lowly: Socio-Historical Interpretations of the Bible*, ed. W. Schottroff and W. Stegemann, 57–77. New York: Orbis Books.

De Boer, P. A. H. 1977. 'A Note on Ecclesiastes 12:12a.' In *A Tribute to Arthur Vööbus*, ed. R. Fischer, 85–8. Chicago: Lutheran School of Theology.

Delitzsch, F. 1980. 'Ecclesiastes.' In *idem, Commentary on the Old Testament*, 6 Grand Rapids, Mich.: Eerdmans. [Orig. pub. 1875.]

Devine, J. Minos. 1916. *Ecclesiastes, or The Confessions of an Adventurous Soul*. London: Macmillan & Co.

Dillon, E. J. 1895. *The Sceptics of the Old Testament: Job, Koheleth, Agur*. London: Ibister and Company.

Dornseiff, F. 1935. 'Das Buch Prediger.' *Zeitschrift der deutschen morgenländischen Gesellschaft* 89: 243–9.

Eaton, M. 1983. *Ecclesiastes*. Tyndale Old Testament Commentaries. Downer's Grove, Ill.: InterVarsity Press.

Eichhorn, David Max. 1963. *Musings of the Old Professor: The Meaning of Koheles – A New Translation of and Commentary on the Book of Ecclesiastes*. New York: Jonathan David Publishers.

Ellul, J. 1990. *Reason for Being: A Meditation on Ecclesiastes*, tr. J. M. Hanks. Grand Rapids, Mich.: Eerdmans.

Erdrich, Louise. 1995. 'The Preacher.' In *Out of the Garden: Women Writers on the Bible*, ed. C. Büchmann and C. Spiegel, 234–7. London: Pandora.

Etting, Emlen, illustrator. 1940. *Koheleth: The Book of Ecclesiastes.* New York: New Directions.

Eybers, I. H. 1977. 'The "Canonization" of Song of Solomon, Ecclesiastes and Esther.' In *Aspects of the Exegetical Process*, ed. W. C. van Wyk, Ou Testmentiese Werkgemeenskap in Siud Afrika, 20: 33–52. Pretoria West: NHW Press.

Farmer, K. 1991. *Who Knows What is Good? A Commentary on the Books of Proverbs and Ecclesiastes.* International Theological Commentary. Grand Rapids, Mich.: Eerdmans.

Fisch, H. 1988. 'Qohelet: A Hebrew Ironist.' In *idem, Poetry with a Purpose: Biblical Poetics and Interpretation*, Indiana Studies in Biblical Literature, 158–78. Indianapolis: Indiana University Press.

Fisch, M. 1995. 'Ecclesiastes (Qohelet) in Context – A Study of Wisdom as Constructive Scepticism.' *Boston Studies in the Philosophy of Science* 162: 167–85.

Fischer, Stefan. 2002. 'Qohelet and "Heretic" Harpers' Songs'. *Journal for the Study of the Old Testament* 26.4: 105–21.

Fox, M. V. 1977. 'Frame-narrative and Composition in the Book of Qohelet.' *Hebrew Union College Annual* 48: 83–106.

—— 1989. *Qohelet and his Contradictions.* Journal for the Study of the Old Testament Supplement Series, 71. Sheffield: Almond Press.

Fox, M. V., and B. Porten. 1978. 'Unsought Discoveries: Qohelet 7:23–8:1a.' *Hebrew Studies* 19: 26–38.

Fredericks, D. C. 1993. *Coping with Transcience: Ecclesiastes on Brevity in Life.* The Biblical Seminar, 18. Sheffield: JSOT Press.

Frydrych, T. 2002. *Living under the Sun: An Examination of Proverbs and Qoheleth.* Leiden: Brill.

Garstang, Walter. 1886. *My Heart's Fruit Garden, Wherein Are Divers Delectable Adages and Similes of the Prince of Doctrinal Ethics: A Translation, out of the Ancient Biblical Hebrew of the Book of Koheleth . . .* London: Simphkin, Marshall & Co.

Goldin, J. 1966. 'The End of Ecclesiastes: Literal Exegesis and Its Transformation.' In *Biblical Motifs: Origins and Transformations*, ed. A. Altmann, 135–58. Cambridge, Mass.: Harvard University Press.

Good, E. 1978. 'The Unfilled Sea: Style and Meaning in Ecclesiastes 1:2–11.' In *Israelite Wisdom: Theological and Literary Essays in Honor of Samuel Terrien*, ed. J. Gammie et al., 59–73. Missoula, Mont.: Scholars Press.

—— 1981. 'Qoheleth: The Limits of Wisdom.' In *idem, Irony in the Old Testament*, 168–95. Sheffield: Almond Press. [Orig. pub. 1965.]

Gordis, R. 1955. *Koheleth – The Man and his World.* New York: Bloch Publishing.

Greissinger, James A. 1909. 'The Worst Understood Book.' *Methodist Review* 91: 734–41.

Grossberg, Daniel. 2000. 'Form and Content and their Correspondence.' *Hebrew Studies* 41: 47–52.

Harrison, C. R. 1997. 'Qoheleth among the Sociologists.' *Biblical Interpretation* 5.2: 160–80.

Harsanyi, M. A., and S. P. Harter. 1993. 'Ecclesiastes Effects.' *Scientometrics* 27.1: 93–6. [A witty application of Ecclesiastes to various scenarios in academe.]

Haupt, Paul. 1905. *The Book of Ecclesiastes: A New Metrical Translation, with an Introduction and Explanatory Notes*. Baltimore: Johns Hopkins University Press.

Hengel, M. 1974. 'Koheleth and the Beginning of the Crisis in Jewish Religion.' In *idem, Judaism and Hellenism*, tr. J. Bowden, rev. edn, 2 vols., 1.115–30. London: SCM, Press. [Orig. pub. 1973.]

Isaksson, B. 1987. *Studies in the Language of Qoheleth*. Acta Universitatis Upsaliensis, Studia Semitica Upsaliensia, 10. Uppsala: Almqvist & Wiksell.

Jastrow, Morris. 1919. *A Gentle Cynic; Being a Translation of the Book of Koheleth, Commonly Known as Ecclesiastes, Stripped of Later Additions; Also its Origin, Growth and Interpretation*. London: J. B. Lippincott.

Johnston, D. 1880. *A Treatise on the Authorship of Ecclesiastes*. London: MacMillan and Co. [Anonymous edn.]

Kaiser, O. 1995. 'Qoheleth.' In *Wisdom in Ancient Israel: Essays in Honour of J.A. Emerton*, ed. J. Day, R. P. Gordon and H. G. M. Williamson, 83–93. Cambridge: Cambridge University Press.

Knopf, Carl S. 1930. 'The Optimism of Koheleth.' *Journal of Biblical Literature* 49: 195–9.

Krüger, Thomas. 1993. '"Frau Weisheit" in Koh 7,26?' *Biblica* 73: 394–403.

Kushner, H. S. 1987. *When All you've Ever Wanted Isn't Enough*. Sydney: Pan Books.

Lauha, A. 1978. *Kohelet*. Biblischer Kommentar Altes Testament, 19. Neukirchen–Vluyn: Neukirchener Verlag.

Lessing, Doris. 1998. Introduction. In *Ecclesiastes, or the Preacher*, Pocket Canon, pp. vii–xii. London: Canongate Books.

Levine, Étan. 1997. 'The Humor in Qohelet.' *Zeitschrift für die alttestamentliche Wissenschaft* 109.1: 71–83.

Loader, J. A. 1979. *Polar Structures in the Book of Qohelet*. Beihefte zur Zeitschrift für die alttestamentliche Wissenschaft, 152. Berlin: de Gruyter.

Lohfink, N. 1990. 'Qoheleth 5:17–19 – Revelation by Joy.' *Catholic Biblical Quarterly* 52: 625–35.

——2003. *Qoheleth: A Continental Commentary*, tr. S. McEvenue. Minneapolis: Fortress Press.

Longman, Tremper. 1998. *The Book of Ecclesiastes*. New International Commentary on the Old Testament. Grand Rapids, Mich.: Eerdmans.

Loretz, O. 1963. 'Zur Darbietungsform der "Ich-Erzählung" im Buche Qohelet.' *Catholic Biblical Quarterly* 25: 46–59.

——1964. *Qohelet und der Alte Orient*. Freiburg: Herder.

Marcus, P. 2000. 'The Wisdom of Ecclesiastes and its Meaning for Psychoanalysis.' *Psychoanalytic Review* 87.2: 227–50.

Margoliouth, D. S. 1911. 'The Prologue of Ecclesiastes.' *Expositor* 8.2: 463–70.

McKenna, John E. 1992. 'The Concept of *hebel* in the Book of Ecclesiastes.' *Scottish Journal of Theology* 45: 19–28.

McNeile, A. H. 1904. *An Introduction to Ecclesiastes*. Cambridge: Cambridge University Press.

Merkin, Daphne. 1987. 'Ecclesiastes: A Reading out-of-Season.' In *Congregation: Contemporary Writers Read the Jewish Bible*, ed. D. Rosenberg, 393–405. San Diego: Harcourt Brace Jovanovich. [A novelist and critic, Merkin brings a uniquely literary perspective.]

Mills, Mary. 2003. *Reading Ecclesiastes: A Literary and Cultural Exegesis*. Aldershot: Ashgate.

Moore, J. W. Brady. 1924. *Koheleth*. London: Arthur H. Stockwell.

Moser, Barry, illustrator. 1999. *The Viking Studio Edition of the Pennyroyal Caxton Bible*. New York: Penguin Putnam. [Illustration, 'The Preacher,' p. 546.]

Murphy, R. E. 1990. 'The Sage in Ecclesiastes and Qoheleth the Sage.' In *The Sage in Israel and the Ancient Near East*, ed. J. G. Gammie, 263–71. Winona Lake, Ind.: Eisenbrauns.

Newsom, C. 1989. 'Women and the Discourse of Patriarchal Wisdom: A Study of Proverbs 1–9.' In *Gender and Difference in Ancient Israel*, ed. Peggy L. Day, 142–60. Minneapolis: Fortress Press.

Odeberg, H. 1929. *Qohaelaeth: A Commentary on the Book of Ecclesiastes*. Uppsala: Almqvist & Wiskell.

Ogden, G. 1980. 'Historical Allusion in Qoheleth iv 13–16?' *Vetus Testamentum* 30: 309–15.

—— 1987. *Qoheleth: Readings*. Sheffield: JSOT Press.

Paterson, J. 1950. 'The Intimate Journal of an Old-Time Humanist.' *Religion in Life* 19.2: 245–54.

Pawley, D. 1990. 'Ecclesiastes: Reaching Out to the Twentieth Century.' *Bible Review* 6: 34–6.

Payne, M. 1988. 'The Voices of Ecclesiastes.' *College Literature* 15: 262–8.

Perry, T. A. 1993b. *Dialogues with Kohelet: The Book of Ecclesiastes*. University Park, Pa.: Pennsylvania State University Press.

Plumptre, E. H. 1880. 'The Author of Ecclesiastes.' *Expositor* 2: 401–30.

—— 1881. *Ecclesiastes or the Preacher, with Notes and Introduction*. Cambridge: Cambridge University Press.

Polk, Timothy. 1976. 'The Wisdom of Irony: A Study of *Hebel* and its Relation to Joy and Fear of God in Ecclesiastes.' *Studia Biblica et Theologica* 6.1: 3–17.

Porter, Lawrence B. 1969. 'Bankruptcy: The Words of Qoheleth, Son of David, King in Jerusalem.' *The Bible Today* 44: 3041–6.

Renan, Ernest. 1882. *L'Ecclésiaste: traduit de l'hebreu avec une étude sur l'âge et le caractère du livre*. Paris: Anciennes Maison Michel Lévy Frères.

Rudman, D. 2001. *Determinism in the Book of Ecclesiastes*. Journal for the Study of the Old Testament Supplement Series, 316. Sheffield: Sheffield Academic Press.

Rudolph, W. 1959. *Vom Buch Kohelet*. Münster: Aschendorf.

Ryken, L. 1987. 'Ecclesiastes.' In *idem, Words of Delight: A Literary Introduction to the Bible*, 319–28. Grand Rapids, Mich.: Baker Book House.

—— 1993. 'Ecclesiastes.' In *A Complete Literary Guide to the Bible*, ed. L. Ryken and T. Longman, 268–80. Grand Rapids, Mich.: Zondervan.

Salyer, Gary D. 2001. *Vain Rhetoric: Private Insight and Public Debate in Ecclesiastes.* Journal for the Study of the Old Testament Supplement Series, 327. Sheffield: Sheffield Academic Press.

Sawyer, John. 1975. 'The Ruined House in Ecclesiastes 12: A Reconstruction of the Original Parable.' *Journal of Biblical Literature* 94: 519–31.

Schloesser, S. 1989–90. '"A King is Held Captive in her Tresses": The Liberating Deconstruction of the Search for Wisdom from Proverbs through Ecclesiastes.' In *Church Divinity*, ed. J. Morgan, 205–28. Bristol: Cloverdale Corporation.

Schoors, A. 1992. *The Preacher Sought to Find Pleasing Words: A Study of the Language of Qoheleth.* Orientalia Lovaniensia Analecta, 41. Leuven: Peeters.

Scott, D. Russell. 1929. 'The Lure of Ecclesiastes.' In *Proverbs, Ecclesiastes, Song of Songs: A Little Library of Exposition*, ed. H. Maclean et al., 65–90. London: Cassell & Company.

Seow, C.-L. 1995. 'Qohelet's Autobiography.' In *Fortunate the Eyes that See: Essays in Honor of David Noel Freedman in Celebration of his Seventieth Birthday*, ed. A. B. Beck et al., 275–87. Grand Rapids, Mich.: Eerdmans.

—— 1997. *Ecclesiastes: A New Translation with Introduction and Commentary.* Anchor Bible, 18C. New York: Doubleday.

Sheppard, G. 1977. 'The Epilogue to Qoheleth as Theological Commentary.' *Catholic Biblical Quarterly* 39: 182–9.

Sheridan, S. 1989. 'The Five Megilloth.' In *Creating the Old Testament*, ed. S. Bigger, 293–317. Oxford: Blackwell.

Short, R. 1973. *A Time to Be Born – A Time to Die.* New York: Harper & Row.

Spina, F. A. 1983. 'Qoheleth and the Reformation of Wisdom.' In *The Quest for the Kingdom of God: Studies in Honor of George E. Mendenhall*, ed. H. B. Huffmon et al., 267–79. Winona Lake, Ind.: Eisenbrauns.

Stone, E. 1942. 'Old Man Koheleth.' *Journal of Bible and Religion* 10: 98–102.

Tamez, Elsa. 2000. *When the Horizons Close: Rereading Ecclesiastes.* New York: Orbis Books.

Taylor, Charles. 1874. *The Dirge of Coheleth in Ecclesiastes xii Discussed and Literally Interpreted.* London.

Viviano, P. 1984. 'The Book of Ecclesiastes: A Literary Approach.' *The Bible Translator* 22: 79–84.

Vlachos, Paul S., illustrator. 1995. *Ecclesiastes: To Everything There Is A Season . . .*, tr. Bronwen Martin and Micheál Ó hOdhráin. Dublin: Philomel Productions.

Whitley, C. F. 1979. *Koheleth: His Language and Thought.* Beihefte zur Zeitschrift für die alttestamentliche Wissenschaft, 148. Berlin: de Gruyter.

Whybray, R. N. 1982. 'Qoheleth, Preacher of Joy.' *Journal for the Study of the Old Testament* 23: 87–98.

—— 1988. 'Ecclesiastes 1.5–7 and the Wonders of Nature.' *Journal for the Study of the Old Testament* 41: 105–12.

—— 1989. *Ecclesiastes.* New Century Bible. Grand Rapids, Mich.: Eerdmans.

Williams, J. 1987. 'Proverbs and Ecclesiastes.' In *The Literary Guide to the Bible*, ed. R. Alter and F. Kermode, 263–82. London: Collins.

Wilson, G. H. 1984. '"The Words of the Wise": The Intent and Significance of Qohelet 12:9–14.' *Journal of Biblical Literature* 103.2: 175–92.

Wright, A. G. 1968. 'The Riddle of the Sphinx: The Structure of the Book of Qoheleth.' *Catholic Biblical Quarterly* 30: 313–34.

—— 1980. 'The Riddle of the Sphynx Revisited: Numerical Patterns in the Book of Qoheleth.' *Catholic Biblical Quarterly* 42: 38–51.

—— 1983. 'Additional Numerical Patterns in Qohelet.' *Catholic Biblical Quarterly* 45: 32–43.

Wright, J. S. 1982. 'The Book of Ecclesiastes.' In *New Bible Dictionary*, ed. J. D. Douglas et al., 2nd edn., 295–96. Leicester: Inter-Varsity Press.

Zimmermann, F. 1973. *The Inner World of Qohelet*. New York: KTAV.

OTHER SECONDARY SOURCES

Auerbach, E. 1974. *Mimesis: The Representation of Reality in Western Literature*, tr. W. R. Trask. Princeton: Princeton University Press. [Orig. pub. 1953.]

Baker, Brian. 2005. 'Ray Bradbury: *Fahrenheit 451*.' In *A Companion to Science Fiction*, ed. D. Seed, 488–99. Oxford: Blackwell.

Balnavez, John. 1997. 'Bernard of Morlaix: The Literature of Complaint, the Latin Tradition and the Twelfth-Century "Renaissance".' Unpublished PhD thesis, Australian National University. [Traditionally known as Bernard of Cluny, Morlaix composed an influential *De Contemptu Mundi* reading, *c.*1140, and this study is a good resource for its intellectual climate. Full text available at http://www.prosentient.com.au/balnaves/johnbalnaves.]

Barr, James. 1973. *The Bible in the Modern World*. London: SCM Press.

Battis, Emery. 1962. *Saints and Sectaries: Anne Hutchinson and the Antinomian Controversy in the Massachusetts Bay Colony*. Chapel Hill, NC: University of North Carolina Press.

Beck, Avent Childress. 1995. 'The Christian Allegorical Structure of *Platoon*.' In *Screening the Sacred: Religion, Myth, and Ideology in Popular American Film*, ed. J. W. Martin and C. E. Ostwalt, 44–54. Boulder, Colo.: Westview Press.

Beckwith, R. 1985. *The Old Testament Canon of the New Testament Church*. Grand Rapids, Mich.: Eerdmans.

Besterman, Theodore. 1970. *Voltaire*. London: Longman.

Bono. 2004. *Bono Quotes*. http://www.angelfire.com/band2/u2megbael/quotes/bonoquotes.html.

Brigden, Susan. 2000. *New Worlds, Lost Worlds: The Rule of the Tudors, 1485–1603*. London: Viking.

—— 2004. 'Howard, Henry, earl of Surrey (1516/17–1547).' In *Oxford Dictionary of National Biography*. Oxford: Oxford University Press. http://www.oxforddnb.com.

Brueggemann, Walter. 2005. *The Book that Breathes New Life: Scriptural Authority and Biblical Theology*, ed. Patrick Miller. Minneapolis: Fortress Press.

Cady Stanton, Elizabeth. 1985. *The Woman's Bible*, 2 vols. Edinburgh: Polygon Books. [Orig. pub. 1898.]

Callaway, Mary. 2004. 'What's the Use of Reception History?' Conference paper, Society of Biblical Literature Annual Meeting. [Available at http://bbibcomm.net.]

Cameron, Euan, ed. 2001. *Early Modern Europe: An Oxford History*. Oxford: Oxford University Press.

Carleton, Kenneth. 2004. 'White, John (1509/10–1560).' In *Oxford Dictionary of National Biography*. Oxford: Oxford University Press. http://www.oxforddnb.com.

Cavalli-Björkman, Görel. 2002. 'Vanitas-Stilleben als Phänomen des Krisenbewußtseins.' http://www.lwl.org/LWL/Kultur/Westfaelischer_Friede/dokumentation/ausstellungen/cgorel_II_V.

Cheney, Liana De Girolami. 1992. 'Dutch Vanitas Paintings: The Skull.' In *The Symbolism of 'Vanitas' in the Arts, Literature, and Music: Comparative and Historical Studies*, ed. Cheney, 113–76. New York: Edwin Mellen Press.

Clifford, James L. 1955. *Young Samuel Johnson*. London: William Heinemann.

Cohen-Bacrie, Pierre. 2000. 'Montaigne.' http://pages.globetrotter.net/pcbcr/montaigne.html. [Includes a comprehensive list of the quotes painted in Montaigne's study, several of which are derived from Ecclesiastes.]

Connors, Tim. 1997. 'ByrdWatcher: A Field Guide to the Byrds of Los Angeles.' http://ebni.com/byrds.

Deacon, Lois, and Terry Coleman. 1966. *Providence & Mr Hardy*. London: Hutchinson & Co.

DiTommaso, Lorenzo. 1999. 'Redemption in Philip K. Dick's *The Man in the High Castle*.' *Science Fiction Studies* 26.1. http://www.depauw.edu/sfs/backissues/77/ditommaso77.htm.

Edwards, A. S. G. 2004. 'Neville, William (b. 1497, d. in or before 1545).' In *Oxford Dictionary of National Biography*. Oxford: Oxford University Press. http://www.oxforddnb.com.

Edwards, Michael. 1990b. 'The World Could Not Contain the Books.' In *The Bible as Rhetoric*, ed. W. Martin, 178–94. London: Routledge.

Ferrell, William K. 2000. *Literature and Film as Modern Mythology*. Westport, Conn.: Praeger.

Flaubert, G. 1976. *Bouvard et Pécuchet*, tr. A. J. Krailsheimer. London: Penguin Books. [Orig. pub. 1881.]

Fosdick, Harry Emerson. 1965. *A Guide to Understanding the Bible: The Development of Ideas within the Old and New Testaments*. New York: Harper & Row. [Orig. pub. 1938.]

Frank, Daniel. 2000. 'Karaite Exegesis.' In Sæbø 2000: 110–28.

Fraser, David. 2000. *Frederick the Great*. London: Penguin Press.

Froehlich, K. 2000. 'Christian Interpretation of the Old Testament in the High Middle Ages.' In Sæbø 2000: 496–558.

Frye, Northrop. 1982. *The Great Code: The Bible and Literature*. Toronto: Academic Press Canada.

Gibbon, Edward. 1909. *The History of the Decline and Fall of the Roman Empire*, ed. with introduction by J. B. Bury, 7 vols. London: Methuen. [Orig. pub. 1896.]

Gilman, Ernest B. 1980. 'Word and Image in Quarles' "Emblemes".' *Critical Inquiry* 6.3: 385–410.

Ginzberg, L. 1968. *The Legends of the Jews*, 7 vols. Philadelphia: Jewish Publication Society of America.

Haak, Bob. 1984. *The Golden Age: Dutch Painters of the Seventeenth Century*, ed. and tr. Elizabeth Willems-Treeman. London: Thames & Hudson.

Halperin, D. 1982. 'The Book of Remedies, the Canonization of the Solomonic Writings, and the Riddle of Pseudo-Eusebius.' *Jewish Quarterly Review* 72: 269–92.

Hingley, Ronald Francis. 2004. 'Chekhov, Anton (Pavlovich).' In *Encyclopaedia Britannica*. Standard Edition CD-rom.

Höltgen, Karl Josef. 2004. 'Quarles, Francis (1592–1644).' In *Oxford Dictionary of National Biography*. Oxford: Oxford University Press. http://www.oxforddnb.com.

Howard, W. Scott. 2005. 'Collins, An (1630 (?)-1670(?)).' In *The Literary Encyclopedia*. http://www.litencyc.com.

Hunter, J. Paul. 1979. 'The Insistent I.' *Novel: A Forum on Fiction* 13.1: 19–37.

Jarman, Mark. 1997. *Questions for Ecclesiastes*. Ashland, Ore.: Story Line Press.

Jenkins, Gary W. 2004. 'Smith, Henry (c.1560–1591).' In *Oxford Dictionary of National Biography*. Oxford: Oxford University Press. http://www.oxforddnb.com.

Karp, Abraham J. 1991. *From the Ends of the Earth: Judaic Treasures of the Library of Congress*. Washington, DC: Library of Congress. [The portion on Ernest Bloch, composer of an Ecclesiastes composition, is available at the Jewish Virtual Library, http://www.jewishvirtuallibrary.org/jsource/loc/Bloch.]

Keeble, N. H. 2004. 'Bradstreet, Anne (1612/13–1672).' In *Oxford Dictionary of National Biography*. Oxford: Oxford University Press. http://www.oxforddnb.com.

Kelly, J. N. D. 1975. *Jerome: His Life, Writings and Controversies*. London: Duckworth.

Kemp, Peter. 2005. 'English Literature.' In *Encyclopaedia Britannica*. Standard Edition CD-rom.

Kraeling, E. G. 1955. *The Old Testament since the Reformation*. London: Lutterworth Press.

Kugel, James. 1979. 'Some Medieval and Renaissance Hebrew Writings on the Poetry of the Bible.' In *Studies in Medieval Jewish History and Literature*. ed. I. Twersky, 3 vols., 1.57–81. Cambridge, Mass.: Harvard University Press.

Küng, Hans. 1992. *Judaism: The Religious Situation of our Time*. London: SCM Press.

Langbaine, Gerard. 1691. *An Account of the English Dramatick Poets, or Some Observations and Remarks on the Lives and Writings, of All Those that Have Pubblish'd . . .* Oxford: Printed by L. L. for George West and Henry Clements.

Leiman, S. Z. 1976. *The Canonization of Hebrew Scripture: The Talmudic and Midrashic Evidence*. Hamden, Conn.: Archon Books.

MacIntyre, A. 1967. 'Existentialism'. In *The Encyclopedia of Philosophy*, ed. P. Edwards, 147–59. New York: Macmillan.

McKay, Elaine. 2001. 'The Diary Network in Sixteenth and Seventeenth Century England.' *Eras* 2. http://www.arts.monash.edu.au/eras/edition_2/mckay.htm.

McNeil, Russell. 1999. 'Vindication of the Rights of Women: Mary Wollstonecraft, 1792'. www.mala.bc.ca/~mcneil/vinda.txt.

Miegroet, Hans J. Van. 1996. 'Vanitas.' In *The Dictionary of Art*, ed. Jane Turner, 31.880–3. London: Macmillan.

Mitcham, Judson. 1991. *Somewhere in Ecclesiastes*. Columbia, M.: University of Missouri Press.

Moran, Terence P. 1974. 'Public Doublespeak: On Beholding and Becoming.' *College English* 36.2: 190–4, 199–201.

Nicholls, Rachel. 2005. 'Is *Wirkungsgeschichte* (or Reception History) a Kind of Intellectual *Parkour* (or Freerunning)?' Conference paper, Society for the Study of the New Testament. [Available at http://bbibcomm.net.]

Nulman, M. 1996. *The Encyclopedia of Jewish Prayer: Ashkenazic and Sephardic Rites*. Northvale, N.J.: Jason Aronson.

Parry, Graham. 1989. *The Seventeenth Century: The Intellectual and Cultural Context of English Literature, 1603–1700*. London: Longman.

Peake, A. S. 1904. *The Problem of Suffering in the Old Testament*. London.

Phillips, Catherine. 2004. 'Bridges, Robert Seymour (1844–1930).' In *Oxford Dictionary of National Biography*. Oxford: Oxford University Press. http://www.oxforddnb.com.

Puyvelde, Leo Van, and Thierry Van Puyvelde. 1970. *Flemish Painting: The Age of Rubens and Van Dyck*, tr. Alan Kendall. London: Wiedenfeld & Nicolson.

Ravenal, John B. 2000. *Vanitas: Meditations on Life and Death in Contemporary Art*. Seattle: University of Washington Press.

Sæbø, M., ed. 2000. *Hebrew Bible/Old Testament: The History of its Interpretation*, vol. 1: *From the Beginnings to the Middle Ages (Until 1300); Part 2: The Middle Ages*. Göttingen: Vandenhoeck & Ruprecht.

Sambrook, James. 2004. 'Bradick, Walter (1705/6–1794).' In *Oxford Dictionary of National Biography*. Oxford: Oxford University Press. Http://www.oxforddnb.com.

Schama, Simon. 1991. *The Embarrassment of Riches: An Interpretation of Dutch Culture in the Golden Age*. London: Fontana Press.

Sherwood, Yvonne. 2000. *A Biblical Text and its Afterlives: The Survival of Jonah in Western Culture*. Cambridge: Cambridge University Press.

Simpson, James. 2004. 'Martyrdom in the Literal Sense: Surrey's *Psalm Paraphrases*.' *Medieval and Early Modern English Studies* 12.1. http://www.sogang.ac.kr/~anthony/mesak/mes121/06.htm.

Smith, R. G. 2005. 'Lights, Camera, *Action*: Baudrillard and the Performance of Representations.' *International Journal of Baudrillard Studies* 2.1. http://www.ubishops.ca/baudrillardstudies/vol2_1/smith.htm.

Starkey, D. 2000. *Elizabeth: Apprenticeship*. London: Vintage.

Tillich, Paul. 1955. *The New Being*. New York: Charles Scribner's Sons.

Waters, John. 1994. *Race of Angels: Ireland and the Genesis of U2*. Belfast: Blackstaff Press.

Watson, Francis. 1994. *Text, Church and World: Biblical Interpretation in Theological Perspective*. Edinburgh: T. & T. Clark.

Wiesel, Elie. 1996. *Memoirs: All Rivers Run to the Sea, 1982–69*. London: HarperCollins.

——2000. *Memoirs: And the Sea is Never Full, 1969–Present*. London: HarperCollins.

Yarchin, W. 2004. *History of Interpretation: A Reader*. Peabody, Mass.: Hendrickson.

Young, B. W. 2004. 'Wollaston, William (1659–1724).' In *Oxford Dictionary of National Biography*. Oxford: Oxford University Press. http://www.oxforddnb.com.

Appendix – The Quotable Qoheleth: Ecclesiastes in Popular Discourse

Reference	Page first discussed	Text – the 1611 Authorized Version	Indirect quotations
1:2; 12:8	98	Vanity of vanities, saith the Preacher, vanity of vanities; all is vanity.	
1:3–5	143	What profit hath a man of all his labour which he taketh under the sun? One generation passeth away, and another generation cometh: but the earth abideth for ever. The sun also ariseth, and the sun goeth down, and hasteth to his place where he arose.	
1:7	145	All the rivers run into the sea; yet the sea is not full; unto the place from whence the rivers come, thither they return again.	
1:9	148	There is nothing new under the sun.	
1:15 (cf. 7:13)	162	That which is crooked cannot be made straight: and that which is wanting cannot be numbered.	
1:18	154	For in much wisdom is much grief: and he that increaseth knowledge increaseth sorrow.	
2:24 (cf. 5:18; 8:15)	25	There is nothing better for a man, than that he should eat and drink, and that he should make his soul enjoy good in his labour.	Eat, drink and be merry.
3:1–8	164	To every thing there is a season, and a time to every purpose under the heaven:	
		A time to be born, and a time to die . . .	
		A time to love, and a time to hate; a time of war, and a time of peace.	
3:20; 12:7 (cf. Gen. 2:7; 3:19)	178	All go to one place; all are from the dust, and all turn to dust again./ and the dust returns to the earth as it was, and the breath returns to God who gave it.	Ashes to ashes, dust to dust.

Reference	Page first discussed	Text – the 1611 Authorized Version	Indirect quotations
4:2	180	Wherefore I praised the dead which are already dead more than the living which are yet alive.	
4:6	—	Better is an handful with quietness, than both the hands full with travail and vexation of spirit.	
4:9–12	182	Two are better than one; because they have a good reward for their labour. For if they fall, the one will lift up his fellow: but woe to him that is alone when he falleth; for he hath not another to help him up. Again, if two lie together, then they have heat: but how can one be warm alone? A threefold cord is not quickly broken.	
5:15 (cf. Job 1:21)	—	As he came forth of his mother's womb, naked shall he return to go as he came, and shall take nothing of his labour, which he may carry away in his hand.	You can't take it with you.
7:2–4	190	It is better to go to the house of mourning, than to go to the house of feasting: for that is the end of all men; and the living will lay it to his heart. Sorrow is better than laughter: for by the sadness of the countenance the heart is made better. The heart of the wise is in the house of mourning; but the heart of fools is in the house of mirth.	
9:4	207	For to him that is joined to all the living there is hope: for a living dog is better than a dead lion.	
9:7	211	Go thy way, eat thy bread with joy, and drink thy wine with a merry heart; for God now accepteth thy works.	

9:10	213	Whatsoever thy hand findeth to do, do it with thy might; for there is no work, nor device, nor knowledge, nor wisdom, in the grave, whither thou goest.	
9:11	214	I returned, and saw under the sun, that the race is not to the swift, nor the battle to the strong, neither yet bread to the wise, nor yet riches to men of understanding, nor yet favour to men of skill; but time and chance happeneth to them all.	
10:1	218	Dead flies cause the ointment of the apothecary to send forth a stinking savour.	A fly in the ointment.
10:20	219	Curse not the king, no not in thy thought; and curse not the rich in thy bedchamber: for a bird of the air shall carry the voice, and that which hath wings shall tell the matter.	A little bird told me.
11:1	219	Cast thy bread upon the waters: for thou shalt find it after many days.	
11:7	221	Truly the light is sweet, and a pleasant thing it is for the eyes to behold the sun.	
11:9	221	Rejoice, O young man, in thy youth; and let thy heart cheer thee in the days of thy youth, and walk in the ways of thine heart, and in the sight of thine eyes.	
12:1–7	225	Remember now thy Creator in the days of thy youth, while the evil days come not, nor the years draw nigh, when thou shalt say, I have no pleasure in them . . . . Then shall the dust return to the earth as it was: and the spirit shall return unto God who gave it.	
12:12	251	And further, by these, my son, be admonished: of making many books there is no end; and much study is a weariness of the flesh.	

Illustrations

Acknowledgements

The editor and publisher gratefully acknowledge the permission granted to reproduce the copyright material in this book:

Yehuda Amichai, 'A Man in his Life', from *The Selected Poetry Of Yehuda Amichai*. Berkeley: University of California Press, 2004. Reprinted with permission of Copyright Clearance Center.

Phoebe Hesketh, 'After the Sun', from *The Leave Train: New and Selected Powms* by Phoebe Hesketh. London: Enitharmon Press, 1994. Reprinted with permission of Enitharmon Press.

A. M. Klein, 'Koheleth' and 'Out of the Pulver & the Polished Lens', from *Complete Poems* by A. M. Klein. Toronto: University of Toronto Press, 1989. Reprinted with permission of University of Toronto Press.

Louis Untermeyer, 'Koheleth', from *The Nation*, 28 February 1928. Reprinted with permission of *The Nation* (www.thenation.com).

Every effort has been made to trace copyright holders and to obtain their permission for the use of copyright material. The publisher apologizes for any errors or omissions in the above list and would be grateful if notified of any corrections that should be incorporated in future reprints or editions of this book.

Name Index

Note: italicized page numbers appear in the Bibliography.

Subject Index